Emotion as Meaning

Emotion as Meaning

The Literary Case
for How We Imagine

Keith M. Opdahl

Lewisburg
Bucknell University Press
London: Associated University Presses

Associated University Presses
440 Forsgate Drive
Cranbury, NJ 08512

Associated University Presses
16 Barter Street
London WC1A 2AH, England

Associated University Presses
P.O. Box 338, Port Credit
Mississauga, Ontario
Canada L5G 4L8

The paper used in this publication meets the requirements of the American National Standard for Permanence of Paper for Printed Library Materials
Z39.48-1984

Library of Congress Cataloging-in-Publication Data

Opdahl, Keith M., 1934–
    Emotion as meaning : the literary case for how we imagine / Keith M. Opdahl.
        p. cm.
    Includes bibliographical references and index.
    ISBN 0-8387-5521-6 (alk. paper)
    1. Emotions in literature. 2. Fiction—History and criticism I. Title.

PN56.E6 O54 2002
809'.93353—dc21
                                                                2002023833

To Michael and Cristina,
who make a father proud.

Contents

Preface

EMOTION IS A STRANGE PART OF OUR EXPERIENCE. WE SPEAK OF IT AS though it were separate from our selves, like the figure of Cupid coming from the outside to overwhelm us. Yet emotion is the heart of our identity. We are the emotions we feel. We are he who is angry, she who is cooperative; she who is lonely, he who is ambitious. We never feel surer of our identity than when we feel strong emotion, never understand others better than when they feel strongly—a subject to which we are exquisitely attuned.

Emotion is central to our experience, then, as several recent books have claimed. Daniel Goleman's *Emotional Intelligence* places what we once called "emotional maturity" firmly at the center of human success. Antonio Damasio's *Descartes' Error* documents the inseparability of emotion and thinking, offering a new model of the mind that he develops in *The Feeling of What Happens*. And in *Paradoxes of Emotion and Fiction* Robert J. Yanal explores the contradictions involved in the reader's reaction to the fiction, showing that emotion is central to the experience of reading.

Books like these reflect the new respectability that the subject of emotion now enjoys. They also—with the work of authors like Susan Feagin, Robert Solomon, Martha Nussbaum, William Lyons, Norman Denzin, Walter Kintsch, and Peter Stearns—form a body of knowledge that is fascinating in its own right. This book belongs to this group with one important difference. I examine emotion not as reaction but as mental representation, or the medium within which we construct and display our internal, imagined experience.

I began this project as an old-fashioned study of literary style, examining the relationship between words and images. Was there, I wondered, any way in which the two are equivalent? No less an authority than Henry James claims (in "The Art of Fiction") that "the analogy between the art of the painter and the art of the novelist is, so far as I am able to see, complete." As I explored this analogy, however, I encountered the fact that we do not form actual images within our minds. How could we, without eyes inside our brain? But if we do not form actual mental images, how do we imagine? Even today this remains a controversial question. If our mental constructs exist in the form of a code, what is that elusive set of signals, and how does it appear to consciousness?

I soon found that this problem cuts across all specialties, requiring an interdisciplinary approach, especially since no single one of them supplies a definitive answer. And so I range widely, making use of as many disciplines as I can. I begin by returning to a body of knowledge that has now been more or less forgotten: the understanding, shared by romantics like William Wordsworth and William Hazlitt, that emotion plays a functional role in thought. I share the view of the cognitive psychologist P. N. Johnson-Laird that we form mental models, and adopt the structure offered by the contemporary psychologist Allan Paivio, who documents our use of mental codes.

I am also indebted to the philosopher Robert Solomon, who shows that emotion is integral to every perception. But though I draw on a panoply of thinkers, ranging from the philosophers Paul Ricoeur and Eva Brann to the critic Wolfgang Iser and the cognitive scientist Gerald Edelman, I rely ultimately on my own, personal experience as a reader. In the midst of many conflicting opinions, I can at least know what my own mind does (or appears to do). In this sense, this book is a report on how one person imagines. It is phenomenological and so, in the general sense, empirical. It is subjective but rationally so. I analyze my mental construction of six very different fictional narratives, asking how their language directs my imagination. How do I form that vivid world inside my mind that extends over time and that seems to occupy a space of its own?

Our current thought offers two conflicting answers to this question. Up until about twenty years ago, many believed that we imagine within the medium of language exclusively. Then psychologists like Allan Paivio and Stephen Kosslyn showed that we think also by means of images, triggering a vigorous debate between the propositional-ists, who define thought in terms of idea (or word), and the imagists, who insist we think in picture-like ways.

I show that neither the propositional nor the imagistic code is sufficient, either alone or in tandem with the other, and that the imagining mind requires a third code, capable of representing those elements idea and image cannot. I make my case by surveying exist-ing theories of mental representation and testing them against the language of actual literary texts, analyzing the processes that control our reading of those texts.

It is true that the emotional code is almost completely unknown. In *The Nature of Emotion,* Paul Ekman and Richard Davidson do not include representation among "The Functions of Emotion." Mette Hjort and Sue Laver ignore the subject in their anthology, *Emotion and the Arts*. And in his recently published book, *Knowledge Representation*, the psychologist Arthur B. Markman does not even mention emotion in his index. Most discussions of emotion treat it as reaction.

But it is also true that emotional representation is natural and even inevitable—a process we all understand even if we are not aware of it. Emotion is meaning because it represents first the significance of the object and then the qualities that create that significance—which is to say, the object itself. Our anger refers back to what makes us angry and so represents that cause naturally, in a process important to the novelist. Katherine McCormick's sense of her husband's innocence and helplessness, in T. S. Boyle's *Riven Rock*, gives those qualities to the reader—and so the character they define.

Why don't I leave this subject to cognitive science, which may some day explain it scientifically? Because many believe that our feelings are too fleeting and personal to be studied, the humanities have a special contribution to make. How can one stabilize an emotion long enough to examine it? How make what is exquisitely private public? The answer lies in the work of literature, where emotion is *there*, on the page, embedded in language. We can walk around it, studying it from all sides. We can come up close to feel its texture and stand back to view it in context. In prose narrative emotion is stable and public and so uniquely accessible.

I'm sure different readers will focus on different dimensions of this book. Some will view it as a survey of the literature on emotion and mental representation, since those subjects are indeed of great interest. Others will find value in the chapters on individual novels or in the definition of emotion criticism, which not only works, as I demonstrate, but solves important problems in our present criticism.

But my primary purpose in this book is to show that the affective code exists. I demonstrate that emotion is not only expressive, giving voice to our immediate feelings, but depictive and perhaps even symbolic, as it stands for something other than itself. And this, I believe, is what is important. Whatever elements I might have left out, or whatever flaws might exist in my argument—however disruptive this fact is to present assumptions about the mind—the basic phenomenon is real. It is real to the many thinkers I survey, and it is real to the constructing mind that could not imagine without it. Certainly it is real within the language of these texts. People differ, of course, and some imaginations employ the affective code more than others. But all people employ it sometimes, as an analysis of these fictional narratives makes clear.

Acknowledgments

I WOULD LIKE TO THANK SEVERAL SCHOLARS WHO AT ONE TIME OR
another gave me encouragement and advice: Jane Tompkins, Eva
Brann, Robert Solomon, William Lyons, Ed Casey, Francis Dunlop,
and Rudolph Arnheim. I am grateful to DePauw University and its
president, Robert Bottoms, for time for research, and to a gaggle of
friends—among them Bruce Sanders, Shawn Phillips, Felix Good-
son, David Herrold, Terry Boesen, and Doug Colwell—who read the
manuscript with good-natured and critical eyes. To my wife, Martha
Donovan Opdahl, who provided unstinting support of every kind, I
will always be grateful.

Emotion as Meaning

Part I
The Mental Construction of Meaning

What a writer of fiction provides is verbal guidance that will start up the theaters of our brains, stimulating them to construct a certain coherent experience.

—Keith Oatley and Mitra Gholamain, "Emotions and Identification"

We actually translate from the text to a diegesis, substituting narrative units (characters, scenes, events, and so on) for verbal units (nouns, adjectives, phrases, clauses, etc.)

—Robert Scholes, *Semiotics and Interpretation*

1

Imagining the Text

Nick drove another big nail and hung up the bucket full of water. He dipped the coffee pot half full, put some more chips under the grill onto the fire and put the pot on. He could not remember which way he made coffee. He could remember an argument about it with Hopkins, but not which side he had taken. He decided to bring it to a boil. He remembered now that was Hopkins's way. He had once argued about everything with Hopkins. While he waited for the coffee to boil, he opened a small can of apricots. He liked to open cans. He emptied the can of apricots out into a tin cup. While he watched the coffee on the fire, he drank the juice syrup of the apricots, carefully at first to keep from spilling, and then meditatively, sucking the apricots down. They were better than fresh apricots.

—Ernest Hemingway, "Big Two-Hearted River"

I

MOST READERS WOULD AGREE THAT THIS PASSAGE FROM ERNEST Hemingway's "Big Two-Hearted River" is vivid. "You smell or hear or touch or see everything that exists," Malcolm Cowley says of the story. "You even taste Nick Adams' supper of beans and spaghetti"—in this case Nick's dessert of canned apricots. Because Hemingway does not provide a dramatic situation to give these sensations importance, however, it has to be his style that creates this vitality. But how? What does Hemingway do with language to achieve his vivid effect? To ask this question is to ask how the mind reconstructs the meaning of the language, and that is a process about which we know little. How do we as readers absorb the information on the page and then make that subject matter present to our minds?[1]

19

We do not simply translate Hemingway's words into ideas, since this passage is a fictional narrative, which requires us to experience its events vicariously. Instead we *embody* the meaning we read, constructing a model of the author's world so tangible that we can imaginatively enter it.[2] Many critics would explain Hemingway's power by means of his concreteness and specificity. He is famous as our most palpable stylist.[3] And it is certainly true that Hemingway embraced an aesthetic of the concrete detail, finding poetry (like Chekhov and Joyce) in fresh particulars. It is also true that his reticence makes the reader focus on even the smallest component. His flat tone makes us seek out his meaning, which makes *everything* important.[4]

Yet the critically accepted view that Hemingway is specific and concrete is misleading. Hemingway's words are in truth general and relatively abstract. He talks of a "tree" instead of a birch or a white pine. He cites a generic "nail" and "pot." Each of the small actions he names in the second half of the paragraph above—"opened," "emptied," "watched," and "drank"— signifies a cluster of actions and sensations that would take a paragraph to describe. To open a can requires many movements, and on a camping trip can be a dramatic event, as the lumpy fruit tumbles into the cup with a splash.

Hemingway's style is not as general as that of Jane Austen, of course, who gives Mr. Wickham "all the best part of beauty, a fine countenance, a good figure, and very pleasing address."[5] Hemingway does indeed write about the physical world, giving his characters practical tasks. But when we look closely at Hemingway's prose, we discover that he leaves out a great deal. Do we in the passage above know what Nick looks like or where he positions himself?[6] Do we know what kind of opener he uses? Does he brace the can on his knee or work between outstretched legs? Hemingway does not tell us. When Nick "drove another big nail and hung up the bucket full of water," Hemingway describes something close to an impossibility. Hammering a nail requires two hands—one to hold the hammer and one to hold the nail—and Nick cannot set the bucket of water on the ground because it is made of collapsible canvas. Does Nick find some other place to hang it? Does he (as many would do) hold the bucket and the nail in the same hand? Hemingway writes only that Nick "drove a nail."

If literary criticism does not answer my question, perhaps science does, since it is learning more about the brain every day. Thanks to new techniques like Magnetic Resonance Imaging, scientists can actually see (on their screens) the place within the brain where each thought is processed. They have discovered that thinking an idea involves not the whole brain, as one might suppose, but specific areas: the brain is modular, with different sections controlling different mental functions. Within each area, knowledge resides in coded patterns or "maps" of synapses. Significantly, the same part of the brain lights up whether one experiences or imagines, suggesting that imagination and perception are parallel.[7]

Such information is obviously valuable, and yet I ask about not the wiring of the brain but the nature of our experience. How does an imagined story *appear* to us? In what medium does the mind display the reconstructed story to itself? In a way I'm asking about the basic, psychic "stuff" of the story as it is imagined. Is it true, as more than one thinker has suggested, that the imagined scene is simply a replay of what would have been the original sensations? I find it convenient to say that I "see" Nick's campfire. But when I examine that process, I find that my image is far different from what we generally assume. We talk a great deal about the mind's eye; just how much do we know about this remarkable mental "vision"?

II

Let me approach this question in a different way. In his play *The Sea Gull*, Anton Chekhov has a character claim that the evocation of a scene in the reader's mind is easy. "A broken bottleneck glitters on the dam, and the mill wheel casts a black shadow—and there you have a moonlight night." These two details evoke the scene because that is how we perceive in real life: we note not the parts of the scene but the whole, not separate sensations but their meaning. Because the perceiving mind always extrapolates the whole from the part, a small part of the text—a couple of details—makes the imagined mill yard bloom.[8]

But even Chekhov's theory does not answer my question. For if the mill wheel and bottleneck give the scene, how does the mind construct *them*? Each detail is itself a whole, which means that Chekhov offers an infinite regress, with increasingly minute specifics creating increasingly tiny wholes.

When I try to imagine Chekhov's moonlit scene, moreover, I find that the process is odd. I do represent the scene in a physical form, experiencing it vicariously, but I have to renew my construction continuously. It flickers and fades, threatening to disappear. And then the medium within which I imagine is maddeningly elusive. In what mode does the imagined mill appear to me? As Thomas Hobbes put it so famously, our imaginings are "decayed sense," or a faint copy of some original perception. But my sense of the moonlit mill wheel is so general that I am hard-pressed to describe the nature of its display. Am I seeing? If I close my eyes, I witness something like an image, but it is vague and blends with the random lights that flash behind my eyelids. Am I intellectualizing? As I read, I reconstitute Chekhov's scene as meaning, but it is one that I experience almost like a sensation.

The process becomes even more odd if I imagine an object within my memory. When I visualize my own house, I conjure up not the structure I have seen a thousand times but a photograph I have barely examined. My wife, on the other hand, imagines our house as a feeling of the cedar siding, especially its texture and color. When the two of us visualize our house on a drizzly day, I imagine not the house but the lights and shadows on the street in front of it. Nor does my wife do any better. Although she is a visual artist, she surprises us both by visualizing not the building but the letters of the word "drizzly." And on other occasions, the process is odder still: we do not actually imagine our house but only know that we can—what we call imagining is our awareness of our capability.

Is it any wonder that experts call our knowledge of the mental display of meaning confused? As the psychologist Ned Block puts it, the nature of our mental image "is one of those problems where everything is up for grabs, including precisely what the problem is."[9] Our knowledge of the mental reconstitution of meaning is a tower of Babel, involving fields as different as philosophy, psychology, semiotics, literary criticism, sociology, and psychoanalysis. Each of these disciplines teaches us something about the imagination, but none of them achieves a definitive model, in large measure because each grabs only that part of the process relevant to its specialty. This is true of even literary studies, which has turned from the imagination as a subject to doubts about language (among aging deconstructionists) or a fascination with political issues (among almost everyone else). It is less true, I am happy to say, of a group of cognitive psychologists, linguists, and critics engaged in the empirical study of narrative. Although this group, identified with the International Society for the Empirical Study of Literature (and publishing in journals like *Poetics* and *Cognition and Emotion*), does not offer a model of the imagination, it does examine the reader's construction of the narrative text, providing solid insight.

Even if the subject of mental representation were not difficult, however, it involves some tricky problems. We know for a fact that individuals differ in how they imagine, even when they interpret a given work in the same way. How can one explain such simultaneous similarity and diversity? And how explain the incredible complexity of the act of imagining itself? Reading a fictional text requires the construction of elements as different as the city of Chicago and the mole on the back of a hand. Readers must mentally construct the act of walking, the voice of a neighbor, the expression of a man eating a meal. They must imagine a word, a memory, a continent, a sensation—the fictional text that is so clear in one's imagination involves a mind-boggling number of different subjects united within a seamless whole.[10]

Literary critics do give me terms for what I am asking. Roman Ingarden calls the reader's construction of the text "concretization," and David Bleich calls it "symbolization," as we translate words into meaning. Wolfgang Iser emphasizes the connections drawn by the reader to form the whole or gestalt, using the term "autocorrelation" to denote the reader's construction of a consistent story.[11] And in *Semiotics and Interpretation* Robert Scholes writes that readers of fiction "actually translate from the text to a diegesis, substituting narrative units (characters, scenes, events, and so on) for verbal units (nouns, adjectives, phrases, clauses, etc.)." In Scholes's view, "diegesis" is the reader's combination of words, sentences, and paragraphs into larger imaginative units. Readers build characters and actions and then fuse them to form the total scene. "The text is not the diegesis. The story is constructed by the reader from the words on the page by an inferential process—a skill that can be developed."[12]

As a semiotician, Scholes examines the codes that govern mental construction. I seek to understand the process that employs those codes, or how one actually forms a mental model of the text. Because one constructs the story in order to present or display it to consciousness, I will refer to the whole process of translation and reconstitution as "construction" or "display." I want to know how one constructs the fictional world in one's mind and then displays it to oneself, holding it steady for reference or revision. I want to know how one can vicariously enter the world of the narrative. In what form does the diegetic story appear to consciousness? In the next three chapters I will survey what we presently know about diegetic display, showing that our knowledge is inadequate. I will then, in Part II, offer my own explanation of how we imagine, exploring its place on the intellectual scene and working up a model I can demonstrate. In Part III I will offer that demonstration, examining several novels, and in Part IV I will explore its practical implications for the reading of fiction.

What is the short answer to the question I am asking? I will show that one of the modes in which we display our construction of the author's world is emotion. In actual practice, affect performs many of the same mental functions as image and idea. But before exploring that point, let us first examine the nature of mental construction and display.

The reader's passions are never sensibly moved till he is thrown
into a kind of reverie; in which state, forgetting that he is reading,
he conceives every incident as passing in his presence, precisely as
if he were an eye witness.

—Lord Kames, *Elements of Criticism*

2
The Mental Display of Meaning

I

BEFORE TURNING TO WHAT EXPERTS SAY ABOUT THE MENTAL DISPLAY
of the imagined text, I want to ask what I can learn from my own
reading experience. Is there something I can know about mental
representation as a subject in its own right, free of the assumptions
and methods of specific disciplines? Can I learn something from my
own imagining of Chekhov's sentence? I find that I can make four
points, once I have acknowledged a couple of assumptions.

The first assumption is that in constructing the text we draw upon
our memory in a complicated way. We have to employ our previous
experience, of course, though our memories often seem vague, raising the problem of how we achieve precision. I will assume that we
invent the text by combining what we already know in new ways,
though we occasionally fabricate entirely new material. My second
assumption is that we represent a given subject by either symbolizing
it, as in words or signs, or duplicating it with some kind of mental
facsimile. The philosopher Eva Brann summarizes the possible
modes of representation by saying that the mind can symbolize a
subject, mirror it, reproduce it in a mental code, or represent its basic
presence.[1] I shall assume, as many do, that the mind reading fiction
forms a mental model of that world.

To turn to my four major points. The first concerns our attitude
toward the **appearance** of the imagined scene. To some thinkers, it
makes no sense to worry about the way our thought appears to us,
since that appearance is simply a translation of a code. Because we do
not have eyeballs or ears within our mind, every image or speech has

24

to exist in some sort of special mental language. Would not that basic, invisible code—the elemental medium of all thought—be the important point? What difference does it make if the construction merely appears in the form of image or speech?

Cognitive scientists in particular posit one basic medium or code beneath all kinds of thought.[2] Such a code need not be conscious or even formed by society, since it could be a biological connection among the neurons of the brain. But whatever such a code might be, the way it displays its meaning within the mind—the way that meaning appears—does indeed count for a great deal. After all, what appears to consciousness is what we actually experience. It is all that we know. Moreover, those who talk about an elemental code end up discussing appearance anyway, since the nature of the elemental code determines the nature of the display. One can discover the basic code—if at all—only by working back to it from the medium within which it displays its meaning.

In an extended review the philosopher John Searle makes this important point:

> No, you can't disprove the existence of conscious experiences by proving that they are only an appearance disguising the underlying reality, because *where consciousness is concerned, the existence of the appearance is the reality*. If it seems to me exactly as if I am having conscious experiences, then I am having conscious experiences.[3]

Searle refers to consciousness per se: if we are conscious of being conscious, then we are conscious. But I take him to refer also to the way in which we are conscious, or the mode in which our conscious experience appears to us as readers. In the mind, "*the existence of the appearance is* indeed *the reality.*"

This principle is important because the nature of the medium influences the nature of the content.[4] As the psychologist Stephen Kosslyn puts it, "The mind evidently stores information in media, and properties of the medium affect how we can store and use information." Eva Brann, who posits a "mental theater," or the place of our imagining, would agree: mental images, she says, require "an appropriate field or medium upon which to appear, just as material pictures need a canvas. Such a medium will set a limit of resolution."[5]

It is true that our experience is rich and varied. We see, hear, taste, touch, and think, and each of these different modes of perception probably offers a different medium of display and so a different way of thinking. But the basic point remains: the nature of the medium influences content. To visualize is to think according to the principles of sight, for example, which at the very least requires one to choose and organize one's subject according to those principles. The visual stresses physical relationships and place rather than cause. To verbalize, on the other hand, is to think within the limits and potentialities of language, and so to choose and organize one's subject matter by those particular lights.[6] One need only remember how the syntax of language determines our assumptions about causation. Nor is the influence of the way we imagine negligible. If the basic method of creative thought is trial and error, or the construction and evaluation of alternatives—and research, as recounted in books like Johnson-Laird's *Mental Models,* shows that it is—then the medium within which one constructs those alternatives plays a large role in the nature of our thought.

To visualize Chekhov's sentence, I focus on the light and the contrasting shadow. To verbalize the sentence, on the other hand, employing words and ideas, I focus on the logical relationship between the bottle and the wheel. In such ways the medium determines the content and so defines the nature of my mental experience.[7] Or does the nature of the content simply determine our choice of the mental medium?

II

My second point is that we **construct** a model of the fictional world in our mind. The word "construct" misses the ease with which we imagine, but it does express what readers actually do. To construct Chekhov's sentence is not to unwind a memory tape passively, or to submit to a fantasy. It is to perform a task, as Gerald Edelman has suggested, having chosen to do so. It is to *act,* building an imaginary scene from assorted words on paper. We can see the complexity of this process, perhaps, in the four steps that it logically requires. Readers first translate the marks on the page into meaning, forming words, phrases, and clauses. They must complete that meaning, since it is usually incomplete, and then construct a model of it, forming the world the author describes. I take this to be the diegetic whole mentioned by Robert Scholes. And finally, they *display* that model within the mind, first as they read, and then when they later recall what they have read.[8] Much of what we call "a novel" or "a memoir" is really our memory of the model we originally constructed while reading.

These steps do not have to be separate, and I am sure the mind conflates at least a couple of them. Yet each is necessary if we would imagine the text. To read is to construct new wholes on an ascending level, making words of letters, sentences of words, and characters and scenes of sentences. Of course, it is true, as scientists insist, that our immediate experience of the world is itself a mental construction: the nervous system carries nerve impulses from the sense organs to the brain, which then translates them into the perception that we know. For this reason our daily experience is a *re*-presentation by the brain of what the world presents to our senses. The developmental psychologist Josef Perner calls the construction of the immediate world the "primary representation" and the reader's construction of the text a "secondary representation."[9] Although they are generally parallel, the imagined construction differs from the actual perception in three crucial ways. I **choose** to imagine, first of all, while I do not choose to experience sensation. It is true that some fantasies overwhelm my will, and I can stop sensation by closing my eyes or covering my ears. I can also pay special attention to particular senses. But by and large, I decide to imagine while I do not decide to experience sensation.

Imagination also differs from perception in its **duration.** After all, one might read a narrative over a span of several months and so have to recall material constructed previously. When I pick up *Adventures of Huckleberry Finn,* having set it down the previous night, I must remember the earlier descriptions of the Mississippi River. I have to refer to my original construction and even summon up parts of it, demonstrating the durability of that construction. It is remarkable, I think, that we have a great deal of flexibility in this regard, since Huck's Mississippi can exist within the mind in more than one way. We can reconstruct Twain's previous description, taking the time to complete a model of the river, or we can represent it without replicating it in detail, as an unobtrusive presence, quietly forming the background.

Finally, the imagined construction is not only willed and durable but **sovereign**—a thing apart, to be examined as itself. It occupies mental space, permitting us to walk around it. It is *there,* a mental model and so available for study, itself an object of consciousness. In real life I sometimes act spontaneously and so do not need a deliberate mental construction, as when I reach into my pants pocket for my keys, say, or reach for a cup without looking. I know the location of these objects automatically, much as I "know" the state of Wisconsin without picturing the map. I need not construct or display the object. But at other times I must hold certain information in my head in order to reflect upon it. When I yearn for a cup of coffee while working in the stacks, I visualize my coffee cup back on my desk. When contracts come out, I mentally display the numbers of my gross salary, holding them in position while I subtract taxes and insurance.

And when I read, I imagine Chekhov's sentence or Hemingway's paragraph in the same way, as worlds to be entered. I can walk about the mill yard and even pick up the littered bottle, studying it. I can join Nick by the fire, tasting Hopkins's version of coffee, and review the scene again and again.[10]

Do all readers construct the same mental models? Obviously people differ greatly in background, language, skill, and motivation. A novel forced on a young reader is an entirely different experience from one chosen by an elderly shut-in. Because no two individuals are alike, no two constructions can be exactly alike. And yet it *is* just one text that everyone reads, mechanically duplicated by as many as a million copies. A well-known novel is in some ways the epitome of community, as hundreds of thousands of readers share a body of intimate experience. Clearly any theory of reading must accommodate both the differences among readers and their similarities—a requirement fulfilled by a recognition of all three mental codes, as we will see in chapter 5.

III

The imaginative construction of the fictional text is complicated further by **reader identification,** a subject vastly more important (and interesting) than our culture assumes.[11] We simply do not read a novel in the same way we read history or an essay. Fiction (and perhaps any narrative) asks us to identify with the characters, taking on their identity and experience as our own. We work as partners with the author, as Georges Poulet explains in his essay, "Criticism and the Experience of Interiority," giving life to the fiction even as the author's fiction directs the reader's consciousness.[12] Poulet stresses the remarkable way in which reader and author each "loan" their consciousness to the other, and in doing so extend rather than limit themselves, creating an imagined text that is different from the minds of either one. It takes a certain self-confidence to extend the boundaries of one's identity.

In *The Nature of Sympathy* Max Scheler observes that readers can either lose their own identity within that of the character or absorb the character's identity within themselves. In either case, the fictional text provides a special *kind* of experience, as readers merge with the character. Reading fiction (or similar narratives) requires a double consciousness, since readers remain aware of themselves and their surroundings even as they lose themselves in the story. They feel at once engaged and detached, empathetic and analytical, identified with the character and yet themselves. And they gain a special source of knowledge, since they know the other person from the inside.

Unfortunately, Poulet and Scheler do not address a logical inconsistency that worries philosophers. How can one "become" a person one knows is imaginary, or experience events one knows are unreal? How can one feel actual emotions when witnessing fictional events? As the philosophers put it, how can one believe in a text without adopting its beliefs? In her recent book, *Reading with Feeling*, the philosopher Susan L. Feagin offers a persuasive answer to these questions. She notes that empathy involves a mental changing of gears. When we pick up a novel, we feel our minds move into a new mode of experiencing—a point each reader can corroborate for himself. I find, as I approach the text, that I open myself to it, softening the focus of my awareness—softening my concern with myself—to identify with the protagonist. It might sound strange, but I lead with my feelings, looking for cues (or clues) to how the character feels. Sometimes I put myself into the character, feeling what the author describes the character feeling. At other times I project myself into the character's world, feeling what *I* would feel within that circumstance. In either case, I compare the feelings of the character with my own—still an important reason to read fiction.

Readers can do this in a story they know is unreal, Feagin says, because they simulate the world the author describes.[13] They construct the model provided by the author *as though* it were real. Such simulation enables them to live imaginatively in a world in which they do not believe. It also enables them to imagine a world without knowing everything about it. Because readers construct a model of the text, they can enter it temporarily, feeling real emotions even though they know the simulated world is not real.[14]

I have only one reservation to the claims of Poulet and Feagin. In my view identification is a larger, more sweeping activity than even these two philosophers acknowledge. It involves more people and a greater intensity than most thinkers recognize. Whether we are female or male, we identify with others (of either sex) all the time.[15] Almost all people can read the facial expressions of others and know the emotions they signal, laying the foundation for an empathetic sharing of those emotions. As Charles Darwin says in *The Expression of the Emotions in Man and Animals*, knowing the motives of one's companion has great survival value. And it has great social value as well, since we always interpret the meaning of another's words in the context of what we perceive to be their state of mind.[16]

Victor Nell recognizes the intensity of identification in his aptly named study of reading, *Lost in a Book*, when he equates reader identification with hypnosis. In the following, Nell paraphrases and then quotes from J. R. Hilgard's *Personality and Hypnosis:*

> For the involved subject, the distinction between the subject and the object of the experience breaks down; there is a total immersion in the experience, which, for the reader, means being "transformed or transported by what he reads . . . swept emotionally into the experience described by the author."

Surely this is true even today, long after Pirandello asked his characters to break the empathetic illusion by speaking directly to the audience (replacing one illusion with another). To read a novel is to enter a trance-like state.[17]

Nell offers several theories of vicarious experience or "daydreaming," noting that readers vary considerably in the attention they pay to the story. Freud believed that fiction provides cover for readers to fantasize forbidden material—one source of our intensity. Readers also have the pleasure of imagining dangerous activity while remaining passive and safe. Some thinkers stress that daydreaming is adaptive, since it provides a means of problem solving. Certainly it is therapeutic, ventilating emotions. And then, as I have said, it has many of the qualities of hypnosis.

What does reader identification mean for mental construction? Certainly we can take identification itself as a mode of display: to identify with Nick is to construct Nick's character by becoming him vicariously, feeling what he feels. Whether I submerge my identity within Nick's or imagine his experience as I would live it, I reconstitute Nick and his world.

How does such identification fit Eva Brann's mental theater of images? It probably does not, since our empathetic construction is a much closer, more engaged form of display than vision. To see, one usually stands back from the subject, creating distance (though this is not necessarily true of the other senses). One stands apart, looking *at.* To empathize, in contrast, one closes with the subject emotionally. One feels *with*, vicariously accepting the other's experience as one's own.

IV

Finally, I have a clear sense as I read that I imagine the passage as **meaning.** It is not that what I imagine has meaning, though it does, but that I imagine the meaning directly. I imagine Chekhov's mill as not a visual scene whose meaning must be discovered but the meaning itself. Tantalizingly, this meaning is not an idea, though I can reduce it to one. Rather it is embodied, full, more concrete than an abstraction. It is something lived—I am back to the notion of the fictional text as experience. As I read Chekhov's sentence, I *experience* the author's meaning. The moonlit mill has a significance that I feel.

This notion is curiously subjective. How could one imagine meaning directly? And then, how do I define "meaning" anyway? *Webster's Seventh New Collegiate Dictionary* defines the word as "the thing one intends to convey, especially by language," which sounds pretty much like factual denotation. But I use "meaning" to include not so much the signification of facts as the significance or felt value of those facts. The meaning of Chekhov's mill yard is not only the locale and the building but their importance, and I would include within that term their importance to the character, the author, and the reader.[18] The meaning of the mill yard is why individuals pay attention to it, and so, once expressed, can represent the reasons (the facts) that lie behind it.

How is it possible to imagine the mill yard by imagining such meaning? The answer is that we perceive and then imagine impressionistically. I imagine not the mill yard but a meaning-laden impression of it. In the paragraph by Hemingway quoted in chapter 1, I get an impression of the campfire as comfort and safety, and so construct it in that way: I imagine the scene by feeling those qualities—which imply the facts that cause them. The impression is quick, facilitating the flow of reading, and thematic, since it includes the point Hemingway would make. And it is useful, since it enables me as a reader to give body to Hemingway's words, filling them out even as I read rapidly, with little time to conjure up detail. As a rule, I do not lay down the book and laboriously "picture" Nick Adams's fire. Instead I *surmise* Hemingway's point, understanding the significance of the fire within this context and imagining not the details but their meaning.[19]

This point makes sense because in many cases the facts are less important than their significance. The facts are often illustrative, pointing to a meaning beyond themselves, which suggests that meaning can serve as a shorthand for them, representing the literal element by expressing its significance. What is Lake Superior? It is a hard fact, obviously, but it is also a meaning or significance that, when expressed, can stand for the factual entity. We sometimes remember Lake Superior as a single telling detail, like the pebbly surface of a particular beach, but even then what counts is what the detail means, or its value within the context of our larger memory.

More than one wit has observed that we would be crippled if our minds were not highly selective. The specifics of our experience are simply so numerous that they threaten to paralyze thought. How better avoid that danger than by remembering (or imagining) by means of meaning? If we read for meaning, understand as meaning, and remember as meaning, why should we not represent by meaning? Psychologists have long known that we perceive in terms of meaning, and critics like Wolfgang Iser believe we complete the text by means of meaning, claiming that the reader supplies "what is meant from what is not said." [20] This point is especially convincing when we realize that such meaning offers an index to more detailed memories and imaginings.

I see another way in which the direct imagining of meaning is efficient. What if I am ignorant of the author's referent? To imagine meaning rather than fact is to be able to keep reading. When I read the phrase "Black Forest," for example, I might have no knowledge of the Bavarian mountains. But I would not, as a rule, stop to look up the term, since I can gather the general meaning of the phrase from the context. I might have a feeling of rural Germany. Or more elaborately, I might imagine the Black Forest as a sense of old trees and deep shade, since the forest is "black." Such tentative interpretation does not require a large investment of energy or time and permits me to proceed for the moment, ready to alter or fill out the construction as the narrative progresses.

Even if I knew the Black Forest accurately, moreover, I would not have the time to imagine it in detail. This is the key point. The Black Forest is a complex entity that could take hours to represent mentally, if one so wished. And the same is true of Chekhov's Russian mill, which involves hundreds of visual details I could not duplicate even if I did have the time, not to mention the mill's history and mechanics.[21] As I read, I pick up Chekhov's tone and meaning from the context, extrapolating from what I do know. I understand moonlit nights and the poignancy of isolated, glinting objects, and so gain a pretty good idea of Chekhov's meaning—let's call it an impression of the whole—even though I haven't the slightest idea what a Russian mill actually looks like.[22] It is the role of meaning as an imaginative construct that permits me to read.

Such are the notions I can glean from my own experience of reading. I hope they will prove useful, laying out certain parameters, and yet they raise still other questions. I myself have begged the question, for example, for if we imagine as meaning—a notion I'm sure many readers would accept—how does that meaning appear in the mind? How does the mind display such a construction? And what does it *mean* to imagine meaning? I think it is time to turn to the experts.

I think the wreckage is brought about by our having a fundamental misconception of the nature of the mind's eye. If you think through the process of having a mental image, you grasp at once that mental images aren't remotely related to the physical images in front of your face.

—Jonathan Miller, *The New Yorker*

3

The Debate: Theories of Mental Construction

To ask how one mentally constructs a scene like Hemingway's is to ask how the imagination works, which is a controversial subject. Philosophers do not agree on whether the imagination exists, let alone how it works. To some, the imagination is the capacity to conjure up what is not present, and so is not a faculty but a mental capacity. Here we might include the philosopher David Hume and the British associationists, who believe that ideas are built up from the association of sensations, permitting us to form new combinations.[1]

To other thinkers, the imagination is the faculty that attributes meaning to the otherwise inchoate or meaningless world, and so dominates and shapes all human experience. Here we find "the constitutionists," who follow Kant's view that the mind contributes some of what is perceived. Modern neo-Kantians like Mary Warnock and Mark Johnson emphasize the role of imagination in the structure of our perception, viewing it as the capacity not only to discover but to create patterns.

Although these philosophers have much to teach us, they are too busy arguing the existence of the imagination to pay close attention to the actual process by which it works. In the last two decades, on the other hand, a lively debate has broken out between two competing models of mental representation. The participants are not only philosophers but psychologists, computer scientists, and literary critics, many of whom express their own personal experience.[2] I'm talking about the imagists and the propositionalists, whose debate has so dominated the subject of representation that it provides a definitive context for our discussion. The propositionalists include many who want to define the mind as computer-like, while the imagists reflect our common experience, which speaks of "the mind's eye" and "seeing" the truth. Do we imagine as idea or image? Between them, the two schools pretty much define current thought about the imagination, some of it technical but all of it revolving around the competing claims of idea and image.

I should confess that I find neither theory adequate. Each school grants a small role to the other, but both tend to overreach, claiming to be the exclusive medium of thought. The propositionalists are especially guilty of this. Is it possible that what appears to be a mental image is actually a proposition or idea? Conversely, could what we know as an idea actually be an image? Such claims seem unnecessarily complicated and violate personal experience. It is true that some thinkers define the proposition as an invisible code unavailable to consciousness and so beyond the ken of this discussion. But others—the subject of my remarks—define the proposition as an alternative medium within the imagination, in some way parallel to image. In the following pages I will look at several examples of these two schools, surveying current thought on mental construction and explaining why I find them insufficient.

I do agree with both parties on one important point. Both the imagists and the propositionalists define imagination in terms of function, looking at what actually occurs within the constructing mind. Imagination is the capacity not only to discover patterns within our experience but to construct a representation of it. It is not only structure, association, and meaning, as different thinkers have argued, but the way in which the mind displays its constructions to consciousness.[3]

I

The contemporary debate was started by the cognitive scientists, whose definition of the mind as computer-like seemed to conflict with the awkward fact of visualization. Until recently, when enormously powerful computers became available, it was difficult to represent pictures with strings of zeros and ones. How, the problem seemed to be, can one reconcile serial computation and mental images? The propositionalists found a solution by defining the basic mental code as not image but idea. We think ideas, after all, and in reading seem to construct the meaning of words as idea. Why should the mind not employ idea or word as its fundamental medium? To the propositionalist, what the mind takes to be an image is an illusion created by a list of factual propositions—in *Ghosts in the Mind's Machine,* the psychologist Stephen Kosslyn numbers them at seven, since that is the number of propositions that the average human being can remember.[4] When we understand that the mental image has to be in code anyway, since we do not have eyes inside our brain, the notion seems reasonable. Why should the mind not use the code it already employs as idea?

Of course, many people besides cognitive scientists believe we think in ideas. One such group I will call the verbalists, or those who believe that the mind displays meaning primarily in the form of language. Many students of literature are verbalists. "You can't have the idea if you don't have the word," I remember telling freshmen writers, asking them to build their vocabularies.[5] Even in silent reading, according to the famous psychologist, John B. Watson, the reader's voice box flexes, suggesting that an idea is in some measure a vocalized word.

Two of the most prestigious verbalists today are the philosopher Richard Rorty and the literary critic David Bleich—or so I will take them, acknowledging that their thought transcends such easy labels. Rorty does not address mental display directly, but he does embrace Wittgenstein's view of language as the defining residence of our humanity, claiming that it is within language that we create the world. While most philosophers insist upon searching for external foundations to truth, Rorty believes that such foundations do not exist. We create truth ourselves by the narratives we form with words.[6] Rorty argues that we always understand in terms of context, which is why philosophers should always "recontextualize," or lay out the context that defines their point—a natural part of narrative.

In *Subjective Criticism* David Bleich argues that it is within language that the mind reconciles the objective and the subjective. On the one hand, language embodies motive, since the meaning it expresses is determined by the motives of the speaker and listener. This means that language embodies subjectivity. On the other hand, language represents what the society considers objective. It names the object, "objectifying" it, and gets that name from the society that defines what is real. Thus it is within language that the mind negotiates the respective claims of the subjective self and the external world—it is within language that we imagine.

Obviously such verbalistic views have much to recommend them. Everyone has read the words of a passage soundlessly, reconstructing their meaning in a silent mental voice. And everyone has discovered his ideas as he spoke or wrote, as though words were the natural medium of thought. Who could deny that language contains within itself the values and conventions of our culture and so the shape of our children's minds? As the theorist Gerald Edelman puts it, language comes right after the formation of the self, since at that point "a world is developed that *requires* naming and intending."[7] In my view, Rorty is correct in saying that we understand in terms of a context defined by language, and Bleich is correct in saying that the word fuses the objective and the subjective.

Still, it is difficult to believe that the fluid, embodied experience we enjoy while reading is primarily verbal. To the extent that Rorty and Bleich represent the verbalistic position, I must disagree with their general conclusion. My vicarious experience strikes me as more "real" than words. It is a concrete whole that exists on its own, deeper than language. It is well known that babies enjoy mental experience before they can speak and that adults think without putting their thought into words. If one acts immediately, one might not verbalize one's idea at all.

I do verbalize more with age. But it is indisputable, I think, that we make complex judgments without verbalizing. Certainly we translate the words of the text into an embodied meaning that does not exist as a conventional, internalized language. It is for such reasons that the psychologist Rudolph Arnheim charges in *Visual Thinking* that "purely verbal thinking is the prototype of thoughtless thinking, the automatic recourse to connections retrieved from storage. It is useful but sterile."[8]

II

The most devoted propositionalists today are the cognitive scientists, by far the most colorful—and notoriously self-confident—of these groups. They are on the one hand relentlessly mechanistic, as they reduce everything to digital choice, and on the other almost giddy in their playfulness. In a book like Robert Cummins's *Meaning and Mental Representation,* one finds analysis interspersed with cartoons, arguments leavened by whimsy. Examine Roger Schank's analysis of mental scripts in *The Connoisseur's Guide to the Mind,* and he will teach you how to cadge a bottle of wine in an expensive restaurant.

Such humor reminds somber Americans how much the Oxbridge thinkers, who are prominent in this group, value wit. Such wit might well belong to scholars who, as Hubert L. Dreyfus puts it, continue to receive large grants in spite of repeated failure. Yet the ultimate reason for such high jinks must be the exhilaration of discovering that complex living forms can be broken into smaller, simpler—and therefore understandable—units. As Marvin Minsky puts it, the working mouse trap is nothing but six pieces of dead wood arranged in a certain way: the integral whole always consists of simple mechanical units.[9] Perhaps those units could be as simple as zeros and ones—the discovery of such mechanization is a little like discovering the secret of life.

For my purpose, the cognitive scientists lay a necessary foundation for an understanding of mental construction. While behaviorism warns scientists away from the internal mind even today, and literary criticism has abandoned the subject, cognitive science takes our intangible mental processes as a legitimate study. It is the cognitive psychologist who asks probing questions about the mental representation of meanings, putting the subject on the national agenda. It is also the computer specialist who demonstrates the centrality to thought of relationship.

Thus it is ironic that cognitive science provides its greatest insight into mental display by showing what the computer *cannot* do. That is, it is the failure of artificial intelligence (at least so far) that reveals what is essential to human thought. In *Mental Representations* the psychologist Allan Paivio complains that cognitive scientists are unclear in their definition of the proposition. They do not explain how experience gets translated into propositions or how propositions get translated into mental images. And they create an unnecessarily complex and rigid system. This is especially true of the analog computer, as it works with images: Paivio charges it with an unseemly complexity, since computer images are built from components, in stages, and each stage requires a complex set of codes.

Jerome Bruner, a psychologist, and Hubert L. Dreyfus, a philosopher, join Paivio in analyzing the failure of artificial intelligence to handle meaning. Although the computer deals easily with accumulations of fact, these thinkers argue, it has a devil of a time with significance, which attaches itself to everything in a constantly changing kaleidoscope. One perceives this point in the importance of the frame or context, which defines the meaning of its content and which computers cannot handle. Lacking the intuitive knowledge of human beings, computers take shadows for rocks, in the famous experiments for the US military, or ironic statements for straight ones. They cannot handle the subtle and fluid context in which facts appear.

Nor do computers do any better with *purpose*, which often defines the larger context. Both our acts and our perceptions find their meaning in our individual purpose at that time. Computers can mimic mental processes, and so are a terrific aid to human thought, but they must be given a direction and a set of values by the person who programs them.

It is revealing that meaning and purpose are subjective elements. Such and such has meaning *to me. I* have a purpose. The meaning may be grounded in the external world, and so be justified objectively, but it still belongs to the person and so is colored by her personal needs. I stress this point because the limits of artificial intelligence imply that subjective elements play a functional role within the mind. Paivio, Bruner, and Dreyfus would not necessarily agree with this statement, but their arguments suggest that even the most rational human thought is dependent upon subjectivity. The emotional, the intuitional, and the personal—all those messy elements we would want to repress—are absolutely necessary to the working mind. *They* express meaning, and so facilitate memory retrieval. *They* represent context, and so determine the meaning that is necessary to understanding what is before us. Cognitive scientists have made progress in programing emotion, which could theoretically fill some of these gaps. But right now the living flow of human thought, which fuses logic and feeling, fact and private need, personality and perception, appears to be beyond the capacity of artificial intelligence.

What does this mean for the mental construction of the literary text? I don't mean to argue against precision or objectivity, let alone computer science. My point is that context, purpose, and retrieval all involve meaning, which is fluid and alive. To discern meaning, the mind at any moment makes a hundred adjustments, many of them transcending a purely literal or rational level of thought. If we would understand how the mind constructs and displays the page of fiction, we must understand this kind of intuitive understanding. The computer teaches us that the imagination is wonderfully alive and complex—and subjective.[10] In chapter 4 I will discuss two cognitive scientists who recognize just this fact.

III

The propositionalists who have most thoroughly examined mental display are the semioticians, or those who, like the well-known critics Jonathan Culler and Robert Scholes, study the transformational rules—the conventions, codes, and systems—that govern our translation of the text. My central question is semiotic, since it involves not the interpretation of the text (which Jonathan Culler dismisses as passé) but the processes by which readers create meaning.[11]

Robert Scholes illustrates this point in his concept of "narrativity," or the capacity of the text to be constructed by the reader. In *Semiotics and Interpretation* Scholes offers first a literal account of the process:

> To enter fictional space through the medium of words we must reverse the processes of perception, generating the images, sounds and other perceptual data that would be available through our senses if we were in the presence of the named phenomenon.[12]

Scholes assumes the mental display of the text to be a replication of sensation, or a kind of mind-movie duplicating real life. But as we have seen, he soon recognizes the actual complexity of the process in his discussion of "diegesis." As readers give body and form to the text, converting language into an imaginative whole, they are directed by social codes contained within the text, including conventions like irony and the "rules of inference." Scholes says that this conventional organizing and stabilizing process provides a foundation to semiotic studies, since it smoothes out time and carries the "weight of culture and tradition and the needs of memory itself" (114). In *The Pursuit of Signs* Jonathan Culler names as determinants of meaning such semiotic conventions as unity, parallelism, irony, climax, and the particular and the general.

What can I carry away from semiotics? When Scholes defines the text as "a set of signals transmitted though some medium from a sender to a receiver in a particular code or set of codes," he focuses on the production of meaning within the mind and thus lays a foundation for a study of the mental process (149). And when he speaks of the words becoming narrative units like actions and characters, he raises the question of how the mind constructs and displays such units.

While semiotics provides a basis for the study of diegesis, however, it ends where I would have it begin. It studies not the mental process of imagining but the social codes that direct it, and so does not examine diegesis as a mental process. *After* the mind has translated words and sentences, understanding them in terms of social convention, how does it present that constructed meaning to itself? How does it display it? Scholes says that the diegesis exists as idea, citing E. D. Hirsch's compilation of research showing that "memory stores not the words of texts but their concepts, not the signifiers but the signifieds" (113).

Scholes leaves the matter there, but even if he pursued it, I don't think he would solve the problem I am considering. For in my view semiotics makes two mistakes in regard to mental construction and display. First of all, it misunderstands the way in which we read fiction. Studying signification, semiotics assumes that meaning is derived rationally, in the recognition of literal and conventional meanings. It forgets that reader identification leads one to construct meaning in a nonliteral, nonanalytical manner.[13] One enters a world of feeling, of nuance, of vicarious sensation that is more fluid and alive than semiotics seems able, with its rational bias, to recognize.[14]

Secondly, semiotics embraces an idea that clashes with reader identification, at least by implication. To Jonathan Culler the semiotic reader is a conglomerate of codes, or a creature who exists only in the social conventions that direct meaning. The reader is not the person who imagines but the signs and conventions themselves, since the human mind is formed by these social codes. And yet what better evidence of a real person than the ability to imaginatively become someone else? The two notions need not be mutually exclusive, but they do offer different definitions of our human identity.

What does all this mean for propositionalism? Some would define *anything* that occurs in the mind as idea, of course, and so settle the matter right there. But that is playing with words. Because propositions are invisible—playing DOS, say, to the WordPerfect of the conscious word or image—we cannot be sure they are not the basic code. Scholes has good reason to define diegesis in terms of idea. And yet, as I have suggested, the fact of reader identification rules out ideation as the basic mode of those constructions we show to ourselves. Reader identification provides the reader with an *experience,* involving levels of mental activity much fuller and deeper than just idea or language. Certainly we imagine ideas within the vicarious experience, as in a character's dialogue, and certainly we later think ideas about what we have read. But our vicarious experience is just that, experience, and so different in kind from abstract thought.

Does any of this apply to the proposition that lies (hypothetically) *beneath* the level of awareness? Could an invisible, abstract proposition, or even seven of them, as in Kosslyn's formulation, provide our vicarious experience? Allan Paivio makes a lot of sense when he charges that propositions of any kind require an awkward amount of translation. Certainly the principle of parsimony suggests that the mind would use a code that requires as little translation as possible. And this includes the translation necessary to provide the mind its conscious experience. If we "live" the text, vicariously experiencing emotions and sensations, the mind would do well to employ a code that lends itself to such diegesis. Ideas are valuable as a medium of thought because they are abstract, and so free from the complexities of the senses. But this rules them out as the mode within which the mind displays an embodied meaning to itself.

IV

What about the image? Does reading create a kind of mind-movie, as images evoked by the novelist flash within our minds? This notion is one of our most deeply held popular assumptions, and certainly describes an actual experience, especially if one includes senses other than the visual (which remains dominant). Even now the preponderance of philosophers writing on the subject embraces the image, as in the books of Mary Warnock, Ed Casey, and Eva Brann (see note 1 in this chapter). So too does a large number of other experts. The aesthetic psychologist, Rudolph Arnheim, argues persuasively for not verbal but *Visual Thinking*. After all, the root of "imagine" is the word "image," and has been since before 1340, when, as the *Oxford English Dictionary* tells us, "ymagyn" first appeared. And so does the critic Ellen Esrock, who complains that literary criticism has been linguistic in nature ever since William Empson. In *The Reader's Eye* Esrock argues that readers visualize the narrative text. Significantly, in this regard, neurological researchers cite the duplication of rudimentary visual patterns by brain waves pictured on a MRI scanner.[15]

In literary studies those who have thought hardest and longest about the reader's display of the text are the reader-response critics, many of whom accept the notion of visualization. Although I cannot follow these thinkers all the way, I base much of this book on their methods. And it is true that among the different disciplines I examine here, the reader-response critics come closest to answering my question. Early commentators such I. A. Richards and Louise Rosenblatt call attention to the reader's construction of meaning, while subsequent critics such as Norman Holland, Stanley Fish, David Bleich, Jane Tompkins, Michael Riffaterre, Steven Mailloux, and Michael Steig have all analyzed parts of the process. Nevertheless, the two thinkers who have investigated the reader's reconstitution of the text most thoroughly are the pioneer Roman Ingarden, writing in the 1930s, and his disciple, Wolfgang Iser, writing in the 1970s. While their thought is more complex than a simple label, they offer good examples of the imagist view.

In *The Literary Work of Art* Roman Ingarden offers a phenomenological theory of reading, asking how the reader "concretizes" or mentally constructs the text. Ingarden breaks the literary work into four levels: the sound of the words, their meaning, the object to which that meaning refers, and the implied meanings, or those aspects inherent in the contextual "schemes" of the work. The first three levels are straightforward enough, but in the fourth Ingarden wrestles with the complexity and fluidity of mental construction. He sees that the implied meaning involves not merely objects and qualities left out of the description but large networks of uncon-cretized material. As an example he cites a novel that takes place in Paris. The mere name of the city stands for and so evokes immense amounts of data, though readers do not construct all or even a substantial part of it.

Ingarden performs a valuable service by focusing on "concretiza-tion" or the mind's display of the embodied text. He recognizes the inevitable incompleteness of the text and the reader's use of a vast reservoir of personal knowledge. He also copes with the complexity and fluidity of the living text in his notion of "places of indeter-minacy," or gaps in the information in the text, saying that such gaps mark the difference between the text, which is always incomplete, and our construction of it, which fills in what is left out.

And yet Ingarden's theory suffers from an important flaw, as his disciple and popularist Wolfgang Iser makes clear. In *The Act of Reading* Iser finds Ingarden's theory of construction to be too literal, largely because the pioneer defines the constructed mental image as photographically accurate, right down to the color of the hair and eyes. In contrast, Iser claims, "the mental image of [an] old man can be just as concrete without our giving him grey hair." The inevitable indeterminacies of the text "may *stimulate* but not . . . *demand* com-pletion from our existing store of knowledge."[16]

Iser defines a looser, more impressionistic mental image than In-garden, doing justice to the fluidity and speed of actual reading. Clearly he wants to open up the process. And he goes even further than Ingarden, arguing that the gap or "place of indeterminacy" in a writer's description is precisely what makes it powerful. The writer leaves gaps or "blanks" in his narrative in order to force the reader to fill in the details. Paradoxically, perhaps, it is by means of such gaps in the text that the author controls the reader.

What might seem a damaging absence in the text, then, becomes essential to the reader's mental construction of it. Readers construct the text according to the social and literary conventions ("the reper-toire") that they share with the author. They organize this "actu-alized" material—this imaginative reconstruction of the text—

according to principles of organization that Iser calls strategies and which involve the relationships between background and fore-ground, theme and context or horizon. As we read, we look back-ward to the previous sentence and forward to the future one. We have a "wandering viewpoint," or a fluid state of mind that incorporates a large number of variables.

In such ways Wolfgang Iser's elaboration of Ingarden explains the act of reading. Because no one can deny that readers complete the text, the logic of the reader-response critics is impeccable. Readers translate marks on a piece of paper into a meaning they then embody in a felt, vicarious experience. I find Iser's focus on the interaction of reader and text, on blanks or gaps, and on the fluidity of the text to be illuminating. It is within the mind of the reader that a novel finds its life, in a process we would do well to understand.

I must also appreciate Iser's belief in reader visualization, even if I ultimately disagree. We know we can visualize because we do so, whether it be the winter lodge we plan to visit or the walk last spring along the river. And images have a special credibility: our ability to solve visual problems has great practical value, since images parallel the objects they represent. Psychologists note that we can always identify the image we have, which is not true of words or even ideas. An image also presents a large amount of information at a glance, depicting relationships with a special ease. Many claim sight to be our dominant sense—certainly we use vision as a metaphor for all thought.

V

As valuable as Iser's ideas are, however, the view that we imagine visually runs into great difficulty. Compared to the mental tasks we must perform daily, images are bulky and awkward: any given image is too rigid to permit one to think flexibly. The psychologist Victor Nell makes an important point when he says that images are more important to authors than readers, because the author needs a detailed mental image of her world while readers do not have the time to construct such particularity. Nell cites William Gass's com-ment concerning a mnemonist: "to imagine so vividly is to be either drunk, asleep, or mad."[17] For the reader, images take effort, particu-larly since they are fleeting and fragile; one must work at sustaining them, an effort incompatible with the ease with which we read.

For the purpose of the novel, moreover, the image is "inarticulate," requiring interpretation. The image *shows* rather than tells, offering a meaning most often absorbed on the unconscious level. Such facts made the Wurzburg School in the 1930s argue that people have images but do not use them in thinking. The philosophers H. Pierce, Gilbert Ryle, Edmund Husserl, and Max Scheler claim we have no images at all.

Iser's thought illustrates the difficulty of the image in two other ways. If Roman Ingarden is too literal in his description of mental display, Iser is too rationalistic. Iser, too, misses the point that fiction is experience. He believes, for example, that images are "ideated," a term he at one place defines broadly but at another uses narrowly. In a footnote Iser defines "ideate" as the German *vorstellen*, "which means to evoke the presence of something which is not given" (137). Such evocation could mean an embodied representation, involving vicarious experience, but Iser also uses "ideate" in the sense of intellectualizing in an abstract and disengaged way. One might suppose that the gap would make the reader who fills it *act* and so participate in the fiction, increasing belief. But Iser believes the opposite: the gap creates not a suspension of disbelief, intensifying the illusion, but an increase in consciousness. "This distance, opened up by impeded ideation," he says, "is a basic prerequisite for comprehension. . . . The resultant break in *good continuation* intensifies the acts of ideation on the reader's part" (189). Rather than pull the reader into the story, the gap pushes him out, generating not empathy but the distance required by conscious analysis.

Iser's second mistake illustrates what I believe to be the main difficulty with the image as the definitive unit of mental construction. The problem is not that we have no images but that it is impossible to define the image in a credible way. Most of those who champion the image are forced to define the term so broadly that it has no meaning.[18] Iser illustrates this point when he says that we imagine the literary text by means of images that exist halfway between experience and abstract thought, and then—as the facts demand—offers this explanation:

> Our mental images do not serve to make the character physically visible; their optical poverty is an indication of the fact that they illuminate the character, not as an object, but as a bearer of meaning. Even if we are given a detailed description of a character's appearance, we tend not to regard it as pure description, but try and conceive what is actually to be communicated through it. (138)

The literature on mental display is full of phrases like "optical poverty," as thinkers cope with the strange nature of the phenomenon. Almost everyone, for example, agrees that the image is not photographic in its precision, a point of definitive importance. Many researchers and philosophers agree with the psychologist Alan Richardson, who says that our inner image is "a hazy etching, often incomplete and usually unstable, of brief duration and indefinitely localized." Referring to Kurt Koffka's account of the representative detail, Rudolph Arnheim observes that "this sort of incompleteness is typical of mental imagery. It is the product of a selectively discerning mind, which can do better than consider faithful recordings of fragments."[19]

Everyone agrees that the "image" is a representation of any of the senses.[20] But sight is dominant and therefore a convenient example with which to pursue this important issue. If the image is not "a faithful recording," just what is it? If indeterminacy does not "demand completion," how and what do we imagine? Of course, given the necessary leisure, we *can* construct a detailed image. We must remember that the novel is cumulative, permitting the reader to build up a complex image over time. But even on the level of the whole novel, the mind cannot imagine a large number of distinct visual (or aural or olfactory) specifics simultaneously. Thus the manner in which the mind represents a complex whole while reading is obscure. We have a visual capability of sorts, but it is essentially "non-optical" and concerned with not images but *meaning*—once again we encounter the notion of imagining meaning directly. Even as Iser wrestles with the difficulties of ideation and image, he understands that the mind constructs in terms of a whole that is defined by its meaning. We imagine not specifics but something else, something that provides an illusion of the concrete and yet articulates the significance of the passage. What is that "something'?

What do these several thinkers tell us? Although we assume that we imagine in either an imagistic or ideational medium, that assumption is false. The mental display of narrative cannot be idea, for ideas are too abstract to provide the experience known to the reader (though they can, of course, trigger the process of completing them). Nor can such display be the image, which is too rigid to satisfy the needs of thought and too vague or confusing (in almost all of these accounts) to explain our mental experience of the text. Reader-response critics like Wolfgang Iser focus on "narrativity," and probe deeper than the semioticians, but they too, confronted with inconsistencies and the difficulties of definition, leave the subject up for grabs.

When I image my living room, it is as if I am actually seeing it, and no one could convince me otherwise. The experience alerts me that *something* is going on in my mind. Experiences are, to use the philosophers' own term, *incorrigible*. You cannot be wrong about whether you feel pain, for instance: If you feel it, you feel it. You can be wrong about the *source* of the pain, but not about the fact that it hurts.

—Stephen Kosslyn, *Ghosts in the Mind's Machine*

4

Double Your Pleasure: Paivio or Kosslyn?

I MUST LOOK AT ONE MORE POSSIBILITY. IF NEITHER IMAGE NOR IDEA alone is adequate as the mode in which we imagine, why not the two combined? Such dualism would make a great deal of sense. After all, we have in real life the capability of both vision and speech. Why not in mental display? Image and idea could supplement one another and even interact synergistically.

In this chapter I will look at two theories that combine the two modes, and in doing so I will raise several questions. If the mind employs both image and proposition, how does it decide which to use? How does the mind move from one mode to the other? I am investigating the reading of fiction, which places the answer to these questions within the actual reading of a passage. I will first examine these two dualistic theories and then test them against a reading of the Hemingway paragraph I took as an example earlier. Word by word, line by line, how does the reading mind translate and reconstruct the meaning of the text? Are the image and the word sufficient *together?*

Like those we examined in the last chapter, these two theories recognize the fact of mental construction. But unlike the previous ones, they also recognize the multidimensional nature of that construction. People have tended to assume that their thoughts appear in either a single mode like the image (as did the philosophers David Hume, Bishop Berkeley, and John Locke), or a gestalt, involving consciousness as a whole. If we experience as a visual and intellectual

46

whole, including our many senses and emotions, why should we not also imagine that way (and so use both image and idea)? I might add that these two theories address mental construction in all its forms, including memory, the fabrication of alternatives, *and* reading narrative. Thus they unite the activities of reading and thought. They also address the unique way we form and display any kind of element, from a remembered object, like one's first tennis racket, to Chekhov's purely imagined bottle.[1]

I

Perhaps the best model for the mental construction of meaning is the one first proposed over twenty years ago by the psychologist Allan Paivio. In *Imagery and Verbal Processes* (1979) and *Mental Representations* (1986) Paivio offers a basic structure within which we can approach all human thought, including that of representation. Paivio begins by observing that psychologists like William James and Edward Titchener examined mental images back in the nineteenth century. But early in the twentieth century the behaviorist J. B. Watson persuaded his colleagues that images are too subjective to study. Watson claimed instead that we think in words, a view that dominated psychological thought for half a century. In his two books Paivio surveys existing research in order to restore the image to its rightful place, and in doing so, argues that the mind thinks in both word and image.

As Paivio puts it, we think at any moment by means of one of two "alternative coding systems, or modes of symbolic representation, which are developmentally linked to experiences with concrete objects and events as well as with language."[2] Paivio calls these systems codes or tracks. How does the mind decide which to use? Paivio argues that each code provides a set of advantages that suits it to a particular task: the reader's mind shifts from one code to the other according to the specific requirements of the passage. Like Rudoph Arnheim in *Visual Thinking*, Paivio says that the image offers speed, freedom, and easy association. It offers a complex set of spacial arrangements at a glance, showing both the object and its relationship to its surroundings (391). The image is also flexible. "The retrieved information . . . [has] relative freedom from sequential constraints, and it can be reorganized or transformed in various ways." Such characteristics, Paivio says in *Mental Representations*, "imply that imagery contributes richness of content and flexibility in the processing of that content."[3]

Verbalization, on the other hand, is suited to the representation of cause and effect. Because words follow one another in a line, they provide sequence, direction, and organization. They are exceptionally well suited to the retrieval of information and its analysis.[4]

By what mechanism do we shift from image to word? We simply make the decision, following our disposition or the requirements of the content. We can do this, research shows, because images can convert into words just as language translates into mental images. The two codes also interact, supplementing one another. "Situations may be represented imaginally, but their elements organized verbally. . . . Words may also arouse nonverbal images of static objects as well as of action and transformation." In any given mind, words and images work together, the two of them giving the mind the breadth to represent all human experience. If "images are particularly effective in promoting rapid associations while verbal processes give them direction," then the combination of the two modes in rapid sequence provides both association and direction (38). In such ways Paivio does justice to the variation and comprehensiveness of the representing mind.

I find Paivio's model persuasive because it recognizes our human variety. Each of us knows that in the course of the day we think imagistically *and* verbally, depending upon the circumstance. Yet most of us have a personal preference for one mode over the other, based on our particular ability, training and temperament. Some people are "visual" and some "verbal," just as we know them to be in daily experience. Paivio's theory admits novelists and architects, physicists and folk singers, hunters and musicians, acknowledging our differences even as it explains our commonality.

Paivio's theory also squares with our experience. I do indeed shift from one code to the other in rapid succession, though I often feel a residual influence of the previous code, experiencing the echoing presence of language, say, as I visualize. I find that the image and the idea are at once distinct and yet intimately connected. Although I will criticize Paivio's theory shortly, I find that he does justice to the intimate and fluid relations between the two codes.

The author of the second theory is better known than Allan Paivio. Certainly he is more fashionable, with his deep interest in artificial intelligence. In *Ghosts in the Mind's Machine* (1983)—a book whose theory remains current even today—the psychologist Stephen Kosslyn explores the nature of images by measuring the amount of time subjects take to imagine a given image. He also pays attention to the angle of vision and the position of objects within the image, techniques that reveal some of the principles that govern our image-making.

Like Paivio, Kosslyn (in this book) defends the existence of the image against the propositionalists, believing that the mind remembers by means of both image and proposition. By "proposition" Kosslyn means an idea that exists first of all in display. The great difference between image and proposition, Kosslyn says,

> makes it all the more significant that people can *choose* in many cases whether to use an image or a propositional format to remember something. It appears that whether we think of ourselves as "mainly visual" or "mainly verbal," most of us have the capacity to shift our thinking in the other direction when it is useful to do so.[5]

How exactly do we choose between the proposition or the image? Kosslyn considers three models: using the image first and then the proposition; using the proposition first and then the image; or using the image and the proposition at the same time. Though it is hard to conceptualize the point, Kosslyn says, "the mind retrieves and uses images and propositions at the same time," choosing whichever mode gives the answer (or forms the representation) first.[6]

Kosslyn sometimes describes the proposition as a kind of unconscious foundation to the conscious image. Because images fade, Kosslyn says, they provide only a short-term memory that periodically requires renewal. Kosslyn believes that this renewal is accomplished by a long-term memory bank that employs the propositional mode. Information from the propositional bank directs the short-term imagistic faculty in its creation and manipulation of images, providing the mind with the advantages of both modes. In his book, *The Imagery Debate* (1992), Michael Tye calls these banks "cells," viewing Kosslyn's thought from the point of view of artificial intelligence. But what is important is that the propositional code supplies information that the visual cannot, particularly for long-term memory. Propositions serve as our mental index, for example, facilitating the retrieval and construction of images. In this way, Kosslyn's "image" enjoys the unique capabilities of both the visual and the ideational.

I am primarily interested in Kosslyn's notion of the simultaneous construction of image and proposition, a theory attractive because of its sophistication. While Paivio has the mind choosing between the image or idea, Kosslyn describes the two codes as intertwined. We all know that images embody ideas and words form images. Kosslyn also explains why the image or the word flows so easily in much of thought and reading: on a level just below consciousness the mind makes both codes available for use. I find that all my imaginings include something like an image, however vague. Kosslyn's theory also facilitates the process of retrieval.

In spite of such advantages to Kosslyn's theory, however, I can't help believing that Paivio's model makes the most sense. Though Kosslyn's notion of forming both ideas and images at every juncture is ingenious, it strikes me as overly complicated and even exhausting, particularly because images require an effort that ideas do not.[7] Surely readers do not laboriously form images over and over, or expend two different levels of energy (on image and idea) simultaneously. At least they do not in what we commonly mean by the image, which we have seen is comparatively difficult to form. In contrast, Paivio uses the natural advantages of image and word as a self-selecting, self-regulating process. Paivio also keeps the proposition and the image separate and distinct, so they are free to interact, which I think is an important strength. Because Kosslyn's elements are always present, their interaction on the level of mental display would seem awkward.[8] I also like Paivio's view of mental storage and display: we can indeed remember as images, it seems to me, and then put those images into words, or remember as words and then display that memory as an image. If images fade in display, it does not follow that they must fade within memory.

II

May we claim that the basic code for imagining is some combination of image and idea? The best way to determine the sufficiency of such a combination is to look at our mental construction of an actual passage, for which Hemingway's description of Nick's camp in "Big Two-Hearted River" will serve. Do we translate this language into images and propositions at the same time, as Kosslyn suggests, or do we move between image and proposition, as in Paivio's model? What does the language *require* us to do? In the following pages I will examine my own construction of Hemingway's paragraph, reporting what I imagine as accurately as I can. Though I claim to be normal (some would say stubbornly), and so mean my construction to be more or less typical, I offer it as a point of comparison, since the experience of each reader must be paramount. Let us see if our experiences are similar.

Of course, the reader would normally approach this passage within the context of the story, having already identified with Nick Adams. Right from the beginning I distort Hemingway's meaning by taking the passage out of context—reader identification transforms the way in which one reads. And yet coming to this paragraph cold makes my point harder to demonstrate. I will show that reader identification makes even the combination of image and idea inadequate: *neither* the theories of Paivio or Kosslyn are sufficient to the mental construction of a text. Here is the paragraph from Hemingway's *In Our Time*.[9]

> Nick drove another big nail and hung up the bucket full of water. He dipped the coffee pot half full, put some more chips under the grill onto the fire and put the pot on. He could not remember which way he made coffee. He could remember an argument about it with Hopkins, but not which side he had taken. He decided to bring it to a boil. He remembered now that was Hopkins's way. He had once argued about everything with Hopkins. While he waited for the coffee to boil, he opened a small can of apricots. He liked to open cans. He emptied the can of apricots out into a tin cup. While he watched the coffee on the fire, he drank the juice syrup of the apricots, carefully at first to keep from spilling, and then meditatively, sucking the apricots down. They were better than fresh apricots.

I visualize Hemingway's first two sentences in a rather surprising manner. If I read the first sentence slowly, taking my time, I visualize each of the simple actions. "Nick drove another big nail and hung up the bucket full of water." But if I read at a normal pace, as though passing to this paragraph from the one previous to it, I skip over the first half of the sentence, absorbing it as idea, and then form a mental image of "the bucket full of water" that Nick hangs. I do the same thing in the second sentence, intellectualizing the first two clauses and visualizing the last phrase, in this case the pot on the grill over the fire. "He dipped the coffee pot half full, put some more chips under the grill onto the fire and put the pot on." Perhaps my imagination is lazy. Or perhaps I construct the last thing mentioned because the stop at the end of the sentence gives me time to form the image. Or perhaps ideation takes so much less effort than visualization that I construct the comparatively rushed early clauses as idea.

When I say I visualize, I mean that I "see" an image that is so vague that it could not possibly account for the precision that I feel. Yet the main point stands: even in these first two sentences, it is Paivio who seems correct. I pass easily *between* ideation and visualization, and do so according to the requirements of the sentence (though they are different from what Paivio described). I have no sense of constructing simultaneous images and ideas—as Kosslyn might agree that I should not, since the foundational proposition remains unconscious. Of course, these simple actions could be constructed as *either* an idea or image: one can both "see" and think hammering "another big nail." One can both visualize "the bucket full of water" and think the idea. But the time available differs from clause to clause, and so determines the code, as though I would visualize whenever I had the time.

With the third sentence of Hemingway's passage, however, I encounter something quite different. When Hemingway writes, "He
could not remember which way he made coffee," I have no image, for
how does one visualize "remember?" The end of the sentence gives
me time to form an image, and I do linger over that word, "coffee."
But "remembering" is a mental action that has no visible correspondent. I am not about to imagine a big question mark, say, or a face
with eyes raised and finger on the chin. And then "Nick could not
remember." How does one visualize a negative? Even if I had a visual
equivalent to "remember," how could I visualize its absence?

Nor do the next three sentences permit visualization: "He decided
to bring it to a boil. He remembered now that was Hopkins's way. He
had once argued about everything with Hopkins." Again the text
offers not physical but mental action, which we cannot see. We know
almost nothing about Hopkins, but that is all right, since the passage
does not ask us to construct Hopkins. He is merely a point of reference. (Or do some readers "see" a Hopkins of their own devising? In
passages such as this, people often report using faces they know,
visualizing . . . if they have the time.)

If these sentences are not images, are they ideas? According to our
commonly accepted assumptions today, they would have to be. One
visualizes or one intellectualizes. And yet this is narrative, as I have
said, and so a form of concrete experience. To imagine the scene is
not to think Hemingway's language but to *embody* it, entering it
vicariously. What is more, the sentence "He could not remember
which way he made coffee" invites me to assume the identity and
experience of Nick (as he performs this mental activity), and so
suggests a mode of construction other than image or idea. If in this
imagined narrative I cannot visualize "remembering" or think the
bald idea, I can at least feel myself remembering as though I *were*
Nick. I can vicariously become Nick and so construct as my own the
feeling of his experience. And as I say, I would in the normal course
of reading have already identified with Nick Adams by now.

Thus it is revealing that even this short passage pushes me into
identification. Is it Hemingway's language that "makes" me empathize? Do I respond to the conventions of reading narrative? Because
Hemingway places his meaning within Nick's thoughts, I have to
identify with the character if I would understand the literal meaning.
As Nick, I feel myself fail to remember and then remember after all,
briefly duplicating the protagonist's experience. I do not imagine
these actions in full, since that would require too much time, but I do
feel an abbreviated sense of such actions. I live within the story.

Some might argue that one can empathize with a character in a visual or ideational manner, but I find that impossible. I do not visualize myself as Nick, even though I am in the story with him. Nor do I imagine myself wearing Nick's face on my body, which is grotesque and at any rate not an option, since Hemingway offers only the vaguest notion of Nick's appearance. And again—since this is a key point in my analysis—I cannot empathize by thinking, since empathy is an experience and ideas are abstract. I cannot *say* or *think* I am Nick—it is something I have to feel.

What happens if I resist this tug to identify, adamantly staying outside of the character? Hemingway's language in the ensuing sentences will not permit me to keep that distance.

> While he waited for the coffee to boil, he opened a small can of apricots. He liked to open cans. He emptied the can of apricots out into a tin cup. While he watched the coffee on the fire, he drank the juice syrup of the apricots, carefully at first to keep from spilling, and then meditatively, sucking the apricots down. They were better than fresh apricots.

I construct "while he waited for the coffee to boil" as an idea, hurrying on to the main clause, "he opened a small can of apricots," which I visualize, perhaps because I once stacked such cans on a grocery shelf and so can visualize their elaborate labels. Thus I revel in the visual . . . until the very next sentence, which offers yet another mental state. "He liked to open cans." Once again Hemingway refers to an internal action that requires me to feel with Nick. Once again he pushes me into empathy, just in case the repetition of the pronoun "he" did not do the job. The next two sentences are visual, but I have by now entered an identifying mode and so construct them as though I were Nick. This is especially true of the words that denote motive or emotion: "he drank the juice syrup of the apricots, carefully at first to keep from spilling, and then meditatively, sucking the apricots down." I can back away from this campfire, visualizing Nick drinking and eating. But words like "carefully" and "meditatively," together with the sensuous act, "sucking the apricots down," encourage me to feel what Nick feels.

Thus these last four sentences describe actions that I perform vicariously because they require it. And I can say much the same for the next and final sentence. "They were better than fresh apricots." This is a thought that cannot be visualized from the outside, since it belongs to Nick, and it is something Nick experiences rather than thinks (though one could argue that Nick makes a conscious note of it).[10] It describes the *taste* of the apricots (judging the flavor) even as it makes a statement that surprises. As an expression of Nick's satisfaction, moreover, the sentence provides a confirming summation of Nick's experience. Yes, these canned apricots are superior to fresh apricots. Yes, it has been a good dinner.[11] In even this last, short, sentence Hemingway places me within Nick's head.[12] Even if I have refused to identify with Nick so far, I now must feel this feeling (or at least think this idea) as though I were within Nick's mind.

Of course other readers are bound to have a somewhat different reading of this passage. Some readers will be more empathetic than I, and others will be less. It might be possible to construct this passage exclusively on an intellectual level. Yet it is clear that for almost everyone, image and idea cannot do justice to Hemingway's meaning. Readers visualize what Nick sees, and think the ideas that Nick thinks, especially if those ideas are verbal. But reader identification often requires a construction beyond those two codes. And Hemingway's citation of mental states has much the same effect. How, we must ask, does a reader imagine not only a negative but the *experience* of a negative? Hemingway's language requires more than the two codes can supply.

In this way a concrete passage of fiction reveals even the combination of two codes to be insufficient. Or let me make the same point in a different way. Paivio defines idea and image as symbols pointing to a meaning beyond themselves. But as I said in chapter 2, I have a sense of imagining Hemingway's meaning directly, without symbolization. If such a thing is possible, I imagine the meaning itself. I *live* it—surely a point worth exploring. And then I imagine the whole, which is another important fact to be understood.[13] I imagine the specifics of the paragraph within a sense of the whole, represented in an unobtrusive way; and then, when I have finished reading, I remember the passage as a whole as well, as a synthesis that lies beyond the capacity of either an image, which is too detailed, or an idea, which is too abstract, to represent gracefully. What is more, the paragraph consists of a myriad of relationships that elude either image or idea, and a body of meaning that exists only as implication, found "between the lines" in a shadowy realm that is not quite conscious.

What conclusion can we draw? If I can take my personal construction of Hemingway's language as typical, then the dual codes of Paivio and Kosslyn are superior to any single code. I see no way that I as a reader could either visualize the total paragraph or intellectualize it. I need both codes. And of the two versions of duality, Paivio's seems the most accurate. I do indeed move from image to idea, as Paivio suggests, though I find that the word evokes a vague image, giving some credence to Kosslyn's notion of simultaneous construction.

But in the end neither of these two dual theories is sufficient. Because Hemingway's paragraph requires feats of mental construction that even the combination of image and idea cannot perform, it requires a third code to fill the gap. Hemingway's language requires a code that expresses meaning in a way that is experiential and fits human interiority, displaying what cannot be seen. It requires a code that can construct quickly and precisely in a way that we as readers intuitively understand. Such a code must mix gracefully with image and idea, which also play a substantial role in display.

III

I might add that the need for more than image and idea is not lost on several other computer scientists, confirming my point. The cognitive scientist P. N. Johnson-Laird, for example, posits what he calls *Mental Models* (1983). These models may include image and idea but transcend them, offering yet another level that captures the *structure* of the represented subject. Mental models represent not a static image of the object but the unfolding process that defines it. They also include such subjective elements as the intention of the speaker and the larger context of the event. They include, Johnson-Laird says, both determinate elements (like a group of two people) and indeterminate ones (like a crowd of two hundred, which we are unable to construct in detail). And they exist within the mind on an unconscious level, giving meaning to language and a point of reference to images. We know them without consciously constructing them. They are "just there," like computer algorithms.

Though Johnson-Laird recognizes the insufficiency of image and idea, however, he does not really answer the questions I am asking. I think he is correct in perceiving that *something* performs these various functions. It's just that he posits an entirely new order of representation, and an abstract one at that: he does not locate the mental model in our concrete daily experience. For my purposes, moreover, he seems to beg the question: granting that such a model rises above the verbal or imagistic (even though it partakes of them), how do we know it when it appears in the mind?

Another cognitive scientist aware of the limitations of image and idea is Walter Kintsch, who in "The Role of Knowledge in Discourse Comprehension" posits the "situational model" of comprehension (and representation). Readers understand first the words, Kintsch explains, and then the larger unit that those words form. But these two levels are not enough, since we learn the meaning of what we read from the context of the situation (both in the text and in the world). And we construct that meaning in two steps, both of which are supported by current research: a rough, commodious translation of language, which includes extraneous and even incorrect interpretations of certain words, and the unification of the whole, based on context, which filters out the erroneous or irrelevant (from the first step) and keeps what is necessary to the whole. In this way, Kintsch says, the mind comprehends according to principles that can be duplicated by artificial intelligence, but remains flexible and open.

Clearly Kintsch's stress on the dependence of understanding on context, reminiscent of the views of Richard Rorty, offers a key element in human cognition. And in fact, another psychologist, R. A. Zwaan, employs Kintsch's theory to define the nature of literature, arguing in *Aspects of Literary Comprehension* that one knows the literary by the controls it employs on the second, filtering level.

But then Kintsch, too, does not answer my question. If we understand any given perception in terms of context, how does the mind represent (that is, display) that context? To recognize the large number of very different elements that enter into the process of thought is to wonder how the mind could possibly represent them all. How does the mind represent both the determinate and the indeterminate—both the accurate and the tentative—at the same time in a way that is clear? Kintsch makes good sense in positing an early, "rough," draft, and recognizing the mind's drive toward consistency, but he finally raises as many questions as he answers.

I know of a way to meet the insufficiency of the image and proposition without such complications or problems. In the next chapter (and all of Part II), I will describe a third code that provides precisely what is missing in dual representations. It is a code that meets the needs of the constructing mind in an efficient and relatively simple way, working in tandem with image and idea. Although our culture has been reluctant to admit that it exists, the works of fiction that we read—the actual books themselves—demonstrate its existence. Let us now turn to it.

Part II
The Affective Code

In thinking thoughts we think the things to which the thoughts refer. In feeling emotions we feel the things to which emotions refer.

—John MacMurray, *Reason and Emotion*

I suppose that what I am saying is that I would rather have an acknowledged and controlled subjectivity than an objectivity which is finally an illusion.
—Stanley Fish, "Literature in the Reader"

5
Feeling Our Way: Emotional Construction

I NEVER DO DISCOVER THE FACTS ABOUT NICK ADAMS IN "BIG TWO-Hearted River." I do not learn what Nick looks like or where he is from or what he does for a living. Remarkably, I do not miss this information. For as I read, I experience a sense of Nick's presence, or an emotional apprehension of his identity. From his thoughts and sensations, his voice and his experience, from his attitude toward the world and Hemingway's attitude toward him, I absorb a feeling that represents him. In my mind Nick is my sense of his character, in this case the feeling of a quietly obsessive (or fussy) person. I can convert this feeling into an idea, putting it into words (as I have just done), or I can find an image for it, perhaps making use of a face I already know. But Nick Adams exists in my mind as a feeling or emotion. My mind translates Hemingway's words into images, ideas, *and* emotions—emotions that are as representational as ideas or words. I construct Hemingway's meaning as an emotion and display it to my conscious mind as an emotion.

This fact seems perfectly normal. After all, as a reader I identify with Nick, imaginatively living his experience, and so share the emotions that he feels. I also react to Nick with emotions of my own, which define his meaning to me—why not represent him in that way? Why not represent Nick by the meaning that I feel? I construct even Nick's setting as an emotional presence, in this case the special feeling that is (and so represents) the working campfire in the growing dusk.

Of course, our culture views emotion as problematic. It believes it to be vague, as in our moods, or violent, as in our sentimental action movies. It views it as something to be manipulated. Emotion is pe-

ripheral, subjective, decorative, vestigial—doesn't it reside in the rep-
tilian brain stem? No wonder the philosopher Alison Jaggar says that
our society always dismisses the current lowest class as emotional. No
wonder our culture defines truth as the absence of emotion, as in
scientific objectivity, and finds personal strength in the repression of
emotion, as in our impassive movie heroes.

Nor is emotion an easy subject to study. Because emotions are
locked within the mind, they seem to be inaccessible. We do not
know how to measure or even identify them.[1] Worse, emotion is not
only a part of our humanity but an *important* part, expressing our
motives and reactions. If emotions are everywhere, how could they be
distinct enough to represent meaning?[2]

Yet it is a fact that some readers at some times imagine in the
medium of emotion. This is true in spite of our general silence on the
subject.[3] Even as I lectured my class years ago on the equivalence of
idea and word, I could feel my thoughts rise to consciousness in a
special way. My words sprang to my lips, yes, but they translated a
meaning that rose into my mind in the form of what I will shortly
define as emotion. Even as I stated one idea, I could feel the next one
pressing behind it, as a feeling, and that includes, ironically enough,
the notion that an idea can exist only within words.

For such reasons I believe that at least some readers imagine fiction as I do, employing not only idea and image but feeling. I believe
that emotion forms a third mental code or track, operating according to the same principles Allan Paivio attributes to image and idea.[4]
To read the word "ball" is to think it as a word, visualize it as an image,
or feel it as a mild emotion. Because the third code consists of the
feeling *of* something, which carries a great deal of information of a
uniquely experiential kind, it is well suited to the expression (or
construction) of certain meanings.

I will call this third code the affective code, noting its emotional
nature. Where does that emotion come from? It belongs originally to
the authors, of course, and to the characters that they create, but my
concern is with the readers, as they live the text vicariously. To read
even a single paragraph like Hemingway's is to encounter a large
number of emotions, ranging from the author's subject and tone to
the reader's reaction. Emotion surrounds the images and ideas in the
text, qualifying their meaning and forming a pool of feelings, all of
which fuse to form an essentially new entity, the representing
emotion.

How does a reader get from Huck Finn's feeling of loneliness, say,
to her mental construction of the scene in which that feeling occurs?
Huck himself may feel so strongly that the feeling just naturally domi-

nates the event. And of course, we identify with Huck, sharing many of his mental processes. We construct him as the emotions that he feels and so might well construct the scene that he describes in the same way. Huck's feeling defines the meaning of the scene, moreover, and that meaning shapes what we imagine. As the psychologists E. W. E. M. Kneepkens and Rolf Zwaan have demonstrated (in "Emotions and Literary Text Comprehension"), one's emotions direct one's construction of the text. To share Huck's loneliness (as the dominant emotion in the passage) is to construct a scene that demonstrates loneliness.

I might add that I am talking about the immediate act of reading rather than our later contemplation of it. Once we have finished a fiction, we can relive our vicarious experience, summoning it up for the purpose of analysis. But my concern right now is our construction of the story as we read it for the first time.

How do the many emotions evoked by a passage fit together? Just as the parts of an image combine to form the whole, and just as minor ideas combine to form a major thesis, so the several emotions felt by the reader of a text combine to form the larger emotion that represents it. The result is not just what we feel *about* the ball but our feeling *of* the ball, which incorporates along with our reaction a sense of particular facts, like the feeling of roundness, say, or the feeling of a leather surface.[5] Nor do we start from scratch with each construction. Because we know what a ball is, we have a fund of representing emotions available in our memory, formed by our personal and social experience. We may use a variation of an emotional translation we have used before—this has got to be quite common. We "recognize" our feelings. And we obviously learn all kinds of emotional values from our society, since that attribution is one of the important works of a culture.

On some levels, of course, the affective code is private. This kind of feeling serves as a personal notation, representing an object to oneself alone. Perhaps emotion was originally a private code that has evolved into a public medium. It is more likely, however, that emotion was originally a public expression, as in those emotion-laden sounds that carry meaning so dramatically. One has only to hear the calls of primates to suspect that this is the case, especially since the meaning of those calls is so clear.[6] It is also true that much of our relationship with the larger society resides in our emotions, as in our attitude toward our country. But whether emotion was originally private or public, the artist finds an important purpose in making the private public and, by the force of her style, the public private.

This, then, is the focus of this study: does the feeling *of* an object really serve to represent that object? If it does, can it be specific enough to do the object justice? How do our disparate feelings combine to form the affective code and how do we move to emotion from idea and image? And what do I mean by emotion, anyway? In the rest of this chapter I will define "emotion" and "feeling," which are controversial terms, and then revisit Hemingway's passage to see if the affective code can represent the meanings that image and idea cannot. I will define several specific tasks completed by the affective code and then a surprisingly general one, without which reading would be impossible.

II

I use the word "emotion" with hesitation. *Something* provides a third mental code, but calling it emotion asks for trouble. We all know emotions like jealousy, love, and surprise, but we have little agreement on their precise nature or their role within the mind. Sigmund Freud defines emotion as the product of conflict within the unconscious, while Jean-Paul Sartre defines it as our attempt to transform an unpleasant world by magic. William James defines emotion as our awareness of changes in our body; Karl Marx defines it as our reaction to capitalism. The philosopher William Lyons sorts these disparate theories into three groups: the cartesian, which views emotion as a feeling, the behavioristic, which would dismiss emotion, and the psychoanalytic, which views emotion as a powerful messenger. In *What is an Emotion?* Robert Solomon and Cheshire Calhoun break the definitions of emotion into five groups, based on sensation, physiology, behavior, evaluation, and cognition.

For my purpose, the best of these many definitions is that of the neurophysiologist J. Allan Hobson, who in *The Chemistry of Conscious States* (1994) approaches emotion from the point of view of sleep and dreams. Hobson's research shows that we feel emotions even in our dreams, as though such feelings were the point of dreaming. Interestingly, men and women differ little in how much or how often they dream emotion. Both genders—in what is Hobson's key point— employ emotion as communication. Hobson understands that emotion carries information within the body and mind, alerting the muscles to possible action or (as William James put it) informing the mind of bodily changes. Emotion also carries messages outside the body, to other people. To feel an emotion is to receive a message—a stunningly suggestive point. Certainly Martin Heidegger would agree, with his definition of mood as the communication of our perception of "how we are doing in the world." And so would Charles Darwin, who, as I have said, understood that people read the emotion registered on the other person's face as an expression of their motives.[7]

In Hobson's words,

> Emotion is not only a signal to ourselves. It is a behaviorally coded message to others about our brain-mind states. Emotions communicate our availability, our approachability, and our affability in a language that is often more clear and direct than our words.

This definition is radically different from the popular assumption that emotion is reaction or effect—something that happens to us. To Hobson emotion makes things happen. It is not simply a mental state but a stimulus of mental states. Hobson goes even further than Darwin to argue that individuals live with emotions set at the particular pitch that defines their personality. People know one another by their emotions—it is by emotion that we communicate who we are. "Emotion is not just a reaction to the world, it is a spontaneous and constantly present component of our subjective experience, and of ourselves, that others pick up, read, and describe as our personalities."[8]

Hobson's definition of emotion finds support in the earlier research of the psychologist Ross Buck. In *The Communication of Emotion* (1984) Buck argues that we perceive in two modes or mental "tracks," the symbolic and the spontaneous. By the "symbolic" Buck means the verbal and the visual, which he defines as abstract and conceptual. By the "spontaneous" Buck means the emotional, which is the basic biological system underlying the symbolic. This system is immediate and unmediated and consists of the perception of emotions in the other person. To most people this focus is second nature. Buck also claims (like many other thinkers) that emotion is communicated directly by "contagion." We tend to answer the laughter of our companion with laughter of our own, an automatic response that underlies the ability of emotion to communicate. Anger stimulates anger, and fear, fear—emotions have the capability of flowing directly from one person to another. Whether this ability is learned, as the social constructionists believe, or innate and biological, as Buck sees it, the revelations of face and body offer an immediately understood code. Because the spontaneous track is basic and undiluted, it communicates effortlessly, carrying intensity and credibility.

Together J. Allen Hobson and Ross Buck provide the affective code with a foundation. If we perceive on an emotional level, we might

expect to construct meaning on an emotional level. Buck recognizes
that emotion is a distinct mental track, and Hobson understands that
emotion conveys more detailed or literal information than the
merely unmediated and spontaneous. Though neither Hobson nor
Buck talk directly about mental construction and display, and limit
the meaning communicated to attitude and motive (instead of the
factual content I am arguing), their insights combine with those of
Allan Paivio to form a coherent model of the imagining mind.

It is still quite a leap from perception to display, however, or from
facial expressions to complex meanings on the printed page. And I
should stress that I do not mean "emotions" in the sense of passions
like love or hate, but as feelings that are mild and controllable. They
are what William James calls "the subtle emotions." They are "mental" in that they are not visceral, and though they draw on our other
emotions, we might well call them a special kind of emotion, suited
to the expression of meaning. In Part III I will argue that they are
precise and even objective.

Several philosophers would prefer to call such emotions feelings.
Paul Ricoeur defines emotion as physical, for example, and feeling as
linguistic and textural, as in "poetic feelings." The emotion looks
inward, Ricoeur says in his essay "The Metaphorical Process," toward
the self and its needs; the feeling looks outward, "toward some objective state of affairs." In *Freedom and Nature* Ricoeur says that "feeling
aims at the very expression of things, it is not aberrant. With emotion
this authentic feeling for the affective nuance of things retreats before the appearance of a magic world."[9] Understanding that emotion
can be trouble, Ricoeur uses his definition of "feeling" to dispose of
an unruly emotion and so preserve precision and control. It is a
useful strategy.

Yet other philosophers use these words in the opposite (and more
conventional) way. "Feeling" in the strictest sense refers to physical
sensation, and has come to refer to the perception of any event
within the body, including those not connected to any particular
organ or locale.[10] For this reason many use "feeling" to refer to not
only sensation but certain mild and seemingly intangible emotions,
and most particularly to those associated with perception.[11] I would
join them. Although "emotion" is a difficult term, and though it is
convenient to isolate a special class of precise emotions, I see no
justification to rejecting the common usage.

Instead, I will follow the basic definition of *Webster's Dictionary*, in
which emotion, feeling, and affect are roughly interchangeable.
What is important in my view is the position of emotion on a sliding
scale of intensity. Thinkers like the philosopher Robert Solomon and

the critic Neal Oxenhandler are correct in positing a continuum that ranges from passion (so intense that it dissolves control) through emotion (potentially controllable) to feeling (mild and therefore controllable). Emotion is sometimes passion and sometimes feeling or affect, with gradations in between, and if that complicates our version of the mind, so be it. Though its projection within the mind is usually mild, the affective code makes use of all of the degrees of emotion, however intense. This fact corresponds to our experience of the fluidity of emotion. It also permits me to cast my net wide, examining all of the emotions evoked by a text, even as it presents the challenge of understanding how these many emotions combine or coexist.

I should add that I believe the emotions felt by the reader to be real. The reader knows the text to be fiction, of course, raising the logical problem I mentioned earlier. If the story is unreal, shouldn't the reader's reaction be less than actual? Robert Yanal in *Paradoxes of Emotion and Fiction* offers yet another answer to this question, observing that we have active and inactive beliefs. When we read, we can hold our beliefs inactive. We often react emotionally to untrue thoughts in real life, Yanal says; why not when reading fiction? Yanal also recognizes what I think is the key factor: because we identify with the characters in a narrative, we *experience* the story.

The important point, in any case, is that emotion is a mode of consciousness that expresses meaning. *This* is what is revolutionary in our understanding of emotion in the twentieth century. In his book *The Passions* Robert Solomon argues that emotion shapes perception, defining its meaning at the very moment at which perception occurs. The mind receives sensations *as* something, in a context of meaning that we know as a feeling. Significantly, the emotion not only coexists with the sensation, providing it with shape and significance, but is one with it.[12] This fact gives credence to the notion of an affective code and explains my sense of imagining the text as meaning. If the emotion exists simultaneously with the thought or sensation, it is but a step for it to represent the subject of that thought.

This coexistence means that the emotion is grounded in the world. It is, as the German philosopher Franz Brentano first put it, "intentional." Brentano argued that all mental activity is directed towards something. The emotion we feel is always *about* something, whether it be an object in the world or (as we sometimes forget) some quality or need within ourselves. We fear that emotion is nonintentional because feelings can appear to float unattached, and people do indeed like to feel for its own sake. But those emotions always come from somewhere—the issue is not that the emotions are unattached but that the individual (or the artist) ignores or misunderstands their source. Or attempts to evoke them by spurious means. This inevitable attachment of emotion to object bears on the claim that emotion is precise and impersonal.[13]

III

Even if emotion carries information, as Hobson suggests, we must ask if that task is necessary. Does the language of a passage of fiction *require* an emotional construction? Let us take one last look at the now rather well-thumbed passage I examined in the last chapter, from Ernest Hemingway's "Big Two-Hearted River," keeping the affective code (and its unique strengths) in mind.[14]

> Nick drove another big nail and hung up the bucket full of water. He dipped the coffee pot half full, put some more chips under the grill onto the fire and put the pot on. He could not remember which way he made coffee. He could remember an argument about it with Hopkins, but not which side he had taken. He decided to bring it to a boil. He remembered now that was Hopkins's way. He had once argued about everything with Hopkins. While he waited for the coffee to boil, he opened a small can of apricots. He liked to open cans. He emptied the can of apricots out into a tin cup. While he watched the coffee on the fire, he drank the juice syrup of the apricots, carefully at first to keep from spilling, and then meditatively, sucking the apricots down. They were better than fresh apricots.

If you remember, I found that even a combination of image and idea cannot construct certain elements within this paragraph. Hemingway requires a reader identification that is neither visual nor ideational and provides a language that requires readers to *embody* his meaning, giving it flesh and bones. That means that however much we may reflect after reading, we really cannot construct the text in the medium of abstract thought. We would not be imagining. Hemingway also names mental states and relationships that we cannot see in our mind's eye.

Does the affective code fill these gaps? Absolutely. The very act of identifying with a character is an affective way of knowing, as one summons within oneself the emotions felt by the character. In the unique mental state that a fictional narrative requires, readers hold their emotions open, ready to mirror those of the character. They *lead* with their emotions, looking for cues in the text to shape them, and so feel pretty much the same feeling as the character does, only less intensely. They feel a "twinge" of anger or a prick of jealousy, replicating not the volume but the quality of the passion, or what it is like to feel that passion without losing themselves in it.[15] And as I have said, such emotions are real. Does Romeo love Juliet? When I read the play, I feel not Romeo's passion but a pang of love or a sudden sense of Juliet as my beloved. I feel either a mild version of the original emotion or what it is like to feel that emotion.

When I read Hemingway's passage, identifying with Nick, I feel the same elements that Nick does. Because I *am* Nick Adams, heating dinner by the fire, I read the word "pot" as not an idea but a concrete object that I pick up. The pot is simply there, involving sensations and associations, though as it happens, Nick does not really look at it, either. He passes his eye over it without thinking, or reaches out for it without looking, and the imagining reader does too. This is why Hemingway can simply name these objects without describing them. The pot over there on the grill is the feeling of its presence.

In such ways emotion displays meaning in a concrete form. Feel Hemingway's meaning and you have not only understood but experienced it—emotion has a special capacity to carry meaning and create experience at the same time. Of course the image can do this also, since we can enter an image even as we understand its meaning. But vision creates distance, requiring us to look *at*, while emotion (as a feeling *of*) brings us close. This makes the affective code especially suited to vicarious experience, since it helps create the vicarious belief—or at least, as Samuel Coleridge put it, a suspension of disbelief. In daily life, we even doubt that something is real until we feel it emotionally, suggesting that the affective code may confer reality upon its subject.

Paradoxically, perhaps, emotion also provides a concrete experience of an intangible mental state. While we cannot *see* "remember" or "not remember," we can *feel* them, or feel how it feels to remember. We know how it feels to run or walk or drink water. Why not remember? This is particularly true in the case of *not* remembering (understood too well by some of us, I fear). "Jim will not go to the store." I can visualize going to the store, using an image from my own memory, but I'm not about to visualize Jim at home in a rocking chair. I have to *feel* the negative.

Much the same is true of emotions named in the text, since they too are states of mind. If Hemingway were to write "Nick felt happy," for example, the phenomenon of contagion would make us feel a twinge of such happiness even if we did not identify with Nick. How else represent an emotion than by the affective code? This is especially true if Hemingway uses the affective code to summarize a number of actions within the text. Hemingway denotes the complex act of opening a can, for example, by writing "He liked to open cans." To like is a reaction, but to one imagining the fictional act of opening a can, the emotion serves as a summary of the event. Feel Nick's pleasure and you feel the actions that provide it. "He liked to open cans."[16] We "like" the special heft of the can and the easy bite of metal into metal. We "like" the evenly crimped lid rising up from the contents and the special sound of the opener seizing the metal around the edge. When Hemingway says "like" he reminds us of all these specifics, though in the heat of reading they remain submerged within the emotion.[17]

What could be more intangible than a relationship? The relationship of Nick and Hopkins is almost impossible to visualize, but it can be felt, as it must be, especially since it is almost purely dramatized. As Nick remembers his arguments with Hopkins, and finds it hard to remember which side he had taken on the coffee issue (which tells us a great deal about those arguments), we get a sense of the relationship between the two men. And that relationship is just one of dozens of all kinds to be found in a narrative and that (as I argue in chapter 13) require the affective code.[18]

Can a felt sensation be a state of mind? It is certainly a mental state, and, in any case, it finds its own representation by the affective code. We as readers feel the feeling *of* the sensations mentioned. It is significant that both emotion and sensation are "felt." We feel sound and taste and feeling and sight. Perhaps we feel smell. We *feel* the pot pulled dripping from the water and the fat chip slipped beneath the grill. We *feel* the metallic bite of the opener on the can and the smooth fullness of the apricots. We feel either a sense of these sensations, as entities in their own right, or what it is like to feel such a sensation.

IV

All of these applications of the affective code flow from the fact that emotion is experiential.[19] While words and images work as symbols and so mean something other than themselves, requiring interpretation, emotions are themselves. We feel their meaning directly and involuntarily. The image must be explained, but the emotion is itself the message, and often a subtle one, involving relationship or significance.[20]

Of course, I am talking about emotion as representation, which means that it too represents something other than itself. But it does so by offering an experience of the thing—a semblance of the original experience—and that fact provides a special advantage. When I read the word "ball," I have to know that those four letters signify a round missile. When I view an image of the ball, I have to recognize the likeness and place it within the context that defines its significance. But when I have a feeling of the ball, I know its meaning directly and without effort. I feel the feeling I would have had in the presence of that subject. Better yet, I have a feeling *of* the subject. It is true that the emotion is stimulated by the words, and in that sense is dependent upon the idea or image that the words evoke. It is also true that we are sometimes unaware of how we feel about a subject, or are puzzled by the source of our emotions. An emotional meaning is not always clear. But for the most part our emotions are self-explanatory. We understand them automatically, since we feel them *as* meaning.

This particular quality of emotion gives the affective code the capacity to work on two different levels. On the one hand, as we saw in the last section, affect is specific, representing the particular. Such emotions are hard, clear, and seemingly detailed. I have a feeling of my blue fountain pen or my friend, Doug Colwell, or the tightly stretched canvas of Nick's tent.

On the other hand, the affective code works in a more general, less particularized way—one essential to our capacity to think and read. The affective code can give the reader a feeling of not only the object itself but its general presence. Emotion can represent the object without a lot of distracting detail, making us feel only that it is "there." Sometimes this object is shadowy or undefined, simply occupying space. We don't need to know any more. At other times, we know very well what it is, though it remains merely the feeling of a presence. Such feelings may be vague, but they are necessary to perception and thought. As we focus on a subject in daily life, we are aware of the existence of objects on the periphery. Their presence is important, but the specifics of their identity may not be, requiring only a general representation.

It is remarkable how precise such general feelings can be and how large a role they play in our understanding, as in the following description of a character, Henry Crawford, in Jane Austen's *Mansfield Park*.

> When they first saw him, he was absolutely plain. . . . The second meeting proved him not so very plain; he was plain to be sure, but he had so much countenance, and his teeth were so good, and he was so well made, that one soon forgot he was plain.[21]

This appears to be a visual description, since Austen tells us what people saw. I assume (filling a gap in the text) that "teeth so good" are white and regular, but how does one visualize a "plain" face or "so much countenance"? How would one visualize the *disappearance* of such plainness? Clearly a visual construction will not suffice.

Austen's use of repetition reveals how we construct her meaning. As Austen repeats the word "plain" four times, in a kind of incantation, we feel that quality without seeing it. We represent it by a flash of feeling that we know is accurate. I know what such "plainness" is, and especially the kind of plainness that disappears with extended acquaintance, though I could never visualize it. And even if I could, such an image would require an arduous act of construction. To put the notion into words—to express it abstractly—would take several sentences. But I can feel the feeling of the experience.

It is remarkable how often readers have to represent large bodies of information in an unobtrusive way. A page or so into a text and we must represent what has gone before even as we focus on the present events. We must keep such facts "in mind," acknowledging their presence. And then every narrative refers to a body of knowledge outside of itself, forming its context, which we must again make present without bogging down in detail—a function especially important if Walter Kintsch is correct about how we know. In addition, every text forms both gaps that the reader must fill and a whole that the mind must represent economically. How better represent the unparticularized presence of such elements than by the affective code?

This means that we read narrative quite differently than we think we do. Although we obviously construct much of the text, we do not even begin to construct all of it. That which we do not construct we know as a sense of presence—a feeling that the object exists, over there, say, though this feeling sometimes involves a quick sense of the object's identity. Just as I do not keep all of the previous events of Hemingway's story in mind as I read, since so much detail would be overwhelming, so I do not construct each and every object in the present text.

But even my use of the feeling of presence is not the end. For as William Hazlitt understood, we often feel even the presence of large bodies of information in an abbreviated form—perhaps yet another level of representation even more attenuated than those I have already described. In Hemingway's passage, I have a sense of what I know without constructing a feeling of its presence, since I understand that I can summon it at will. When I read Hemingway's passage, I know I "have" a coffee pot within my imagination (or memory), and so absorb Hemingway's words as not a construction of the pot, or of its general presence, but merely a sense that it is somewhere within me, waiting to be tapped. This sense of a potential presence is tricky, since I do feel something of the object's identity. But it is of great use to the mind: we as readers represent even particular elements in the quickest and briefest way, which is to say, almost not at all. We imagine the coffee pot as our confidence that we could make it present, or as a quick flash of feeling that marks our capability, with perhaps just a fleeting sense of its special quality.

It is as though we skipped from peak to peak as we read, aware of a large base of unconstructed meaning supporting each point of contact. We know it is there and what it is. Or say rather that our affective construction serves as an index to the larger body of information. We feel—in the briefest way—what we have stored (or know we can invent). What is Hemingway's passage to me? To a substantial degree, I do not so much construct the scene as "have" it, feeling that I could construct it if needed. I experience an impression of the whole that represents what could become the imagined scene if I took the trouble to pull up the specifics. "While he watched the coffee on the fire, he drank the juice syrup of the apricots, carefully at first to keep from spilling and then meditatively, sucking the apricots down." As I read this sentence now, I construct only parts of it, like the fire and the lumpy apricots, but I know that I could construct the rest of it if I took the time.

In such ways the affective code works on several levels. It can be specific; it can provide the unparticularized presence of an object; and it can serve as a marker for the large body of information that remains unconstructed in one's imagination or memory. Of course, such capacities make it invaluable to the act of reading, let alone thinking. They fill the gaps defined by Ingarden and Iser. And they explain our sense of imagining in terms of meaning: all three levels offer a feeling of the elements' meaning, creating the impression that we imagine as meaning. We feel the presence of the object as a feeling of its meaning or significance.

V

Am I trying to have it both ways, claiming that the affective code is both precise and indeterminate? The truth is that we imagine in different ways at different times. My feeling of Asbury Hall, here on my university campus, is highly specific. Within the privacy of my mind, it seems as detailed as an image or idea. But if I think of the campus in general—as the backdrop to some event, say—Asbury Hall fades into a general presence: it becomes a building over there, across from Harrison Hall.

Even so, the notion of an affective code will strike some as absurd. How does an emotion like grief become an accurate mental representation of some person, place, or event? How could something so central to human behavior serve also as representation? In our popular culture, emotion is vague or self-delusional. It is sentimentality or road rage, self-pity or paranoia. Certainly, if I am to make my case, I must document the presence of the affective code in a number of narratives, which is what I will do in parts III and IV. I must also survey those several thinkers who have glimpsed the affective code, as I will do in the next two chapters.

And I must make use of the research into emotion done by psychologists in the last forty years. It is true that these researchers study the emotions with which we react, while I study the use the mind makes of those emotions. Yet these thinkers offer a valuable body of insight. I'm thinking of not only psychologists like R. B. Zajonc or Israel Scheffler but their predecessors, like Charles Osgood, who sought to quantify the affective meaning of language; George Mandler, who studied the cause of emotions; or Gordon Bower, who studies emotion and memory. I'm thinking also of a group of psychologists and literary critics centered around the International Society for the Empirical Study of Literature, which includes members from Holland, Scandinavia, Belgium, Germany, and France. These researchers use the techniques of cognitive psychology to document the presence and function of affect in literature, pinning down subjective facts that would otherwise remain conjectural.

Researchers like G. Hansson, Mark Sadowski, D. S. Miall, and Keith Oatley have all contributed to this body of work, in some cases even hinting at a connection between representation and affect. Thus Ellen Esrock, in her defense of the image, spends a chapter exploring the contribution of affect to the image. Andrew Ortony says that our personal representations of the poem must include affect. And Gernsbacher, Goldsmith, and Robertson show that readers mentally represent the emotions felt by fictional characters.

To be more specific, in the article "Emotions and Literary Text Comprehension," E. W. E. M. Kneepkens and Rolf A. Zwaan distinguish between the emotions one feels within the text, in the course of identifying with the characters, and those one feels about the text as an artifact. Both kinds of emotion direct our construction of the author's fictional world. In "Story Processing as an Emotion Episode," collected in *Naturalistic Text Comprehension*, Ed Tan documents the many different kinds of emotion evoked by a text and explores their role in cognition. "Emotion requires appraisal, but it also motivates and controls the construction of a particular meaning, lending the force of belief to it, and enforcing it to awareness."[22]

The neurophysiologist Antonio Damasio, who belongs in a category all of his own, shows that the very nature of consciousness is founded on feeling. In *The Feeling of What Happens* (1999), Damasio argues that we have a feeling of knowing that tells us when we know. We also have a feeling of the self that does the knowing. Such feelings enhance our mental constructions by sharpening our focus on them.[23] They also help form the very nature of consciousness. Is it not likely that we also have a feeling of *what* is known? Damasio assumes without comment that the feeling of knowing represents the act of knowing, pointing to a bona fide example of emotional representation.

These researchers leave no doubt that the narrative is an affective device. In this sense, even though my method is different, I build upon the foundation they provide. If the text is designed to awaken emotions within the reader, and if those emotions exert control over the story—if the story in large part consists of emotion—why shouldn't emotion be the mental medium of that construction? From one perspective the focus of these pyschologists on emotional reaction obscures the fact of emotional representation. One must go beyond the preliminary functions of emotion. And yet the work of these psychologists opens the door to the subject of this study: from the larger perspective, the affective code defines one more way in which emotion facilitates cognition.

The only way of expressing emotion in the form of art is by finding an 'objective correlative'; in other words, a set of objects, a situation, a chain of events which shall be the formula of that *particular* emotion; such that when the external facts, which must terminate in sensory experience, are given, the emotion is immediately evoked.

—T. S. Eliot, *The Sacred Wood*

6

The Intellectual Landscape I

THE CONCEPT OF AN AFFECTIVE CODE IS ALIEN TO OUR USUAL WAY OF thinking. For at least a hundred and fifty years we have defined the mind as intellect, dismissing emotion as a distraction. We *resist* the notion that emotion plays a functional role in thought, as one can see in Eva Brann's *The World of the Imagination,* which rejects the emotional mode as an acceptable option. And how could it be? Following the lead of the cognitive scientists, our contemporary intellectual world has marched resolutely away from our ordinary experience (dismissed as "folk knowledge") toward a faith in innate ideas and abstract theory.

Yet emotion is truly a functional part of the human mind. The affective code is *already* a part of our thinking, in fact, if we but recognized it. It is one of those ideas that exist on the periphery of our collective awareness, known and yet unacknowledged, understood and yet not quite conscious. Quite a few thinkers have glimpsed it, though usually on the way to making another point.

In a discussion of Sartre's theory of emotion, for example, the philosopher Mary Warnock ventures that "what seems clear or strong, in the case of a good imitation, is not a picture which is a good likeness, but a *feeling.*" And Sartre himself, in *The Psychology of Imagination,* speaks of the representation of a woman's hands: "those hands that present themselves to me *under their affective form.*" In his *Psychology* William James is highly conscious of a "halo" of emotion around the image: "The significance, the value, of the image is all in this halo

74

or penumbra that surrounds and escorts it,—or rather that is fused into one with it." No wonder that James Hillman recognizes representation in his book, *Emotion,* or that *The Encyclopedia Britannica* covers "aesthetics" by setting the headings of imagination and emotion side by side.[1]

Nor should such a fact surprise us, since emotion performs many tasks that imply that it is a mental code. It unites the private and public realms, for example, providing the cement that makes community possible—especially if the community determines meaning. It also provides the basis for our sense of the whole, which we call the impression, as well as filling the gaps in the narrative recognized by Roman Ingarden and Wolfgang Iser (see chapter 8). The capacity of emotion to express meaning would alone make it a natural medium for diegetic construction.

In addition, the affective code explains aspects of the mind that are otherwise ambiguous or mysterious. It is emotion in its representational function that offers an almost perfect definition of a "nonoptical image." When Wolfgang Iser says that images "illuminate the character, not as an object, but as a bearer of meaning," he points to emotion, since, as Henry James tells us, "in the arts, feeling is always meaning." As Mary Warnock says, "the emotion-laden 'seeing' of the image (whether inner or outer) is identical with 'seeing' the truth."[2] Because emotion has an almost infinite capacity for fusion, as I argue in chapter 11, it completes Samuel Coleridge's famous definition of the imagination, explaining *how* the imagination reconciles or unites Coleridge's long list of "discordant qualities."

Accordingly, I now turn to thinkers in several disciplines who in some way corroborate the affective code. What can we learn from them? Not all of these writers would accept the affective code, and none of them have championed or developed the notion. Yet at least a half dozen of them (if I include the philosophers discussed in chapter 9) understand emotional representation to be a fact. Together they indicate, if only in the aggregate, that *something* is there, performing like an affective code. They show that the notion is acceptable and perhaps inevitable. I understand that they discuss genres other than prose fiction, ranging from poetry to daily thought, and yet the basic function of construction and display remains much the same in all genres, permitting me to range among several categories. All of these thinkers have something to teach us, not the least of which is how to struggle successfully with our cultural prejudice against emotion.

I. Wordsworth and Hazlitt

As one might expect, the first thinkers to understand emotional construction are the romantic poets. Surprisingly, however, Samuel Coleridge is not the leader in this understanding. Coleridge believed that the imagination permits the poet to feel, binding emotion to thought, but he was interested in emotion as subject and reaction. The point of *Lyrical Ballads*, he writes in *Biographia Literaria*, was "the interesting of the affections," and his own task was to do so by means of the supernatural, or "by the dramatic truth of such emotions, as would naturally accompany such situations, supposing them real."[3]

Instead it was William Wordsworth who understood the representational function of emotion, and did so in a strikingly practical and hard-headed way. By defining poetry as "the spontaneous overflow of powerful feelings," the preface to the second edition of *Lyrical Ballads* (1802) becomes nothing less than an essay on the role of emotion in poetry. Wordsworth uses the language of common men, he says, because such people use their "simple and unelaborated expressions" to "express their feelings and notions." He claims a moral purpose to his poetry because it educates the reader's emotions, connecting them "with important subjects, till at length . . . his affections [are] strengthened and purified."[4]

Most of all, Wordsworth identifies emotion with the production of poetry, giving his now famous account of how emotion works within the imagination. Poetry

> takes its origin from emotion recollected in tranquility: the emotion is contemplated till, by a species of reaction, the tranquility gradually disappears, and an emotion, kindred to that which was before the subject of contemplation, is gradually produced, and does itself actually exist in the mind. (740)

This famous description is plain enough except for one point: Wordsworth speaks of contemplating not the original subject, as one would suppose, but the feeling it produced.[5] "The *emotion* is contemplated. . . ." What is more, the result of that contemplation is a reconstitution of not the original scene but the original emotions. The poet thinks about the remembered emotion until he feels it again, and *that* is the poem! Wordsworth cites an emotion precisely where one would normally cite the object. In both meaning and text, the emotion (i.e., the affective code) stands for the subject.

For this reason the central document of English romanticism describes the affective code. Emotion represents the poet's subject first in the poet's memory and then in the moment of writing ("and an emotion . . . is gradually produced"). Emotion also represents the poet's meaning within the reader's mind, where readers duplicate the writer's process in reverse. Just as the poet moves from memory to emotion to emotional representation to language, so the reader moves from text to emotion to affective code to represented object.

It is true, of course, that some scholars interpret "The Preface" as a discussion of image or word. Yet it is not an *image* that is "recollected in tranquility." It is not a word that is "gradually produced." While the poet works with language and image, he has

> an ability of conjuring up in himself passions which . . . do more nearly resemble the passions produced by real events, than anything which, from the motions of their own mind merely, other men are accustomed to feel in themselves. (735)

Why do we not hear more about this particular process of affective representation? One reason lies in Wordsworth's recognition of the many other functions performed by emotion. Wordsworth valued emotion for its own sake and then for its special connection to spiritual insight,

> that serene and blessed mood
> In which the affections gently lead us on,
> Until . . . we are laid asleep
> In body, and become a living soul[6]

Among such experiences, the role of emotion as construction easily gets lost, illustrating what is perhaps the greatest obstacle to our recognition of the affective code: the many functions emotion plays in human experience. Yet it is indisputable that Wordsworth speaks in the preface of "such objects as strongly excite those feelings," which in turn represent the poet's meaning (735). In "The Prelude" Wordsworth speaks of "obscure feelings representative of things forgotten."[7]

A second romantic writer, the English essayist and critic William Hazlitt, is even more explicit about emotional representation. In his essay "On Genius and Common Sense," Hazlitt recognizes the role of the affective code in the judgments people make in daily life. How, Hazlitt asks, do we represent the vast amount of experience and knowledge we bring to bear upon a decision? In asking this question, Hazlitt identifies what the psychologist Rudolph Arnheim would call 150 years later "one of the most astonishing gaps in the program of modern psychology," a gap Arnheim defines when he says that "the mere fact that so many of our judgments of right and wrong are made before we know why we make them should alert the profession."[8]

As I mentioned in the last chapter, our store of unconscious knowledge is a problem because it is vast. How could we possibly recall, reconstruct, and ponder each and every memory? Instead, Hazlitt tells us, articulating the very key of diegetic emotion, we know our past experiences as the feeling that synthesizes them. "In art, in taste, in life, in speech, you decide from feeling, and not from reason; that is, from the impression of a number of things on the mind, which impression is true and well-founded, though you may not be able to analyze or account for it in the several particulars." Hazlitt equates "feeling" with the "impression" because both synthesize complex bodies of information.[9]

We "decide from feeling" because that is how the mind communicates what is held in memory. We depend upon our "impressions" because (as in the first impression) they reduce a complex scene to an overview, the meaning of which we feel as an emotion. In this way Hazlitt explains how we are able to use our vast residual knowledge without pushing everything else out of our minds.

How does this work in daily life? When we need to buy a vacuum cleaner, we have a great deal of relevant information in our head. We use our past experience vacuuming, our present needs, and our knowledge of the vacuum machines available. And how do we do it? We synthesize and display our knowledge by means of the affective code. We have a feeling that an upright is more powerful or that one should avoid plastic accessories or that Hoover is a solid company. Such feelings express the meaning of our complicated experience, and as I say, they work as an index, offering a summary of our knowledge. They are "common sense," as Hazlitt says, or a representation of the vast sum of data stored in the unconscious mind.

What do Wordsworth and Hazlitt teach us? They do have their differences. Wordsworth sees the poet as exceptional, while Hazlitt defines the "common sense" of all people. Wordsworth describes the process of imagining in detail while Hazlitt points to the phenomenon as a whole. Yet both discuss the same process, even if they do not develop it in detail. Both recognize the basic fact that emotion represents meaning, whether it be an ecstatic experience or a homely memory. Both understand that emotion *distills* meaning, reducing complex subjects to a useful form (much as an idea offers an abstract counter for its referent). This is a key function in human thought. And both recognize the capacity of such emotion to serve as an index to memory. I might note that in the second part of "On Genius and

Common Sense," Hazlitt defines the imagination as empathy, or the ability to feel within oneself the emotions felt by another.

II. T. S. Eliot

Such ideas about the affective code are quite different from the views of aestheticians like Joseph Addison and Shaftsbury in the eighteenth century, or Walter Pater and John Ruskin in the nineteenth. These four essayists focus on emotional reaction. They celebrate emotion for its own sake, sometimes as a kind of meaning (Shaftsbury on the sublime) or a kind of energy (Pater's burn with a "hard, gem-like flame"). While Wordsworth and Hazlitt do not deny such notions, they define emotion as not just motive or reaction but one of the codes within which we think.

Unfortunately, the insights of Wordsworth and Hazlitt did not make it into the twentieth century. The scientific method has no use for emotion, and as the historian Peter Stearns observes, our citizens strive to be "cool." And yet, wonder of wonders, the twentieth century may someday be known for its quiet rediscovery of emotion. A number of its thinkers examine the emotional dimension of language, and in doing so offer support for the affective code, even though they have to struggle mightily with contemporary prejudices. Several thinkers make emotion acceptable to our culture by insisting that it is impersonal.

We see this strategy in our most direct description of emotional communication, T. S. Eliot's theory of the "objective correlative." In his famous essay "Hamlet and His Problems," Eliot claims that the specifics and patterns in a text evoke emotion in the reader.

> The only way of expressing emotion in the form of art is by finding an "objective correlative"; in other words, a set of objects, a situation, a chain of events which shall be the formula of that *particular* emotion; such that when the external facts, which must terminate in sensory experience, are given, the emotion is immediately evoked.[10]

We can glimpse Eliot's difficulty with this doctrine in how passé the notion of a formula seems now. The theory appears mechanical and has been largely forgotten: as *The New Yorker* art critic Adam Gopnik would put it, making fun of such theories, Eliot is one of those who were "earnestly dopey in their insistence that abstract art mechanically encrypted particular emotions, with big red blotches equalling excitement, droopy forms making you feel sad, and so on."[11] Yet the truth is that Eliot voices an important insight into reading: it is a fact that language evokes an emotion that is functionally important.

What seems strained or excessive in this concept, in my view, derives from Eliot's attempt to convince our recalcitrant culture.

For one thing, Eliot had to strain to make poetry fit the new doctrines of modernism. He understood that painters such as Kandinsky and (to a lesser degree) Picasso were moving from the literal representation of objects to the pure color and form that evoke (or express) emotion directly. He also knew that both cubism and fauvism distort the surface appearance of the object in order to express an essential feeling. No doubt he understood that such painters find kinship with the sculpture of Henry Moore and the music of Igor Stravinsky, who also moved beneath the surface of their subject to express the essential emotion.

One could argue that the objective correlative *is* modernism. Modernist art exists, as Eliot says, to evoke emotion directly in its audience. Sometimes this emotion exists for its own sake, as in Archibald MacLeish's view that "A poem should not mean but be." One reads not for ideas but to experience the emotions the poem evokes. At other times the emotion evoked by the work expresses its meaning. In his essay on "Hamlet" Eliot refers to the emotional motivation of the character, and in the poem "The Love Song of J. Alfred Prufrock" he expresses an emotion that defines an era.

But how does a poet, who uses words that refer to the world, craft a literary version of the abstract visual process of modernistic painting? Gertrude Stein and James Joyce might seek to use words as sound, creating a verbal art approximating music or abstract painting, but most writers (and those two as well, to tell the truth) continue to write referentially. Confronted with this dilemma, Eliot bridged the gap between pure form and referential language by treating the named objects and patterns of literature as sources of emotion in themselves. He realized that the referential meaning of words creates emotion in its own right, especially if the usual syntax is fragmented. If the painters would create emotion by form and color, Eliot would create it by allusion and reference—by using snatches of song or phrase or idea as well as the "set of objects, a situation, a chain of events," to which the words refer. Nor is this process as mechanical as it seems. While Eliot seems to treat words and forms as buttons to push, he is quite aware of the living process. He understands, as he says, that the feelings expressed in the poem are discovered in the act of writing and so belong to just those words expressed in just that way. The act of writing transforms the original emotions.

At the same time that Eliot attempts a modernistic description of poetry, working to bridge the gap between art and literature, he struggles to fit emotion into our scientific age. It is this effort especially that creates the strain in Eliot's thought, as he uses the concept of the "objective correlative" to make poetry impersonal (and so scientifically acceptable). The poet's mind, Eliot says in "Tradition and the Individual Talent," is like a chemical catalyst. The emotion that the poet and the reader feel is as precise and hard as a mathematical formula. "It is in this depersonalization that art may be said to approach the condition of science."[12] And it is in this emulation of science that Eliot becomes formulaic.

Like Paul Ricoeur fifty years later, Eliot also distinguishes between feeling and emotion, which enables him to jettison whatever is uncontrollable or sloppy. In "Tradition" he defines emotion as the personal, or the expression of individual needs, and feeling as the impersonal, rising above the individual. Readers experience emotion as they react to the text, but the point of the work is the creation of (the more scientifically respectable) feeling, which is attached to words and images and "which was probably in suspension in the poet's mind until the proper combination arrived."[13] Feelings are precise, less intense than emotion, and representational. They are "impersonal" in the sense that they convey information to the reader in an accurate way.

What does T. S. Eliot contribute to an understanding of the affective code? He places emotion at the center of the poem, like Wordsworth, and then adds what we may take as the enabling mechanism. His equation of language with emotion moves the representational emotion out of the writer's head and onto the page. It also explains how emotion moves from artist to text to reader. Eliot describes the artist expressing the emotion that he feels by finding the proper object and naming it, and implies that the reader will follow the process in reverse, finding in the word the object that evokes the emotion.[14] To both author and reader (as Wordsworth said) the poem lies in the feeling. In this regard it is pertinent that the philosopher F. H. Bradley, on whom Eliot did his Ph.D. thesis at Harvard, believed that the mind knows experience as a flow of feeling. In what I will show in chapter 11 to be a key concept, Eliot also viewed emotion as a fusion of many strands. When Eliot uses the word "evoke," moreover, he suggests that readers actually feel the emotions involved.[15]

III. COLLINGWOOD AND LANGER

To reconcile the claims of modernism, science, and emotion is a tall order. We see just how tall it is—and how hard a twentieth century thinker about emotion must work—in the views of two prominent philosophers of the 1930s, 1940s, and 1950s. Neither of them accepts affective representation itself, but they do lay a foundation for it. And their attempt to make emotion impersonal illustrates the difficulty of reconciling the facts about emotion with the assumptions and prejudices of science.[16]

The English philosopher R. G. Collingwood defines art as the language of emotion, and in doing so offers several useful insights into the emotional code. Collingwood argues in *The Principles of Art* (1938) that the quality of the work depends upon the quality of the expression of emotion. Good art is that in which the artist discovers his or her emotion, enabling the reader to do the same. Good art also organizes the emotions it expresses in a harmonious way. Like Eliot, Collingwood understands that emotions combine, and claims that the emotion expressed in the work is unique. To Collingwood, moreover, every "sensum" or mental sensation "has its own emotional charge," which provides the key distinction between feeling and emotion. While the emotion proper exists independently of sensation, a feeling consists of both sensation and emotion, which, "thus related, are twin elements in every experience of feeling."[17]

Although Collingwood recognizes the emotion in the work of art, he rigorously excludes it from the interaction of writer and reader. Artists seek not to evoke emotion in the reader but to express their own feelings. Their relationship is with the work alone. Readers discover their own emotions while reading the work, but hermetically, relating to not the artist or his feeling but the text. Both artist and reader are so absorbed in clarifying their personal emotion that they have no time for the other.[18] To both the key word is not "representation" but "expression."

Collingwood insists on this rather curious separation of writer and reader in order to defend the spontaneity of emotion. To represent emotion, he believes, is to make it the object of the writer's craft, and so conscious and manipulated, violating its unmediated and spontaneous nature.

Still, Collingwood provides support for Eliot's concept, recognizing that communication in art is affective. Because the emotion and the factual meaning of a word are "absolutely united," Collingwood has no difficulty with the equation of word and emotion.[19] "The expression of any given thought is effected though the expression of the emotion accompanying it."[20] Collingwood separates the emotions of the writer and reader, in fact, in order to avoid the problems involved in equivalence of word and emotion. Art is not a "formula" but a kind of Rorschach test, in which the emotions are so individual that Collingwood need not explain how they are shared. To Collingwood emotion lies at the center of human communication but remains personal and eclectic.

Not many thinkers would agree with Collingwood on this point. It is true that every emotion contains unique elements, which is how it provides precise representation. But the fact that emotion is highly social, its substance and expression often taught by the culture, would seem to insure a community of feeling. Collingwood might be correct about the hermetic focus of writer and reader, but for all practical purposes, both undergo the same process: what expresses the emotion of the writer evokes that emotion within the imagining reader, suggesting that writers and readers feel much the same emotion. This point is reinforced by Collingwood's belief that the feeling of a given work belongs to just those particular words or colors or sounds—an idea that sounds quite a bit like Eliot's formula.

In *Philosophy in a New Key* (1942), *Feeling and Form* (1953), *Problems of Art* (1957), and *Mind* (1967), the American philosopher Susanne K. Langer also celebrates the role of emotion in art. She too, like Collingwood, shapes emotion to fit the scientific predilections of the past century, largely by defining it as impersonal. To Langer, as to Collingwood, art exists to express emotion: "*All art is the creation of perceptible forms expressive of human feeling.*"[21] Art is necessary, in fact, because discursive language cannot express our subtle and literally unspeakable human feelings. "Verbal statement, which is our normal and most reliable means of communication, is almost useless for conveying knowledge about the precise character of the affective life."[22] Langer recognizes what legions of rational thinkers ignore, which is the richness and power of inner feeling, or

> what we sometimes call the *subjective aspect* of experience, the direct feeling of it—what it is like to be waking and moving, to be drowsy, slowing down, or to be sociable, or to feel self-sufficient but alone; what it feels like to pursue an elusive thought or to have a big idea. . . . Only the most striking ones have names like "anger," "hate," "love," "fear," and are collectively called "emotion." But we feel many things that never develop into any designable emotion. The ways we are moved are as various as the lights in a forest; and they may intersect, sometimes without cancelling each other, take shape and dissolve, conflict, explode into passion, or be transfigured. All these inseparable elements of subjective reality compose what we call the "inward life" of human beings.[23]

Langer's point is irrefutable, I believe, and makes some of the present models of the mind irrelevant. Art is as necessary as science, Langer says, because only the form of the work of art can express such subtle and uncharted feelings. Accordingly, Langer in *Feeling and Form* gives the most extensive analysis of emotion in the aesthetic experience that we have, as she surveys the role of feeling in each of the different arts. And she offers several kinds of support for Eliot's objective correlative. She seconds Eliot's understanding that art is impersonal and, as I say, argues that the *form* of the work serves as a correlative to the emotion felt by the artist—one of Eliot's ideas precisely. In *Mind* Langer perceives feeling to be the foundation of language.

While Langer places emotion at the center of the work, however, she also takes it back. What I call emotion in the act of reading Langer defines as "virtual emotion," or a semblance of the real thing. In Langer's view readers do not feel the emotion in the text. They understand it cerebrally, recognizing it from the outside. "What art expresses is *not* actual feeling, but ideas of feeling. . . . The feeling in a work of art is something the artist *conceived* . . . rather than something he was undergoing."[24] While emotion dominates the work, the reader knows it intellectually, which is to say without the subjectivity or fluidity that bothers critics like Eliseo Vivas.

We can see the attraction of this argument. In a single stroke Langer frees art from what is messy in emotion and resolves a problem long debated by philosophers—the relationship of vicarious and real emotion. And yet Langer misses a crucial element. As Susan Feagin makes clear, the emotion one feels while reading is actual—Langer's "virtual emotion" goes too far. More importantly, Langer misses the immense power of empathy or reader identification, which may sweep up readers in a flow of emotion that is both precise and powerful. Although we know that our reactions to vicarious and actual experience are different, both kinds of feeling are real.[25]

Or put it this way: fiction is fantasy, which means that in the guise of the characters, we actually read—and so feel—about ourselves. These emotions are as real as only one's feelings about oneself can be, and then are especially free, as the fantasy permits us to feel emotions we would otherwise repress. Langer succeeds in her hidden purpose in *Feeling and Form,* which is to refute Collingwood's claim that emotion is hermetic: she certainly does reestablish emotional contact between the author and the reader. But she does so by distorting the reader's emotion in two ways. First of all, she misses (in *Feeling and Form*) the important fact that we feel emotion in degrees. During a single day we feel many different intensities of emotion, and even feel them change within us. Our feeling (of something wrong, say) can grow into an emotion (a conviction of injustice) and even a passion (a drive to change the status quo).

Secondly, Langer underestimates the impressive complexity of emotion, assuming that the reader feels only one emotion at a time. It is more accurate to say that our emotions are usually mixed. Though I find a bullfight repellant, for example, I can still feel the calm and stoicism of the bullfighter, experiencing emotions that are different than my personal reaction. In both art and life, I feel both the personal and the impersonal at the same time, which means that I feel both real emotion, as the personal must be, and a relatively disinterested emotion, as in my sense of the object or my empathy with another character.

Still, Susanne Langer presents several ideas central to the affective code. Like Collingwood, she sees the expression of emotion to be the purpose of art. She also understands that the form of the work expresses emotion, and so stands as the equivalent to it—an objective correlative. In her description of virtual emotion, moreover, Langer (like Eliot) recognizes an impersonality in emotion that is real even if it is counterintuitive. And finally, though she differs from him in many regards, Langer joins Collingwood in wrestling with the difficult issue of emotional expression. She too understands that the mere expression of emotion changes it. To Collingwood the moment of expression, and the emotion expressed, are unique and so cannot be duplicated by the reader. To Langer, the emotions of the text can be shared, thanks to the subtlety of aesthetic form, but the act of writing does indeed transform the artist's original, private emotion.

Everyone knows emotion, yet no one seems to know what it is. It baffles analysis and yet lies in our bosoms. The paradox, I suggest, disappears, if we recognize that emotion is the very essence of quality. It is the very quality of the event itself when this event is voluminous, intense, and highly fused.

—Stephen Pepper, "Emotion"

7

The Intellectual Landscape II

I. WIMSATT AND BEARDSLEY; STEPHEN PEPPER

I TURN NEXT TO SEVERAL THINKERS WHO EMBRACE EMOTION WITH fewer reservations than we have seen so far. Even more than the authors discussed in chapter 6, these writers perceive the qualities of emotion that make the affective code possible. They understand that emotion is precise and objective, that it expresses meaning, and that it expresses the whole (which in several ways evades image and idea). They also understand that emotion exists as an intrinsic part of one's perception, fused to sensation from the very beginning.

This does not mean that these thinkers come together to form a self-consciously coherent body of thought. What is striking as one reviews their writing is how isolated each of them seems—and how isolated their discussion of emotion is from the rest of their work. They all wrestle with the problem of subjectivity, knowing it to be the essence of our human experience in a culture that distrusts it. They all work hard to make emotion acceptable to current thought.

So once again we encounter the prejudice of our culture against emotion, and none so clearly as in a central document of the New Criticism, the critical school that provides the foundation of literary studies even today. In their essay "The Affective Fallacy," the professors W. K. Wimsatt and Monroe Beardsley do indeed repudiate the "impressionism and relativism" of emotion and so appear to reject affect. To assume that the essay makes that point, however, is to be wrong: in one of those quirks of public opinion, the title "The Affective Fallacy" has become more influential than the essay itself. *It* has been embraced while the substance of the essay has been ignored. That is to say, what Wimsatt and Beardsley actually reject is not the study of emotion in the poem but the divorce of emotion from fact. They write to disagree with I. A. Richards and those semanticists who would separate emotion from meaning. Yes, they argue, purely personal emotion in a work is damaging, but emotion grounded in reality (and reaching a level of impersonality) provides the essence of the poem as well as a definition of its quality.

Because the fact is the source of the emotion, and so is equated with it, Wimsatt and Beardsley defend T. S. Eliot's objective correlative. "Poetry is characteristically a discourse about both emotions and objects," they conclude, "or about the emotive quality of objects." The emotions in the poem are "presented in their objects and contemplated as a pattern of knowledge." In this way the authors of this famous essay describe not the rejection of emotion in poetry but how such emotion ought to be approached—insisting that it *should* be approached because it is connected to truth.[1]

What do Wimsatt and Beardsley contribute to a theory of the affective code? Perhaps their largest contribution is their explanation of the role of affect in aesthetic evaluation. They testify to not only the precision of emotion and its position at the center of the poem, but the differences in the quality of emotions within the poem. Emotions unconnected to fact (and so termed sentimental) are aesthetically inferior because they are imprecise and free-floating. One judges a poem by not the personal feelings that it awakens—how it makes one feel, as I. A. Richards argued—but the validity of the emotions the poem employs. The "fallacy" is not the embracing of the affective but failing to take mood or tone or connotation seriously.

Wimsatt and Beardsley also argue that emotion expresses the *importance* of the particular fact, securely tying emotion to the meaning of the statement. Their essay shows that the New Criticism was about emotion as much as about science, restoring affect as a functional part of art and thought. It is true that some readers find Wimsatt and Beardsley's discussion of emotion "contemplated as a pattern of knowledge" to be mechanical. But the authors' distinction between sentimentality and affective knowledge is persuasive, making an acceptance of the objective correlative possible. When people reject emotion (as they do in different ways), they really reject a false or misused emotion. Wimsatt and Beardsley describe one way emotion is grounded in reality and so made authentic.

A philosopher who grappled with emotional representation in the thirties shows even less strain than Wimsatt and Beardsley—while defining the concept that lies at the center of the affective code.

Stephen Pepper provides what is still the best general treatment of emotion, even though his essay, "Emotion," was first published in his book *Aesthetic Quality* sixty years ago. He offers a clear and thoughtful description of what we truly experience, refusing to distort that experience to accommodate our cultural bias. He provides a baseline for our understanding of emotion, offering what we might call the old-fashioned, humanistic description of emotion, or precisely those principles of common human experience that cognitive philosophers dismiss as "folk psychology."

Pepper actually mentions most of the concepts necessary to the affective code. He understands that emotion organizes the text or work of art; that texts evoke emotions in readers in several ways, including simple contagion; that emotion can be precise; that emotion expresses meaning understood by most readers; and that the objective correlative is therefore actual. Pepper also understands that the work of art can be judged according to the aesthetic integrity of the emotion it arouses. Art enjoys a vitality greater than even our daily experience because of its sharp and uncluttered focus.[2]

But most of all, Pepper defines the central concepts of "quality" and "fusion":

> Everyone knows emotion, yet no one seems to know what it is. It baffles analysis and yet lies in our bosoms. The paradox, I suggest, disappears, if we recognize that emotion is the very essence of quality. It is the very quality of the event itself when this event is voluminous, intense, and highly fused.[3]

By "quality" Pepper means *identity*, or what is unique in the event. He means our feeling *of* the individual quality of the event, person and element. How better represent an object than by the "essence" of its "quality"? When Pepper insists that we feel the identity of the art work as a whole, he reminds one of William Hazlitt's definition of the "impression" as the essence of an event. As Pepper puts it in *Principles of Art Appreciation:*

> The distinctive over-all character of each picture remains as something different from the characters of the elements. This intuitively grasped character of the total picture is its fused quality. And to grasp that character is to react emotionally to the picture rather than analytically.[4]

Pepper does not take the next step, which would be to recognize an emotional code, but he comes close. In one's memory "the intuitively grasped character of the total picture" would represent the painting admirably, and that "character" or "essence" calls out for emotion. Pepper seems to say that the mind fuses the many lines and colors—the myriad sensations—of a scene into a whole that we *feel*, an idea not unlike that of William Hazlitt. Pepper also recognizes the ability of emotion to express a complex subject in a flash of feeling. It is emotion that represents the whole created by the fusion of the separate and sometimes conflicting individual elements.

Pepper probably takes this notion of fusion from William James, who views emotion in terms of the fusion of "organic and kinesthetic sensations," and perhaps from R. G. Collingwood, who stressed the fusion of sensation and emotion. As we will see, it is fusion that permits the affective code to synthesize a complex of meanings within a single feeling. It is also fusion that enables the affective code to achieve precision—and that organizes the many separate emotions in a passage into the single, encompassing code emotion.

What can we take from Pepper? He does not describe emotional display as such, perhaps because he did not feel the need to. And he does not ground the qualities of emotion in the mind as a whole—he might well have distinguished among the key functions of emotion. Yet he gives the affective code a solid foundation. If Wordsworth describes the emotional imagination, and Hazlitt extends it to daily life, and Eliot relates it to language, Stephen Pepper explains *why* emotion is suited to these specific functions.

II. Scheler and Leeper

The third thinker who recognizes representation is a European phenomenologist, or one of those who sought to reestablish the primacy of concrete experience. Members of this group, writing mostly in the first half of the twentieth century, include Martin Heidegger in *Being and Time*, Stephan Strasser in *Phenomenology of Feeling*, and (somewhat later) the American, Robert Solomon, in *The Passions*. Because I discuss these three thinkers in other chapters, I will look here at the theory of Max Scheler in *The Nature of Sympathy*, published in German in 1931 and English in 1954. Scheler offers one of our most complete examinations of emotion as cognition, arguing that emotion is as important a way of knowing as reason, since it is by means of emotion that we perceive values. Scheler distinguishes between two sets of emotions: "feeling-states," in which the object of the feeling is not obvious, so that they exist as a state of mind, and "value-feelings," which are a perception of a real attribute or value of the world.

Of course, we see only what we look at, which means that the emotions that motivate us control perception. As we look in one

direction or another, our value-feelings determine what we see and
so control cognition. But Scheler means much more than this. In any
given instance, the emotions that we feel uncover new and otherwise
ignored attributes in the object. When we react with love or hate,
those emotions are perceptions of something real in the object or
event.

I don't think many people would disagree with Scheler on this
point. Forty-eight years after *Sympathy* appeared in English, many
philosophers and psychologists define emotion as "appraisal," or
one's immediate judgment of the object. Philosophers now explore
the cognitive value of "attitude." As a phenomenologist, however,
Scheler believed that we perceive such values immediately, in the way
the ear hears sound or the eye sees movement. Emotion is a direct
perception of values inherent in the object. Scheler catches the important fact that emotion expresses meaning without mediation.

Although Scheler is probably correct on this last point, he represents the losing side in an important debate. For in the conflict in the
sixties between phenomenology, which champions the validity of
individual perception, and poststructuralism, which doubts all perception, the phenomenologists lost. We are just now, at the beginning of the new century, emerging from under the shadow of the
poststructuralist victory in the seventies. But whatever the fate of
phenomenology, Scheler offers several concepts useful to an understanding of the affective code. Because the values reside in the objects, the emotions that discover them are "objective" or accurate.
They are *not* projected, which means that people share them naturally, as they do because of "contagion." Scheler also understands the
large role of empathy in human perception[5] and then hints that the
value-feeling can represent meaning.[6] If we represent an object by
means of our feeling of the whole, as I suggested in my discussion of
Pepper, we can surely represent it by means of our feeling of its
unique value. Phenomenologists believe that such feelings capture
the "thisness" of the object, or what Pepper calls its unique "quality."

The influence of phenomenology in this country may grow in the
future. It has already invigorated the reader-response movement,
toward which critical attention shows some small signs of returning.
But at the middle of the twentieth century, it was not a philosopher
who most clearly recognized emotional representation but a research psychologist, which is fitting enough. As Israel Scheffler explains in his essay "In Praise of the Cognitive Emotions," not a few
psychologists have examined the role of emotion in cognition. If
feeling not only precedes cognition but follows it, as some believe, is
it not possible that it *is* cognition? R. B. Zajonc points out that "it is

entirely possible that the very first stage of the organism's reaction to stimuli and the very first elements in retrieval are affective."[7]

This line of thought was taken to its logical conclusion in the work of Robert W. Leeper, who argued (in books such as *Toward Understanding Human Personalities*, 1959) that emotion is a way in which we organize our experience. While some emotions are disorganizing, Leeper insists that much of our emotion is less intense than passion, and that we have in fact many fine and delicate feelings that we can control—once again making a functional distinction between emotion and feeling. Such feelings not only help organize experience but represent it. Leeper argues that

> emotional processes, rather than being something outside of and distinct from perceptual processes, are one type of perceptual process. They are processes that represent realities, just as other sorts of perceptual processes do, but they are perceptual processes that are motivationally significant.[8]

Not all perceptual processes are emotional, but all emotional processes are perceptual. What is more, emotions may involve a great deal of subtle perception, serving as "feed back mechanisms that can pick up slight clues."[9] Perceptual processes are "motivationally significant" because the emotions they represent are the same human feelings that can motivate: love plays a large role in the feeling that represents my partner, and it is that same love that motivates me in our relationship. In such ways, memories make us behave in certain ways.

What does Robert Leeper add to our understanding of the affective code? Though he was once cited as an authority in *The Encyclopedia Britannica*, he is no longer fashionable. To my knowledge, no psychologists have picked up on Leeper's basic insight, though in the 1970s Magda Arnold and her colleagues investigated emotion as appraisal, which would, if explored fully, lead to Leeper's pioneering insight. It is also true that Leeper did not develop this understanding, or work up the evidence that would persuade his colleagues. Yet Leeper did indeed understand the diegetic or representational value of emotion. It makes a lot of sense for writers to represent their meaning by means of an emotion that is "motivationally significant," since such emotion, even as it expresses meaning, encourages the reader to imagine intensely. I confess that such dual functions make me uncomfortable: it is hard enough to pin down one function of emotion, let alone two. But in even this casual claim, Leeper lays a foundation for one of the special strengths of the affective code and describes one of its powerful economies.

III. THE CRISIS OF THE SUBJECTIVE

I turn now to a sizable group of philosophers interested in the emotional side of the imagination, including William Lyons, Robert Kirk, Anthony Kenny, and Francis Dunlop. Of these I choose three thinkers who exemplify recent thought about emotion and who suggest that a recognition of the affective code may be inevitable. Emotion actually resolves a central intellectual issue of the 1970s and 1980s, what we can call the problem of knowledge or the crisis of the subjective. Though we have now moved on, it seems, this issue exemplifies the logic that could lead our general culture to a new and more accurate view of emotion.

The critic David Bleich defines the problem in *Subjective Criticism*, in his summary of the subjective nature of knowledge. Bleich reminds us that the mind does not absorb pure data like so much gravel, waiting to be processed for meaning. Rather, as thinkers ranging from Kuhn to Derrida to Rorty have argued, the mind perceives the world *as* meaning, itself creating a great deal of what it perceives. This occurs in several ways. The mind focuses on one subject rather than another and so satisfies one motive rather than another. Of course, where we look determines what we see. The mind also supplies the paradigm that controls interpretation, and even if it did not, the mind understands meaning in terms of social conventions and values that belong to it rather than to the object examined. And then, Bleich says, the mind interprets within language, which shapes what it expresses—in a surprisingly large number of ways the mind manufactures what it perceives.[10]

For such reasons, we understand that knowledge is subjective or an invention of the individual. And that gives us two choices. On the one hand, we can follow science and several literary theories, viewing the subjective as contamination. Because truth lies outside of the personal, the scientist achieves it by expelling the subjective from the process of knowing—truth resides in the world of objects. On the other hand, we can follow the poststructural critics and their view that the expulsion of the personal is impossible, accepting the idea that the mind cannot really know anything. This means that we must live bravely with no truth or, more realistically, with the truth manufactured by our society. Because society instills conventions that determine perception, epistemology is at bottom community. For such reasons David Bleich agrees with Stanley Fish that what one knows is simply the particular fiction one's culture has accepted.

It is not difficult to associate such limited perception with original sin, as Fish does in his discussion of *Paradise Lost*. Nor is it difficult to relate this view to the self-disgust felt by postmodern novelists like Kathy Acker or Don DeLillo. Certainly the present stress on social construction rests on the foundation of such ideas. But given the subjectivity of all knowledge, we have a third alternative, which is that our subjective perception *is* accurate. It is *not* contamination. The person *does* perceive. After all, our species has survived thus far: however much meaning we invent ourselves, we have understood enough of the world to avoid being eaten. Perhaps the socially invented view is not so much fiction as wisdom, based on collective experience. Perhaps the subjective is not inevitably distorting. In any case, why must a subjective perception, which involves the insight as well as the desires of the individual, necessarily be inaccurate?

To perceive in a subjective or emotional manner, after all, is to see from the inside. It is, as Max Scheler tells us, to perceive elements otherwise obscured. Why should the view from the outside alone be valid? And what makes us think (as Husserl and Foucault remind us) that we *could* get outside even if we wished? Even as they announce their relativism, thinkers like David Bleich (who, as I have said, believes that language embodies *both* the objective and the subjective) adopt a scientific standard of truth. They profess their views in a rational, distanced manner that affirms the objectivity that they declare impossible. They also assume that the only truth that could be valid, were it possible, is the objective one.

In my view they would do better to follow philosophers like Heidegger in asserting that a subjective view of the world yields an accurate vision. Yes, emotion can be corrupting, but so can ideas, especially when defined as self-evident or innate. Conversely, both emotion and idea can be trustworthy if used in the right way. And we have good reason to believe that emotion can be accurate, all things being equal, since it is tied to its object. Certainly our daily experience shows it to be trustworthy.

This general view finds support among some of our most stimulating young philosophers, as they wrestle with the problem of knowledge. In *The Body in the Mind* (1987) Mark Johnson analyzes the relationship between the imagined work of art and the real world, asking how the mind can create part of what it perceives and at the same time know a stable, shared reality. If the imagination creates what the individual takes as actual, Johnson observes, then the uniqueness of each person means that we all live in a separate world unknowable to others.[11] Johnson solves this problem by following Immanuel Kant's definition of the imagination as a structuring capacity. He argues that people share a world because they share the structures the imagination provides. While Johnson gives social agreement its due, he also attributes these structures to the "body in the mind," or the biological nature that we all share.

In this way Johnson neatly turns the problem of knowledge on its head, showing that it is the very fact that we create our own perception that makes communal knowledge possible. What people share is the element they individually contribute to their perception. Johnson underlines this argument by tying it to the human body, which offers a common base, and so opens the door to a common knowledge (and presumably, a kind of truth). And yet, for the purposes of my thesis, Johnson does not walk through that door. He does not quite equate the body with its primary vehicle of communication, emotion. Perhaps he feels he does not have to, since emotion is so clearly identified with the body. Or perhaps like the earlier thinkers we have examined, Johnson shies away from the insight he intuits, defining the body as the patterns and structures of its nervous system rather than the emotions that flow within them. In the end, Johnson clings to the old, impersonal categories of perception.

In *Knowledge, Fiction, and Imagination* (1987), David Novitz is much more explicit about emotion. Novitz analyzes the same problem as Johnson: how the mind's contribution to perception isolates the individual. But he finds his answer in not Kantian structure but the reader's emotional entrance into the work of fiction. Novitz defines the imagination as our ability to combine two separate entities or images, which means that the imagination furnishes our ability to make sense of the world.[12] He is also convinced that knowledge in reading requires the proper emotional engagement with the subject. One can know only when engaged. We must not blindly believe in the text, he says, but we must not stand outside of it either. Rather we must permit the imagination to place ourselves within a book *as though* it were real. In this way the imagination permits us to know a text emotionally—the only valid kind of knowledge—without losing perspective or context. How can we know that our emotional and imaginative knowledge is accurate? Novitz argues that we take as knowledge those imaginative constructs that work. We perceive in a practical world, and test those perceptions by the pragmatic standard of that world.

If Mark Johnson opens the door to an understanding of the mental role of emotion, then David Novitz walks us though it, adding the importance of reader identification and its illustration of the integrity of emotional knowing. I certainly subscribe to Novitz's emphasis upon imagination and the role of emotion within it. I also accept his advocacy of human experience as a test for truth and his definition of the imagination in terms of *doing*. Unlike Susanne Langer, Novitz

sees the emotions of the reader as real, and like Heidegger, he believes that insight based upon distance from the object is incomplete.

Even so, Novitz does not for my purpose go far enough. He recognizes emotion as empathy and reaction, but does not see that emotion represents meaning and so constitutes the third mental code.
Nor does Novitz recognize that emotion in the text directs the
reader's understanding of the words, offering instructions on how to
read. Are the words ironic or straight? Thoughtful or comic? As we
will see, in the reading of fiction, it is tone—the emotions expressed
by the author—that determines the meaning and directs the reader
to it.

Of all of these writers it is Paul Ricoeur who looks most directly at
emotional diegesis, championing the affective code even as he illustrates our cultural inhibitions concerning it. In the essay "The Metaphorical Process as Cognition, Imagination, and Feeling," Ricoeur
describes affective representation in his attempt to salvage the concepts of image and feeling from their dismissal as mere ornament or
"psychology." Within the metaphor these elements express
knowledge—they are not only psychological but semantic, which
means that like word and image they carry (and so represent) meaning. In Ricoeur's words, the metaphor employs feeling "to yield some
true insight about reality."[13] When tempered by cognition and language (and understood to be different from emotion, which is physical), the feeling is representative of truth.

Such feeling is important because of the nature of the metaphor,
which requires us to hold two opposing ideas at the same time: the
literal and the figurative meaning of the words. This is "the split
reference of poetic discourse," or the tension or split between identification and distance (157). "To *feel*, in the emotional sense of the
word, is to make *ours* what has been put at a distance by thought in its
objectifying phase" (156). In a metaphor we have it both ways, as we
engage with the subject emotionally at the same time that we stand
back from it. The function of poetic feeling "is to abolish the distance
between knower and known without canceling the cognitive structure of thought and the intentional distance which it implies" (156).
To put it another way, the metaphor embraces emotion, taking it as
the subject it expresses, and then rejects it as well, replacing the real
emotion with the distance of literature.

In such ways Ricoeur describes something close to what I call the
affective code. Certainly he leaves no doubt that feeling represents
subject matter; the split in consciousness caused by metaphor exists
on the verbal, imagistic, and emotional levels, making them all participants in the representation of meaning. Cognition, imagination,

and feeling inhabit parallel structures. Ricoeur even points to the importance of feeling vis-à-vis the mental image, offering yet another example of the "image" that is not pictorial: "To imagine, then, is not to have a mental picture of something but to display relations in a depicting mode," an action he later attributes to feeling (150).[14]

I should hasten to add that Ricoeur himself would disagree with my appropriation of his description of feeling, since he explicitly rejects the notion of emotional representation. He embraces neither intuitionalism, he says, nor emotional realism, since he insists upon his distinction between feeling and emotion. I do think he equates feeling and emotion in practice, as when he tells us that he uses "feeling" in the "emotional sense of the word." Yet the fact remains that even if we accept his definition of feeling, he does not move from the metaphor (where he describes the three tracks I am arguing) to the mind in general. Ricoeur stops but a step away from recognizing what I am calling the emotional imagination and what he might call the imagination of feeling. His testimony is convincing because he grounds it in his analysis of a specific literary device, but like many of the philosophers we have surveyed, he has to wrestle with the rationalistic assumptions of our culture. He separates emotion, with its ostensible physical crudity, from feeling, with its precision and subtle meaning, in order to sanitize emotion, not unlike Nick Adams positioning all that is unpleasant over there, in the swamp.

How do these three philosophers show that our human subjectivity can be true to the world outside our minds? Johnson argues that private minds share the structures of perception, which presumably carry something true, and Novitz and Ricoeur observe that the mind knows the object emotionally, obtaining both the engaged and the disengaged perspective. Thus all three suggest that a subjective emotion or feeling represents the truth without an inevitable distortion. In this way they resolve the problem of knowledge. If our feelings are "semantic," to use Ricoeur's word, they carry meaning just the same as image and word, which means that they display or represent that meaning. Or do all human beings share the same world because they share the same structural or emotional makeup? For my purpose, what matters is that the affective code accurately communicates what people perceive, whether it be real or delusion. I note that all three of these writers ground their views in human experience—which is where we usually perceive emotion to be central. All three philosophers point to the fact that in art, at least, emotion can be as accurate a representation of the available truth as image and idea.

I have seen *Paris*, but shall I affirm I can form such an idea of that city, as will perfectly represent all its streets and houses in their real and just proportions?

—David Hume, *A Treatise of Human Nature*

I would not say that inner images literally "express" emotion; rather they contain or are suffused or informed by feeling, somewhat, indeed very much, as a music or a fragrance informs space.

—Eva Brann, *The World of the Imagination*

8
The Affective Code: A Model and a Method

ALTHOUGH THE AFFECTIVE CODE IS NOT COMMONLY RECOGNIZED, then, the idea is not really alien to our culture. Those who think about the mind can't help but notice that *something* is there, performing the functions I attribute to emotion. The affective code is like an unseen planet rotating around a distant star: we know it exists because we perceive its effect, in this case our ability to imagine elements that idea or image cannot construct. What is especially convincing, when we look into the matter, is that our personal experience confirms the hypothesis. Shall I vacation in Santa Fe this summer? Thinking about it, I imagine the city much as I might imagine my brother or the year 1967. I have a feeling of the city—of its identity or presence—that carries as much information (of a certain kind) as the comparable idea or image.

I *can* think without constructing a mental replica of my subject. Ask me my Social Security number, and I will recite it immediately, without working up a private mental display. I form the number within the words I speak. Ask me if I am sure about those numbers, however, and I will stop and display them within my mind, fabricating a model that I can read off to you. With some activities I always construct a model, as when I indulge an extended memory or read fiction—whenever I have to refer to or enter the construction. What happened during that Sunday visit to Uncle Fred's apartment? I conjure up the memory, reliving it. In my imagination I enter the living room, where I listen to my father and Uncle Fred arguing politics. Certainly I can visualize the sunlight in the windows or think about the event abstractly. But I can also *feel* the nature of that apartment. I can feel the relationship of my father and my uncle and then the presence of the neighborhood outside. I can represent the larger scene by my feeling of such relationships. I can feel Kimbell Avenue, south of Humboldt Square, as an emotion that is unique to that particular stretch of street.

Such experiences convince me that the affective code is actual even if it is not widely recognized. And yet, if I am to establish my point, I must prove the existence of the code and solve some of the problems that it raises. Is it even possible to talk about emotion? In Part I, I showed the need for a new model of mental construction. So far in Part II, I have offered the affective code as the answer to that need and have examined several thinkers who have glimpsed it. I now want to dig deeper into the code, identifying its governing principles, and by so doing pull together these several strands into a unified model that I can demonstrate in Part III.

I

As everyone knows, the act of imagining begins with the author conceiving his or her fictional world and then putting it into words. Although writing differs from reading, both author and reader employ the same mental process. Writers spend a great deal of their time reading, for example, as they go over and over their sentences, testing them in their own minds. Does the sentence or paragraph produce the effect one originally imagined? As we have seen, the psychologist Victor Nell believes that writers pay more attention to images than do readers, since writers need a detailed map of their world. Yet writers employ the same mental codes as readers. And readers *reconstitute* the writer's text, translating the verbal code back into the constructed vicarious experience.[1] In this way, as French criticism makes clear, readers invent or "write" the text.

Whether we focus on the author or the reader, Allan Paivio's theory of two mental codes provides our model with a foundation. Paivio's description of the unique capabilities of each mode is especially useful, since it makes the shift among the codes self-regulating. If you remember, Paivio shows that the visual is integrated and compact, providing information at a glance, while the verbal or ideational is linear and logical, offering a natural format for the definition of cause. All readers employ both codes, though individuals tend to favor one mode over the other, moving from code to code as the content of the text and their own predilections demand. In this way Paivio accommodates both the unity and the diversity among readers—a highly significant task.

To Paivio's original two codes, I add a third, operating in a manner parallel to idea and image and governed by many of the same principles.[2] Just as mental verbalization is based upon (but not identical to) speech, and the mental image is based upon (but not identical to) the sensations of sight, so mental emotion is based upon (but not identical to) the emotions felt in daily life. Such mental emotion is mild and thus controllable.

How would I summarize the strengths unique to the affective code? I have already described several applications, ranging from a sense of presence to the representation of particular objects and states of mind. To the extent that readers do not construct the whole text, emotion offers an abbreviated representation or marker of what we know we could produce—an absolutely essential function. I now want to step back from these specific occasions to identify the precepts that lie behind them. Three principles in particular summarize the special capabilities of the affective code.

The first is the capacity of emotion to synthesize or **distill** a large body of information within a single feeling. It is not limited to the sense of presence that I discussed in chapter 5, since we often refer to large entities that overflow the bounds of a single word or image. One has, for example, many Chicagos, requiring a remarkable feat of representation. My feeling of Chicago recognizes objective facts ranging from the geography of this city built on a swamp to the texture of its specific neighborhoods as seen from the "El." It includes my awareness that Louis Sullivan designed several of the buildings and my sense of the slums that lie west of the skyscrapers. It also includes elements that have a personal meaning, such as the grammar school that I attended and the houses in which I lived, not to mention the family that raised me.

How represent such a cluster of meanings? Yes, the city could be an idea or a word. This is true whether I'm reading a text or pursuing a memory. But the *feeling* of Chicago is in truth richer and more complex than the idea, largely because it embodies (as T. S. Eliot and Stephen Pepper point out) many strands. And, of course, it is concrete rather than abstract. Chicago could also be an image—of tall buildings, say, rising on the edge of a vast lake. But note how that image is limited to one part of the city or one dimension of its meaning. The *feeling* of the city distills many different parts of it, whether they be the shady lawns of Winnetka or the broken neighborhoods of Milwaukee Avenue. And it captures an essentially internal truth. While the image is "cool," positioning us outside of the city looking in, emotion is "warm," placing us inside. It puts us *there*. Compared to image or idea, emotion adds nuance and complexity.

I am not overtly conscious of these individual elements when I think of Chicago, since I know only the composite emotion. My feeling is like a cable of many strands woven into a single cord. But with reflection I can tease out the individual fibers. While the overall emotion represents the city as a whole, it also permits me, if I take the time, to feel (or identify) the constituent emotions separately. Note that these individual emotions may themselves represent images or ideas, offering the feeling of the sight of Lake Michigan, the feeling of the idea of the "second city." Note, too, that these emotions may include my reaction to the city, which serves as a rough evaluation of it, and then my emotional response to that reaction—a subject I discuss in chapter 11.[3]

Why do we not confuse these different kinds of emotion? Sometimes we do, which is why we are nervous about the affective code. Yet a healthy mind can distinguish between its personal mood and the tone of a companion's voice, between a personal disposition and a reaction to the object before one. We easily separate our feeling of Chicago from our personal reaction to the city—though whether we pay attention to that distinction is another matter. People do get careless or distracted, confusing their personal preference with objective reality. This is a universal human failing. But as Aristotle noted 2300 years ago, such confusions involve ideas (and presumably images) as well. Emotion is not more reliable than reason or visualization, but it is not less reliable either.[4]

II

I should stress that the affective code does not exist in a vacuum. It works in tandem with, and so is reinforced by, the other two codes. The affective code refers to objects and elements in the world, moreover, which counteract any tendencies toward the vague or the general. We know them, like everything else, within their setting. And in actual practice, we relentlessly compare the emotion we feel with the circumstance which gives rise to it, making adjustments as we go. Our emotions strike us as concrete, and so are solid in a way that neither idea nor image can be.

The second principle is the capacity of emotion to **blend** with image or idea. This is probably what we mean when we say that emotion is fluid. Eva Brann uses the word "suffusion" to denote this quality, saying that our inner images are "suffused or informed by feeling, somewhat, indeed very much, as a music or a fragrance informs space."[5] We know what she means. Sometimes the emotion seems to surround the mental image or idea, forming the immediate context that determines its meaning. At other times it seems to penetrate the image or idea, becoming part of it, much as Robert Solomon claims, and so permeating it with the meaning that the emotion expresses.

In other words, William Hazlitt was right: emotion is a special form of consciousness that makes information available to the mind in an unobtrusive way. Such feeling is "there but not there," as I said in chapter 5, available to the mind and yet peripheral, or below the level of specific notice. It is a presence that we can choose to make conscious but that otherwise remains unobtrusive. It permits us to be conscious of the foreground and merely *aware* of the contextual background, as we feel its meaning.[6] It permits the mind to represent a significant body of information even as it focuses on a single object. Emotion expresses our reaction to the perception, after all, and so is designed to accompany and complement the perception.

The third principle makes these first two strengths possible. For when I said in chapter 2 that I imagined **meaning** directly, I was really saying that I imagined in the affective code. What kind of meaning does emotion represent? As the critics Wimsatt and Beardsley point out, emotion expresses importance or significance, a point supported by Robert Solomon's view of emotion as an evaluative framework in which we see things as so and so. We "make" our world by virtue of the value we attribute to what we perceive, and we come by this ability naturally.[7] Scientists tell us that all sensation passes through the amygdala, the seat of emotion within the brain, before it reaches the neocortex, or the seat of reason. This means that emotion provides the first, elemental appraisal of our experience, triggering the appropriate action and thought. To perceive is to feel emotion, and to feel emotion is to recognize meaning; thanks to the amygdala, we actually experience sensation *as* meaning—that is, permeated with the emotion that expresses value.

Neurologists like Antonio Damasio witness the result of this fact when a disease destroys the emotional centers of a patient's brain. In *Descartes' Error* Damasio (head of the department of neurology at the University of Iowa College of Medicine) observes a damaged patient who could think abstractly but could not come to a conclusion, let alone act in his own self-interest. The patient could not even choose a time for the next appointment. "He had the requisite knowledge,

attention and memory; his language was flawless; he could perform
calculations; he could tackle the logic of an abstract problem." But he
lacked the capacity to feel. "There was only one significant accompa-
niment to his decision-making failure: a marked alteration of the
ability to experience feelings."[8]

Why should a loss of feeling become a loss of judgment, leading to
a "perpetual violation of what would be considered socially appropriate and personally advantageous"? In my view the loss of emotion
means a loss of the affective code, and so the loss of the knowledge
that defines meaning (and therefore provides a basis for action).
Destroy the emotional centers and you destroy the individual's sense
of place and past, his expectations for the future and his understanding of his personal values—the subtle knowledge that defines the
meaning of the present by expressing the meaning of the past. You
also destroy the sense of the whole, which gives significance to the
specifics within it. As Damasio puts it, emotion is a form of social
knowledge, providing the basis for our perception of many complicated meanings. Damasio's patient could not perceive the emotions
of another or the significance of a symbol—insights essential to life
within a group.

To recognize that we construct the meaning of the text, then, is to
recognize the necessity of the affective code. Of course, as we have
seen, some thinkers argue that the preeminence of meaning requires
words or propositions. Stephen Kosslyn posits a two-tiered mental
representation precisely because of the inability of the image to express meaning over time. My point, in contrast, is that meaning
might well be represented by feeling, which we can feel even as we
focus on the foreground. What is interesting, I think, is the ability of
our feeling of the significance of an object, which is originally general, to become specific and so representative of just that object at
just that time.

III

I can't claim that William Wordsworth understood the affective code
in just these terms, even though he understood the basic mechanism.
But if Wordsworth is right in defining his memories as feelings—if, as
I would put it, the three codes do exist—we must answer a key
question: what is it that makes the reader choose one code rather
than another? The author controls the process, of course, but
readers enjoy a considerable latitude.[9] Some subjects can be
displayed in any of the three modes, as we have seen: one can visual-

ize, think the idea of, or feel the feeling of Nick Adams's coffee pot. If the context does not require a particular code, readers use the one most convenient, which might be the code required by the previous sentence, or perhaps the one they find most comfortable. Accordingly, some readers visualize much of the time, taking the image as their primary mode of imagining. Others intellectualize—some theoretical critics seem to resist reader identification. And still other readers tend to feel the textual meaning, with all the advantages and the difficulties that it entails.

Interestingly, once the mind has begun to construct in a given code, it tends to remain with it, following a principle of inertia. If we have begun to visualize, we want to continue until the content rules it out. Similarly, we tend also to stick to the code we favor, slipping back into intellectualization, say, as a kind of default mode. This means that the mind pushes the limits of each code, asking it to perform functions that might logically belong to the other ones. We sometimes visualize ideas, as in metaphor, or think feelings, as when we name the emotion directly. Images, which begin with sensation, can be stretched to express category or significance; ideas, which begin with category, can be adapted to convey the concrete; and emotions, which begin with private significance, can be adapted to express a publicly shared meaning.

This is not to say that the nature of the subject does not usually require the appropriate code. Clearly, the greatest determinant of the code we use is the nature of the content we would represent, since it requires a particular kind of knowledge. When Nick slips a pine chip onto the fire beneath the grill, he uses his sight, and so must readers who vicariously share Nick's experience. If Nick speaks to someone, readers would probably employ the verbal track. "We need more wood for the fire," Nick might say, requiring most readers to "speak" those words in an inner voice. And when Hemingway writes that Nick "liked to open cans," many readers will share Nick's emotional pleasure—and represent the act by means of the emotion.

We employ much the same process in memory. It is true that whenever I think of my Uncle Fred's living room, I have the ability to *choose* whether to analyze, feel, or visualize the scene. I can even recall the subject in one mode, visualizing the pale light of Chicago two-flats, say, and then develop it in another, analyzing the number of years my Uncle Fred lived there. But most of the time I shift automatically to the code that best matches the requirements of the content. I use images to represent the physical existence of the subject, as presented to the senses. I use ideas and words to represent the conceptual identity of the subject, signifying its definition and category. And

I use emotions to represent or express its significance or value (and perhaps its literal meaning as well).[10]

<h1 style="text-align:center">IV</h1>

Thus our choice of code depends upon the disposition of the reader, the momentum of the passage, and the nature of the content. It also depends upon our purpose, or the larger use to which we would put the mental construction. If I regard Nick's campsite as a category—as one more of his temporary homes, say—I construct it intellectually. My purpose is to categorize and analyze. But if I read Hemingway's story as fiction, vicariously living it, I construct its physical or visual presence. And the same principle holds if the campsite is its meaning: if I imagine the camp as its value to Nick (as a source of safety, say, or a personal accomplishment), I use the affective code, feeling the camp's significance. Of course, my mental construction can fulfill more than one purpose at any given moment.

But then our choice of code depends also upon timing, since each stage of the reading process involves a different set of functions and so a different code or mix of codes. Our initial construction of character, event, dialogue, or setting is direct and basic: we usually imagine a particular object or event in a single code. But the fiction (or memory) requires us to assemble these several elements into a larger whole, which is a different kind of constructive task: we form a highly flexible and even amorphous whole that can absorb the flow of unfolding specifics.[11] It is this body that Robert Scholes calls the diegetic whole and that we generally take to be the novel or story.

And then, once we have finished reading the story or novel, we form an even larger whole, which is our memory of the narrative and our reaction to it, often distilled into a single flash of meaning (though it can be a complex, extended whole as well).[12] In contrast to our first construction of objects, which is concrete, or our formation of the acting whole, which is flexible, this third level requires a representation with sweep and economy and a special capacity for synthesis, qualities that idea and image muster with comparative difficulty. It is this third level that serves as an index, marking our ability to summon up specific elements.

Such, then, are the factors that determine which of the three codes we use. But I ought to ask another question: could my particular breakdown of these three codes be incorrect? Could what I call a representing emotion be better named an "affective image," say, or an "emotional idea," as though the three codes were different facets of a single mental medium—as though they were not separate after all? I do indeed seem to imagine all three codes at once, suggesting that they come together to form the "mentalese" described by the psychologist Zenon Pylyshyn. Or could what I'm calling three codes exist in some other configuration—as a set of two rather than three codes? Emotion and image both require engagement, for example, and so stand in contrast to the idea, which usually requires distance. Why not argue that feeling and image form one single code, standing against idea? I *feel* both emotion and sensation, and as I say, I do experience those two codes together.[13] I enter the emotions and the images of the text while I remain outside of the ideas that I think. Why not believe that we think with idea and imagine with feelings that can be either sensational (that is imagistic) or affective?

Or is the key the different kinds of abstraction? Emotion like idea expresses a large body of meaning in a single, brief, flash of consciousness, condensing within a feeling what is physical and complicated. In this sense, both the emotion and the idea provide the same function. Why not argue that feeling and idea are forms of abstraction, standing in contrast to the comparatively concrete image? But then the image offers a form of abstraction as well, which leads us back to three separate tracks.

Which is where I think I will leave it, for the present, since the notion of three separate codes has so much to support it. The individual codes of image and idea have strong champions, as we have seen. And an author creates characters who see, think, and feel, requiring the identifying reader to do the same. *Of course* we construct the different elements of a passage in different mediums. How else represent what we know to be individual images, ideas, and feelings? Nor do I see any reason why these three codes cannot exist side by side in the imagination, just as ideas, images, and feelings exist side by side in our ordinary experience. Nick thinks, speaks, visualizes, and feels—when put in that way, the necessity of all three codes as distinct entities seems quite clear.[14]

V

It is one thing to describe the affective code and how it works and quite another to prove that it exists. What kind of evidence can I muster? In the pages that follow, I will continue to consult as many experts as I can find. But most of all I will rely on the experience of reading itself, as I did in the case of the Hemingway paragraph, examining how an actual reader imagines the text. Though such an account is anecdotal, and so not proof in the scientific sense, the novel itself provides good evidence. It is "out there" for all to see. It is also stable, permitting me to search its language for intimations of the affective code. Because the author's words direct the reader's imagination, and often require a particular code, they illuminate the reading process. Surely the writer's language tells us a great deal about the mental event that it triggers.

I don't feel badly about lacking scientific evidence.[15] Such proof will come in due course—perhaps even in the near future—and in the meantime, to examine a complete novel provides several advantages. I can look at a total reading experience, or the complex whole that transcends the small acts that make it up. And I can make that experience the reading of not a group of passages (as in many empirical experiments) but a complete work, which is a unique experience in its own right, as each page builds, cumulatively, upon what went before. To study the reading of a whole novel is to examine such elements otherwise lost as suspense and climax and evolving tone.

And then readers can verify my account themselves. I intend for each reader to compare my reading of these texts with his or her own. We will differ in some particulars, but as I have said, a classic literary text is read by hundreds of thousands of readers. It has been "field-tested," its preeminence among books testifying to the imaginative power of the language, including the fit of the words to the process. How many millions have read *Pride and Prejudice?* A novel also describes the mental processes of its characters, offering yet another model of the imagining or remembering mind.

It is clear that the affective code presents several problems. If affective representation were not on some level counterintuitive, it would have been embraced long ago. In Part III I will confront five different objections to my thesis. Conveniently, each of these difficulties leads to a premise that supports my argument. One might wonder, for example, if words really evoke emotions. Doesn't language express fact rather than feeling? In chapter 9 I will show that *the words in the text evoke emotion.* Are not emotions too personal or too private—too unique—to be shared? In chapter 10 I will show that, all things being equal, *readers share the emotions evoked by the text.* Many would object that emotion is too vague or spongy to convey a precise subject. In chapter 11 I will show that *the emotion employed within the affective code is precise.* And then, in contrast to those who define emotion as purely personal, I will in chapter 12 show that *the emotion employed within the affective code is impersonal or objective.* Why is the affective code necessary? What major task can it alone perform? In chapter 13 I will show that *the affective code is essential to the representation of relationships.*

Other problems remain to be revisited. One, which I have already mentioned, is the leap the mind must take from raw emotion to mental representation. What can we know about this process? Would not the large number of our emotional reactions make affective representation difficult? Emotion offers not conscious ideas (though it is a form of awareness) but experience. It is immediate and absorbing, expressing a meaning that can remain unconscious. How could it serve as a *public* form of communication? Privately speaking, one can represent an object within one's mind any way one chooses, as long as the construction makes sense. But conveying that representation to another person is another matter. And so is sorting out one's experience. In a text, one reacts to the mental image formed by the words: how can I be sure that what I take to be an independent code is not just a reaction to image or word?

To address questions like these, I will study, besides Ernest Hemingway's story "Big Two-Hearted River," the novels *Pride and Prejudice* by Jane Austen, *Adventures of Huckleberry Finn* by Mark Twain, *The Portrait of a Lady* by Henry James, *Beloved* by Toni Morrison, and *The Centaur* by John Updike. Why do I choose these particular works? I like them, for one thing. If all novels employ the affective code, as I believe they do, then a random or eccentric sample is as good as any. But I also believe that these particular novels are great books, with much to teach us about ourselves and the nature of writing.[16] They range over two centuries, two races, and both genders. They are comic and solemn, tragic and melodramatic. They tend to be realistic, reflecting my personal taste, and yet *The Centaur* is postmodern while *Beloved* exemplifies magic realism. I would hope these novels offer a wide enough variety to illustrate the universality of the affective code.

I leave out several kinds of material. I do not study a novel in a foreign language, even though that might be illuminating. Nor do I examine a translation. And I choose the novel as evidence even though I refer often to poetic theory. I do this because the novel requires an extended mental construction and so provides a more obvious kind of example. On the other hand, I think I have done well to choose writers who are reputedly nonemotional. Hemingway is hard-boiled, James intellectual, Austen ironic, and Updike imagistic. If these particular writers employ the emotional code, it seems fair to say, other novelists do so also.[17]

I don't mean to suggest that all of these novelists write in the same manner. Each of them evokes emotion in the reader in a different way. Ernest Hemingway stimulates emotion in the reader by means of fine detail. Jane Austen relies heavily on rhetorical diction and comic characterization. Mark Twain creates his representational emotion by means of Huck's voice, with its unique diction and cadence, and Henry James feeds the affective code by means of images: the creation of a signifying emotion in the reader is often the point of his metaphors. John Updike names the emotion directly, connecting it to the human "atmosphere" that it articulates. And so does Toni Morrison, to whom emotion is as palpable as color. Rather than employ a literary device to evoke emotion, Morrison invents a language that presents emotion directly.

Part III
The Affective Imagination: Five Premises

What's almost never discussed is what you and I have just been talking about: the language in which a book is framed. And there's a good reason. It's hard to talk about. It's hard to write about. And so one receives a broad analysis of, perhaps, the social issues in one's work but rarely anything about the way the writer gets there.

—Don DeLillo, *The New Yorker*

The man is really hateful, the action really mean; the situation really tragic—all in themselves and quite apart from our opinion.
—William James, "The Place of Affectional Facts in a World of Pure Experience."

9

Language as Emotion in "Big Two-Hearted River"

Premise I: Words translate into emotions.

HEMINGWAY'S USE OF EMOTION TO REPRESENT HIS SUBJECT WAS most likely deliberate. The novelist talked often about the emotion created by the text, showing himself—this most macho of writers— to be a connoisseur of feeling. The story exists to give the reader an emotional reaction. More than that, readers construct the text by means of emotion. If knowledgeable and skillful enough, Hemingway wrote in *Death in the Afternoon,* the writer "may omit things that he knows and the reader . . . will have a feeling of those things as strongly as though the writer had stated them." It is because of this that you must know, if you are to write well, "what you really felt, rather than what you were supposed to feel, and had been taught to feel." You must know "what the actual things were which produced the emotion, . . . the real thing, the sequence of motion and fact which made the emotion."[1]

In such remarks Hemingway refers to what I would call the affec- tive code. The "actual things" (the act or person or "sequence of motion and fact") make the author feel an emotion which he then expresses by means of his language; for the reader, the language evokes the emotion that serves to construct the event. Never mind the mechanical nature of this sequence. Hemingway echoes Eliot's description of the objective correlative, posing an equivalence be- tween object or word and emotion, and adds two new ideas. Readers feel what is not explicitly in the text, which is an expansion of the power of emotion to represent. We feel context and implication. And

111

the writer (like the reader) is surrounded by potential falsity, in both his emotion ("what you were supposed to feel") and the world that evokes it ("the actual things").

Is Hemingway correct? Do words really translate into emotions in the reader? And if they do, *how* do they? I can think of several reasons to doubt such an equivalence, not the least of which is the factual meaning of the word. When I mention my coffee cup, I mean not a feeling but a ceramic container. Our systems of words and numbers denote real things. And then, as so many people believe, figures of speech are often visual, suggesting that language triggers not feelings but images. Our metaphor for perception is sight, after all—we *see* the truth.

Fair enough. But we do feel someone's presence. We *feel* something to be true. Our idioms also support the affective code, as does the special and intimate relation between language and feeling.[2] It is not hard to imagine language arising in order to express emotion, in fact, since that is one of our primal needs. As I have said, the raw noises that humans make are intensely expressive: we might well have learned to shape the raw sound into a word that identifies its source, especially if, as physiologists tell us, emotion is the initial expression of the individual's desires and needs. The first words spoken may well have indicated the cause of the expressed feelings. Because sound expresses emotion naturally, moreover, even the most abstract or intellectual words are expressive.

Is it possible that words (or the object that they name) evoke emotions in a stable way? The answer is yes: all things being equal, words evoke emotions in the reader, forming a pool of feeling from which the affective code draws what it needs. Not all people feel the same emotions in the same way, just as not all people understand the same ideas in the same way. The process is not as blindly mechanical as the objective correlative seems to make it. But language does indeed communicate emotion, as the empirical psychologist David Miall, among others, has documented. Clearly emotion plays an important role in our mental construction and display of the narrative.

In the chapters that follow in Part III I will show that the emotions evoked in the reader are shared, precise, objective and necessary. In this chapter I will demonstrate simply that words *do* evoke emotions, forming an equivalence of word and feeling that is stable. I can do this by approaching the subject from three different directions. I will look first at the specific ways words awaken emotion in the people that read them, establishing the basic fact of emotional evocation— and the subtle meanings it expresses. I will then examine Hemingway's short story, "Big Two-Hearted River," which takes the translation of experience into emotion as its very subject, demonstrating the essential equivalence of the word and a particular feeling. And finally, I will examine the views of three philosophers who explain why language *has* to evoke emotion, like it or not, and why that emotion is representational.

I

The difficulty in discussing this subject is not showing that language translates into emotion but sorting out the many ways that it does. Max Scheler, for example, claims that emotions are communicated in several ways: as community of feeling (in which people feel alike), psychic contagion (in which we duplicate the other's emotion), emotional identification (in which we feel with the other person) and fellow feeling (in which we feel for the other person). In *Principles of Art Appreciation* Stephen Pepper says that the artist produces emotion within the audience in still other ways: by stimulating the senses, presenting a symbol with emotional meaning, representing emotional behavior, and expressing emotion directly.[3]

The sheer number of ways words evoke emotion indicates the emotional charge carried by almost every word. Nor are these two lists exhaustive. To them I would add association and connotation, or those feelings that have become attached to particular objects and words. A connotation can be private (the emotional residue of an earlier association, say) or public (emotions learned from the culture), and it is the latter that concerns me here. Think of the large body of emotional meaning carried by the simple word "fish," deriving from both its physical nature, including smell and shape, and its cultural associations. In our European culture we associate the word with fertility, sex, and early Christianity. In the United States around Thanksgiving—to give a perhaps too subtle example—we associate the word with Native Americans burying fish with their corn seed. While Nick Adams associates the trout with feelings of mystery and independence, another kind of fisherman might associate it with sticky scales and bloody newspaper, both associations enjoying a public currency.[4]

Connotation and association mean that every word in a passage floats on a pool of feeling, and that is just the beginning. Contagion, identification, dramatization, reaction and representation all trigger emotions within the reader. Because emotion begins as reaction, in fact, everything from fine detail to the crudest plot evokes it. But what is important is not the number of emotions, but their interaction and the subtle meanings that such exchanges express. This is clear in the distinction between "tell" and "show" taught by all creative writing instructors. The two words describe the writer's general presentation of his or her subject, but they also furnish what may be the most useful principle of organizing narrative emotion.

On the one hand, the text can name or "tell" an emotion directly, offering it as an idea. "But this was good." "He was excited by the early morning and the river." The convention of indirect discourse permits the writer to name the emotions the characters feel, assuming (if we forget reader identification for a minute) that one might read such exposition intellectually. To understand the named emotion as an idea in itself requires skill, since the world of feeling is not always clear, even from a distance.

Yet we do not read even a named emotion in a purely ideational way. "Susie felt a certain chagrin." While in one part of my mind I understand the abstract denotation, in another the process of emotional contagion makes me feel some of the emotion itself.[5] Even as I think the idea, "chagrin," I feel a glimmer of the feeling. In this way, pure signification itself evokes emotion. We may not feel the emotion to the degree that the other person feels it, and we may feel our own version of it. But feel it we do. Thinkers like Max Scheler, Ross Buck, and Stephen Pepper make this clear. Does Nick like his apricots? One feels a flash of pleasure. Does Nick fear the swamp? One feels a sense of the ominous (or of the swamp as ominous). In such ways we feel emotion even before we identify with a character. And of course we do identify, as I have said, becoming fictional characters vicariously and so knowing them as the emotions they feel and we share.

On the other hand, many texts dramatize the story so purely that the emotions remain implicit.

> The trout was steady in the moving stream, resting on the gravel, beside a stone. As Nick's fingers touched him, touched his smooth, cool, underwater feeling he was gone, gone in a shadow across the bottom of the stream.[6]

Even this dramatization names several emotions, such as "steady," or the name given to the unusual touch ("the cool, underwater feeling"). At the same time, one can be so caught up in the event that one feels the intimacy directly, as an experience alone.[7] Hemingway evokes the emotion within us by describing the situation, and if it is a new or unique combination of emotions, we say he has *created* that feeling within us. This kind of emotion is without self-consciousness and is different than identification, based as it is on the reader's direct engagement with the text.

Such feelings are largely our reaction to the story as a whole. We feel the conflict that shapes the tale and the emotional curve of its resolution. We feel suspense and tension and climax and tone—the philosopher Martha Nussbaum is correct in calling narrative an emotional medium. But as I am arguing in this book, these emotions become a feeling of the whole that catches and so expresses its unique quality. Reading a text, we feel not only general reactions, like pleasure or pain, but specific qualities, like vitality or disunity, and then what is unique, like the tension between Nick's freedom and compulsiveness. Whether such feelings belong to the object itself, as William James claims, or belong to the moment of perception, as Robert Solomon claims, they offer a central source of constitutive emotion representing the whole.

What needs to be emphasized, I think, is how various and subtle the feelings in a text may be—and how varied and subtle the meaning they express. Writers may show or tell separately—the critic Wayne Booth reminded us of the expository nature of fiction years ago—but they often do both, in succession, creating a unique and revealing effect. Should one proceed inductively, offering the specifics and then telling their point, or should one give one's point first and then offer the supporting specifics? Different researchers have argued for different sequences, but what is important is the often subtle meaning created by either order.[8]

In the first sequence, the writer may describe the object, as does Hemingway, and then name the feelings it evokes:

As the shadow of the kingfisher moved up the stream, a big trout shot upstream in a long angle, only his shadow marking the angle, then lost his shadow as he came though the surface of the water, caught the sun, and then, as he went back into the stream under the surface, his shadow seemed to float down the stream with the current, unresisting, to his post under the bridge where he tightened facing up into the current.

Nick's heart tightened as the trout moved. He felt all the old feeling.

In the second sequence, the writer may name the feelings and then offer the description that justifies them. F. Scott Fitzgerald signifies the feeling of awe in *The Great Gatsby* when he says that Gatsby's famous car had been noticed by "everybody," and then continues,

It was a rich cream color, bright with nickel, swollen here and there in its monstrous length with triumphant hat-boxes and supper-boxes and tool-boxes, and terraced with a labyrinth of wind-shields that mirrored a dozen suns.

Fitzgerald relishes the adjectives Hemingway cut out, gaining his impression by means of detail (the nickel, the toolboxes) but even more by means of language, as he uses such emotionally loaded words as "bright" and "swollen" and "monstrous." In Hemingway's passage the feeling resides within the text, while in Fitzgerald's it belongs to the narrator's voice.

Fitzgerald makes us imagine Gatsby's car as intensely as we imagine Nick's trout stream, but his description has a different texture. Hemingway creates feelings that are tight and clear while Fitzgerald (describing a kind of decadence) gives a sense of the muddy and the overblown. Hemingway often uses his named feeling to summarize and solidify what went before, crystallizing the description and providing a feeling of precision and order. Fitzgerald permits the named feeling he places at the beginning of his description to swallow up the details that support it, creating an effect that is soft or diffuse. In each case, however, the author creates the effect he needs, evoking the emotion that reinforces—and in effect articulates—his meaning. He skillfully employs the natural processes of emotional construction for the purpose of his passage. In both passages, the emotion catches the essence of the author's vision, providing a halo of feeling that expresses and so represents the meaning.

II

Hemingway published the story "Big Two-Hearted River" as the conclusion of *In Our Time* (1925), a volume reflecting the experimental ferment then current in Paris. It has but one character, Nick Adams, and nothing like a usual plot: Nick gets off a train in Upper Michigan, hikes cross-country, makes camp, and the next morning goes fishing. Yet the story is remarkable in its strategy. For Hemingway records the actions and sensations of Nick Adams without giving their context. He doesn't tell us who Nick is or why he is here, in spite of the fact that his point of view lies within Nick's mind. Nick plunges into a world of specifics without reflecting on the purpose or background of his journey. He looks at the burned town of Seney with no surprise and walks to a bridge from which he peers dispassionately into the water at the fish. As he does so, our suspense mounts, so necessary is context. Who is this character and what does he want? Why does he think so narrowly, without the allusion and perspective that would reveal his identity? What do these events *mean?* We feel buried within Nick's mind and struggle for insight, seeking to understand the emotions that motivate him.

After the trout shoots upstream, "only his shadow marking the angle," Hemingway adds two succinct sentences: "Nick's heart tightened as the trout moved. He felt all the old feeling."[9] Hemingway emphasizes these two sentences by setting them off as a paragraph, and in doing so makes them the climax toward which the first three paragraphs have driven. Nick suddenly has a reaction, revealing something personal about himself. He has a past, since the emotion is "old," and he has a psychology, since the rush of feeling breaks his almost mechanical stolidity. With a sense of relief, we begin to discern a meaning.

If this short paragraph tells us about Nick, moreover, it also tells us how to read this narrative. The exclusion of emotion up to this point gives this sudden feeling a singular importance, confirmed by Nick's own realization. The *trout* creates the feeling, moreover, and that is the key: emotion flows from objects and events. Nick attends to his sensations and emotions with almost painful deliberation, and will control that emotion by controlling the objects and actions he permits himself to experience. He has been badly hurt, though we do not know how,[10] and he has come to this place to heal, perhaps because here, free from social complexities, he can control his experience. When Hemingway tells us in the next paragraph that "Nick felt happy" and that "he was happy," we find our suspicion confirmed: we have a story in which the plot lies in the shifts in Nick's emotion—shifts that Nick himself manipulates. He will repress his memories and will choose with care those objects that make him feel the emotion he needs.

This is to say that Hemingway makes his subject Nick's use of the equivalence of object and emotion.[11] Like a writer crafting his novel, Nick in this story constructs for himself a healing fantasy, carefully choosing those objects that will produce the emotions that will make him healthy. The fire that burns down the Seney saloons, the sand that forms the soil, the sweet ferns and the pine needles and the cold water and the trout—the cleanest of all fish, some say—everything in the story (except the swamp and Nick's own memory) works to form a feeling of aseptic purity. Nick travels to the wilderness to cleanse himself, shutting out all in his life that is muddy; again and again he defers pleasure, as he hikes in the hot sun with a heavy pack, walks a full day before stopping, and makes camp before eating.[12]

To Hemingway these several feelings *are* this fiction. As readers we watch Nick from the outside, witnessing his deliberate activity, but we also participate in those emotions, so that the emotion that is Nick's response (and which we know because we identify with him) provides the foundation for our own construction of the story. The object named by Hemingway evokes a feeling that contributes to the affective code that we use. For the reader, it probably helps to be a Midwestern male familiar with the outdoors. Yet it is remarkable how clear Nick's emotional experience is to everyone. Nick's hatred of mosquitoes, for example, could well be universal, and he is driven by a need for purity that almost everyone understands. Or is the universal point Nick's compulsion for order? One does not have to be shell-shocked to understand the emotions that lie behind Nick's narrow and compulsive focus. Although these feelings are reactions rather than representations at this point, they illustrate the principle of equivalence.

Of course, not all critics agree with my interpretation of this story, and indeed, the criticism surrounding "Big Two-hearted River" makes an interesting tale in its own right. Readers originally took the story to be a simple fishing yarn until Malcolm Cowley and Philip Young pointed out Nick's troubled state of mind. Nick hangs onto himself desperately because he may break down at any moment. On the other hand, a second group of critics *still* find Nick's state of mind to be blissful. To Raymond Nelson, Nick is "bursting with happiness and well-being." To Keith Carabine the story describes "the quiet satisfaction of a mind composedly noting the natural demarcations of the landscape with no attempt to make it particular or glamourous." And to Chaman Nahal, Nick finds a profound tranquility and strength in his awareness of a beautiful world.[13]

Is Nick tormented or serene? Does the story portray an inner terror or a Wordsworthian peace? It is striking (and humbling) that critics offer diametrically opposed interpretations, though such disagreement is not unusual. Significantly, the issue centers on Nick's emotions, though I do think that both sides get it wrong, largely because they ignore the equivalence of word and emotion. To focus on Nick's emotion, as reflected in the objects and acts he names, is to find the two interpretations reconciled within a sharply defined emotion, the expression of which gives the story its point. Hemingway finds his theme in a feeling that encompasses both instability and pleasure: the fragile but reassuring pleasure the wounded take in their own healing. Saul Bellow is quite correct to call Hemingway "the poet of the crippled state."[14] Hemingway dramatizes the deep satisfaction that one feels in the slow but seemingly deliberate process of mending, a feeling especially intense because Nick gives *himself* the emotions that will heal him.

It is for this reason that the story consists of a series of small challenges and healing responses. Gingerly, Nick completes one minor task after another. He travels (and once off the train, must sit down); he hikes (and must take a long nap); he makes camp (and sleeps through the whole night). On each occasion, Nick relishes his small accomplishment as well as the rest that he has earned. And he revels in the profoundly satisfying feeling of his recuperation. He enjoys both the view from the hill he has climbed and the soil on which he hikes, "sandy underfoot." He makes his camp "in the good place" and enjoys a dinner his exertions have made delicious. Again and again, Hemingway repeats Nick's refrain: "It was a good camp." "It was a good feeling." And when Nick has secured his home, and achieved a number of small successes, he risks the emotional challenge of fishing, during which he again monitors his emotion.

Thus "Big Two-Hearted River" dramatizes an emotion—that slightly woozy but comforting sense of convalescence—and while doing so equates object and emotion.[15] Nick is damaged and fearful, but he seeks out the small victories that will heal him. Miss this emotion and you miss the very center of Nick's experience.[16]

III

I turn next to three philosophers who, offering a theoretical basis to representation, explain why Hemingway's equation of object and emotion works. Although these thinkers do not describe the affective code directly, they do define emotion (and cognition) in such a way that the affective code is inevitable. Within the context of their thought, in fact, the notion of an affective code is modest. We can argue that the mind uses emotion to represent the subject because the mind experiences *everything* in the form of emotion. Nor should that fact surprise us, since (as these philosophers claim) emotion lies in the world itself.

The first of these thinkers is the American pragmatist William James, the older brother of the novelist Henry and the founder of American psychology. Even today many of his insights have not been superceded. In his essay "The Place of Affectional Facts in a World of Pure Experience," James argues that emotion fulfills a key function in all perception, unifying the physical and the mental. Because it is the object that creates the emotion, the affective meaning belongs to not just the mind that perceives but the object that is perceived. "The man is really hateful," James writes; "the action really mean; the situation really tragic—all in themselves and quite apart from our opinion."[17] The emotion that we so often dismiss as merely personal derives in fact from the form and sensation and meaning of the object.

James's argument is especially persuasive because he believes that emotions are physical. In *Principles of Psychology* he asserts that emotion is but the name we give bodily changes. Emotion, he says, is our awareness of what our body is doing. Fear is a consciousness of sweaty palms and fast breathing; joy registers our sense of physical well-being. In such ideas, commonly known as the James-Lange theory, James offers the scientifically popular view that emotion is based in the body.

William James is no dreamer: his attribution of objective truth to emotion is as practical or hard-headed as one could wish. And it explains Hemingway's aesthetic process, even though the novelist probably never read the philosopher. Nick lives precisely the intimate relationship between object and emotion that James describes, evoking the emotion by choosing the object, and then revealing the emotion by naming the object. What is interesting is how this equation works in both directions. In real life the object creates emotion inside the observer; in narrative such emotion, in its representational form, "expresses" the object in the reader's imagination. In either case, emotion and object (or at least the word that names it) become equivalents.

James goes even further than the equation of object and emotion. He explains in *Principles of Psychology* that we represent (or think) all kinds of grammatical relationships by means of emotion. In the phrase "on the table," the preposition "on" translates within the mind as an emotion, the feeling of "on." "We ought to say a feeling of *and*, a feeling of *if*, a feeling of *but*, and a feeling of *by*, quite as readily as we say a feeling of *blue* or a feeling of *cold*."[18] If we broaden this insight to include other kinds of relationships, which seems reasonable enough, we may then say that however we mentally reconstitute the nouns in Hemingway's story, we construct the relationships as emotion. We *feel* Nick's relationship to everything around him. And as Robert Solomon reminds us, our real-life emotions, whether they be loving or suspicious, trustful or fearful, determine our relationship to the world and so serve to constitute it.[19]

Another philosopher equates emotion with an even larger relationship and, in doing so, offers another theory applicable to Hemingway's accomplishment in "Big Two-Hearted River." In *Being and Time* (1927) the German phenomenologist Martin Heidegger agrees with James that emotion plays a central role in human perception. In fact, it is emotion that permits us to perceive. In applying some of Edmund Husserl's ideas about consciousness to *Dasein*, or our practical, daily life, Heidegger arrives at the concept of "mood," by which he means something close to our popular usage of the word. To Heidegger, mood is the general feeling we carry to and from our experience. Mood expresses the interaction between our sense of ourselves and the situation before us—our position in the world or "how we are doing." We *feel* who we are and where we are, and the two factors are indissolubly bound within a single emotion. In turn this emotion or mood determines what we perceive and how we act. Thus emotion plays a role in all that we see and do.

What is important for my purpose is Heidegger's view that mood determines what we see. Mood not only motivates us to look in a certain direction but defines the point of view that determines our evaluation of the perceived object. Because that evaluation establishes the meaning of our experience, it is our mood that determines the true meaning of our lives. Nor is our mood merely personal. We learn our mood from the society that teaches us about ourselves and our world, which means that we share with others a body of emotion that embodies cultural values and ideas. A society is defined by the mood its citizens share.

In Heidegger's view, to see conceptually or nonemotionally—to see without mood or objectively—is to distort knowledge, because such effort splits thought from emotion, offering only a reductive view of the subject. Emotion provides knowledge from the inside of the experience. Emotion in the form of mood is also authentic, driving home the truth of a situation we are all too prone to deny or distort. In this way anxiety can be seen as necessary to clear vision.[20] In this way, too, we understand how the self and the world, the subjective and the objective, the emotional and the "factual" all form a single unity. We know ourselves as beings in the world, and we know the world as the situation in which we find ourselves. And this amounts to representation, since it is as emotion or mood that we experience such insight.

Like the ideas of William James, Heidegger's ideas explain Hemingway's aesthetic in "Big Two-Hearted River." Because what Nick sees is the product of what he is, or of the mood that expresses it, we know Nick's character by knowing his world. Even an ostensibly unemotional sentence, such as "Nick drove another big nail and hung up the bucket full of water," expresses mood.[21] Its tone of calculated simplicity and directness embodies Nick's sense of himself and his situation. Hemingway describes bare actions because they are all that the troubled Nick will permit himself. Hemingway internalizes nature, discovering its meaning in Nick's emotional needs, and objectifies Nick's emotions, giving them an external form in nature. Thus the story unifies the objective and the subjective. If we know about Nick and his emotions from the world in which he resides, we know about the world from our understanding of Nick's emotions.

On the surface, at least, Hemingway's story seems to miss Heidegger's conviction that mood reflects society and so connects one to it. Nick Adams has fled his society to the burned town of Seney. Yet a moment's reflection shows that Nick actually expresses socially constructed values and strategies. For example, he exemplifies the American view of a healing nature in contrast to a corrupting society. And he illustrates an American view of illness as something to be conquered. In his camping and fishing skill, Nick exemplifies the American love of technical mastery.

In the more recent past (in his book *The Passions,* 1976), the American philosopher Robert Solomon has built upon the basic insights of Heidegger. Solomon rejects what he calls the "hydraulic" model of emotion, in which our emotions rise up within us like a liquid that must be expelled, because he believes that emotion is an integral part of consciousness. Indeed, like Susanne Langer in *Mind,* he writes at times as though emotion *were* consciousness. Emotion, he says, is constitutive of experience—it is literally the way in which we create the world we perceive.[22] We choose our emotions, for example, and in doing so create ourselves, or the one who perceives the world. Again, because emotions motivate us to look at one thing and not another, they determine what we see. More than that, Solomon says, emotions are judgment—they function in the mind as not an expression of judgment but the act of judging itself. Since judgment defines meaning or value, it is emotion that provides the meaning of the experience.

Thus Solomon argues that whatever enters our consciousness is already felt as an emotion—is *already* judged and given a meaning, which explains the dynamic of Hemingway's story. The author can describe Nick's actions without comment, confident that they reveal the judgment within them and so their meaning (and so the point of the story). By choosing his emotions, Nick creates himself, just as Solomon claims. Likewise Hemingway reveals Nick's character by describing his world. Hemingway sometimes gives Nick's appraisal of his experience after it has happened ("It was a good camp"), but the fact remains that the judgment informs the description, and so occurs to Nick and the reader simultaneously with the experience. Even a statement as neutral as "Nick drove another big nail and hung up the bucket full of water" embodies in its tone an implied judgment of the tasks performed, in this case a feeling of satisfaction.

Solomon also claims that emotion imbues the world with a sense of reality. And like James and Heidegger, Solomon believes that the emotion we feel is true to the world: because the cause of our emotion always resides in the world, Solomon says, our emotion is "objective." Solomon echoes Heidegger's concept of mood again when he adds that emotion provides the structure that links the individual and the world. To Solomon, the reader absorbs emotion as a matter of course, since that is how human beings perceive.

While none of these three philosophers talks about the affective code, they do explain how emotion represents meaning. Whether it be relationship, mood, or appraisal, the emotion "stands for" a larger body of information, which in this case amounts to a great deal of the fictional text. Does Hemingway make us visualize an image? Certainly. I will always see the small grill over the fire. Does he make us think ideas? Of course. Yet Hemingway's language also depends upon the equivalence of word and emotion, as the meaning of the word evokes the emotion that constructs that meaning. The emotion is *out there*, as James says: name the object and you have the feeling of the object (as interpreted by your culture). The text embodies the Heideggerian mood we know as tone; read the words and you will know their meaning as the tone they embody. Simply experience the object, as Solomon says, and your mind will appraise it in an emotional form automatically.

Such definitions of affective representation should not surprise us. If emotion constructs our actual experience, it would surely construct our imaginative experience. And yet a question remains. Does the word evoke *the same* emotion in all people? What evidence is there that all readers feel the same (or more or less the same) emotions? I suspect that most people would agree that language evokes emotion, but they would not agree that readers share either an understanding or the experience of those feelings. I must now show that I am not describing an affective Tower of Babel.

It is common everyday experience that emotional communication is often better understood than verbal communication. Just as a look or a gesture can make an attitude clear between two people which a thousand words would still leave ambiguous, so with many emotional works of art.

—Stephen Pepper, *Principles of Art Appreciation*

10

Shared Emotion in *Pride and Prejudice*

Premise II: Readers share the emotions evoked by the text.

IT IS EASY TO UNDERSTAND WHY ONE WOULD DOUBT THAT EMOTION is shared. Emotions are personal, fluid, and sometimes uncontrollable. If one does not know how one feels, which is common, how could other people share that feeling? The mere expression of an emotion changes it, moreover, which means that the author transforms her original emotions in the act of writing them down. And then there are still poststructuralists who doubt the authority of the text: if readers of fiction do not agree on the denoted facts, how can they agree on something as subtle and fleeting as emotion?

And yet emotion is actually communicated quite well. We all understand emotion vastly better than our culture recognizes—so well, in fact, that readers often understand emotion *before* they understand the facts, as in the tone of the passage, which tells them how to read the words. For this reason, the literal meaning is dependent upon the emotional meaning. When the facts in the passage are obscure, we can still discover the meaning within the tone, which conveys the author's implied evaluation of the subject (not to mention her attitude toward the world). For a substantial community of readers, emotion is less a problem to be solved than a source of clarity.[1]

To demonstrate this claim, I will look at Jane Austen's *Pride and Prejudice*, which takes the question of human perception as a central concern. I will show first that emotion is the subject of *Pride and*

Prejudice, as one might expect from a plot hinging upon the lovers' misunderstanding of each other's feelings.[2] I will then apply this fact to the most discussed critical issue in the novel, Austen's portrayal of gender, before moving on to two reasons why readers of this novel *must* understand and feel the same emotions.

I don't mean to suggest that the understanding of an emotion is the same as sharing it. One can understand an emotion intellectually without experiencing it. Conversely, one can feel an emotion without "understanding" it. And yet the two functions are related, and not only because one must experience something in order to understand it fully. To understand Austen's story one must understand what her characters feel, which sometimes means sharing those emotions (as one identifies) and at other times means perceiving their significance (and so understanding them).

My focus will be on not the affective code as such but the motives and reactions of the characters, which are the emotions we mutually understand. Because the affective imagination constructs the text from the emotions available to it, of course, readers who share the characters' feelings employ similar affective codes.[3] But what is striking in *Pride and Prejudice* is how Austen's use of emotion as a source of humor shows it to be a lingua franca of human intercourse. To Austen, people are nothing less than emotional beings who know one another as emotional beings: her characters reveal their identities in what they feel and judge others on the basis of what they feel. And the emotions they perceive in others determine the emotions that they feel. Austen shows that for all its private intensity, emotion is a public medium—a primary way in which we know and judge one another.

I

Not a few critics see Jane Austen as an intellectual writer, offering wit and satire rather than emotion. "The Passions are perfectly unknown to her," Charlotte Brontë wrote in a famous letter:

> she rejects even a speaking acquaintance with that strong Sisterhood; even to the Feelings she vouchsafes no more than an occasional graceful but distant recognition; too frequent converse with them would ruffle the smooth elegance of her progress.[4]

Pride and Prejudice offers no walking of the moors, no reckless embrace, no equation of love and death. We do not see Elizabeth and

Darcy overwhelmed by passion, and we understand that Lydia, the sister who *is* overwhelmed, makes an egregious error. What is more, Austen's controlled style and form, based on balance and irony, seems to contain and dissolve whatever emotion is expressed in the book.[5]

Yet this accepted view of *Pride and Prejudice* does not do the novel justice. Charlotte Brontë is correct about the passion but incorrect about the "Feelings," or those mild emotions that the philosopher Susanne Langer identifies as the very stuff of human experience. Here, for example, is Elizabeth's reaction when Darcy's sister asks to meet her.

> The surprise of such an application was great indeed; it was too great for her to know in what manner she acceded to it. She immediately felt that whatever desire Miss Darcy might have of being acquainted with her, must be the work of her brother, and without looking farther, it was satisfactory; it was gratifying to know that his resentment had not made him think really ill of her.[6]

Although this passage offers no emotional fireworks, every clause involves an emotion. Elizabeth is *surprised;* she *feels* the presence of Darcy; she feels *satisfied;* she feels *gratified* at the absence of Darcy's *resentment.*

To go through *Pride and Prejudice* passage by passage is to discover that emotion is the substance of daily experience. It is the very prism through which Austen views the events of the novel. Characters think about emotion when they are alone and talk about it when they meet with one another. They understand each other by perceiving one another's motives and they present themselves to the world as the emotions they feel. To perceive the facts in this novel one must understand the feelings. What is more, Austen knows that emotion shapes the fate of her characters. This is true of not only the Bennet daughters, who must wait for men to propose marriage, but the Reverend William Collins, whose sinecure depends upon the cordiality of Lady Catherine. Because emotion defines the way in which one relates to the world, it determines one's actions and so the fate that flows from them, as in Charlotte's marrying Collins.

For such reasons critics of this novel have long recognized the importance of emotion to it. Because they have not gone far enough, however, they have created confusion, interpreting the role of emotion in conflicting ways.[7] To Marilyn Butler in *Jane Austen and the War of Ideas* and Mary Poovey in *The Proper Lady and the Woman Writer,* Elizabeth's emotionality is a problem. Her early anger keeps her from Darcy, whom she wins only when she learns to be rational. The privileged values in the novel are rationality and distance. To Susan Morgan in *In the Meantime: Character and Perception in Jane Austen's Fiction,* on the other hand, the novel moves in the opposite direction, privileging engagement and emotion. Elizabeth begins as detached and rational and learns to engage and to feel.

Of course, more than one critic has noted that Jane Austen balances her themes so carefully that one finds support for contradictory views. But in this instance, the evidence supports Susan Morgan. *Pride and Prejudice* is nothing less than an exhaustive study of the role of emotion in the human mind. As Jane and Charlotte and Elizabeth ponder the emotions of Bingley and Mr. Collins and Darcy (who in turn ponder the emotions of the women), the novel finds its shape in a sequence of perceptual problems involving emotion. To miss this point is not only to misinterpret Elizabeth's growth but to confront a novel that does not make sense. In the words of Marilyn Butler, "Confusion enters because *as a whole* intelligence is represented as faulty in the novel." The sensible Gardiners define the norm, Butler says, but they play a small role. "The result is that in *Pride and Prejudice* the reader tends to feel himself in a moral limbo."[8] Conversely, if we recognize Austen's point to be a rigorous but celebratory look at emotion—as even the title itself suggests—such problems disappear.

Austen teaches the reader to focus on emotion. The very first scene not only introduces Mr. and Mrs. Bennet but raises the question of their true feelings. Mr. Bennet seems to be kindly, telling Mrs. Bennet that she is "as handsome as any of them," but his teasing threatens to shade into mockery. To her credit, Mrs. Bennet is open and direct: Mr. Bennet is "tiresome," she says, and abusive of his children.

> "You take delight in vexing me. You have no compassion on my poor nerves."
> "You mistake me, my dear. I have a high respect for your nerves. They are my old friends. I have heard you mention them with consideration these twenty years at least." (52)

Focus on Austen's comic tone, and this is light-hearted banter. Mr. Bennet's voice sounds playful, particularly since married couples often speak to one another frankly. But focus on Mr. Bennet's mockery, along with his claim that most of his daughters "are all silly and ignorant like other girls," and the tone is biting and even angry. "I have heard you mention them with consideration these twenty years at least."

Such ambiguity forces the reader to study the emotions the author portrays, particularly since the plot of the novel derives from Eliz-

abeth's misunderstanding of emotion. As Alison Sulloway percep-
tively reminds us, Elizabeth mistakenly extrapolates the whole person
from a revealed emotion—a fault that reveals Elizabeth's mode of
perception. "Because Wickham is tender toward Elizabeth, she assumes that he has integrity—which he does not. Because Darcy is
crassly arrogant, she wrongly assumes that he lacks integrity in family
matters."[9]

And yet, in spite of such errors, Austen celebrates Elizabeth's ability to know what others feel. Elizabeth's skill exhibits her intelligence,
which in this novel, for all its reputed rationality, is an emotional
intelligence. When Jane returns home glowing from a walk with
Bingley, Elizabeth immediately perceives Jane's new love. When Collins turns his eyes upon Elizabeth once too often, she reluctantly—
and with horror—reads him as well. She is not fooled by the blan-
dishments of Miss Bingley and Mrs. Hurst, and though she mistakes
his motive, she is correct in suspecting that Darcy spirited Bingley
away from Jane.[10] Elizabeth might well see these emotions from the
outside, interpreting their visible signs, and so be more rationalistic
than empathetic—a point that is debatable. But even if she does not
identify with her companions, Elizabeth is sensitive to their internal
life.

Elizabeth also earns our trust because of her own stable emotions.
When Darcy insults her at the ball, Elizabeth shrugs off the sting with
a joke. When Wickham pays attention to her, she responds cautiously,
and for all of her appreciation of his "amiability," is aware of the need
for corroboration. Moreover, critics have not done justice to the
unpleasantness of Elizabeth's life in the Bennet household, where
she is a pawn in the conflict between her parents ("—Your mother
will never see you again if you do *not* marry Mr. Collins, and I will
never see you again if you *do*"). Surely Elizabeth feels suffocated
amongst her silly mother and sisters, with only her books and a
couple of friendships to lighten a life that shows no promise of ending. To her father, Elizabeth is a favorite, but to Mrs. Bennet she is
"the least dear to her of all her children."[11]

Elizabeth also looks good because the other characters in the novel
look bad, making *Pride and Prejudice* a compendium of the errors
people make in regard to emotion—a constant source of humor.
Mrs. Bennet, for example, often feels emotions incommensurate to
their cause.

> "Yes indeed," cried Mrs Bennet. . . . "I assure you there is quite as much of
> *that* going on in the country as in town." Everybody was surprised; and
> Darcy, after looking at her for a moment, turned silently away. (88)

Although Mrs. Bennet is right to worry about her daughters' future, Austen takes pains to show that her emotions are extreme and inconstant. When she hears of Lydia's marriage to the rake Wickham, she is not only joyful (since any son-in-law is better than none) but immediately slides from the marriage into the subject of Lydia's clothes. Jane Bennet, on the other hand, shows too little emotion, which is one reason Bingley fears she does not care for him. And Charlotte shows too little as well, since her loveless marriage to Collins illustrates the self-destruction inherent in the denial of passion, though it is interesting that Austen does not show her to be unhappy.

For his part, the Reverend Collins professes emotions that are patently false. While he is abject before Lady Catherine (as that Lady would prefer), he pretends to a humility that his pathetic pride belies. Collins is so false, in fact, that one must doubt that he feels anything. "But before I am run away with by my feelings on this subject, perhaps it will be advisable for me to state my reasons for marrying—." Collins is like Mrs. Bennet and Lady Catherine, who feel emotions so inappropriate that they seem spurious. Humorously, Austen has these characters claim the deeply felt emotion that confers stature—and that they chastise Elizabeth for lacking ("Unfeeling, selfish girl!").

What makes unjustified emotion so damning is its impact on perception—a point Austen makes again and again. If our emotion determines what we see, as Heidegger claims, then false emotion blinds us. So once Elizabeth feels differently about Wickham, having learned the truth, "how differently did every thing now appear in which he was concerned!" Emotion that is too strong can shut out all perception, moreover, as when Elizabeth, suddenly meeting Darcy at Pemberley, "distinguished no part of the scene." The evolution of Elizabeth's love for Darcy is actually a study of the way feeling determines perception. When Elizabeth is angry with Darcy, she sees him as a bore. When she feels gratitude, she sees him as attractive.

How, in the face of so much misunderstanding, does Jane Austen prove that readers share an understanding of emotion? Perhaps the best answer lies in Austen's humor. It is true that she finds her humor primarily in the inability of her characters to understand the emotions of one another. Collins misreads not only Elizabeth but (in a delicious scene) Darcy; Bingley misreads Jane, and Lydia misreads Wickham. Mrs. Bennet misreads just about everyone—and of course, Elizabeth misreads Darcy. But in each of these cases, Austen makes the emotions missed by these characters clear to the reader. *She* ensures that we see what the comic character is missing, whether it be Elizabeth's revulsion or Darcy's indifference. *She* communicates the emotion to the reader, and so demonstrates the viability of emotional communication. The novel would make no sense to us if she did not—and it certainly would not be funny. At almost every point, almost all readers commonly understand what these characters are feeling.

Nor does Elizabeth's mistake in regard to Darcy disprove our general ability to share knowledge of emotion. We make mistakes about ideas, after all—the issue is not whether one is infallible but whether a reasonable, shared understanding is possible. And on every page of its narrative, *Pride and Prejudice* shows that it is. Certainly at the end we have reason to believe that Elizabeth and Darcy understand one another emotionally. Thinking about the other women who pursued Darcy, Elizabeth tells him, "I roused, and interested you because I was so unlike *them*." For his part, Darcy reveals that he had visited Longbourn at the end to read Elizabeth's emotions. "My real purpose was to see *you*, and to judge, if I could, whether I might ever hope to make you love me."

II

Austen also shows that emotion can be shared in her treatment of gender—the most-discussed issue in *Pride and Prejudice*.[12] It is true that Elizabeth Bennet comes close to becoming a feminist heroine. She reads; she is intelligent, rational, and witty; she is independent and unconventional, as in her hike to her sick sister's side; and she is impulsive and warm-hearted, qualities that subvert the usual social conventions.

But it is equally true that Elizabeth Bennet finds her happiness in marriage to a fabulously rich landowner. She tempers her cutting wit in order to become the conventional—and subordinate—wife. At no point, it seems, does Austen question the role of women within the society or its controlling institutions. Elizabeth Bennet rises above the feminine stereotype only to fall back into it.

Is it possible that *Pride and Prejudice* accepts the cultural stereotypes for men and women? The answer is yes, on the surface. As a male, Darcy is public, political, powerful, and rational; as a woman, Elizabeth is private, domestic, dependent and emotional. Of course, one could resolve the issue of Austen's conservatism by showing that the private issues in the novel are really public ones. In her book *Jane Austen*, Claudia Johnson shows that gender roles are connected to the larger cultural and political conflicts of the time and so reflect Austen's essential participation in liberal thought.

What is important to my purpose, however, is the dependence of questions of gender upon questions of emotion. Austen might have failed to challenge the stereotype in her portrait of Elizabeth, but she succeeded in her portrait of Darcy. For when we look closely at Darcy, we find that he is not at all the purely rational patriarch the stereotype would make him. In fact, Darcy is masculine *because* he is emotional. In 1813, when *Pride and Prejudice* was published, Jane Austen dissolved an arbitrary and artificial definition of gender for at least one of the sexes.[13]

I don't want to overstate my case. As I say, Austen describes Darcy's strength as his "judgment," presenting him as a rational man of the world. Darcy is also an English estate owner, which makes him a public person even if we do not see him perform his duties. And then Darcy confesses to a certain (and stereotypical) emotional disability: he is unable to read people, he tells Elizabeth, and is too often insensitive to the emotions of others.

But this view of Darcy is far from the complete story. For in virtually every scene in which he appears, Darcy is driven by his emotions. His rude behavior at the ball, for example, flows from his frustration at his own inability to make small talk—though I must say that I find his bad temper inexcusable. Later, when he has fallen in love with Elizabeth, he hangs about her in a silence created by his emotion. In the next to final chapter, Elizabeth asks,

> "Why especially, when you called, did you look as if you did not care about me?"
> "Because you were grave and silent, and gave me no encouragement."
> "But I was embarrassed."
> "And so was I." (389)

Darcy's problem is not that he does not feel but that he feels so deeply. What makes his first proposal obnoxious is his naive revelation of not only his passion for Elizabeth but his less complimentary feelings about her family. He explains that "disguise of every sort is my abhorrence. Nor am I ashamed of the feelings I related. They were natural and just." In time Elizabeth recognizes the truth in Darcy's view of her family, tactless as it may be. But the point is that Darcy confesses all of his emotions because he is so deeply wrapped up in them. In Darcy's insensitivity, Austen shows what Henry James would later show in Isabel Archer's suitors: strong emotion can serve as an obstacle to the very human relationship it seeks.

Whenever Darcy appears, Austen describes his emotional reaction. "His astonishment was obvious." "He came towards her in an agitated manner." "Mr. Darcy stood near them in silent indignation." Even when Austen does not describe his emotions directly, Darcy's actions reveal them, as when Elizabeth played the piano and he "stationed himself so as to command a full view of the fair performer's countenance." Darcy is inexpressive, certainly, and shy, but Austen, who may well have taught Hemingway the power of the stiff upper lip, makes it clear that Darcy's very silence means he is swept by feeling.[14]

Of course, Jane Austen describes *everything* in this novel in terms of emotion—it is the currency of these relationships. And it might imply nothing about men in general. Darcy's emotions are necessary to the love story, after all, and he is lovesick. The hesitation he feels in the face of the Bennets' modest status (and large impropriety) simply intensifies his feelings; Darcy is emotional in the way that only conflicted people can be.

Yet the fact remains that Darcy is an emotional person. If he finds parties painful, it is because he can not detach himself from them as Mr. Bennet does, taking his neighbor for sport. If Elizabeth charges that he is not a gentleman, he broods about her words. "—I cannot think of it without abhorrence. . . . How they have tortured me." Darcy changes in the novel by moving (like Elizabeth) from one emotion to another, shifting from irritation to interest to shame and then to conflicted love. At any point, we know him as disdainful or angry or dutiful or shy.

Nor is Darcy alone in this emotionalism. It is interesting that the man who is most relentlessly public and rational and so closest to the male stereotype is Collins. But Collins is actually captive to his feelings of inferiority and conceit, as we have seen—a serene young bogus, floating on a cloud of banal and ostentatiously rational conversation. Wickham is enslaved by his feelings (shallow as they may be), and so too is Bingley, though his passivity gives Jane much pain. Mr. Bennet fulfills the masculine stereotype in that he regards the world with detachment, but he too is actually driven by emotion. He might employ humor to make the best of a bad marriage, but it is not hard to see the sorrow and the frustration behind his facade. He retreats into his study because he is afraid of his own feelings, and there he appears, on one level at least, an ironic embodiment of the female stereotype: the man of the house, certainly, and yet passive, private, and emotional.

Such privacy and passivity suggest other ways in which Austen's men violate the stereotype. While Mr. Bennet and Darcy have public power (which they exercise as their natural due), both are extremely private people. Like Mr. Bennet in his study, Darcy has made Pemberley a private haven, which is precisely what Elizabeth sees when she visits the tastefully appointed estate.[15] She penetrates not the public role of the man but his private self. And then all of these men are passive. Bingley is a pawn of his sisters and friends; Mr. Bennet is ineffective; Wickham is supported by others and passive before his appetites; and Darcy, the decisive man of affairs, is a lovesick supplicant. It is significant that on their last walk together, it is Elizabeth who speaks first, taking control of their mutual fate.

While Elizabeth holds her tongue at the end of the novel, then, forbearing to tease Darcy, we should not make too much of it. Darcy's devotion to her is total, and the danger is not that he will dominate her but that he will submit to her too easily, falling into that other stereotype, the subordinate husband. Despite Darcy's great public power—which again, must not be underestimated—the danger in this relationship (if danger there must be) is matriarchal. Elizabeth now takes the lead. Darcy must learn how to read emotion, she says, and as she does so, we have no doubt about the strength of her will. Why not take her softening as the relaxation of one confident in an equal and so healthy companionship? Elizabeth's devotion to Darcy responds to his devotion to her. They chat easily, in these final pages, and with an intimacy that bodes well for the future.

The truth is that our culture is schizophrenic about the male identity. It insists that the stereotypical man be both unemotional and intensely emotional. The gentleman is known by the quality of his feeling—Wickham is a scoundrel because he is "devoid of proper feeling." And as I say, Darcy is masculine *because* he feels strongly. When he complains that he is poor at catching tone and feigning interest, defining himself stereotypically, Elizabeth corrects him. She is not as good a pianist as some, she says, "But then I have always supposed it to be my own fault—because I would not take the trouble of practicing." Everyone can learn to communicate emotionally, as both Austen's women and men must do: emotion is not the province of women but the faculty of all. And we understand that. We understand that men, for all their reticence, are especially emotional, no doubt because they have been taught to bottle up their feelings. We understand not only the emotions they openly express but—as Hemingway so well knew—many of those that they conceal or repress.

III

In such ways Austen's dramatization of the difficulty of sharing emotion demonstrates the actuality of such sharing. And yet to examine emotion as a subject, as Austen does, does not guarantee that her readers share or understand those emotions. So many of the characters in the novel misread emotion, in fact, that I must dwell upon this point. I'm confident that Elizabeth would share the emotion expressed in a literary text, understanding the author's intentions, but surely Lydia, Mr. Collins, or Mrs. Bennet would not. Some people never identify with a literary character, it would seem, and others shut emotion out of their lives so rigorously that they do not notice what other people are feeling. It is true that most readers feel themselves to be highly competent in emotional matters. But then, so do Mrs. Bennet and Lady Catherine and Mr. Collins, who have no clue. The sharing of textual emotion among readers is clearly an issue.[16]

If the self is a social construction, however, or an aggregate of values and conventions absorbed from the culture, then readers in the same culture would naturally share the emotions taught them. Dozens of psychologists and anthropologists have discovered emotions unique to a given society, and so offered evidence that our culture teaches us our emotions. The Japanese feel *amae*, for example, which is the parents' "sweet cuddling" of the child.[17] The anthropologist Michelle Rosaldo describes the Philippine society of the Ilongo, which teaches its members that emotion exists outside of the self in the world at large. Where Westerners would say that a person acts out of anger, an Ilongo would say that the person discovers the anger that lies in the world. In the same vein, the anthropologist Jean L. Briggs claims that certain Eskimo tribes do not recognize the emotion of anger. And other thinkers, such as the philosopher Michel Foucault, argue that we internalize as emotion a panoply of cultural elements—values, ideas, strategies, social distinctions—that then rise unbidden to imprison us. Certainly we learn not only specific emotions but the role emotion can play in daily life. Emotion is not something private or hermetic but public and knowable, if we have but the courage and skill to discuss it.[18] And it is something that we share so deeply with the other members of our society that we can define the society by it.

In respect to *Pride and Prejudice*, our Anglo-American culture has probably developed new emotions since the novel's publication in 1813. But we still share many of the same feelings about courtship, gender, family roles, the self, and society—about the taboos surrounding Lydia's sexual escapade (which has now changed) as well as the glamour surrounding the military (which has not). What is important is that the greatest number of these feelings are unconscious, or so much a part of us that we take them for granted.[19]

To me the best example of a socially shared emotion in *Pride and Prejudice* lies in the famous Pemberley description, in which our culturally shared conventions and values permit us to share Elizabeth's feeling. When Elizabeth first sees Darcy's house, it stands across a valley with trees behind it,

> and in front, a stream of some natural importance was swelled into greater, but without any artificial appearance. Its banks were neither formal, nor falsely adorned. Elizabeth was delighted. She had never seen a place for which nature had done more, or where natural beauty have been so little counteracted by an awkward taste.

The key words here, of course, are "natural" and "artificial."[20] Pemberley is neither formal, harking back to the eighteenth century, nor artificially wild, in the manner favored by the romantics. The estate gives a feeling of a graceful and unobtrusive composition that addresses the feelings we have been taught about the natural. An unimproved scene would bespeak laziness, perhaps; a total make over of the river would be contrived. More to the point, the scene addresses our intense but conflicted cultural feelings about power and passivity. Elizabeth judges Darcy by a vista constructed by a light and thoughtful hand. She sees that the sensibility that shaped this vista (and which must have shaped Darcy) is sensitive to what exists: the residents of Pemberley enhance rather than dominate the given.

Of course, literature is itself one of the instruments by which a culture teaches emotion, and in this passage Jane Austen does just that. As we identify with Elizabeth, we share her feelings of harmony or balance born of restraint. If we had not felt such a feeling already in our lives, we feel it now—what we currently know as organic form.

Did Jane Austen herself understand the social construction of emotion? The answer is probably no, though the question of Austen's attitude toward society is a matter of long-standing controversy. Some readers of *Pride and Prejudice* believe that the novel shows that Elizabeth must accept certain social values while other readers— correctly, in my view—believe that *Pride and Prejudice* is resolutely antisociety.[21] The book satirizes society, after all, and the worst characters are those who speak most forcibly for contemporary mores—Mrs. Bennet, Lady Catherine, and Mr. Collins, who believes that Lydia's violation of social decorum requires her death. Elizabeth is a loner, and she tells Darcy that the two of them are alike—"we are each of an unsocial, taciturn disposition, unwilling to speak, unless we expect to say something that will amaze the whole room."

How does this relate to the reader's sharing of emotion? Austen makes us see the truth of this society, which is corrupt because its feelings are corrupt. Austen treats the society of Longbourn as a character in its own right, in fact, exposing it as frivolous, fickle, and chronically mistaken in its judgments—emotionally unstable. At the ball, the group first admires Darcy. "The report . . . was in general circulation within five minutes after his entrance, of his having ten thousand a year." But the group soon turns against him. "He was the proudest, most disagreeable man in the world, and everybody hoped that he would never come there again." It is not hard to hear an echo of Mrs. Bennet in this group voice, particularly since the group shares her volatility and difficulty with fact. This is the same social group that, when Wickham has left the village with unpaid debts, "began to find out, that they had always distrusted the appearance of his goodness."

Austen divides the characters in this novel into two groups, distinguished by their use (or misuse) of emotion. Those who speak for the Longbourn society are unsympathetic because their emotions are inappropriate. Thus *Pride and Prejudice* illustrates an important point: we are highly sensitive to the emotions felt by the characters and judge them according to the fit of those emotions to the circumstance. Such evaluation is one of the very first acts we perform, whether socializing or reading, and is possible only because we all share a certain mutual understanding of the emotion at hand.

IV

Readers also share emotion because they share biology: as Ross Buck notes in *The Communication of Emotion,* emotion is traditionally associated with the body. It is true, of course, as Foucault tells us, that the body takes definition from our culture. And yet the physical continues to exist in all its stubborn consistency. Once we have granted every argument to social construction, the purely biological still remains an important force, setting the perimeters within which culture must work.[22] This is especially true in the communication of emotion, which depends upon the biological base we all share. Readers feel the same emotions while reading a fiction because they share the same biology.

It is not hard to show that *Pride and Prejudice* recognizes the biological. The novel is about mating, after all, and at least one critic speaks darkly of Darcy's sexual desire. The novel also recounts Elizabeth Bennet's rise above her biological origins. When Darcy speaks of "the family obstacles which judgment had always opposed to inclination," he refers to not only the Bennet's low status but an innate pattern of behavior—"that total want of propriety so frequently, so almost uniformly betrayed by [Mrs. Bennet], by your three younger sisters, and occasionally even by your father." I take Darcy's comment to be his worry about the Bennet family genes. Elizabeth and Jane spring from the loins of their mother, after all, and are the sisters of Kitty, Mary, and Lydia.

Such facts make *Pride and Prejudice* a study of the relative importance in human affairs of social and biological elements. The elopement of Lydia and Wickham, like the courtship of Elizabeth and Darcy, obviously embodies such a conflict. And it is significant that Jane Austen describes her characters in biological terms. Although she is well known for the abstraction of her style, Austen is like that other intellectual writer, Henry James, in the attention she pays to her character's bodies. She makes us more conscious of physical presence than does Ernest Hemingway. Wickham has "a good figure" while Elizabeth's features are "coarse and brown." Even the correct Darcy teases Miss Bingley and Elizabeth: "you are conscious that your figures appear to the greatest advantage in walking."

As her adjectives testify, Austen uses physical reference to make her readers feel certain emotions. More than that, Austen ties the emotion Elizabeth sees in a character to its physical expression. When Elizabeth baits Wickham with her knowledge of his perfidy, his "alarm now appeared in a heightened complexion and agitated look." Jane, having been with Bingley, "met her with a smile of such sweet complacency, a glow of such happy expression, as sufficiently marked how well she was satisfied with the occurrences of the evening." Although these physical phenomena take meaning from our social values, they have a physical center, as Charles Darwin well knew and Paul Ekman has recently documented in *The Face of Man*.[23] If we read one another's facial expressions, we might well read the same emotions in the descriptions of a fictional character. We might disagree in our appraisal of an event, and so react differently, but one of our novelists' tasks is to make their readers share *their* appraisal of events.

In this as in all novels, the greatest evidence of a biologically originated emotion lies in the effect of aesthetic form. Physiologists know that colors produce a predictable emotional effect on people, and our personal experience tells us that certain forms do the same. Short sentences obviously create an effect of tension; long, flowing sentences, with many qualifiers, create an effect of unhurried thoughtfulness. The important point is that we feel such formal effects involuntarily. We feel a crowded paragraph, a balanced chapter, a sudden ending, even as we attend consciously to the content of the passage. Critics all seem to know that Jane Austen means the ending of *Pride and Prejudice* to be a happy one, for example. And how do they know? Elizabeth has made a good marriage, and the tone (itself embodied in form) is triumphant. But the effect is also established by Austen's arrangement of the concluding material, as she works through the fate of the characters one by one. We feel the rhythm of the series, the passage of time, and the author's closing benediction.

This reminds us that in any narrative we feel both the climax and the rising and falling action. The rhythms of narrative echo the physical rhythms of conflict and resolution, bewilderment and discovery, sexual desire and release.[24] Martha Nussbaum addresses such facts in her essay "Narrative Emotions: Beckett's Genealogy of Love," arguing that narrative embodies the physical structure of the emotion, becoming a paradigm for it—the narrative operates as a kind of objective correlative.[25]

Finally, Jane Austen offers yet another set of biological emotions based upon the story itself. Virginia Woolf disagreed with Charlotte Brontë about the presence of emotion in *Pride and Prejudice,* commenting that

> Jane Austen is thus a mistress of much deeper emotion than appears upon the surface. She stimulates us to supply what is not there. What she offers is, apparently, a trifle, yet is composed of something that expands in the reader's mind and endows with the most enduring form of life scenes which are outwardly trivial.[26]

I find that in at least one instance I feel more passion in *Pride and Prejudice* than in *Jane Eyre*—for Mrs. Bennet is a monster. I do appreciate the way that she stands up to her husband, giving voice to what he would merely imply. And she certainly has good reason to worry about her unmarried daughters. As a comic character, she is to be taken lightly, of course, and she does stimulate an affectionate laughter. But Mrs. Bennet is not only shallow and false—"a woman of mean understanding, little information and uncertain temper," as Austen puts it—but she betrays her own daughter. She violates this biological (and cultural) tie and so evokes emotions that have biological roots. Though Elizabeth is clearly more intelligent and mature than her sisters, Mrs. Bennet is quite prepared to throw her away. Jane can have Bingley, since she is good-looking, but Elizabeth must settle for Collins. Among brothers and sisters, such discriminations trigger passions that are as strong—and as clearly perceived—as any we feel.

When Elizabeth refuses Mr. Collins, moreover, Mrs. Bennet's reaction is extreme. "—And so I warn you. —I have done with you from this very day. —I told you in the library, you know, that I should never speak to you again, and you will find me as good as my word." Elizabeth knows that this is just talk, and yet has to understand the rejection her mother expresses. Mrs. Bennet is the wicked stepmother to Elizabeth's Cinderella, and we resent the older woman precisely to the extent that we identify (or even sympathize) with Elizabeth.[27] For all of the humor, Mrs. Bennet proves to be not harmless but a threat, since she provides Darcy with a reason to stay away from Elizabeth. And for all of Jane Austen's irony and wit, the novel on this level reaches something close to a fantasy of love and hate.

I feel uncharitable in saying this. Mrs. Bennet is a victim, with her five marriageable daughters and the entail. Yet her judgment is so consistently bad and her behavior so detrimental to Elizabeth that it is hard not to feel a visceral resentment. More than that, Austen shapes the novel to create those strong resentments, dividing the characters into two camps, as I have said, and reminding us of the division. At every juncture Mrs. Bennet sides with the group we find mediocre and reprehensible. She thinks that Mr. Collins is "a remarkably clever and good kind of young man" and that Mary is a good musician. Wickham is her favorite son-in-law (as he is—wittily—Mr. Bennet's) and Lady Catherine is a model of the aristocracy. Mrs. Bennet always takes a position in conflict with that of her husband and Elizabeth. Thus the passion is there, if we identify with Elizabeth, and it is a passion that we all understand quite clearly. To anyone with brothers or sisters, it is resonant.

I cannot deny that the expectations of parents and children are learned from the culture, of course, which makes this emotion socially constructed. One could imagine a culture requiring a rejection precisely like that of Elizabeth by Mrs. Bennet. And yet the relationship between parent and child finds its root in the child's biological dependence upon the adult, just as sibling rivalry is fueled by the physical arithmetic of families.

I should conclude by adding that it is the *combination* of these sources of emotion in the text that ensures that readers understand them. We can misunderstand the social references in a novel, say, and still feel the rhythms of the prose, absorbing the emotions even when we do not perceive their source. We can fail to respond to the form of the work and yet understand the emotions felt by the characters. As we actually read, we confirm and reconfirm our emotions continuously, absorbing and responding to the logic of the story, the social meanings we recognize, the biological elements we absorb. It is because of this interpenetration of several factors, and the wonderful capacity of the mind to mediate among them, that readers understand the emotions that determine the meaning of the text. As Stephen Pepper puts it, talking about the many sources of emotion in a work of art: "How far these are learned or natural, no one knows, but in every culture they constitute an emotional language of great reliability for those who have been brought up in it."[28]

We talk as if thought was precise and emotion was vague. In reality there is precise emotion and there is vague emotion. To express precise emotion requires as great intellectual power as to express precise thought.

—T. S. Eliot, "Shakespeare and the Stoicism of Seneca"

11

Precise Emotion in *Adventures of Huckleberry Finn*

Premise Three: The affective code is precise.

I

IN HIS CHARACTERIZATION OF HUCKLEBERRY FINN, MARK TWAIN tells us something important about the human mind. Huck is "thoughtful" or brooding, as he narrates his adventures, but he does not think in the way we usually define the term.[1] He does not analyze his relations with Jim, or review their history together, or place their relationship in the context of Southern society. He does not define a problem or review solutions or develop a hypothesis. Instead Huck lives in the immediate present (or, when a threat arises, in the near future), and when he pauses to think, he attends to his emotions. "Miss Watson she kept pecking at me," he says in the first chapter, as he goes to his room.[2]

Then I set down in a chair by the window and tried to think of something cheerful, but it warn't no use, I felt so lonesome I most wished I was dead. The stars was shining, and the leaves rustled in the woods ever so mournful; and I heard an owl, away off, who-whooing about somebody that was dead, and a whippowill and a dog crying about somebody that was going to die. . . . I got so down-hearted and scared I did wish I had some company. Pretty soon a spider went crawling up my shoulder and I flipped it off and it lit in the candle; and before I could budge it was all shriveled up.

141

Huck thinks about his situation by focusing on his emotions.[3] He tries to make himself cheerful, but his feelings only get worse: he moves from "lonesome" to "scared" to the implied terror of the shriveling spider. Because Huck is melancholy by nature, we understand that he brings these emotions to the window himself. But in another sense he opens himself to his feelings, which become a kind of meditation. The emotions he permits to flow over him serve as what psychologists call an appraisal of his situation—an evaluation of his present life. Huck reflects the basic fact that much of our thinking consists of a *re-*feeling of our persistent emotions.

But what is really striking is Huck's connection of his emotions to objects and events outside of himself. He tries "to think of some*thing* cheerful" (italics mine). He catalogues the objects and sensations that equal his melancholy. The owl and dog and "whippowill" illustrate what he is feeling, but they also evoke that feeling within him— and the reader. They are both illustration and cause. Read the word "lonesome" as an idea, feeling nothing, and the owl and the dog make you feel that emotion anyway. Feel "lonesome" as you identify with Huck, and the stars and leaves will confirm and clarify your emotion. It is not hard to understand why Hemingway, who was skilled in the affective code, praised Twain's prose in *The Green Hills of Africa,* claiming that "all modern American Literature comes from one book by Mark Twain."[4]

Twain also confirms the insight of William James. The leaves *are* mournful, the owl *is* grieving. Emotions and objects *are* equivalent. Nor is this passage atypical of Twain's prose. A few chapters later, on Jackson's Island, Huck again names an emotion and the objects that support it. Having recently escaped from pap, Huck lies in the grass

> feeling rested and ruther comfortable and satisfied. . . . There was freckled places on the ground where the light sifted down through the leaves, and the freckled places swapped about a little, showing there was a little breeze up there. (41)

Huck obviously notices the details that reflect his mood. His original feelings make him notice the beautiful shadows. But Huck also reacts to his surroundings, feeling the emotions that *they* create in him. It would be hard not to feel comfortable in such a place and with such flickering shadows, just as it would be hard not to feel lonesome at night by his window listening to an owl hoot and a dog cry.

It is this equivalence of object and emotion that demonstrates the affective code. In real life, the objects evoke emotion; in the act of reading, the emotion (evoked by the mental objects) provides the basis of our mental construction (or reconstitution) of the objects named in the text.[5]

But Huck's window vigil also illustrates one of the key problems of the affective code. Huck feels not just one emotion here but many. In this single passage he feels lonesome, mournful, down-hearted, scared, and terrorized. He feels a desire to die. Surely, it would seem, these emotions jostle one another, getting into each other's way. Is Huck sad or is he terrorized? Is he lonesome or is he fearful? When we say, as we must, that he is all of these things, we raise the question of how so many emotions fit together.

It is my contention that these many feelings, for all of their potential for confusion, create an important kind of precision—the precision that is necessary if the affective code is to perform its job. In the following pages I will first document the large number of emotions generated by even a single paragraph. I will then examine how the mind organizes those feelings, achieving, instead of tumult and sloppiness, order and precision.

II

I don't know anyone who would deny that readers feel many emotions simultaneously. If each emotion is unique, of course, such coexistence is hard to understand, especially since we have not thought about the subject very much. Accordingly, at the risk of belaboring the issue, I want to look at an inevitable source of emotion in all narrative passages. I will take as my example a passage that is as famous as many great poems, Twain's idyllic description in *Huckleberry Finn* of dawn on the river. In the passage, which I quote below, Huck and Jim float on the raft away from the bloody Shepherdson feud.

Two or three days and nights went by: I reckon I might say they swum by, they slid along so quiet and smooth and lovely. Here is the way we put in the time. It was a monstrous big river down there—sometimes a mile and a half wide; we run nights, and laid up and hid day-times; soon as night was most gone, we stopped navigating and tied up—nearly always in the dead water under a tow-head; and then cut young cottonwoods and willows and hid the raft with them. Then we set out the lines. Next we slid into the river and had a swim, so as to freshen up and cool off; then we set down on the sandy bottom where the water was about knee deep, and watched the daylight come. Not a sound, anywheres—perfectly still—just like the whole world was asleep, only sometimes the bullfrogs a-cluttering, maybe. The first thing to see, looking away over the water, was a kind of

dull line—that was the woods on t'other side—you couldn't make nothing else out; then a pale place in the sky; then more paleness, spreading
around; then the river softened up, away off, and warn't black any more,
but gray; you could see little dark spots drifting along, ever so far away—
trading scows, and such things; and long black streaks—rafts; sometimes
you could hear a sweep screaking; or jumbled up voices, it was so still, and
sounds come so far; and by-and-by you could see a streak on the water
which you know by the look of the streak that there's a snag there in a
swift current which breaks on it and makes that streak look that way; and
you see the mist curl up off of the water, and the east reddens up, and the
river, and you make out a log cabin in the edge of the woods, away on the
bank on t'other side of the river, being a wood-yard, likely, and piled by
them cheats so you can throw a dog through it anywheres; then the nice
breeze springs up, and comes fanning you from over there, so cool and
fresh, and sweet to smell, on account of the woods and the flowers; but
sometimes not that way, because they've left dead fish laying around, gars,
and such, and they do get pretty rank; and next you've got the full day,
and everything smiling in the sun, and the song-birds just going it! (129–
30)

Practically every word here is designed to convey Huck's feelings,
and yet, as they say, that is not the half of it. As we read about Huck's
emotion and then share it, reacting with emotions of our own, we
also feel (unconsciously, for the most part) the many feelings evoked
by form, or Twain's arrangement of his words and ideas.[6]

Perhaps the best example of such form lies in Twain's rhythm.
Adventures of Huckleberry Finn is shaped by its pulse, as it alternates
between the serious and the comic, fear and peace, the river and the
shore, one father figure and then another. Huck creeps close to an
adult and then flees; he lives alone and then joins a group and then
flees again. As Twain wrote to his wife, Livy, he was deeply interested
in pacing and contrast: in the "running narrative-plank" of his
speeches, he would like to drill holes "six inches apart, all the length
of it," and then "make plugs (half marked 'serious' and the other
marked 'humorous') to select from and to jam into the holes."[7]

Sometimes Twain uses rhythm to create excitement, as when he
begins the description of the dawn with a series of short clauses that
build tension by holding back the flow, until they break into a crescendo of longer, flowing sentences. (We get ten stops in the first two
hundred words and then, in the rest of the passage, only four stops,
all semicolons.) At other times Twain uses such felt rhythm to express
nothing less than complex themes. One perceives this in Twain's
rational organization, for example, as Huck states his topic sentence
and then develops it methodically, creating the effect of order. Having chosen the silent arrival of daylight as his subject, Huck divides

the event into three stages, each of which he supports with detail. "The first thing to see," he says, is "a kind of dull line," which gives way to the second stage, as "the river softened up, away off, and warn't black anymore, but gray." In the third stage, the mist rises "and the east reddens up" and he can make out detail all the way across the water.

At the same time that Twain evokes feelings of order, he evokes a sense of a dynamic and natural fluidity. As is proper to the moment of first light, the description begins slowly with a sparseness of sensation. Twain gives the impression of silence, of that time when nothing moves—but then the sensations break and come tumbling one after another as the light increases and the breeze comes up and the sounds arrive, to reach a crescendo that includes all of the senses. As many critics have noted, Twain moves from darkness to light, from silence to sound, from gray to color and from a scarcity of sensation to a bursting climax—fittingly expressed in the quick accumulation of clauses.

And then the very sequence of perception generates an emotion, as Huck gives first the sensation and then its meaning, moving back and forth between the emerging sight and the act of cognition. When he sees "a dull line," Huck explains "that was the woods on t'other side; you couldn't make nothing else out." When he sees "dark spots drifting along, ever so far away," he recognizes them immediately: "trading scows." The streaks are rafts and the white streak is a snag and the log cabin with wood piled brings forth a veritable torrent of ratiocination: "being a woodyard, likely, and piled by them cheats so you can throw a dog through it anywheres."

III

All of these formal emotions *coexist* within the reader's mind.[8] As we read Twain's passage, we feel the ease of the rhythm and the control of the organization, the fluidity of the light and the satisfaction of Huck's recognition of objects. We feel these emotions simultaneously even as we feel those evoked by Twain's content—feelings of the light and the shore and the contents of the river, not to mention the water on which Huck has traveled and the culture that extends on either side of it. Because we identify with Huck, we also feel what *he* feels. And then, backing away, we feel his presence and even the presence of ourselves, as the novel has shaped us and as we know ourselves to be.

Not every reader will feel all of these emotions, and many will feel them without becoming conscious of them. But it is a fact that a single passage like the river dawn evokes dozens and perhaps even hundreds of feelings. And then, as if those were not enough, we react to what we experience with yet other emotions: we have feelings about our feelings.

I'm not being flippant. Just as readers have ideas about the ideas that they read—that a concept is insightful, say, or complex—so readers feel emotions about their emotions, a notion understood by thinkers as different as the philosopher Johann Tetens and the sociologist Norman Denzin.[9] In fact the latter defines our social experience as a chain of emotional expression, reaction, and new reaction. In real life we show our mood and disposition on our face, triggering the emotional reaction of our companion, which is revealed on his or her face, to which we then react again. How long might such a chain continue? As long as we remain in each other's company or think of one another. We are so used to such exchanges that we are unaware of them.

Much the same occurs when we read fiction, though it remains within a single mind. However we construct the author's words, we react to the experience that the construction provides.[10] And then we react to how that experience makes us feel, developing a feeling about our feeling, which influences our aesthetic judgment. Does the river dawn make us feel serene? We *like* that, and so feel positively about what Twain makes us feel.

Such reactions to our feelings may be purely personal, as we like stories that make us feel good, say, but they also define the special or unique quality of the text. When we read the description of the river dawn, we feel the freshness and precision of Twain's style. Huck describes not sunrise, which is the cliché, but first light.[11] Depending upon the passage, we feel qualities like control or suspense, tension or spontaneity, harmony or disharmony. We feel the *relationships,* which William James has told us we know as emotions. And those feelings in turn define the essence of the passage, or perhaps the nature of its internal form, contributing to the emotion that expresses the passage as a whole. In this way our feeling about how we have been made to feel is sometimes a judgment of the experience and sometimes a definition of what is unique in the passage, but in either case it is an expression of its significance.

IV

I go into these many emotions because they create a problem. In *Feeling and Form* Susanne Langer complains that emotions evoked by real things named in the text "obscure the emotional content of the form."[12] If she is correct, the large number of emotions evoked by a passage would create an even greater obscurity. How does the mind keep them all straight? Doesn't their sheer number threaten to form some kind of affective mess?

We have at least two theories to explain how these many emotions come together, both of which are helpful. In *The Principles of Art Appreciation* the philosopher Stephen Pepper defines four ways in which textual emotion is organized, all of which we can recognize in Twain's river dawn. Huck unites his specifics within what Pepper calls a "dominant emotion," which in this case is fluid ease. Huck also uses a "natural emotional sequence," or a generic unfolding of feeling, as in the movement from confusion to meaning. Because the sequence occurs gradually over time, building to the emotional climax of new light and sensation, it also exemplifies Pepper's third category, "gradation," or the gradual change in the intensity of emotion. And because that process involves the juxtaposition of the paired feelings, it illustrates Pepper's final organizational category, "contrast."[13] Again and again, Huck contrasts the pleasant and the disturbing, the near and the far, the dark and the light.

Clearly these four kinds of organization explain a great deal. We see them everywhere. While defining them in the *Principles*, however, Pepper assumes that they are sequential, no doubt because he is thinking about emotion in a linear way. Readers feel first one emotion and then another.[14] But a purely linear account overlooks what must be the key, which is that readers feel the several emotions of a passage simultaneously. For this reason the European philosopher Stephan Strasser is even more helpful than Pepper when he claims that emotions form coexisting layers or strata.

In *Phenomenology of Feeling* Strasser argues that emotions organize themselves in a vertical order, stacked in the sequence of their development. At the base lie pre-intentional emotions, or those that look inward, expressing the individual's needs and motives. Then come those that are focused on the object, or the intentional, looking outward, forming the larger part of our emotions. And finally come those of "apprehension," in which the object exists in its own right, without reference to anything else, offering a sense of its independent "thingness."[15]

I have no doubt that Strasser's model is true to at least some of our experience. Clearly, we begin with emotions of the self, like mood and motive and need, and move outward to the object and the emotions centered on it. We attend to our own feelings and then to the object, to which we react. And if we are mature, we perceive the object on its own terms. It makes sense to say that each level of emotion incorporates the feeling before it, so that we feel all of these emotions at once.

While we cannot think two ideas at the same time, then, or visualize two images simultaneously, we *can* feel two or more emotions at once, and do so on a continuing basis. We talk about levels of emotion all the time, making a general use of Strasser's notion of stratification. To read is to feel several currents of emotion flowing forward simultaneously, a point reflected in our recognition of emotional composites like love and hate. In such cases, the individual strands maintain their identity even as they bind together.

Often the two joined emotions form a unique relationship. The lover's gratitude to his mate intensifies his admiration of her. The employee's boredom with her job diminishes her loyalty to the firm. The separate parts of the composite emotion can contradict, modify, qualify, or enhance one another, and, as Susanne Langer says of our inner life in general, are anything but static: "The ways we are moved are as various as the lights in a forest; and they may intersect, sometimes without cancelling each other, take shape and dissolve, conflict, explode into passion, or be transfigured."[16]

V

Yet even Strasser misses the ultimate point, which is that such emotions coexist in not only the aggregate but (as Pepper says elsewhere) *fusion*.[17] Emotions *meld*, each submerging its identity within the newly formed whole. When Wolfgang Iser talks about imagining foreground and background, he believes that the two combine to form a single unit, and this is especially true when we imagine in the affective code. As readers, we do not feel one specific emotion for the subject and another as the background, but both together, as a single unit. We feel the subject *as* it exists within the context; we feel the background *as* the context for this particular subject. In the description of the river dawn, we feel not Huck and then the river but Huck-watching-the-river. We feel not the river and then the continent through which it flows, but the river as part of the continent. Reading about Huck's hidden campsite, we experience feelings of the raft, the water, the concealing cottonwoods, the sandy river bottom, and the dawn all fused into our feeling *of* the camp.

On this level, the affective code is like the human palate, which physiologists tell us combines four basic tastes into many unique flavors. The mind combines a number of basic emotions—Paul Ekman's count of seven seems as good as any—into our fused, representational emotions. When we remember that each emotion can vary in degree, from the strongest passion to the lightest feeling, we can appreciate the almost infinite variety available. Here the work of the social determinists is of interest, since society teaches us unique feelings by combining the basic emotions in new ways.

What does a fused emotion look like in the text? We may discover it in a single detail, as in the snag that stands out in the water in Twain's passage, where it orders space even as it disrupts the surface, and so fuses feelings of order and disorder. Or we may discover it within a general characteristic of the scene. The largeness of the river offers both danger and protective cover, for example, which Twain's language encourages us to fuse. As Huck and Jim make camp, feeling comfortable and nurtured by the river, Twain uses the words "run" and "hid," fusing feelings of danger with those of comfort. The water under the towhead is "dead" and in camp the two fugitives are "laid up"—to the feeling of safety such words add feelings of danger.

Another example of fusion lies in the feelings of vastness and intimacy. Twain says that the river is immense ("a monstrous big river down there—sometimes a mile and a half wide") and the sky is even larger. Yet Huck discovers a surprising intimacy. The night encloses him; the water washes over him; the breeze brings the smell of the far shore and the light brings the sight of distant objects. The water makes distant sounds near, and then entertains Huck as well, since Huck needs only to sit in the shallows to watch the parade of rafts and boats.

Even the fact that Huck watches people unawares contributes to this intimacy, since he witnesses their private moments. And then Huck speaks to the reader in a confidential whisper, forming a community of two, as he describes shapes that even before he identifies them seem familiar. Because of this duality, we have not read very far in the paragraph before we have a sense of these two feelings joining together in a fruitful tension. When Huck, as he hides by the shore, witnesses a change in the enveloping light, we feel an intimate vastness or an intimacy intensified by awe.

Readers might combine these emotions in different ways. Some might feel them in sequence, which is one of the ways in which they appear in the text. As Huck describes first "the monstrous big river," then his private camp, and then the river once again, we feel first awe, then intimacy, and then awe again before the vast and timeless river.[18] Other readers might imagine these two emotions as parallel strands (much as Strasser describes his strata), flowing in tandem as Huck records emerging detail. We carry our sense of a vast space forward, through even Huck's making of camp; we carry our feeling of intimate comfort forward, as Huck stares at the river and describes the darkness lifting. And then, as I say, still other readers will fuse the two emotions into a single and unique feeling, forming a new emotion all together—call it the feeling of an intimate vastness. And because at some point our memory becomes a single whole, all readers must do this eventually.

The very number of emotions that might cause confusion, then, makes precision possible. For however we put the two emotions together, the combination makes for precision. The combined feelings work like two intersecting lines, locating a precise spot. It is just *these* emotions fitting together in just *this* way. One feels not intimacy but intimacy intensified by the vastness of water and sky. One feels not vastness but a vastness witnessed from a position of intimate safety. When the combining emotions contrast, their differences sharpen and dramatize one another. And when they overlap, their coalescence confirms the meaning (offering a special clarity and pleasure). We may also feel the particular relationship of the combined emotions, whether it be a sequence, a parallel, or fusion. And then, below the level of immediate consciousness (though we may bring them to awareness), we may feel the individual feelings interact with one another, forming a symbiosis that generates a meaning of its own. When the number of emotions is three or more, of course, the precision is even greater.

Perhaps the best example of fusion in the river dawn also expresses Twain's thesis: more than anything else, the river dawn evokes a feeling of fluid ease or harmony. "I reckon I might say they swum by, they slid along so quiet and smooth and lovely," Huck says. How exactly do these days "swim by"? The current flows silently; the time flows effortlessly; the sound travels over the water easily: the light emerges mysteriously. Each of these specifics offers a different kind of fluid ease that contributes to the overall, elemental feeling. And they all fit together with an invigorating precision that reinforces Twain's theme—and makes it impossible to avoid. Miss the days swimming by, and one has the water with its steady current. Miss the flowing water and one has the light gliding in silently. Miss the movement of the raft, and you may catch the flow of time. Miss all of these elements, moreover, and you may catch Huck's basic experience, as the sensations wafting across the water carry the whole world to Huck as he cools himself on the river's sandy bottom.[19]

Timing means a lot here. I'm describing fusion as it occurs at the moment of reading. But as I have said, after we have read this passage, we take away a sense of the seamless whole that represents it.

What is the river dawn *after* we have read it? It is a tapestry of affect, in which all kinds of elements—voice, idea, image, rhythm, reaction, memory, anticipation, connotation, association—translate into emotions that blend to form the single, comprehensive emotion. It is a unique composite, existing in just this form and just this time—and so precise. Because we all feel certain personal reactions, we each have our own unique composite feelings, though in the case of this passage, the feeling of liquid ease must play a prominent role in most of them.[20]

The mind of the poet is the shred of platinum. It may partly or exclusively operate upon the experience of the man himself, but, the more perfect the artist, the more completely separate in him will be the man who suffers and the mind which creates, the more perfectly will the mind digest and transmute the passions which are its material.
—T. S. Eliot, "Tradition and the Individual Talent"

12

"The Rest is Just Cheating": Objective Emotion in *Adventures of Huckleberry Finn*

Premise IV: Emotion in the affective code is objective.

I

To say that emotion achieves objectivity within the affective code seems absurd. Emotion is the heart of subjectivity, expressing the individual's desires and needs and reactions. It defines the essence of the private self. How could it possibly achieve fidelity to the perceived object? As *Webster's New Collegiate Dictionary* puts it, objectivity gives the "reality apart from personal reflections or feelings," and so is defined as the absence of emotion. Clearly, it would seem, "feelings" cannot do justice to the object.

I am going to show that *Webster's* is wrong. I don't mean that emotion is the language of mathematics or the product of a double-blind experiment. I do mean that emotion does not have to be only personal: the feelings evoked in the reader can do justice to the object. After all, we are talking about representation, or the mind's reconstruction of the world of the fiction. All things being equal, such emotion can reflect the object accurately, as it exists in the physical world.

Or perhaps I should say that I agree with those thinkers who have already argued that emotion is objective. Stephan Strasser and T. S. Eliot, for example, claim that emotion is objective *in itself*. Strasser speaks of an "unqualified objectivating feeling," by which he means something like William James's "feeling of rationality," or a state of mind that shapes perception. We perceive objectively when we adopt an objectifying state of mind or attitude. And that attitude produces a dispassionate or accurate feeling *of* the object.

T. S. Eliot argues that poetic emotion is emancipation from personality, since, as Eliot says in "Tradition and the Individual Talent," such emotion reflects not the writer's personal desire but the object he would describe. The poem is produced within the mind by a purifying fusion of many separate personal feelings, transforming them into the objective. Although Eliot uses the metaphor of a chemical catalyst to explain this effect, one could argue that such feelings also triangulate, producing objectivity at the point at which they intersect.

We have already heard William James tell us that the emotion belongs to the object outside of the self. James offers another source of objective accuracy in the fact that emotion is concrete:

> So long as we deal with the cosmic and the general, we deal only with the symbols of reality, but *as soon as we deal with private and personal phenomena as such, we deal with realities in the completest sense of the term.* (italics by James)[1]

Our private experience is objective because it makes us feel the object as it actually exists, in all its complexity. In this regard, even our imagined experience is concrete, providing not a symbol of the object but a special sort of facsimile. James also understood (as Martin Heidegger would later do) that one's experience includes the interior facts—the *"private and personal phenomena as such"*—that lie deeper than physical appearance. It includes a sense of how the object works—the principles that guide it—as well as what the object means to the person, information that reveals a great deal about the object.

In his essay, "The Metaphorical Process as Cognition, Imagination, and Feeling," Paul Ricoeur explains that feeling (along with image and idea) involves engagement and detachment simultaneously. We experience the object and yet (because it is a mere reproduction) remain dispassionate. Such duality gives the affective not only objectivity but the special accuracy of a double focus. We know the object in both a personal and an impersonal way. To Ricoeur's "metaphorical process" I would add the process of reader identification, which also combines passion and distance: to feel the emotions of another person is to engage with that person, sharing his or her emotions, and yet to move beyond one's own personality. It is to be emotional in a nonpersonal way.

Finally, we could argue that everything is subjective anyway. That is, a purely "objective" perception, freed from all personal thought, would consist of a meaningless jumble of lines, colors, and textures. It is the individual's *mind* (including his or her feel of things) that identifies and organizes the disparate sensations that form a tree or auto or person. It is also the subjective mind that supplies the context that defines meaning. For such reasons every objective perception requires a subjective element to be complete—it is emotion that makes objectivity possible.

II

Are such theories correct? *Is* emotion objective, or at least accurate in regard to the physical characteristics of the object? Fortunately, we can test this notion by returning to *Adventures of Huckleberry Finn*, which as a first-person narrative consists of precisely those "personal reflections and feelings" that define the subjective.

What makes *Huck Finn* a useful test is the famous issue regarding the last third of the novel, which takes place on the Phelps farm. Although any single paragraph in the last seventy pages appears all right, the Phelps episode feels wrong. Something is amiss, something to do with the emotion involved, so that the more vividly we have imagined the first part of the book, it would seem, the more deeply we resent the last third.

What goes awry? Most critics argue the issue on the grounds of theme. In the final section Tom Sawyer just happens to visit the Phelps farm after the family has captured Jim and mistaken Huck for their nephew. This coincidence permits Twain to reunite the two boys in their attempt to free their old companion. But Twain now makes a joke of Jim's flight to freedom, betraying the values he had established in Huck's earlier decision "to go to hell" for Jim. As Leo Marx argues, "the author, having revealed the tawdry nature of the culture of the great valley, yielded to its essential complacency."[2]

Some critics argue that the Phelps section does not go awry, and it is true that many themes bind the book together: at the end Twain circles back, as these scholars argue, returning to situations and characters that served him well at the beginning. Huck begins and ends subservient to Tom Sawyer—he was willing to go to hell, let us remember, if that was where Tom went. Huck begins by playing a prank on Jim (rewarding him with a nickel) and ends by playing pranks on him again (rewarding him with forty dollars). As Richard Hill puts it, "the more one looks at the ending of *Huckleberry Finn,* the tighter draws the noose of theme and plot."[3]

Yet the problem with the Phelps episode is not the theme but the style, which returns us to the affective code. While Huck's language is personal in the first two-thirds of the novel, it becomes *im*personal or objective in the last third, providing a basis for comparison of the two. Which narrative strikes us as more accurate or credible? Which is more true to the objective or physical facts of the situation?

Of course, one could say that the novel is a fiction and so has no "objective" reality anyway. But that is to misunderstand the nature of the novel as a genre. Twain places *Huck Finn* within the actual world, after all, and describes events we know very well could have happened within these circumstances. The novel is "objective" in that it must conform to what hundreds of thousands of readers know of the world—readers who are exquisitely sensitive to distortion. Yes, we know that the story is fantasy, and yet we demand psychological verisimilitude. We will believe in the narrative only if the tone and the detail and the language earn our trust. We demand *more* than objectivity, in fact, requiring not only representation of but insight into the world.

In the pages that follow, I will first document Huck's subjective presence, showing that it dominates the first two-thirds of the novel. I will then analyze Twain's shift to an ostensibly objective account of the Phelps episode, explaining why it is the early style that is really the more objective.

III

Huck's early narrative is centered on Huck's sensations and feelings.[4] In the first chapter Huck feels lonely in the widow's parlor and then sits alone in his room. In the last third of the novel, in contrast, Huck is seldom alone, and when he is by himself, he does not give the texture of his experience. He records events rather than sensations, even when the sensations are as memorable as butter melting under his hat. The Huck who in chapter 2 fights his need to scratch while hiding under Jim's nose ("There was a place on my ankle that got to itching, but I dasn't scratch it; and then my ear begun to itch; and next my back, right between the shoulders")—the Huck who goes on about his itching for two solid paragraphs ("My nose began to itch. It itched till tears came into my eyes")—this Huck later freezes under Aunt Sally Phelps's gaze with no sensation at all. When in the later episode the butter drips down his skin ("the butter beginning to melt and run down my neck and behind my ears"), Huck gives not the tickling he must feel but what Aunt Sally sees. "A streak of butter come a-trickling down my forehead, and Aunt Sally she see it and turns white as a sheet."

Such changes mean that the last third of the novel—somewhat astonishingly, I agree—ceases to be a first-person narration. Huck remains the technical narrator, but the story moves outside of him, where Huck describes not his private sensation but the public or external event, in a shift that makes a large difference in our mental construction of the text. Twain in the later novel, for example, must fill in the specifics Huck would earlier have summarized. Without Huck's personal experience as a center, unifying the action and permitting him to dip in and out of events at will, the later Twain must give a detailed chronology. He must shift the densities of the text, giving less of Huck's reaction (which usually enlivens the story), and more exposition and occurrence. Twain must now *explain,* and his labor is not lost on us. "Why, Aunty," Tom Sawyer says, "it cost us a power of work—weeks of it—hours and hours, every night, whilst you was all asleep. And we had to steal candles and the sheet and the shirt. . . ."

The early Huck has a gift for graceful and efficient summary. In the first chapter of the novel, for example, Huck covers *The Adventures of Tom Sawyer,* Mr. Mark Twain, his supper, the Widow Douglas, Miss Watson, and his sensations by the window of his room. He shifts easily from the general to the specific, using a brief scene to illustrate his overall point. On the Phelps farm, in contrast, Huck recites Tom's exhaustive account of their pranks as though he sought to order or explain his narrative. Twain now takes the boys step by step through actions he would earlier have summarized—though the text still suffers from several purely factual gaps. The Phelps have three children, for example ("and behind her comes her little white children"), but once Huck is settled at the farm, we see almost nothing of them, as Tom and Huck pursue their pranks in comparative solitude.

Yet the matter of density or length is not quite the point, either. For when we compare Tom and Huck watching Jim in chapter 2 with the boys watching Silas in chapter 37, we discover that Twain's earlier description is the longer of the two. The early prank takes six paragraphs, while Silas in the cellar takes only three. What changes in the two passages is the role of Huck: in the early scene Twain places him (with his horrendous itch) center stage. Jim addresses the boys (whose identity is unknown to him) and significantly interacts with them.

> "Say—who is you? Whar is you? Dog my cats ef I didn't hear sumf'n. Well, I knows what I's gwyne to do. I's gwyne to set down here and listen tell I hears it agin."
> So he set down on the ground betwixt me and Tom. He leaned his back up against a tree, and stretched his legs out till one of them most touched one of mine. My nose begun to itch. . . . I reckoned I couldn't stand it more'n a minute longer, but I set my teeth hard and got ready to try. Just then Jim begun to breathe heavy; next he begun to snore—and then I was pretty soon comfortable again. (5–6)

Huck and Tom are *in* this scene, which quickly becomes one about Huck himself, and Jim's proximity to Huck gives the passage both focus and drama. In the later description of Silas, on the other hand, Twain concentrates on the older man exclusively:

> He went a mooning around, first to one rat-hole and then another, till he'd been to them all. Then he stood about five minutes, picking tallow-drip off of his candle and thinking. Then he turns off slow and dreamy towards the stairs, saying:
> "Well, for the life of me I can't remember when I done it. I could show her now that I warn't to blame on account of the rats. But never mind— let it go. I reckon it wouldn't do no good."
> And so he went on a mumbling up-stairs, and then we left. (279)

Silas neither talks to the boys nor approaches them, so they remain passive observers, watching from the outside. Nor does Huck experience any personal sensations. The description is competent enough, and we hear Silas's voice, but we miss the striking verisimilitude of Twain's earlier description of Huck's fresh and yet familiar itching. Even as he describes Silas, Huck is not himself in the scene.

IV

I don't want to exaggerate Twain's shortcomings in the Phelps episode. Writing that is mediocre by Mark Twain's standard reaches a high level by other measures. One could argue that Twain in this final episode changes just a little, choosing the wrong joke and letting it go on a shade too long. Twain cuts his description somewhat short and permits his speaker to talk at too great a length. He ceases to alternate between action and quiet, melodrama and humor, adopting a single farcical tone. Having shifted his tone when he should not have, Twain sustains it when he needs variety, and such misjudgments make Huck, the narrator, look bad.

Nor can I deny that this effect might be an illusion. Huck is such an attractive character that the loss of his experience probably means more than it should. Early on Huck exhibits a comic ignorance that makes us not only like him but understand the humorous point of the narrative. "The widow she cried over me," Huck says, "and called me a poor lost lamb, and she called me a lot of other names too, but she never meant no harm by it." Huck is also humorously judicious. Disappointed by the lack of Arabs and camels in the raid on the "caravan," Huck tries to be reasonable: he allows that Tom Sawyer might have believed it was a caravan, "but as for me I think different. It had all the marks of a Sunday-school." Even generosity is funny when it is rigid.

Or is it the loss of cruel adults that makes the difference? If the dishonesty of pap, the king, and the duke highlight Huck's own honesty, then the loss of those rogues would change the nature of the illusion. Silas and Sally Phelps simply do not deserve the hard treatment Twain's narrative supplies. I might add that I disagree with the critic Gerry Brenner, who claims that Huck's pretense to emotions he does not feel makes him as duplicitous as the duke and king.[5] The duke feigns a sorrow that is unjustified, pretending to have lost his aristocratic position, while Huck represses a resentment that is all too justified. The duke adopts his emotion for gain; Huck adopts his, when he does, in order to survive.[6]

But whatever the reason, Huck by the Phelps episode has really changed. In contrast to the earlier, generous Huck, the later Huck adopts a sarcastic tone that makes him sound peevish and middle-aged. "So drat him," Huck says of Tom at the Phelps farm, "we went along but I didn't like it much." On another occasion Huck exclaims, "Don't do nothing of the kind; it's one of the most jackass ideas I ever struck." In such comments Huck has the voice of an older man.[7] Nor is such a shift surprising, when we look at the facts of the composition of this novel. Mark Twain began *Huck Finn* in the summer of 1876 and completed it in a single push during the summer and autumn of 1883. It would be remarkable if Twain's style or frame of mind hadn't changed during those seven years.

V

And yet the loss of Huck's personal experience is no minor matter.[8] Not only does the greatest American novel misplace its narrator, surprising as that fact must be, but that loss precipitates a change in style so dramatic that we can identify the point at which it occurs. In the first paragraph of chapter 32, Huck approaching the Phelps farm is pretty much his old self, which is to say frightened and lonely and superstitious.

> When I got there it was all still and Sunday-like, and hot and sunshiny—the hands was gone to the fields; and there was them kind of faint droning of bugs and flies in the air that makes it seem so lonesome and like everybody's dead and gone; and if a breeze fans along and quivers the leaves, it makes you feel mournful, because you feel like it's spirits whispering—spirits that's been dead ever so many years—and you think they're talking about *you*. As a general thing it makes a body wish *he* was dead, too, and done with it all. (240)

Huck is present in this passage, telling us not what the scene looks like but how he experiences it. He names a feeling ("all still and Sunday-like") and then supports it with detail (the "faint droning of bugs and flies in the air"). Once again he equates physical details with emotion ("it makes you feel mournful"), moving back and forth from the one to the other. But then he moves into such despair that the passage becomes overwhelmingly subjective, which may be why Twain suddenly shifts tone.

For when Twain hurries on in the next paragraph to describe the Phelps farm, his writing changes. And the change is, as Huck would say, considerable:

> Phelps's was one of these little one-horse cotton plantations; and they all look alike. A rail fence round a two-acre yard; a stile, made out of logs sawed off and up-ended, in steps, like barrels of a different length, to climb over the fence with, and for the women to stand on when they are going to jump onto a horse; some sickly grass-patches in the big yard, but mostly it was bare and smooth, like an old hat with the nap rubbed off; big double log house for the white folks—hewed logs, with the chinks stopped up with mud or mortar, and these mud-stripes been whitewashed some time or another; round-log kitchen, with a big broad, open but roofed passage joining it to the house; log smoke-house back of the kitchen; three little log nigger-cabins in a row t'other side of the smokehouse; one little hut all by itself away down against the back fence, and some out-buildings down a piece the other side; ash-hopper, and big kettle to bile soap in, by the little hut; bench by the kitchen door, with bucket of water and a gourd; hound asleep there, in the sun; more hounds asleep, round about; about three shade-trees away off in a corner; some currant bushes and gooseberry bushes in one place by the fence;

outside of the fence a garden and a water-melon patch; then the cotton
fields, begins; and after the fields, the woods. (240–41)

Huck is present at the beginning of this paragraph, as he provides
an impressionistic generalization ("they all look alike") and the
meaning of the details ("for the women to stand on"). And it is the
old Huck who provides a couple of similes ("like barrels of a different
length" and "like an old hat with the nap rubbed off"). But Huck's
voice quickly fades: the last three-quarters of the description, beginning with "big double log house," could have been written by anyone.[9] Although Twain sprinkles in a few spelling and grammar errors, the voice becomes genteel, as in "some currant bushes and
gooseberry bushes in one place by the fence; outside of the fence a
garden and a water-melon patch." Twain also offers a Huck who is
tired, eliminating verbs and articles ("bench by the kitchen door,
with bucket of water") to plunge us into a mass of detail—for as Huck
says, "these little one-horse cotton plantations . . . they all look alike."

Huck never again describes a setting like this or employs emotion
to represent it. He ceases to be the butt of Twain's humor (as he has
seldom been since the arrival of the duke and king) and no longer
describes his own sensation. In short, the novel moves from Huck's
felt experience to the world that supplies it, and the result is an
obvious change in the quality of the style.[10]

I must admit that this judgment violates our common assumptions
about writing. The personal Huck who earns our trust revels in ap-
proximation, using phrases like "kind of" or "sort of," as his emotions
practically bury the given facts. He describes his life with pap "as kind
of lazy and jolly, laying off comfortable all day, smoking and fishing,
and no books nor study." He describes the covered walkway of the
Grangerford house as "a cool, comfortable place. Nothing couldn't
be better. And warn't the cooking good, and just bushels of it too!"
Huck is so intent on giving his feelings, in fact, that he makes up
words that catch the impressionistic or identifying emotion: the
houses in the Arkansas town, he says on another occasion, are "old
shackly, dried up frame concerns."

In composition courses we would call such phrases sloppy and
impressionistic. "Use precise language," we might write in the mar-
gin. How is it that such subjective phrases strike us as unusually vivid
and complete? Why do we believe we are reading a detailed description of these buildings even though Twain tells us little about them?
Twain's narration at the beginning of the book strikes us as fuller and
richer than at the end. His tone is sound and his writing is vivid.
Twain's prose at the conclusion, for all its intellectual unity with the

rest of the novel, strikes us as thin and strained. Somehow the writing that is centered on Huck's feelings is more accurate and precise than the style that is centered on the object or fact. As Ernest Hemingway put it: "You must stop where the Nigger Jim is stolen from the boys. That is the real end. The rest is just cheating."[11]

VI

Three factors explain the superiority of the subjective style. The first lies in the nature of emotional repression. *Huck Finn* shows that in art, at least, one cannot represent reality *without* "personal reflections and feelings." Openly confront your personal feelings, and you can work with them, making sure they are true to yourself and the event. Banish your personal feelings, on the other hand, and you risk their return in an uncontrollable and even damaging form, which is what happens in the Phelps episode. The novel turns "emotional," in the pejorative sense, meaning that Twain now expresses an unjustified and uncontrolled emotion. The emotions that have heretofore lain buried within Huck's relationship with adults now show up in unjustified and brittle turns of plot.

We sense their source outside of the book, in Twain himself (because they have no valid source within the novel), but the result is confusion, as the narrative spins out of control. For many readers the Phelps episode takes on the quality of a dream, focusing on not character but comparatively extreme or mechanical events. What had been personal in the early part of the book (and so, paradoxically, contained and controlled) becomes nightmarishly impersonal and disconnected. Has Huck felt a certain conflict with adults? Tom Sawyer now threatens the Phelps with armed robbery. Has Huck been frightened by adults? He is now shot at by sixteen farmers. Has Jim supplied a fantasy of parental love? Jim now gives up his very freedom—the company of his own wife and child—to ensure Tom Sawyer's recovery. The story is marred by a subterranean self-pity that has no justification within the text.

The second explanation of Twain's shift in style is Huck's own character, which is remarkable in its emotional skill—and its exemption from the ravages of repression. As Twain put it in his notebook, Huck has "a deformed conscience" but "a sound heart." Modeled on the real Tom Blankenship, a disreputable but good-hearted youth back in Hannibal, Huck is emotionally gifted. He hits the correct tone in the way a gifted singer sounds a flawless note, using emotions the reader senses are inevitable. He has perfect pitch, which means

that Twain as an author rose above himself, in one of those remarkable moments that make great art. Huck is, as T. S. Eliot put it, one of
"the great discoveries man has made about itself."[12]

I would like to think that Huck's emotional virtuosity is one reason
we find him so attractive. Almost everyone agrees that Huck is su-
premely fair-minded. Though an abused child, Huck remains calm
and good-natured, feeling melancholy where others would feel resentment and anger. This could be psychologically unhealthy (and
probably would be, in real life), but in the novel it is less injurious
than advantageous: by remaining calm and good-natured, Huck continues to see clearly.[13] And of course, he earns our trust.

Does the high quality of Huck's emotions affect the quality of the
reader's mental construction of his story? It is true that many readers
will visualize or intellectualize Huck's feelings. But it is also true that
we tend to imagine in kind, as I have said, constructing the physical as
an image, the abstract as idea, and the emotion as affect. Because
Huck speaks in the first person, describing his feelings, we are likely
to imagine affectively—in a very real sense, Huck's reactions become
our representations. And because Huck's emotions are clear and
just—resonating with an unusual force—our affective constructions
are clear and resonant. Lose Huck's first-person narrative and you
lose those vital emotions and the imaginative vitality they provide.

VII

The third—and for my purpose, the most important—factor is the
capacity of affect to achieve an objectivity on its own. Emotion is,
after all, a way of seeing.[14] It determines where we look and how we
interpret what we see. More than that, it interprets *how* we perceive:
because emotion defines our relation to the world, it is a disposition
to perceive in a certain way.

One could argue, like William James, that we treat the object
dispassionately because we adopt that frame of mind. Or one could
argue, like Paul Ricoeur, that the imagining mind is both engaged
and dispassionate at the same time—the categories of subjective and
objective distort the actuality. But I want to go further: all things
being equal, emotions are intrinsically objective or accurate. They
can be grounded in concrete detail, for example, and so belong to
the physical world.[15] They can exist within the act of reader identification, and so require the reader to transcend his or her own personality. And they can fuse into a new entity that leaves the purely
personal behind. In Huck's description of the cornfield, we blend

the feelings of stillness, Sunday, heat, and sunshine into a representing emotion that rises above any one of the elements, including Huck's personal feelings. As T. S. Eliot so rightly understood, such emotions are transformed into the objective by the catalyst ("the mind of the poet") that fuses them.

Such emotions are also impersonal because they are public. Most of us have encountered Huck's feelings before in our own lives (or what society has taught us), so that we come to the text with such feelings pre-formed. They are impersonal because we have learned them from our culture. We know that a teenage appetite is amusing ("just bushels of it, too"). We know that a fly buzz expresses emptiness, as it is used by writers ranging from Emily Dickinson to Saul Bellow. And certainly we know what a summer Sunday is like, shaped as it is by our customs and institutions. We may have experienced these things, and so have personal reactions and impressions to revisit, but those are influenced by the public attitudes and emotions we have absorbed.

But the matter need not be complicated. It is as simple as the fact that one can have an accurate or objective feeling of the object. Sometimes this objective feeling is a sense of general presence, as I have said, and so remains broad and unparticularized, evoking Huck's world quickly and efficiently. At other times it is highly particular: the field really is still, Sunday-like, and "sunshiny." Such representational feelings are not only what one would feel in the presence of the object (as I. A. Richards has told us) but feelings of the object itself. In Twain's hands, moreover, such feelings surprise us: Huck moves from his boyish generalities to an observation so insightful that it startles—to note the "Sunday-like" stillness of a summer day is to remind us of what we know but have not made conscious.

John MacMurray calls such impersonal emotion "rational emotion," and Susanne Langer includes it within her concept of "virtual emotion."[16] It is what Stephan Strasser calls an "objectifying feeling." Besides capturing meaning, which is itself a considerable representation, such feelings capture the *texture* of the object, as we can see in Huck's fabrication of the word "sunshiny," which gives away the writer's secret. Twain evokes the texture of the scene by naming the feelings that express that texture—and that fuse to give us the feeling of the whole. We *feel* heat, stillness, light, and "Sunday-like." It is no accident that Twain gives us the general feeling of the scene first, or a sense of its texture, before describing the literal facts.

And finally, the subjective style, employing the affective code, offers a unique *completeness* of representation. Accuracy involves not only fidelity to the facts, after all, but inclusion of all those that are necessary. As William James pointed out, the personal account offers not only the appearance of the object but how it works and where it comes from—not only the physical details but their meaning. Huck's exclamation of "just bushels" of good food gives not only the fact but its significance, providing in the combination of object and reaction the equivalent of binocular vision.

This is not to make Huck Finn into a rocket scientist. Huck's accuracy of description belongs to the nature of his character, which is exactly what science would exclude. Nor do I mean to equate art and science: science studies what is real while art creates the illusion of the real. And yet that aesthetic function creates a special obligation. Art must not only be true to the world (as is all art, in different ways) but make the reader believe in that truth. Art must in some manner be more convincing, more complete, and so more accurate than science—all in the service of what is not real. *Huck Finn* is but one novel, of course, but if we take it as typical, it shows how the writer achieves a more intense, more complete verisimilitude by means of a personal or affective style.

We ought to say a feeling of *and,* a feeling of *if,* a feeling of *but,* and a feeling of *by,* quite as readily as we say a feeling of *blue* and a feeling of *cold.*
— William James, *The Principles of Psychology*

An emotion is a decision to have a certain relationship.
— Robert Solomon, *The Passions*

13

Relation in *The Portrait of a Lady*
Premise V: The affective code is required to construct relationship.

THE REPUTATION OF THE NOVELIST HENRY JAMES ILLUSTRATES THE kind of problem that occurs when one leaves emotion out of the equation. For James's reputation suffers from a puzzling anomaly. Even in his middle period, James is famous as an intellectual novelist who uses abstract language in a prose that is, as Richard Bridgman says of the later novels, "of almost unrelieved abstraction and attenuation."[1] Yet James also creates an illusion of his characters' bodies that is as concrete as that of any other writer. Reading Ernest Hemingway, we remember the crabbed courage of the protagonists. Reading Henry James, we remember physical positions and gestures, like Isabel in the doorway or Quint on the tower, Waymarsh sitting on a bed or Major Monarch standing erect. James's novels are grounded in place and his characters' actions are physically memorable, whether it be Lambert Strether staring up at Chad's apartment, or Merle and Osmond communing silently in Isabel's sitting room.

How can James render the physical so memorably and still deserve a reputation for abstraction? In "The Art of Fiction" James claims that abstractions are concrete, confessing that "a psychological reason is, to my imagination, an object adorably pictorial."[2] Yet the major point is that James gives not a physical description of his characters' bodies but the *impression* those figures make. He gives the reader a "sense" of

165

his subject, much as William Hazlitt suggested, or a feeling of it, an emotion, and in the mind that amounts to the concrete. To portray Henrietta Stackpole in *The Portrait of a Lady*, for example, James gives the feeling of her robust physical presence. Look at James's style as style, and it is abstract; look at the effect of the style, or what readers experience, and it is concrete. Of all the writers I analyze in this book (excepting perhaps Toni Morrison), it is Henry James who best understands the affective code.

James also illustrates a principle of emotional representation that makes the affective code necessary. He would create his protagonist, Isabel Archer, he says, by portraying her as the sum of her relations to other characters. Does he succeed? The question has become a major issue because several critics find her characterization inadequate.[3] In truth James's portrait of the young American, like the plot of *Huck Finn*, exposes the usually hidden process by which we imagine the narrative. Does James's focus on relationships create a living character? In the following pages I will examine first James's use of the affective code, much as I have done so far, studying Isabel's mental construction of the suitors.[4] Like Hemingway, Austen, and Twain, James employs language that requires an emotional construction. I will then examine the reader's construction of Isabel, based on James's announced use of her relation to her fellow characters. While the concept is not part of our popular vocabulary, it is relation, in all its different forms, that defines meaning and so drives much of our language and thought. And it is the expression of relation, more than any other single function, that makes the affective code necessary.

I

Even though some readers have complained of Isabel Archer's intellectualism, it is clear that she is an emotional person. She chooses Gilbert Osmond, after all, because "a certain feeling took possession of her." "I have only one ambition," she says, "—to be free to follow out a good feeling." Nina Baym confirms this point in her article "Revision and Thematic Change in *The Portrait of a Lady*," showing that Isabel is more emotional in the first edition of 1881 than in James's revision of 1908. In the first edition, Baym says, "the vagueness of her feelings lead directly to many of her mistakes." The critic Joel Porte disagrees, claiming that in the revised edition "not a sob or a tear is excised" and that Isabel feels even more "erotic feeling."[5]

In either case, Isabel's emotional nature influences her mental construction of the three men who seek to marry her. Isabel knows the first suitor, Caspar Goodwood, as the combination of his effect on her and her attitude toward him.[6] "He seemed to deprive her of the sense of freedom. There was a disagreeably strong push, a kind of hardness of presence, in his way of rising above her" (ML, 113). Isabel refers to touch, but what is important is the emotion. We *feel* the deprivation of freedom. We *feel* Goodwood's hard presence. On another occasion, as Isabel awaits Caspar's arrival, she names the emotion he triggers directly: "the feeling was oppressive; it made the air sultry, as if there were to be a change of weather." Although such feelings contain nothing of Caspar's identity or background, they give us his character.

Characteristically, James evokes the necessary emotion by naming an image, and he seems to do the same for the second suitor. When he writes that Lord Warburton's radiance "surrounded him like a zone of fine June weather," it sounds visual. But one does not see "fine June weather." One sees a certain quality of light, or an abundance of green, but one *feels* the weather, since it is a summarizing whole, and so one constructs it emotionally. On the same occasion, James names the emotion directly: to Isabel, James writes, Warburton's smile "was peculiarly friendly and pleasing, and his whole person seemed to emit that radiance of good feeling and good fare which had formed the charm of the girl's first impression of him." James gives Warburton's own mood ("friendly and pleasing") and then the impression that he makes ("that radiance of good feeling and good fare"), and in doing so offers the emotion by which we may know him. What is remarkable, perhaps, is how vividly such feelings represent the character.

Where Twain might evoke emotion by means of Huck's voice, then, James uses an image. James often reinforces the defining feeling by repetition of that image. Having represented Caspar as "a disagreeably strong push," Isabel later feels Caspar "beside her on the bench and pressingly turned to her" (ML, 113, 586). Other characters feel much the same rigidity or hardness, as in Osmond's description of his conversation with Caspar: "It wasn't easy at first, you had to climb up an interminable steep staircase up to the top of the tower; but when you got there you had a big view and felt a little fresh breeze." In Osmond's "steep staircase" we recognize the same man whose "jaw was too square and grim and his figure too straight and stiff"—Caspar is whatever is difficult and angular and aggressive.

Of course, Isabel's construction of her suitors is private, needing to make sense only to her. Yet descriptions like these of Warburton and Caspar illustrate how public such representing emotions can be, and how precise and consistent. In each case the constructing emotion captures the suitor's attitude toward the world, which makes sense. If we create ourselves by the emotions we permit ourselves to feel, as Robert Solomon argues, then others would certainly know us by those feelings.

In contrast to these first two, the third suitor, Gilbert Osmond, takes charge of his own effect. His manipulation of Isabel shows that like all natural processes, the affective code can be abused. Osmond is narrow and dishonest—a thoroughly despicable person—but the style he manufactures makes him attractive.[7] He illustrates the principle James dramatizes in "The Real Thing": because art suggests rather than reproduces, it is more convincing than the real. When Mrs. Touchett says of Osmond that "there is nothing of him," she puts him into the same category as Miss Chum in "The Real Thing," who could adopt various identities because "she had no positive stamp."[8]

What makes Osmond so skillful? Although he himself is so controlled he appears devoid of emotion (while secretly feeling several childish ones), he is a master of manipulating emotion in others. He knows that emotion is a primary mode of communication and so takes care to hit just the right tone. "He always had an eye to effect," James writes, "and his effects were elaborately studied." While the other suitors struggle with their passion, Osmond, with his "well-bred air of expecting nothing, a quiet ease that covered everything," is gracefully considerate of Isabel's needs (ML, 246). Caspar and Warburton are too much in love with Isabel, too much in need to have much style, but Osmond appears to be all grace and poise. "He never forgot himself, as I say; and so he never forgot to be graceful and tender, to wear the appearance of devoted intention."

Osmond understands that emotion is representational. He knows that just a hint of revealed emotion creates an illusion of the total person, especially if one has captured the imagination of one's audience. Thus his well-bred demeanor—his "high spirit attuned to softness"—makes Isabel imagine an attractive and civilized individual.[9] What is more, Osmond hits the tone that bespeaks a poised and sensitive inner self, creating a psychological chiaroscuro that makes him interesting. Again and again he is full of contrast—a relatively penniless man who loves fine things; a man of high intelligence and self-regard who has remained, as he says, quiet; a man of poise and style who touchingly needs Isabel. He is diffident and self-conscious, Isabel notes, but he is also "full of the effort (visible only to a sympathetic eye) to overcome this disadvantage."

What construction of himself does Osmond instill in Isabel? He makes Isabel feel not the nasty Osmond that James shows the reader but a mature man who is patient where the others are hasty, easy where they are awkward, and open where they are possessive. More than that, Osmond wraps himself within the very beauty of Italy, equating his appearance in Isabel's life with "the atmosphere of summer twilight." "What a long summer afternoon awaits us. It's the latter half of an Italian day—with a golden haze, and the shadows just lengthening, and that divine delicacy in the light, the air, the landscape. . . ." The fact that this passage echoes both the opening of the book and the shadowed peace of Gardencourt reveals its importance.[10] Osmond knows that Isabel is attracted to a private heaven, which happens to be what he can offer her. Among other things, *Portrait* is a study of how such peaceful but private refuges turn sour.

Isabel discovers that Osmond's fine style has consequences. Once married, she finds herself controlled by her husband, as in the scene following Osmond's surprise incarceration of his daughter Pansy in the convent. Pansy is punished for speaking to her lover, Rossier, but Isabel believes that the issue is not really Pansy's transgression. "She was convinced that the whole proceeding was an elaborate mystification, addressed to herself and destined to act upon her imagination."

Osmond understands that tone determines meaning. In this scene he skillfully strikes the tone that justifies his action, even as it puts Isabel on warning. "Osmond spoke deliberately, reasonably, still with his head on one side, as if he were looking at the basket of flowers." His tone is "that of a man not so much offering an explanation as putting a thing into words—almost into pictures—to see, himself, how it would look." By setting the tone he can manipulate meaning ("The convent is a . . . school of good manners; it's a school of repose.") and at the same time warn Isabel against challenging it. As Osmond talks, Isabel and Gemini travel from the surface of his statement (I am a sensitive father) to the truth of his motives (I am punishing *you*) and then still deeper, to his threat that he would rather harm Pansy than tolerate Isabel's disobedience. "If he wished to be effective," James writes, "he had succeeded; the incident struck a chill into Isabel's heart."[11]

II

We can learn even more about James's concept of the imagination in a famous chapter that James felt to be "the best thing in the book," Isabel's vigil after she has glimpsed Osmond and Madame Merle in the sitting room.[12] Merle stands and Osmond sits, their eyes locked familiarly. In an instant, James writes, Isabel "had received an impression." She had glimpsed a truth, but she is not sure what it is. "Their relative position, their absorbed mutual gaze, struck her as something detected."[13]

Isabel then sits alone through the night, her candle dripping and the clock chiming, as James portrays her marriage in just a few pages—a considerable feat that also dramatizes the mind in the act of constructing meaning. But what is most remarkable, perhaps, is how differently the critics interpret the nature of Isabel's thought. In *Person, Place and Thing* Charles Anderson writes that "in the reverie-under-stress, as in dreams, the mind understands in pictures rather than by logically ordered recapitulation." In *Literary Impressionism,* on the other hand, Peter Stowall complains that Isabel is not truly visual: "She suppresses her impressions in favor of a conceptualization, which she arrives at later and which fits her own preconceived needs." And in *The Phenomenology of Henry James* Paul Armstrong agrees that Isabel conceptualizes, but regrets that she does not do more.[14]

Because Isabel (like everyone) employs both the imagistic and verbal codes, each of these critics is correct in his way. Isabel thinks imagistically, as she is "assailed by her vision," and abstractly as well, even if she could be more reflexive about her motives. But Isabel also employs the affective code. Shaken by her glimpse of Merle and Osmond, Isabel represents her marriage as the feelings of "terror" or the "hideously unclean," the feelings of a "dark alley" and a "dead wall"—reactions that within Isabel's mind represent the original. Once again James evokes such feelings by means of metaphor, but Isabel does not so much look at these images as enter them, reliving her impression of Merle and Osmond and the marriage they illuminate. Three times she moves from her original feelings toward Osmond to his feelings toward her, translating those reactions into representational feelings that express the memory of the marriage. She feels much more than she knows.

For this reason, the vigil illustrates the value of the affective code, since it permits Isabel to relive her whole marriage in a short time. Isabel's emotions lead her thought, providing the central concept ("that sense of darkness and suffocation") that organizes the detail. And they provide her with insight, strengthening and clarifying her understanding of her marriage. As Paul Armstrong points out, James believed that the impression (which we have seen to be emotional) has "almost miraculous revelatory power."[15] Isabel recognizes Osmond's true feelings toward her, crystallizing a group of scattered impressions into knowledge. She also comes to understand her feelings toward him, as her review places her marriage in perspective.

Although Isabel does not act right away, the vigil plays a key role in James's plot. For in facing up to the truth of her marriage, Isabel gains a large source of strength. She realizes that Osmond would die rather than appear in the wrong, which gives her a great deal of power over him. Because Osmond is a slave to convention, in fact, Isabel returning to Rome at the end of the novel is not defenseless. Just as Osmond had controlled Isabel by controlling her emotions— "he believed he should have regulated her emotions before she came to that"—so he now loses control over her by virtue of her new emotional understanding.[16] The emotions that had made Isabel vulnerable now furnish the insight that saves her.

III

If Isabel represents her experience by means of emotion, so do we as readers. In *Portrait*, however, the process is not without a problem. Some readers agree that Isabel comes alive as a character, but others, as I have said, find her lacking. On the one hand, Leon Edel includes Isabel among those heroines who have "taken on a life of their own— Becky Sharp, or Dorthea Brooke, the Lady of the Camillias or Jane Eyre, Anna Karenina or Emma Bovary. It was as if they had really lived." On the other hand, critics such as F. W. Dupee find Isabel elusive: just when we think we know her, she slips away—at least in the first half of the novel. "In her energy and meaning, it must be admitted, Isabel is far from easy to reconstruct." As Virginia Smith puts it, "we look for Isabel at the end and she isn't there." It is significant that James in "the preface" called Isabel "an apparition," a "slim shade," "a figure who hovers."[17]

Such disagreement is not unusual among literary critics, but in this case it derives from a significant phenomenon. For still other readers of *Portrait* (including myself) find that Isabel develops from an initially vague or incomplete character into a precise or realized one. In my experience, Isabel gains identity and depth right before our eyes, and she does so in a way that illuminates the role of the affective code in characterization.

What is the difference between James's early and late treatments of Isabel? One difference is thematic, since the early Isabel keeps other people at a distance. To James in "the preface" Isabel begins the novel "still at large, not confined by the conditions, not engaged in the tangle, to which we look for much of the impress that constitutes an identity."[18] When Isabel later permits people to come close, she becomes a more accessible and so a fuller character. Isabel also comes to understand that her identity is contingent upon the world, fulfilling Madame Merle's well-known description of the self as

> the whole envelope of circumstances. There is no such thing as an isolated man or woman; we are each of us made up of a cluster of appurtenances. What do you call one's self? Where does it begin? Where does it end? It overflows into everything that belongs to us. (186)

Another difference between the early and late Isabel lies in James's style or technique.[19] We know the early Ralph Touchett and Henrietta Stackpole better than Isabel because James gives them simple, dramatic characteristics that are easily imagined. Ralph Touchett keeps his hands in his pockets and gives off an aura of sickliness: "His gait had a shambling, wandering quality; he was not very firm on his legs." In contrast Isabel Archer is "a tall girl in a black dress, who at first sight looked pretty"—a bland, general description. In the opening scene James reveals Isabel to be independent and alert ("she was looking at everything, with an eye that denoted clear perception"), but we neither see nor feel these qualities with the definition that adequately evokes character. The feeling of alertness is especially abstract. James does better when he connects Isabel's alertness to her body ("her flexible figure turned itself lightly this way and that"), but Isabel remains elusive. As she stares at her surroundings, our eye travels away from her, in the direction of her glance.

Even when James presents the inner Isabel, he does not give a feeling of her self. James says in chapter 3 that Isabel likes the "strange and lonely room" in which she reads. She remembers hearing schoolchildren inside a neighborhood school; she detests human nastiness and is somewhat dry in manner. Though James gives a great deal of information, however, he fails to strike a spark. His concept of Isabel at this point is too abstract to be imagined whole; he counts too much on what he called his "American type," the fresh and bold young American woman.

But in the later novel James does provide memorable traits and details, evoking a clear and coherent representing emotion. He moves from emotions that are thin and vague—and that construct an insubstantial character—to those that are substantial and precise, illustrating the connection between the quality of the characterization and the quality of the representing emotions. (A feeling of an alert young woman does not resonate with the same force as the feeling of a disappointed but persevering older woman.) He evokes a precise feeling of Isabel, for example, by giving her a recognizable voice—one of our most direct and unmediated contacts with a character. In time Isabel's voice becomes quick and sharp, in the tradition of Mrs. Touchett, with a masculine tone that reminds one of Hemingway's Brett Ashley. Isabel says nothing like "you chaps," but she is direct and androgynous, with the charm of the tomboy turned beauty. Quite often she is tart. "You are beating around the bush, Ralph. You wish to say you don't like Mr. Osmond, and yet you are afraid." Behind these words we hear Isabel's own feelings, which is to say we hear the person behind the language. This is true whether we identify with her or remain outside.

As one would expect, James also evokes a precise feeling of Isabel by means of his imagery. Here is Isabel's reaction when Madame Merle tells her she is resilient: "Isabel received this assurance as a young soldier, still panting from a slight skirmish in which he has come off with honour, might receive a pat on the shoulder from his colonel." The image of the young soldier is vivid because it reveals the soldier's emotion. Yet few readers would visualize the metaphor, since the image of Isabel as a soldier is incongruous. Are we to see her with her hair tucked under her cap? In a khaki shirt and combat boots? The metaphor compares the *emotions* of Isabel and the soldier, and defines a relationship between Isabel and Merle that is emotional in nature. By such images James builds up not a visual portrait of his protagonist but a feeling of her presence, in this case of a praised and pleased subordinate.

All of these strategies help to characterize the later Isabel. But there is one more that is especially—and even strikingly—effective. While James often places Isabel within space, as she stands within a doorway or walks across a lawn, he also defines the space within Isabel, making her a complex and mature character. And in both cases the effect is the same. In the opening paragraph of the novel James uses the chiaroscuro of creeping shadows on a tufted lawn to make us imagine spatially.[20] In the last third of the book Isabel herself creates a distinction between the surface of her manner—of her face, say—and the depth of her feelings, making us imagine the character dimensionally. She conceals her real feelings from Osmond, of course. Before Ralph, Caspar, and Warburton, she puts the best face possible on her marriage. And in her relations with Pansy she distinguishes between her feelings and her duties. In the vigil she creates internal space by looking at herself from a distance. And on several other occasions, such as the final kiss by Caspar, she feels depths in herself that she does not consciously understand.

Once Isabel has married Osmond, James dramatizes these facts in the attempt of secondary characters to guess Isabel's inner state from her appearance. Everyone examines her, hoping to glimpse what she hides, and she herself represses so much that she wonders what she feels. In this way *Portrait* focuses the reader's attention on Isabel's dual existence. Isabel becomes increasingly aware of the many ironies in her life, and irony is a kind of double consciousness. She becomes increasingly adept at combating Osmond by virtue of her self-control, or the purposeful division between what she feels and what she shows. She increasingly feels the intolerable conflicts within her, between freedom and duty, passion and flight, confidence and timidity, happiness and self-sacrifice. In short, Isabel increasingly discovers her identity in the space between what she shows and what she feels, between her conscious mind and the depths that she does not understand and would conceal.

IV

Such duality is ironic in the young woman who was determined that "her life should always be in harmony with the most pleasing impression she should produce; she would be what she appeared, and she would appear what she was." But it is just this division that gives Isabel a strikingly dimensional life as a character. Paradoxically she achieves "reality" when she becomes false—a phenomenon that takes some explaining. How can a split in her psyche give Isabel life as a character? Once again James offers an anomaly, as he creates the illusion of a whole character by describing concealment and fragmentation.

Of course, one could argue that Isabel springs to life in spite of her internal split. The simple arithmetic of reading, which is cumulative, explains how a portrait would deepen with time. We can see this in the many parallels between events in the first and second halves of the novel. Isabel visits a park or stands in a doorway or walks in London and her action recalls—often ironically—earlier visits or walks or postures. Isabel's visit to Pansy in the convent raises an echo of her earlier visit to Pansy in Osmond's villa. Isabel's approach toward Ralph in his bed at Gardencourt echoes her approach toward Ralph on the chaise in Florence, where she swore she would never tell him she was unhappy. Readers may not always be conscious of such parallels, but they feel them. The first event gives meaning and resonance to the later one.

True as such factors might be, however, the most important reason for the growing actuality of Isabel's character is James's focus on *relation*. Because the secondary characters know Isabel in relation to themselves, James could portray Isabel as the accumulation of those relationships. To evoke "the sense of a single character," James tells us in the 1908 preface to *The Portrait of a Lady,* he would give "the view of her relations to those surrounding her. Make it predominantly a view of *their* relation and the trick is played: you give the general sense of her effect."[21]

While this approach permitted a middle-aged bachelor like James to portray a young woman, it also recognized a key fact about human perception. By "relation," of course, I mean the comparative position or interaction of two or more elements. Cognitive scientists believe that perception is dominated by the discovery of relation, as in the relation between what we expect and what we find, or in the relation between new sensation and preexisting mental structures or "maps." To Gerald Edelman, in fact, it is the processing of such relation that gives rise to consciousness. Decades ago, moreover, Ferdinand de Saussure taught that words find their meaning in their relation to other words.[22] We think of language as verbs and nouns, referring to acts and things, but even those elements are actually relations (to act upon, to be). Language is designed to portray relationships because relations define meaning.[23]

Both our daily lives and our literary texts are filled with subtle, complex relations that define the essence of the experience.[24] How does the mind represent such relationships? Once again the image and the idea are alone insufficient, since one imagines dozens of relationships that are nonspacial or nonintellectual. Certainly we have no word for many of them. How fill the gap? As we have seen, William James claims that we represent relationships by means of "feelings of relation." The mind constructs conjunctions, prepositions and some adverbs as not ideas, since they are patterns of existence, but feelings. "We ought to say a feeling of *and,* a feeling of *if,* a feeling of *but,* and a feeling of *by,* quite as readily as we say a feeling of *blue* and a feeling of *cold.*"[25]

It seems fitting that William's brother would create Isabel by giving the feeling of her relation to many other characters. And it works: in between her external appearance and internal actuality, Isabel comes to life. We feel we "have" Isabel when we feel her concealment—we know her as the feeling of putting up a false front. And this is true of the secondary characters as well, all of whom feel Isabel's concealment of herself. To Caspar, Isabel is elusive right from the beginning, concealing her feelings so that she may escape him. To Warburton, the Isabel who originally flirts chooses to evade him. To Ralph, the true Isabel is also concealed, as his surprise at her marriage might suggest. And to Osmond, Isabel is elusive because she is independent, with a mind of her own, which the egotist finds abhorrent.

Although the feeling of a concealed Isabel does not reveal the self that is hidden, it gives a definition by which we may know and construct the character. Isabel is she-who-conceals-herself. The feeling also requires us as readers to employ the affective code: if Isabel is a composite of her different relations, then we must construct her as a composite of the emotions that represent such relations. William James implies that we *have* to construct such relationships in the affective code, for reasons of speed and efficiency. And in his preface Henry James agrees, suggesting that he constructed Isabel as an emotion, and that the flexibility of such emotion—its capacity for combining into complex units—facilitates the reader's construction of the text.[26] James gives, he says, not only the "effect" or the impression that Isabel makes, which is one level of emotion, but "the general sense of her effect," or the feeling of her effect on others—he would give the feeling of all these feelings.

This point should not surprise us. Just as we construct the relationship among the words, filling in the spaces within the sentence, so we construct the relations among the characters, setting and events, filling in the story. A number of reader-response critics, moreover, recognize the importance of relation in the reader's construction of the text. In *The Expense of Vision* Laurence Holland builds his whole theory upon E. H. Gombrich's description of a picture as not a duplicate of the subject but "a relational model" that captures the relationship of the original parts. Holland argues that the language of the literary text portrays not the substance of the object but the form of its internal relationships. For readers that means that the Isabel we construct is once again a composite of emotions, since readers imagine relationships as emotions. It also makes Isabel a vivid character, since the concealment provides a sharply defined internal relation to be represented.

Wolfgang Iser also believes in what he calls a "relational model," claiming that the reader's filling of the gap "brings about an interaction of textual patterns."[27] Isabel's concealment of herself creates a gap where her self would be, and it is precisely such a gap, as we have seen, that impels the reader to enter the world of the text in order to fill it. James makes it clear that Isabel begins as pure potential, or something of a blank slate, and ends with her ambitions still unfulfilled—her slate in this sense still blank. Innocent and without self-concern, Isabel is also what a colleague calls an "empty vessel." And she is a woman, which means that she must live within a vacuum of opportunity. Readers fill all such gaps by extrapolating from the rest of the text as well as projecting from their own experience and desires.[28] In doing so they call up a complex of patterns that form highly complex relationships among themselves—patterns we are likely to feel.

In *Fictional Truth* Michael Riffaterre takes the relational model even further. Focusing on the reader's mental construction of the text, Riffaterre agrees with Holland that the text provides the illusion of real life by creating the process of reference within itself. Texts "parallel in language the cognitive processes we use in everyday life."[29] Once writers have established the fictionality of their text, Riffaterre says, they provide a body of truth inside the novel to which the text then refers. Thus writers duplicate in their fiction the pattern of real-life perception, triggering in the reader feelings of confidence and recognition. They evoke a sense of reality by reproducing a key relationship. In *Portrait* James establishes Isabel's concealed self as the anchoring truth and then creates an illusion of verisimilitude by referring to it. Even as the Riffaterrean reader knows Isabel to be a fiction, the process of internal reference instills a sense of credibility. To be more specific, Isabel's act of concealing her inner self actually posits the existence of that self, and for the reader this reference to what she conceals creates the illusion of it. Like Osmond fabricating his persona, Isabel induces the reader to feel the self that she infers.

V

By a stroke of luck or genius, then, James achieved a living portrait by offering a "relational model" of Isabel that matches the way in which readers mentally construct the text. And of all the relations James portrays, the most important one (as he recognized in the preface), is that of Isabel to herself, raising another explanation of her life as a character. If Robert Solomon is correct in saying that we know ourselves as a feeling, then Isabel can grow as a character by developing a feeling of her own identity. She creates herself and uses the affective code to do it. It is striking that in the vigil, coming as late as it does, Isabel thinks about Osmond's emotions more than she does her own. She realizes that *he* felt betrayed. *He* found her independence dismaying. *He* grew to hate her. What is more, the emotions Isabel recalls as her own strike one as impersonal, since they leave out her sense of herself. But once Isabel has learned the truth about Osmond and Merle, and has chosen to disobey Osmond, she develops a feeling of herself. This comes clear on the final train ride to London, on her way back to Gardencourt.

> She saw herself, in the distant years, still in the attitude of a woman who had her life to live, and these intimations contradicted the spirit of the present hour. It might be desirable to die; but this privilege was evidently to be denied her. Deep in her soul—deeper than any appetite for

renunciation—was the sense that life would be her business for a long time to come. And at moments there was something inspiring, almost exhilarating, in the conviction. It was a proof of strength—it was a proof that she should some day be happy again. (517)

Isabel has several emotions in this passage, such as her sense that life holds still more for her, but the key one is a sense of her own unique experience. Having been all attention to others, Isabel now thinks about herself. She "sees" herself, and what she sees is her "attitude"— her emotional relation to the world. When she looks at her desire for death and feels instead an exhilarating desire for life, she can know herself as the feeling of that relation. Isabel is she-who-would-insist-upon-living. She gains a specific sense of her own presence.

It is as though Isabel Archer at first permitted herself to be defined by her relationship with others, but then discovered a relationship to herself—and so imbued the text with the emotion with which we imagine relationships. Of course, James probably did not understand the younger Isabel as well as he did the older—this alone would account for a great deal. Yet the fact remains that Isabel's relationship to herself seems powerful. Stress Isabel's consciousness, James admonished himself in the preface, "stick to *that*—for the centre; put the heaviest weight into *that* scale, which will be so largely the scale of her relation to herself."[30]

Is James's portrait of Isabel Archer a success, then? I think a focus on emotion offers a persuasive answer to the question. I feel Isabel's presence powerfully, so I would say, yes, she is a vivid character. But I must qualify that answer, since Isabel does not really step forth from the page as a specific person. That is, I do not know her as a personality, no doubt because she hides herself. Even her marriage to Osmond is a kind of concealment, since the life of beautiful summer afternoons that he promises shuts out the rest of the external world.

For this reason Isabel is memorable as not a personality but a presence. She has substantial weight, but generically, as a lady. What is most interesting about this point, I think, is how little difference the absence of personality makes. In both life and imagination, we know one another quite differently from what we suppose, often using just one or two traits to stand for the whole. Although we think we perceive individuals as such, psychologists reveal that we move from the general to the specific, measuring deviation from the stereotype. Some of the time, of course, we stand pat with the general. This is why critics like Millicent Bell and Virginia White are correct in perceiving something unfinished within Isabel, even as others of us find her complete. Nor is this lack of a finely delineated character incompatible with James's intention. By the end of the novel Isabel has made one choice that turned out badly and another in which the party died, and has not yet decided what to do next. Although she has made a start, she has not really chosen who she will be.

The affective code is able to represent fully formed personalities, of course. One has a feeling *of* Osmond, Ralph, or Henrietta. As I have said, a human personality is one of those complex entities, like a city, that the affective code does especially well, fusing the many complex elements into a single flash of feeling. What is remarkable in *The Portrait of a Lady* is how clear and even precise we find Isabel's *general* presence. Think of her as a personality and she is elusive. But imagine her as a lady, as the aptly chosen title suggests—as that mature figure scrutinized by all her friends—and she exists with the fullness of a great literary character. As Riffaterre would put it, the internal reference to Isabel makes her seem real.[31]

Part IV
Toward a Practical Criticism

Emotional reactions . . . are the main component of the literary experience. This is the prickly fact that critics have to deal with if they want to talk about readers as well as texts.
—Jane Tompkins, "Criticism and Feeling"

Whatever marginal legitimacy literary emotion may have won in recent years, the fact remains that we have no thoroughgoing affective criticism as such. Although emotive terms serve to locate certain crucially sensitive areas in the reading process, they themselves have never become the locus of a sustained theoretical account.

—Neal Oxenhandler, "The Changing Concept of Literary Emotion"

Emotions are neither more basic than observation, reason, or action in building theory, nor are they secondary to them.

—Alison Jaggar, "Love and Knowledge: Emotion as an Epistemic Resource for Feminists"

14

An Affective Criticism

I

WE ALREADY HAVE AN AFFECTIVE CRITICISM, OF COURSE, BASED ON the reader's focus on emotion. We have always had it, going all the way back through Hazlitt and Shaftsbury and Addison to Aristotle himself, who defined tragedy in terms of the emotions of the audience.

Much of what is excellent in literary criticism today, in fact, includes a general focus on emotion—as in the film reviews of Pauline Kael, say, who examined the emotions of both the characters and the audience, or in the essays of Helen Vendler, who often focuses on the emotion in the poem. Obviously these critics discuss more than feeling, and yet it is their awareness of emotion that grounds their criticism and gives it life. Other critics are more explicit. In her essay, "Criticism and Feeling," Jane Tompkins asks for a criticism based upon a comparison of the reader's and the author's reaction to events. In "Narrative Emotions: Beckett's Genealogy of Love," Martha Nussbaum presents what she calls "emotion criticism," based on the novelist's own model of emotion and the critic's deconstruction of it. In *Readings and Feelings* David Bleich works out an analysis of emotion in the classroom, laying a foundation for his later study of *Subjective Criticism*. Michael Steig also examines emotion in *Stories of Reading*, again focusing on the classroom. And in *Emotion and the Arts* Mette Hjort and Sue Laver have gathered a collection of critical essays based on the study of emotion. Although these several critics differ, as one might expect, their thought shares a common orientation. They all analyze emotion in at least one of its several forms within the work—the basic criterion of affective criticism and so my subject in this chapter, as I examine the different ways emotion appears in the text.[1]

Other academic disciplines today show an even greater interest in emotion. Philosophers like William Lyons, Amélie Rorty, Francis Dunlop, Robert Solomon, Ronald DeSousa, David Novitz, Alison Jaggar, Robert Yanal, and Susan Feagin examine emotion from several different perspectives. Psychologists like Magda Arnold, Ross Buck, R. Herré, and Josef Perner probe the role of emotion in the processes of thought—and psychologists like Edward Tan, Rolf Zwaan, Walter Kintsch, and D. S. Miall, to name just a few, analyze the role of emotion in literary texts. Philosophy now has two anthologies of essays on emotion, one edited by Amélie Rorty and the other by Solomon and Calhoun, and psychology has two, one edited by Herré and the other by Ekman and Davidson. Sociologists like Norman Denzin investigate the role of emotion in the social encounters of daily life. The historian Peter Stearns examines emotion as an expression of the age. And neurologists and cognitive scientists like Antonio Damasio and Steven Pinker ponder the role of emotion within the wiring of the brain.

Prominent as these many voices are, it is still true that an affective criticism violates the temper of our time. For the past thirty years literary criticism has privileged theory, slighting the concrete work, or political causes, subordinating the specific novel to the issue. Neal Oxenhandler is correct in saying that most critics ignore affect.[2] Perhaps technology has made individual novels less important, or perhaps the need for social justice must override every other traditional concern. Whatever the reason, the result of these trends is to devalue the individual work as the object of study. Such trends detach the reader from the novel, dissolving what for many readers is an otherwise valuable imaginative and emotional immersion in the story.

Is it possible that we now have a generation of readers who do not enter the text emotionally? The general tenor of literary criticism suggests that it is. In the last twenty years a great many critics have privileged distance and abstraction over engagement and experience. Today we are all conditioned by the visual, which encourages us to look at the subject from the outside rather than constructing it from within. More and more, it seems, authors themselves stand back from their characters, dramatizing their own self-consciousness. Perhaps we have come to believe that the literary work is best approached intellectually, as a repository of ideas.

This last view has been the argument of the well-known critic Gerald Graff. In his essay "Disliking Books at an Early Age" (later published as a chapter in *Beyond the Culture Wars* [1992]), Graff confesses that he must as a reader intellectualize the novel in order to make it interesting. Describing his youthful "dislike and fear" of books, Graff recounts his inability to relate to

> any of the other books my father brought home—detective stories, tales of war and heroism, adventure stories with adolescent heroes (the Hardy boys, *Hans Brinker, or the Silver Skates*), stories of scientific discovery . . . books on current events. Nothing worked.

As a boy Graff simply could not identify with a character so intensely that he forgot himself. "What first made literature, history, and other intellectual pursuits seem attractive to me was exposure to critical debates."[3] It was not the narrative that engaged him but the *ideas.*

Other readers have a different experience, since they live the story vicariously. They engage in the narrative emotionally, as David Novitz so persuasively argues, and in doing so experience not ideas in the abstract but a vicarious form of actual experience. Such readers might even "teach the issues," as Graff recommends. But they also understand that ideas are but a shorthand for the concrete event— existing not for themselves but as a language referring to the actual emotional and imaginative experience.

I don't want to be unfair to Graff's position. Because he wants the contemporary novel grounded in social fact, he too champions the concrete. Yet the tendency to deal with ideas rather than texts, abstractions rather than characters, and causes rather than the human experience is quite real and damaging. In contrast to Graff's concentration on ideas, affective criticism asks the reader to engage with the text and so honor the individual fictional experience. It focuses on the concrete work, addressing what we might term the whole mind. One simply cannot do justice to a work of fiction without imagining it, and one cannot imagine a work of fiction without feeling it. If the code in which one constructs the text influences what one can know, moreover, it is important for readers to use all three codes. Exclude the emotional and you exclude an important kind of knowledge. You also destroy the claim literature makes to being a discipline in its own right, or a unique way of knowing.[4]

We can't really know if the recent interest in emotion will become something larger. Perhaps affective criticism is like feminism in that it is best integrated into all critical ideologies. It should be part of our general sensibility. Yet a focus on emotion in general, moving beyond the affective code alone, offers a separate critical approach worth examining. In the following pages I will offer a comprehensive model of an affective criticism, basing it on the study of not specific emotions, which is the usual strategy, but the functions that our emotions perform within the text. This approach makes emotion manageable and bridges the gap between affect and the writer's narrative technique. I will discuss what I find to be the four main functions of emotion within the text, defining their role, and will then show how an affective criticism grows naturally out of the dominant critical schools. I will next identify the tools or methods that affective criticism borrows from these movements. And I will conclude by examining the neglected subject of our judgment of the work, to which emotion, which rises in the mind as appraisal, leads us.

II

Is an affective criticism possible? Isn't emotion a kind of quicksilver, changing shape the minute one touches it? Perhaps the greatest obstacle to an affective criticism is the many roles that emotion plays in the text. Certainly emotion performs many different tasks, some popularly recognized and some not, and does so simultaneously, as a single emotion provides both the subject and the tone of the work, say, even as it expresses the reaction of a character. I've already argued that the emotion by which the reader remembers the work is an amalgam of the several emotions evoked by the passage.

While such multiplicity makes the role of emotion in the text complex, it also offers the key to understanding and using affect: we can always identify an emotion by the function it performs in the text at that moment. One can sort out these functions in different ways, but I perceive four basic ones: subject, tone, reaction, and representation. I could add motive, though that is often the writer's subject, or I could break reaction into its constituent parts. The point is that such functions permit one to focus on one emotion at a time. Each function identifies and limits the emotion in question and yet admits flexibility, since it does not deny the simultaneous existence of other functions or emotions. I'm talking about emotions that are mild, of course, and so more subtle and complex than many of our daily passions.

Three of these functions are so familiar to us that they have a history. We all pay attention to the emotions felt by the characters, for example, and so examine emotion as a subject. What we do not do, as a rule, is investigate all four of these functions in a single text, even though they fill different roles and so offer different kinds of knowledge, placing us in different positions vis-à-vis the narrative. We look at emotion from the outside when it is the subject, and take it as a direction on how to enter the work when it is tone. We become conscious of our own response (and values) when the emotion is reaction, and we in some manner replicate the original experience when the emotion is representational. (Note that the four functions of emotion in the text offer four different ways of relating to the author's meaning: to look at it, as subject; inhabit it, as tone; respond to it, as reaction; and replicate it, as representation.)

I want to stress the flexibility of an affective criticism. It encompasses whatever emotion lies within the text and embraces whatever offers insight into it. Defined in this broad way, affective criticism provides a great deal of freedom, and can easily adapt to art forms other than the novel, including drama, cinema, and the visual arts. It also studies what I would call the emotional economy of the work, or the ways in which the author or protagonist copes with emotion in itself. That is, at the same time that we feel specific reactions, we have personal strategies for dealing with our emotions, and those strategies influence our perception and thought. Martha Nussbaum shows that such strategies are a prominent feature of every work of art (not to mention every culture).

Emotion is a **subject** of the work, first of all, or what the writer looks at, and it is an especially good one, since the emotions of other people fascinate us. Such feelings are so intimate that they constitute a secret—we often hide our own emotions as we strive to perceive those of others. And we find the challenge of discerning another's emotions engrossing, perhaps because such understanding is a source of power. In fiction not a little plot suspense hinges on the obscurity of a character's feelings. Like D. H. Lawrence in *Women in Love*, moreover, writers often define their era by expressing the precise feeling of living in it. Not a few authors seek to put into words a specific feeling of a place or a time or a person, knowing that it reveals meaning.

The critic Eve Kosofsky Sedgwick offers a good example of the analysis of emotion as a subject in her essay "The Beast in the Closet: James and the Writing of Homosexual Panic." Arguing that the gay

experience is central to American culture, Sedgwick offers a persuasive new interpretation of "The Beast in the Jungle" by analyzing the
sexual nature of the protagonist's fear. The meaning of James's famous story depends upon the study of the emotion it takes as its
subject.[5]

If the subject of the work belongs to the text, the **tone** of the work
belongs to the author, since it embodies his or her meaning. Tone is
implied rather than stated and so is elusive. Yet many have recognized the illumination that it offers. To study tone is to study voice, or
the emotions that lie beneath the literal words, as revealed in diction,
rhythm, organization, and exposition. Tone tells us how the author
evaluates the subject and so how he or she wishes us to read the text.
In this sense tone is meaning, and essential to our interpretation of
the writer's words.[6] In practice the study of tone first involves understanding whether the passage is straight or ironic. Read the passage
one way, and Elizabeth Bennet is emotional and foolish; read it another, and Elizabeth is loyal and deeply feeling. It is that simple. Not a
few critics have made their careers interpreting tone—for whether
Wittgenstein's figure is a rabbit or a hand takes quite a bit of sorting
out.[7]

What I call **reaction** belongs to the reader, as each of us responds to
the passage according to our values and predilections. To some
thinkers, all emotion is reaction, since we always feel *about* or *toward*
something. Even our mood, as Heidegger saw, is a feeling about the
state of ourselves. Conversely, every experience elicits a reaction expressed as emotion, which means that a reaction is always available to
the author and the critic.

What do critics do to examine reaction? They focus on their own
reaction to the work, asking what they feel—not always an easy question, since what we feel may conflict with what our culture prefers us
to feel. Critics also seek out the sources of their reaction in the text,
exploring the significance of those sources. In one of the best examples of this focus, the essay "Criticism and Feeling," Jane Tompkins
defines her reaction to the characters in *The Sun Also Rises* and then
analyzes the text (and her own values) to understand why she feels
the way she does. She then explores the implications of her discovery
for the interpretation and evaluation of the novel. Interestingly, she
offers her conclusion first in the technical, analytical language of
literary criticism, and then in the personal language of affect.

David Bleich also analyzes reader reaction as a way of approaching
the text. Bleich's early but valuable book, *Readings and Feelings,* offers
the added advantage of using the reader's reactions in the classroom.
Bleich asks his students to discover their reaction to the work and

then to make a number of personal associations with it. He regards the act of reading as a source of self-knowledge, and uses the text as a tool in introducing his students to discourse on emotion. Although this approach shifts the focus away from the work itself, threatening to make reading a form of therapy, it gets students to pay attention to their reactions and to think about emotion. Bleich is similar in this emphasis to Hans Robert Jauss, who in "Aesthetic Pleasure" examines the reader's reaction in detail.

Can we *control* our emotional reaction? Thinkers such as Alison Jaggar, William Lyons, and Robert Solomon insist that people choose to feel their emotions, a power borne out by the process of reading. Readers choose whether to identify with or remain distant from the characters. Like Nick Adams choosing his own experience, moreover, they often choose the books that will make them feel the way they desire. And yet much of our response to an object is involuntary, occurring as it does at the moment of perception. And so is our response to narrative form, as we feel the rise and fall of an action. While we can control some of our emotions some of the time, we also find a kind of integrity in emotions that rise within us unbidden. As I have said, such emotions serve as our initial appraisal of the experience.

The disadvantage of reaction as an approach to the work is that it may open the door to personal distortion. In a classroom, it can degenerate into a comparison of indiscriminate associations and impressions—useful cathartically, no doubt, but not illuminating of the novel at hand. Yet the advantages, as Jane Tompkins tells us, are great, and our emotions are not nearly as distorting as we generally fear, if we but keep the specific object in view. We are talking about emotion in literature, after all, where one has time to sort out one's feelings. In the classroom the point must be to focus on the actual text, which is good practice even when not working with emotion.[8]

Finally, readers use emotion to reconstitute or **represent** the text, translating the marks on the page into imaginative experience constructed in the affective code. This point is of course the argument of this book. It is as basic as the fact that we don't know what Elizabeth Bennet looks like even though we feel the special quality of her character. And it is as sensible as the notion that our emotional response expresses the meaning of its object. Although we think of emotion as something that is itself represented, its capacity for mental construction should not surprise us. How better represent a subject than by its essence or meaning? We know other people as the emotions they feel—why not represent them in that way? Because our reactions are normally commensurate to their cause, moreover, they are practically halfway toward corresponding to the subject. We often let an emotion stand in for the subject that triggers it. And then a great deal of an imagined passage lies beyond the literal meaning of its words, in the implicit (and so felt) relations among its parts.

What do critics do when they examine the representational function of emotion? For one thing, they ask whether the author positions the reader to construct the text in a particular way: Does the text require a particular mental code? They also ask how that knowledge affects one's understanding and evaluation of the tale. Certainly, as I have said, the process of reading a text dictates the terms on which we can understand it. It is pertinent to our interpretation of *Pride and Prejudice* to know that the famously ironic Jane Austen shapes her style to evoke emotion. It is also useful to know that Mark Twain elicits emotion by means of Huck's narrative voice, while Henry James does so by means of images. Many of those critics who attacked John Updike's use of myth in *The Centaur* (discussed in chapter 16) may have felt differently if they had understood how myth and reality blend on an emotional level.

What makes these insights possible is the capacity of emotion to bridge the gap between the private and the public. We learn many of the emotions we feel privately, of course, from the culture. And we are joined to our society by precisely those emotions that it teaches us, since they embody values, attitudes, and even strategies. It is for this reason that the affective code can work: our most intimate emotions are not only understood in the public realm but carry information within them.

One could look at many of the chapters in this book as models of these different emotional functions. In chapter 10 I examined Jane Austen's use of emotion as a subject in *Pride and Prejudice,* and in chapter 12 I examined the tone of *Adventures of Huckleberry Finn.* Chapter 16 focuses on reaction, resolving a critical debate about *The Centaur,* and chapter 13 focused on representational emotion, showing how it resolves the issue of characterization in *The Portrait of a Lady.* In the next chapter I will sum up all four of these functions by looking at *Beloved* in terms of all four. But first let me place an affective criticism within the context of the existing critical schools, identifying those critical tools it can adapt to its purpose.

III

An affective criticism did not just suddenly appear. In many ways it represents a culmination of the major critical movements of the last fifty years, addressing many of their concerns and adopting many of their methods. This is true even if such a claim seems exaggerated— emotion is so clearly at the center of human experience that such derivations are inevitable.

Like all contemporary thought about literature, affective criticism begins with the New Criticism that dominated literary thought after World War II. It does so even though the New Criticism seemed to exclude emotion from the reader's focus. The New Critics taught us to examine the poem as if it were a specimen in the lab, an analogy that captures the school's emulation of scientific objectivity. They urged readers to study the language of the poem or novel with rigorous attention. While some New Critics, like I. A. Richards, defined the value of literature by its effect on the reader, others viewed literature as a source of truth, forged by language under pressure.[9]

Even as New Criticism discouraged our awareness of emotion, how- ever, it prepared the way for it. For it was the New Critics who showed that one could analyze subtle textual elements like feeling. In truth the New Critics were implicitly sympathetic to emotion, as terms like "tension," "unity," and "climax" suggest. The New Critics showed how the form of the work creates affect. They also believed that the soul of the poem lies in the experience that precedes analysis, acknowledg- ing that a poem "should not mean but be"—that analysis is auxiliary to the reader's experience of the text.

Most importantly, the New Critics provided the pattern or attitude that dominates criticism even today, which is the belief that criticism uncovers a hidden meaning. *What* is uncovered would define the different critical movements for the rest of the century. Whether these movements concerned race, gender, sexual orientation, lan- guage, or social construction, they would find their rationale in the subject matter they brought to public awareness.

While the New Critics teach affective critics to examine language closely, the reader-response critics teach them to analyze the (often subjective) experience of the reader. I've already discussed the thought of Roman Ingarden, Wolfgang Iser, and David Bleich, and have mentioned critics like Stanley Fish and Michael Riffaterre who insist that the words on the page enjoy no life until the reader recon- stitutes them. Their logic is impeccable. The story or poem is indeed a collaboration between author and reader, asking critics to study not only the text and the reader's imagination but the interaction be- tween the two.

As Frank Lentricchia reminds us in *After the New Criticism*, reader- response criticism almost dominated literary thought in the late sixties. But then Jacques Derrida offered deconstruction, and for reasons we still do not understand, critics shifted their attention from the reader's vicarious experience to the self-reference of language. The claim by deconstructionist critics that texts deny their own meaning, privileging distance, devalues empathy with the text and values the analytical breakdown of its meaning—a source of great fun and power, even if it does erode our appreciation of the masterpieces that define our culture. In this sea change, critics moved from the old humanism, which had a place for emotion and subjectivity, to the relentless world of semiotics (discussed in chapter 3), in which all is convention and the only path to knowledge is self-conscious analysis.

Still, affective criticism can learn a lot from these particular modes of analysis. From the deconstructionists it learns to dig beneath the surface of the text, looking for self-contradiction, and from the semioticians it learns how to expose the code that lies beneath the reader's construction, both useful methods in dealing with emotion. Nor is that all, since deconstruction (or the larger poststructuralism to which it belongs) posits a pluralism that is welcoming to emotion. Our feelings are usually specific to each situation and so the natural constituents of a pluralistic world.

Poststructuralism also prepares for a study of emotion by breaking the positivistic mold, opening the way for a new kind of thinking. And so do other poststructural ideas, such as the disillusionment with objectivity, the exposure of the hidden levers of social and linguistic control, and the conviction that the individual is socially constructed. If the critic would uncover the hidden springs of human action and thought, he or she might well examine the emotions that underlie the text. If science is ultimately subjective, as so many now believe, then the affective life takes on a new respectability.

Poststructuralism also paves the way for affective criticism in several small ways. The body, so often the recipient of poststructuralist attention, is traditionally associated with emotion. And more than one critic has remarked on the emotions created by deconstruction, whether they be the joy of play or the pleasure of demystification. Psychoanalytic critics like Julia Kristeva and Jacques Lacan examine the connection between language and unconscious desire. And while Michel Foucault believes our emotions are often mistaken, he shows in *The History of Sexuality* how analysis serves to heighten the emotional pleasures of sex. In truth, Foucault—like many poststructuralists—discusses emotion without quite acknowledging that he does so.

Many of these same concepts give emotion a valuable role in social constructionism. It is no accident that Martin Heidegger defines emotion as a fusion of self and society. Emotion is the means by which social convention and value direct the behavior of the individual. Emotion is the conduit of social power, internalizing within the individual the values and beliefs of the culture. For this reason emotions themselves may be the proper subject of Foucaultian archaeology. Emotion provides one of the basic ways in which society creates the self.

One could say that the relationship between private emotion and public policy is like a ball floating in water: first one side is up and then the other. If the subjective self is really political, as Stephen Greenblatt puts it—an "ideological product of the relation of power in a particular society"—then even the aesthetic examination of the private self is a political and social activity.[10] Because social constructionism dissolves the boundaries between the private and the public realms, as critics like Claudia Johnson have recognized, the two become identical. Or, to put it another way, if all knowledge is narrative, as Jean-François Lyotard tells us in *The Post-Modern Condition,* and all narrative is an emotional structure, as Martha Nussbaum tells us in "Narrative Emotions," then all knowledge—public *and* political—is emotional.

In any case, emotion is intimately associated with power. Because politicians reach office by touching the emotions of the electorate, one could define politics as the manipulation of those emotions.[11] In all walks of life, moreover, the structures of emotion reflect the structures of power: subordinates survive by perceiving the emotions of those in charge, while the powerful need not bother—the reason feminists equate an emotional blindness with patriarchy.

And that brings us to the critical school of feminism, which has probably done more than any other critical school to keep an interest in emotion alive. Feminism, like the other moral and political schools of criticism, including African American and gay studies, is highly conscious of emotion. It would motivate readers to seek justice for all citizens, and it studies the effect of cultural attitudes toward emotion, connecting emotion and gender. As Alison Jaggar points out in "Love and Knowledge," our society delegates emotion to women and then excludes emotion from the centers of knowledge and power, leaving women on the periphery. Or, as Arlie Hochschild has shown, women are given the "emotional work" in our society, requiring that they muster the correct emotion—the right smile—for public consumption. Feminists perceive emotion to be the vehicle of certain conventions and values that diminish women, even in the emotions they themselves have been taught.

Emotion also means something very positive to the feminist, for it provides women with a notable source of strength. Building on the theories of Nancy Chodorow, some thinkers argue that women, who mature by identifying with the mother rather than separating from her, as men do, are better at cooperation and mutual support. If emotion plays a functional role in the mind, as I am arguing, then women with their natural gift for identification may enjoy an even greater advantage than they thought.

Perhaps the most important feminist contribution to affective criticism lies in the call for a new model of the mind and so a new language in which to discuss it. The old, patriarchal model involves objectivity, distance, authority, and aggression. Many feminists seek to broaden this limited model of cognition to include subjectivity, engagement, relationship, and sharing—to validate a different way of relating to and so knowing the world. And it is precisely such qualities that characterize affective criticism.

IV

From the New Critics, then, affective criticism learns the importance of language and its psychological effect upon readers. From reader-response it learns the possibility of analyzing subjective experience and the importance of the reader-author interaction. From semiotics it learns the very concept of construction, highlighting the reader's display of meaning. From deconstruction it learns the ubiquity of implied and contradictory meanings, and from New Historicism it learns how much of what we are is social conditioning—and can be identified as such. Many of the values that lie concealed in the text find expression in emotion.

Even if affective criticism were the ultimate expression of contemporary critical movements, however, one might wonder why a sophisticated reader should practice it. Never mind the extraordinarily large role emotion plays in the text. What unique insight does a focus on emotion provide? I believe that such a focus takes us more deeply into the novel than any other approach, highlighting the motives of the characters and the tone of the author. It also acknowledges the affective code, which controls a substantial part of the act of reading. And then, as we have seen, it solves several otherwise intractable problems, like the ending of *Huck Finn* or the characterization of Isabel Archer.

I don't want to exaggerate. Emotion is only one of many elements that interact within a text. And as I have said, our emotions are originally private, and so not always suited to public discourse. Clearly they are better at expressing value than fact. On the other hand, readers are hungry for the intersubjective, and so read for emotion, which expresses the meaning of the text with power and efficiency.

To novelists themselves, emotion is a tool that performs specific tasks, many of which I've already implied. Writers employ emotion (evoked by image or word), when they wish to provide a background that does not dominate the scene, including a reminder of what has gone before. Emotion can organize a novel as well as a paragraph, providing the point of the story. It can also invigorate a description— even when the author mentions emotion casually, it makes the passage bloom. Here, for example, is Mark Twain talking about a riverboat that arrives at a village once a day: "Before these events, the day was glorious with expectancy; after them, the day was a dead and empty thing." Norman Mailer in *Tough Guys Don't Dance* describes a dog on the front seat of a car as sitting "as solemn as a soldier going to the front."

A literary critic does well to understand such tools, since they illuminate the novel. It is obviously useful to know how something is constructed. And then emotion answers several questions in the theory of reading, such as how readers fill the gaps in the text or how readers can react simultaneously to the form and the subject of the work. The affective code explains how readers meld the foreground and background of the scene into a single whole, and how they can imagine all kinds of complex meanings simultaneously. It explains how a supposedly fuzzy mental experience (which is an illusion, after all) can provide the effect of precision and solidity.

I will not elaborate upon the value of emotion in interpretation, since I offer examples of it in chapter 9, interpreting "Big Two-Hearted River," and chapter 15, interpreting *Beloved*. It is enough to know that emotion lies at the center of our understanding of the work. Nor will I belabor the value of emotion to literary history: in *Sensational Designs* Jane Tompkins shows that the public attitude toward emotion is often the signature of an era. Peter Stearns documents the same point in histories like *Jealousy* and *American Cool*. Because each age has its own emotional economy, emotion is a natural way to represent it.

What I will examine is an application that is presently unfashionable: our aesthetic judgment of the work.[12] Whether readers are aware of it or not, the act of reading always involves a judgment. The reader's relationship with the protagonist determines the author's meaning, for example, and that relationship is the product of several judgments. In narrative fiction ideas are embodied in characters, which means that the writer conveys her meaning by directing our emotional appraisal of her characters. As we will see in the next chapter, a novel can find its very point in creating an unconventional reader reaction.

An emotion is a judgment in three different ways. The first, which we have already witnessed in the thought of Robert Solomon, is that the emotion is *itself* the evaluation. That is, we react to not the object in the world but the object within our head, where it has already been processed by the senses and the limbic region of the brain. What we experience is already imbued with emotion that expresses our interpretation of the object and what it means. The emotion is part and parcel of the perception and the writer's task is to make the readers feel the emotions that carry her judgment.

The second way involves our subsequent evaluation of the emotion itself. Whenever we feel, we automatically judge the feeling: it is pleasant or unpleasant, desirable or undesirable, "good" or "bad" in any number of specific ways. The philosopher R. W. Hepburn, for example, argues that emotion evoked by art should be specific, appropriate, and discriminating rather than vague, inappropriate, or crude. Hepburn recommends "replacing jaded and repetitive habit-emotions with fresh and keen emotions, coupled logically to new individualized ways of seeing." Other thinkers stress the relationship of the felt emotion to the rest of the self and then to other people. To Margaret Phillips,

> educated emotions are those which are integrated, or organized, in sentiments; which no longer function spasmodically, in isolation or to conflicting ends, but rather work smoothly and consistently together, modifying and reinforcing each other in support of a common purpose.

Still other thinkers define quality emotion to be a true expression of the self (in a world that demands a distorting conformity); to be directed outward toward the world, away from the needful self; and to exhibit a certain coolness or control, avoiding overexcitement. R. G. Collingwood insists that the author's own emotions must be sincere, as we have seen, while Martin Heidegger sees authentic emotions as a first step to authentic being. Susanne Langer observes that we judge intellectual work by means of the feelings surrounding it:

> Strain and expectation, vagueness and clearness, ease and frustration, and the very interesting 'sense of rightness' that closes a finished thought process are really the ultimate criteria by which we judge the validity of logical relations.[13]

Do successful works of art make readers feel these "successful" kinds of emotion? As I said in chapter 12, it seems more than possible. Would not a feeling that is demonstrably "authentic" or "integrated" or "right" create a more vivid or more accurate experience within the reader? It would be more precise, certainly, and so provide a more sharply defined construction. And it would instill confidence in the reader, evoking a general impression of authenticity. Clearly the quality of the emotion evoked by the text, eliciting its own level of judgment, plays a central role in our appraisal of its value.

V

The third way in which emotion involves judgment overlaps these first two and yet defines the means by which we make the evaluation or appraisal. It is true that one feels what one feels: we think of emotions as unwilled and spontaneous and so a direct, noncalculated reflection of the self. How could they differ in quality? We know that we disapprove of many emotions, calling some of them a sin, like envy, and others a source of illness, like anger. But we also understand that an emotion—whatever we may think of its own characteristics—conveys a message about something else. To blame the emotion is to shoot the messenger.

And yet we care deeply about the relationship of the emotion to its context, judging the emotion on that basis.[14] We *always* notice whether the emotion fits the situation at hand, a trait that may have its roots in our need for survival: if the motive of our companion is inconsistent or hidden, we are disarmed or threatened. Whether we are reading or immersed in daily life, we distrust and fear those who feel inappropriately and trust and like those who do not. It is no accident that novels like *Pride and Prejudice* or *Adventures of Huckleberry Finn* are studies of appropriate and inappropriate emotion.

Perhaps the best example of inappropriate emotion is pap Finn's famous complaint in *Huckleberry Finn*.

> "Call this a govment! why, just look at it and see what it's like. Here's the law a-standing ready to take a man's son away from him—a man's own son, which he has had all the trouble and all the anxiety and all the expense of raising. . . . The law takes a man worth six thousand dollars and upards, and jams him into an old trap of a cabin like this, and lets him go round in clothes that ain't fitten for a hog. They call that a govment!"[15]

We find this self-delusion delicious because the match between pap's emotion (outrage and self-pity) and the circumstance (pap's theft of six thousand dollars from his own son) is so perfectly wrong. We as readers are exquisitely sensitive to such inconsistency, judging the fit of pap's feelings to circumstance immediately and automatically, as though such calibration were our very first act when with another person.[16]

If we did not understand Twain's judgment of this character, of course, we would misread this speech and so misread the whole novel. Thus our interpretation of pap (and the story in which he appears) is dependent upon our judgment of him: our appraisal is part and parcel of our understanding—the very foundation of interpretation. This is why Professor Lee Clark Mitchell performs a valuable service in his essay, "'Nobody but Our Gang Warn't Around': The Authority of Language in *Huckleberry Finn*," even though he is (in my view) wrong in his specific argument. Mitchell charges that Huck's decision to go to hell rather than turn in Jim is based on emotions that are unfounded. Because they refer to nothing but themselves, Huck's feelings are self-serving, sentimental and arbitrary.

> The "conscience" of a slave-holding South, however evil, represents at least a coherent social system, just as the Grangerford-Shepherdson feud illustrates a system of prescriptive rules, however vicious. Not so Huck's seemingly humane alternative, which lacks either system or logic that might link "feeling" to something outside the self.

Mitchell is inconsistent, since he demands that Huck ground his emotion in an external reality but then complains when Huck does the same with his words.

> Unlike Tom, who engages language as a play of signifiers, Huck at every point looks for verification to "reality." . . . Events always precede discourse for Huck, and language can do no more than turn us back to that prior order.[17]

Is there some reason why emotion requires a referent while language does not? In any case, Mitchell makes a mistake about Huck's decision for Jim that illustrates an important point about evaluating emotions.[18] Because Huck has been conditioned to believe in the tenets of racism, and so believes that he is stealing property from Miss Watson, he feels guilty about helping Jim escape. But Huck's *experience*, which has revealed Jim's humanity, contradicts this learned racism. In a sense Huck's feeling for Jim operates like the affective code, in that it synthesizes the meaning of a large body of experience. And that experience grounds Huck's feelings.

Still, Mitchell is correct in his larger point. Nothing destroys a work of literature so completely as unjustified or false feeling. Emotion leads our thought, and when the emotion is muddy or unjustified, offered without a clear foundation, the thought is liable to be so too. Certainly unjustified emotion is the source of much bad art, as we see in so many Hollywood movies today. Fiction is fantasy, of course, whether in print or on film, and so offers "spurious" emotion by definition. It satisfies wish fulfillment. Yet the challenge for the responsible writer is to fulfill the needs of fantasy in a plausible way, providing circumstances in which the emotions are justified—not an easy task. *Huck Finn* offers a fantasy of freedom that Twain could manage only so long, for example, reflecting the fact that a realistic fiction is one of the most difficult of arts.

Mitchell also points to a fascinating truth about the affective code, which is the translation into emotion of both our personal experience and our social conditioning. As Foucault understood, emotion carries the values of a culture into the working psyche of the individual. But emotion also expresses one's personal desire (which may of course have been itself conditioned), so that personal needs and social values meet within the mind in the form of felt emotions. Not a little of what we call thinking is the sorting out of these emotions, resolving their difference (or choosing one over the other). Huck feels the guilt he has been socially conditioned to feel; he feels his loyalty to Jim, based on the experience of the past weeks; and he makes his decision by weighing these different emotions.

Of course, Huck does not say to himself, "Here is the world, which views Jim as a stolen possession, and here is my feeling of personal loyalty toward Jim: how shall I resolve this conflict?" Huck feels his loyalty to society and his love of Jim and chooses the feeling that is the strongest. Or he struggles to reconcile his feelings. He might monitor such a decision consciously, and he might second-guess himself. He might make sure that his two emotions are "rational," as philosophers put it, or justified by their object. But in most cases Huck, like most of us, knows that his feelings represent bodies of information and value: he makes his decision according to the dictates of what we have heard William Hazlitt call "common sense," or the reservoir of knowledge and value that we summon forth into consciousness in the form of emotion.

I don't mean to say that we never think in a conscious, rational way, for of course we do, particularly when the stakes are high. When called on to explain ourselves, moreover, we put our reasons into a rational order. Nor do I mean to suggest that the representation by emotion of the self and our society is free from problems. It is precisely the representation of both elements by the same medium that makes us so touchy about emotion: too often we take the personal desire for the public fact or, as Hemingway complained, the public cliche for our private reaction. For this reason critics save their worst opprobrium for those works that offer (as Mitchell says of *Huck Finn*) what appears to be an emotion floating free of its source.[19]

In such ways, affective criticism returns the critic to judgment based upon an awareness of emotion. Although readers make these judgments anyway, as I have said, an understanding of the process— of the role of judgment in interpretation, and the role of emotion in judgment—cannot but make for clarity. The affective critic understands that emotion is in itself a form of consciousness.

I don't mean that an affective criticism is only judgment. In the chapters that remain I will offer examples of affective criticism performing other tasks. No doubt other critics will use the analysis of affect in still other, entirely different, ways, making these examples but one illustration of what is possible. But it is true that a focus on emotion confronts some of the major critical issues regarding these novels. It offers it own insight, and so provides a coherent, valuable approach to the work of art. And it is inevitable, in any case, since interpretation requires judgment and judgment finds expression in emotion.

But whatever may be the cause of sympathy, or however it may be excited, nothing pleases us more than to observe in other men a fellow-feeling with all the emotions of our own breast.
—Adam Smith, The Theory of Moral Sentiments

A painting has to be the experience, instead of pointing to it. I want to have and to give *access to feeling.* That is the riskiest and only important way to connect art to the world—to make it alive.
—David Salle, Letter to Janet Malcolm

15
A Critic's Notebook: *Beloved* and the Functions of Emotion

As a rich and complex novel, Toni Morrison's *Beloved* requires several different critical approaches. It requires exegesis in the New Critical mode, since its meaning is difficult, and then a feminist and an African American analysis as well.[1] Many critics would recommend a study of the semiotic codes that control our understanding of Morrison's language, while still others would focus on the deconstructing contradictions that make its meaning complex. New Historicists would examine the sources of power in the post-Civil War era, understanding that the novel is, in addition to being magnificently written, as political as *Uncle Tom's Cabin.*

I'm sure that many readers would also agree that *Beloved* requires a study of affect, or the numerous emotions Morrison names or evokes. Such a focus permits us to do justice to the human experience Morrison represents, fulfilling her desire to make us *feel* the experience of her characters. Toni Morrison came to believe, she says, that the traditional slave narratives repressed certain facts, no doubt because the black authors did not want to offend their white audience. They dealt exclusively with the external life of the slaves. "Most importantly—at least for me—there was no mention of their interior life."[2] In contrast, Morrison would write about not slavery as such—though she provides what may be our most vivid portrayal of it—but

201

its effect on its victims. In *Beloved* she would add to the external world of historical fact the sensations and feelings of the slaves, and in doing so would present something like a test case for the affective code. Can a focus on what these characters feel give a significant representation of their experience? Do the characters' *reactions* translate into the readers' representations?

Even though *Beloved* was recognized as an American classic from the very moment of its publication in 1986, it raises several critical issues. It recounts the true story of an escaped slave, Margaret Garner, who murdered her daughter rather than permit her to be returned to slavery. Morrison was much taken, she says, by the contemporary newspaper description of the murderous mother as serene. Garner seemed to feel that she had *saved* her child, which is a position that we can understand. As Morrison puts it, the murder was "absolutely the right thing to do, but she had no right to do it."[3]

But critics still worry about Morrison's attitude toward the mother, named Sethe in the novel, whom Morrison both condemns and defends. They also worry about the identity and meaning of the title character, who is presumably the ghost of the murdered baby. Their concern leads them to an examination of the narrative form of the novel, which is innovative, and Morrison's use of language, which some find poetic and others melodramatic or overblown. Morrison sets the novel in Cincinnati some seventeen years after the time of the Civil War, Sethe's escape from the plantation, Sweet Home, and Sethe's subsequent murder of her daughter. She seems destined for recovery when the mysterious Beloved shows up.

My plan is to approach *Beloved* by examining the major functions of emotion, wherever they may lead. Thus I will do self-consciously what many readers do as a matter of course, seeking the insights to be found within subject, tone, reaction and representation. This format permits me to understand how each of the four functions performs, especially in comparison with the others. It also permits me once again to document the affective code. *Beloved* is especially useful in this regard because Morrison takes the affective code to a new level of mastery.

But my main purpose is to illustrate not the affective code but an affective criticism, or at least one form of it, studying the several ways emotion exists within the text. I will show that each of the four functions of emotion can serve as a critical tool, as the word "notebook" in my chapter title might suggest. I want to catch the rough spontaneity of an actual search for insight, portraying an affective criticism in process. I also want to show how basic and straightforward an affective criticism can be: I will trace each function of emotion wherever it may lead, expecting at least one of the functions to provide a useful insight. Characters are what they feel, after all, and they act and speak accordingly. Although one or more of these functions may draw a blank, I am confident that at least one of them will take us to the heart of the novel. In ordinary circumstances I would probably choose the function that seems most promising and follow it exclusively. But working up all four functions gives me the opportunity to compare them and the insights they offer. Let us see what happens.

I

Emotion as the **subject** of *Beloved* is perhaps the easiest of the four functions to examine, and it may prove to be the most fruitful. How does a critic deal with the subject-emotion of a novel? As I said in the last chapter, one steps back from the page to look at the emotion that the text itself examines, whether it be the motive of a character or the feeling of an era. The very title of *Beloved* refers to an emotion, of course, and so does the first sentence: "124 was spiteful." Because Beloved's resentment at her murder lies at the center of events, one could examine the novel as a study of spite. Out of spite the nephews at Sweet Home beat Sethe for reporting their forcible theft of her breast milk. Out of spite the community near Cincinnati does not warn Sethe of schoolteacher's approach (thinking Baby Suggs and Sethe had put on airs by giving their feast). And it is out of spite, possibly, that Sethe—for all her love of her children (and no doubt because of it, as we will see)—deprives schoolteacher of his property, her child, by means of murder. (After all, Sethe's own mother killed her children to deprive their white father of his property.) Such is the horrible arithmetic of slavery.

Like Jane Austen, moreover, Morrison defines her characters as emotional beings. Her characters know themselves by what they desire and their companions by the emotions they see within them. More than that, they find definition in what we might call their personal emotional economy, as in this description of Paul D:

> For a man with an immobile face it was amazing how ready it was to smile, or blaze or be sorry with you. As though all you had to do was get his attention and right away he produced the feeling you were feeling.[4]

Paul D is "the kind of man who could walk into a house and make the woman cry"—perhaps too good to be true, as some reviewers have said, and yet possessed of a capacity found in many men. Paul D may be a fantasy of devotion to Sethe, but his violation of the male stereotype gives him a certain freshness.

To read about these characters is to read about the emotion that defines them. And yet Morrison's subject is not so much the emotion of these characters as the damage slavery has done to it—especially the long-range damage.[5] We find this theme dramatized in the ministry of Baby Suggs, Sethe's mother-in-law, who understands the emotional wounds suffered by the ex-slaves who listen to her. Baby herself learned to repress her feelings when seven of her children were taken from her, and she understands that the other blacks have repressed their feelings also. In the Clearing on Saturday afternoon, Baby Suggs conducts exercises in feeling, asking group after group of ex-slaves to laugh and cry and sing, telling them that their emotions and their bodies are holy. She teaches them to value themselves, which involves accepting (and expressing) their feelings. She leads her people toward emotional health.

Like Baby Suggs's parishioners, Sethe herself is repressed, since "she worked hard to remember as close to nothing as was safe." And that results in damage to her daughter, Denver, who is defined by her loneliness and the fact that she, like Nathaniel Hawthorne's Pearl (also the daughter of a strong mother who has broken the social code), remains an immature creature until humanized by an act of kindness—in this case by the community.

Because of such damage, emotion holds special dangers for this group. After Sethe murders her child, for example, Baby Suggs, feeling defeated, takes to her deathbed. The violence of schoolteacher and her daughter-in-law have vanquished Baby Suggs's message of emotional expression. Paul D betrays Sethe, giving in to his sexual desire for Beloved, because he is emotionally wounded, and Sethe murders her child in an emotional panic, with "hummingbirds pecking in her hair." It is Sethe's own emotional damage that makes her motherhood so intense.

And it is in Sethe's tormented motherhood, of course, that Morrison dramatizes her theme most directly. Sethe's love for her children is, as Paul D says, "too thick." Having been stripped of everything else by slavery, Sethe invests too much of herself in her children. She identifies so completely with her "best thing," as she calls her children, that she forgets to distinguish between them and herself (she planned to kill herself after killing them). And when the young woman, Beloved, shows up, Sethe invests too much—her life—in sacrificing for *her:* having gone to extremes to save her children, Sethe now goes to extremes to expiate her guilt. At one time,

Morrison says, she thought her major theme might be how the good act carries the seeds of its own destruction.[6] Brilliantly, she understood that slavery would intensify even ordinary feelings into something self-destructive.

At the very least, emotional damage distorts perception. Emotion so distorts Sethe's perception at the end of the novel that she mistakes the white man who had helped her for the white man who would destroy her. The character Beloved suffers the delusions created by a bottomless need, and so too do the other characters, who can perceive Beloved only in terms of their own (often self-destructive) emotional needs.[7] To the lonely Denver, Beloved is company. To Paul D, who suffered sexual deprivation most of his life, Beloved is sexual release and a way of escaping commitment to Sethe.[8] To Sethe, who has not yet sufficiently grieved her dead daughter, Beloved *is* that dead daughter, returned to demand the love and the life she was denied. Beloved's avidity matches with a destructive precision Sethe's remorse. Beloved is Sethe's guilt, returned to haunt her, and so the means by which Sethe copes with her crime.

Every novel takes emotion as its subject in some way, of course. And yet one cannot understand *Beloved* without focusing on emotion. The novel is driven by the perfect, ironic fit between the emotional needs of Beloved and Sethe. It is also true that Morrison uses emotion to unite the private experience of these characters with the public culture. Themes such as repression and sublimation belong to whole societies, which always decide what kind of emotional economy is "natural." In this sense Morrison completes the historical account, putting emotional flesh on the bare bones of historical fact. We may take the character, Beloved, as the public appearance of the private or emotional reality. Repress the emotional truth, Morrison seems to say, and it will burst into the open anyway. On the other hand, the schoolteacher riding into the yard carries the public or institutional world into Sethe's private world. On almost every level, *Beloved* posits a tension between the polarities of public and private.

II

Tone embodies the narrator's way of relating to the world and so the emotions that she brings to any interaction. It also returns us to the reader's construction of the text, since it ultimately directs that act. How does one focus on tone? Because it lies mostly in the internal voice that we hear as we read, we need only hear the voice to discover the feelings that shape it. Back away from that voice and one can make those feelings conscious.[9]

I can dramatize the importance of tone by considering a review of *Beloved* that is practically a classic of wrong-headedness. In "Aunt Medea," Stanley Crouch complains that Morrison's tone in *Beloved* requests the reader to feel emotions unjustified by the text. Crouch claims that Morrison would add black women to the list of our society's victims, charging that she has no sense of the human evil that existed before and after slavery, and that "she lacks a true sense of the tragic." Her tone is shallow. Toni Morrison "almost always loses control. She can't resist the temptation of the trite or the sentimental."[10]

Many other reviewers understood *Beloved* to be great *because* of its tone, and I think that they are correct. Morrison uses a voice so distinctive that *Beloved* joins *Adventures of Huckleberry Finn* as a masterpiece of colloquial English. Previous black writers like Richard Wright, Ralph Ellison, and James Baldwin adopted the idiom of the American literary culture, writing about the black experience in white language. Toni Morrison brings to the black experience the daily language of African Americans.[11] Her voice is shaped by not only her detail but a particular black diction, rhythm, and emotion.

This voice finds distinction in its avoidance of precisely those faults suggested by Crouch. Although the events are luridly dramatic, the narrator and characters view them with an authenticating calm.[12] The voice does *not* request a reaction that is unjustified. When the characters feel deeply, as they often do, they fall silent: Morrison lets us surmise their emotions from the context. And the narrative voice operates on the same principle, offering the story in a matter of fact tone. For all the pain and anger caused by these atrocities, the novel regards them in a commonsensical way.

I do think that Toni Morrison skirts the edge of sentimentality. Paul D is a pretty remarkable fellow, after all, and the terrible events recounted here might well elicit an extreme emotion. Sethe's life is saved by the white girl, Amy, who washes her feet and delivers her baby. But Amy is not idealized. With an instinctive sense of human complexity, Morrison makes the comic Amy too insensitive or self-centered to be saccharine. "You gonna die in here, you know. Ain't no way out of it. Thank your Maker I come along so's you would't have to die outside in them weeds. Snake come along he bite you."

Such gruffness is a stock device that might have become cute. "Don't up and die on me in the night, you hear? I don't want to see your ugly black face hankering over me." But Morrison really does hit the right tone, since Amy too has been abused, permitting us to appreciate the young woman's honesty and spunk while revealing her ignorance and racism. Amy is both generous and selfish, a friend and an enemy, capable of turning at any moment. Like most people, Amy is myopically focused on her own affairs.

Humor helps Morrison avoid sentimentality. Though her subject is grim (sixty million dead), her characters almost always find a nourishing source of laughter. Thinking about the murderous practice of slavery, for example, Baby Suggs charges "no bad luck but white people" and then explains, in humorous understatement: "They don't know when to stop." On another occasion, after Sethe has mistakenly tried to kill the white man Bodwin, Paul D and Stamp Paid find an occasion to laugh. Was Sethe crazy? Well, yes, though "'ain't we all.' They laughed then. . . . 'Every time a whiteman come to the door she got to kill somebody?'"

The truth is that Morrison offers events to which, as Roger Sale observes, we do not know how to react. Some of them are so painful that we don't know how to admit them to consciousness. Morrison tempers this material—and so keeps us reading—by making us work to understand what happened: some events are so obscure when first encountered that we don't react right away, feeling the accumulated weight of such atrocities only later. This parallels the way in which the characters themselves endure their wounds, which for all of the immediate pain cause long-range suffering.

Morrison also forestalls the sentimentality Crouch fears by means of ambiguity. Like Henry James in *The Turn of the Screw*, Morrison writes a tale that can be viewed as either a ghost story or a psychological study (or perhaps both at the same time).[13] The character Beloved is either a demonic ghost returned to seek revenge on the mother who murdered her, or, as Elizabeth House argues, an unfortunate young woman who escaped from the white man who imprisoned her. Stamp Paid speaks of a young woman at Deer Creek who killed her sexually abusive master—the identity that I think makes the most sense. Beloved does not identify herself as Sethe's child in her concluding monologue. She says instead that she has been smuggled into this country as a child, which accounts nicely for all of the other events she mentions. Her traumatic imprisonment and sexual abuse explain her immaturity. She has been emotionally stunted. It also explains her sexual knowledge, exhibited with Paul D and in her final monologue, when she remembers that "ghosts without skin stuck their fingers in her and said beloved in the dark and bitch in the light"—the reason that she thinks her name is Beloved. The "ghosts" are without skin, of course, because they are white.

This interpretation underscores the emotional damage done to the slaves, which, as I have said, was Morrison's goal. Sethe *needs* to expiate the guilt she has repressed, and so seizes the opportunity, her need distorting her perception. Beloved *needs* to be cared for, and so clings to the stranger who shows kindness. The two characters fall upon each other in a mutual and self-destructive delusion that dramatizes their emotional wounds. At the end, Beloved flees not because she is a ghost exorcised by the women but because, as her monologue prepares us to understand, she is again (as the women grapple with Sethe) abandoned by her mother in the presence of a pile of bodies at the feet of a white man.

The ghost story is a terrific tale in its own right, of course, and one that Morrison clearly intended, thinking of Beloved as Sethe's daughter come to demand her due.[14] In this view Beloved is a spiritual rather than a naturalistic being, but she exhibits the same psychology, as the greedy child devours the guilty mother. One could also interpret Beloved as an African water spirit, as Karen Carmean claims, or as the archetype of the African diaspora, pulling together such strands of slave history as capture, transport on the death ships, and abuse.

Can we know whether Beloved is a stranger, a ghost, or an archetype? Morrison really seems to mean all three. In any case, such ambiguity or complexity moderates our reaction, setting a tone that pulls us back from the full agony of the characters. Like Henry James in *The Turn of the Screw*, Morrison keeps us up in the air, wondering and so distracted from the full horror. We have to think. And because we can't really know who Beloved is, Morrison's subject becomes the limits of human perception, highlighting not the agony of the two characters, great as it is, but the irony of their psychological fit.

What is the significance of this for the critic studying tone? One might note how quickly such a focus leads to the major competing interpretations and a consideration of the evidence for them. If one would interpret this novel accurately, one must work out the emotions the author tries to make one feel. Because the novel is about emotional repression, moreover, with a character who seems to well up from the unconscious, one studies the tone to work out what Morrison herself felt about these events.

III

Just as tone expresses the author's evaluation of the subject, so **reaction** expresses the reader's judgment of that evaluation. Critics of a novel compare their emotional reaction to events and characters with that embodied in the authors' tone. They also study the author's means of obtaining the reaction she desires. Because authors seek to evoke a particular reaction, a focus on one's response is an important tool in interpretation. To focus on reaction also discourages jargon and ensures modesty, since the critic offers a response that must be tested against the text and the reactions of other readers.

One's reaction in *Beloved* is especially revealing because the novel seeks to evoke a response opposite to what one might expect. That is, one would think that Sethe's murder of her baby with a handsaw would diminish our sympathy for her. At least one critic identifies her with the myth of the destructive mother, and when Paul D learns about the act, he is censorious: " 'You got two feet, Sethe, not four,' he said, and right then a forest sprang up between them; trackless and quiet."

Yet Toni Morrison uses a variety of means to move us from censure to sympathy with Sethe. In Denver's eyes, for example, the appearance of Beloved converts Sethe from victimizer to victim. And even at the time of the murder, Morrison offers several mitigating circumstances. Sethe acts under duress and is a victim of her community, which does not warn her of schoolteacher's approach. And then, as I have suggested, slave mothers sometimes killed the babies forced on them by white males, providing Sethe with a precedent for her act.

It is also significant that death in this novel is not final: Sethe says that "my plan was to take us all to the other side where my own ma'am is." She not only acted without malice, but believed herself to be placing her children on another plane of existence, out of harm's way. This belief is supported in the novel by the existence of spirits and by Morrison's description of a world in which images and emotions linger in the air long after their original appearance. Travelers pass through these residual feelings as through a mist, and their existence as sensations posits a physical world that is spiritually alive.

Morrison reinforces this reaction to Sethe's crime by using the reactions of other characters. Minutes after Sethe has murdered the baby, Stamp Paid confidently hands Denver to Sethe to suckle. Baby Suggs is described as beaten not by the murder but by its ambivalence: "They came in her yard anyway and she could not approve or condemn Sethe's rough choice. One or the other might have saved her, but beaten up by the claims of both, she went to bed."

Personally speaking, I have two reactions to *Beloved* that seem worth exploring. The first is my sense of almost classical tragedy, born of the extremity of Sethe's act and her personal dignity. To me, Stanley Crouch's complaint that Morrison has no "true sense of the tragic" is precisely wrong, since the novel rises to a level of timelessness. The extremity of the murder, the solitude within which Sethe acts, and her desperate reach for self-determination all contain a tragic largeness and inevitability. As both a violation of social mores *and* a defense of individual integrity, Sethe's act is both wrong and courageous.

Sethe herself is "queenly," moreover, or a natural aristocrat. At Sweet Home she has a natural dignity that keeps six males at bay, and even as a slave she insists on as much meaning to her life as she can garner. She consecrates her union to Halle. She reveres her children. She shows enormous stamina in escaping from the farm, wounded and pregnant, and great strength in bearing the loss of her mother, husband, daughter, and (eventually) sons. And she carries on when Baby Suggs chooses to die. On every level, Sethe does what is possible within the circumstance, and if her repentance for the murder is inadequate, she knows *that* about herself as well, as we see in her desperate self-sacrifice for Beloved. When she crumbles before Beloved's will, it is a thunderous revelation, though even her willingness to destroy herself gives her a noble and so tragic bearing.[15]

My second reaction to *Beloved* is more troubling. After Sethe has acknowledged the anger of the ghost—"the baby's fury at having its throat cut"—she remembers how she had given sex to the stonecutter in return for an inscribed gravestone for her child.

> But those ten minutes she spent pressed up against dawn-colored stone studded with star chips, her knees wide open as the grave, were longer than life, more alive, more pulsating than the baby blood that soaked her fingers like oil. (5)

To Sethe the act of giving sex to a stranger for pay is more vivid than the murder of her baby. And she means just that: "Who would have thought that a little old baby could harbor so much rage?" she complains. "Rutting among the stones under the eyes of the engraver's son was not enough."

How does one evaluate this? Are murder and sexual humiliation equivalent? Is Sethe's sexual violation a sufficient penance? My initial reaction is negative, since that equation (which is not meant ironically) strikes me as wrong. Surely the taking of a life is worse than the abusing of a life, bad as it may be, though Morrison offers plenty of support for Sethe's statement. Having been violated at Sweet Home by the nephews, Sethe feels a special horror at yet another invasion of her body (once again intensified by the gaze of a spectator, in this case the engraver's son). Sethe herself says that she honors her dead child by dirtying herself irremediably. She believes, as she does of the murder itself, that her intention defines the meaning of the act.

Within the context of slavery, moreover, sex carries a special meaning. In a key passage late in the book Sethe fears that Beloved will
leave before she can make her understand that death is not the worst
thing:

> worse than that—far worse—was what Baby Suggs died of, what Ella
> knew, what Stamp saw and what made Paul D tremble. That anybody
> white could take your whole self for anything that came to mind. Not just
> work, kill, or maim you, but dirty you. Dirty you so bad you couldn't like
> yourself any more. Dirty you so bad that you forgot who you were and
> couldn't think it up. And though she and others lived through and got
> over it, she could never let it happen to her own. The best thing she was,
> was her children. Whites might dirty *her* all right, but not her best thing,
> her beautiful, magical best thing—the part of her that was clean. (251)

In these terms, sex embodies not only the damage done to the slave's
sexual identity, that most tender area, but her lack of personal sov-
ereignty. The issue is not sexuality but Sethe's horrible choice—on
behalf of her children—between death or humiliation. Loving her
children intensely, Sethe would save them from slavery.
   Even so, I am bothered, or at least puzzled, by Morrison's treatment of sexuality. For sex plays an even more confusing role in the
character of Beloved, who has an extraordinarily strong sexual
charge. Beloved is, in Paul D's words, full of "shining," or the glow of
sexual desire. As the spirit of a baby in a woman's body, returned
from the deprivation of death, Beloved is polymorphously perverse,
or so greedy for sensations that she does not discriminate among
them. And then, as a consequence of either her derangement or her
identity as a ghost, she is sexually bold in a way we feel is demonic.
   I worry that Beloved's sexual aggression threatens to take over the
story. Beloved has real sex with Paul D and metaphorical sex with
Denver, their speech "a duet as they lay down together, Denver nurs-
ing Beloved's interest like a lover whose pleasure was to overfeed the
loved." Beloved tries to have real sex with Sethe when she won't stop
kissing her and metaphorical sex during the woman's sojourn in the
winter cabin. There the sensuous overtones of their claustrophobic
relationship taps into our cultural fears and taboos, as Morrison
seems (like James in *The Turn of the Screw*) to use homoeroticism to
intensify her ghost story.[16] She presents Beloved as a creature whose
appetites are out of control—she has been so badly damaged by
slavery—which makes her seem eerie. Certainly Morrison makes the
cabin episode lurid. Nor am I simply prudish, since the point is not
the sexuality itself but its domination of the scene. The erotic theme
threatens to take over the story, as though Morrison began writing

about slavery and ended up writing about sexuality. Or perhaps the point is Morrison's treatment of the theme: though she uses sexuality as a measure of the emotional damage done to these characters, in the case of Beloved she uses it to dramatize the demonic.[17]

Or so I feel.[18] In the cabin the female community that we expect to be nurturing becomes destructive—a point central to Morrison's thought. Once again Morrison shows how a good thing can become damaging—or how emotional damage twists what is normally good into something destructive. These characters are so damaged by slavery that they cannot fulfill this feminine idyll. But as I read the text, this justification is intellectual: what I *feel* is an excess that sweeps all before it. Perhaps I should blame this affect on the special intensity of Beloved, who as libido becomes an uninhibited and destructive force in her own right, threatening to wrest the novel from its author. Or perhaps Morrison exhibits values and feelings here that she does not fully understand. It is remarkable how sensitive we are to such blind spots, if blind spot it is.

How useful are reactions like these? I don't think there is any doubt that sexuality is an important issue in this book, involving themes that Morrison may not have assimilated. My reaction is useful in that it sets a course of investigation. One wants to track the theme of sensuality (and this repugnance) sentence by sentence. And yet my feeling is also a tribute to the character, Beloved, who is one of those rare literary figures who haunt us. She is powerful not because she is an alien ghost or an avenging child, but because she is ultimately so human, defining the outer extensions of human desire. She is the unconscious, the sensuous, the grasping. She is human emotion itself, when the person is charged and out of control.[19] Certainly she is emotion when it is repressed and so transformed into something destructive. And yet on another, even more basic level, she is simply the essence of the child, dramatizing in extreme form the ruthless neediness every parent will recognize.

IV

Finally, I turn to the role of emotion in the reader's mental **representation** of *Beloved*. What is the character, Beloved, to my imagination? How do I mentally represent her? I can recite the young woman's name, thinking of her as a word or an idea, but that is to ignore her imaginative substance. I can also feel her presence generically, as someone "there"—she is a ghost the way Isabel is a lady—and then even more specifically, as an individual, since her simple neediness is so strong an identity. I feel Beloved's beauty because Morrison insists on it, but I do not construct a beautiful face in my mind's eye. Rather, I feel her satiny, unblemished skin. I also feel the odd phenomenon of a child in a twenty-year-old body, with her greedy demands for sensation and attention. I feel a will out of control, but more than that, and perhaps understandably, since she is a twenty-year-old with seamless skin, I feel her as a babe in the cradle, her breath smelling of milk.

I am unable to visualize such a character, and I can barely think the idea of her. This is especially true because Beloved has a double or triple identity. How can I visualize Beloved simultaneously as the ghost of the two-year-old, the escapee from Deer Creek, and the representative of the slave experience? These three dimensions give depth and complexity to Beloved as a character, but they foil any effort to visualize or conceptualize her in a single stroke. I am practically forced to construct Beloved in the affective code, and must do so in spite of the strong presence in this novel of the other two codes, which I should now recognize. Morrison herself has spoken of the aural quality of her style, as she stresses the voices and so the language of these characters. In a way, in fact, Morrison's style is almost too good, since the calm, colloquial beauty of the language sometimes works to soften the horror of the events.

But then Morrison is really after levels that lie deeper than language. At one point she notes a sound that is nonverbal. As the women pray to expel the devil-ghost from Sethe's life, they move from words to pure sound—the pure expression of emotion. "In the beginning there were no words. In the beginning was the sound, and they all knew what the sound sounded like." Baby Suggs achieves the same raw form of communication in the open field, since she understands that sound transmits emotion directly to the listener by means of contagion. The voice of the novel transmits emotion in the same way, since we hear, just below the literal meaning, a level of feeling that expresses Morrison's definitive meaning. This is to say, of course, that on one level even verbal construction is emotional.

Morrison's style is also highly visual, a fact confirmed by her comment that it is not the emotions that help in writing but the image. "The controlling image is useful because it determines the language that informs the text."[20] Morrison uses vision as a metaphor for perception and representation. "And suddenly there was Sweet Home rolling, rolling, rolling out before her eyes." Just as Sethe employs vision to remember, Paul D uses it to imagine: "With an effort that makes him sweat he forces a picture of himself lying there, and when he sees it, it lifts his spirit."

Yet *Beloved* is ultimately not a visual book, either. To an even larger degree than the earlier novelists we have considered, Morrison uses the visual to express emotion. The point is not the image but the feeling. Thus the color red expresses the spite in the house at 124. The emotion causes the color just as it causes the shaking of the house, but what matters is the result of this causation: the emotion is palpable. It is felt through the senses. It acts on and through the physical world. One could even say that emotion in Morrison's narrative is the very stuff of which the world is made. It is sensation and it is force. In short, Morrison takes the word "feeling" at its full value, making one feel the emotion within both the mind and the senses. The angry light at 124 suggests what many people suspect at one time or another, which is that emotion is somehow an actual physical force, a point understood by any public speaker who has felt the emotion of the crowd wash over the podium like a wave of energy. Or is it just the sound and substance of so many people?

At any rate, when we look closely at Morrison's text, many of the images that we assume to be visual turn out to be emotional, as in this description of Sethe's lost husband. " 'You may as well know it all. Last time I saw him he was sitting by the churn. He had butter all over his face.' " It doesn't matter that we do not know what Halle (or a butter churn) looks like. Nor is the general image of the butter-smeared face important, since Morrison does not specifically describe it. What counts here is not the image but the feeling of the desolate figure disfigured by butterfat and madness. Halle's theft of the white man's butter is a crazy parody of the nephews's theft of milk from Sethe's breasts. Or is Halle crazily attempting to make himself white? One feels the grotesquerie and self-hatred in this act long before one teases out the literal reason.

Beloved offers countless visual images that readers construct emotionally. "Some new whitefolks with the Look just rode in. The righteous Look every Negro learned to recognize along with his ma'am's tit." Isn't the point here not the image of the Look but the emotion that it reveals? "The Look" is in truth "The Feeling." Much like the novelists we have already studied, moreover, Morrison represents her characters by means of the emotions they feel. As Sethe receives Paul D's gaze, she realizes that "not since Halle had a man looked at her that way: not loving or passionate, but interested, as though he were examining an ear of corn for quality." I find this trope quite visual, as I picture the ear of corn, but the image exists to convey the emotion. I feel not only that emotion strongly, with a flash of understanding and special interest, but the presence of Paul D himself, given life by the emotion.

In such ways *Beloved* raises our awareness of emotion and its place in the mind to a new level. Again and again, Morrison directs the reader's construction of the scene by embodying emotion in a specific detail or naming it abstractly and so requesting the affective code. In the course of the novel, in fact, she forges a distinctive vocabulary for just this purpose. "Something in the house braced, and in the listening quiet that followed Sethe spoke." We know and so must imagine this house *as* that emotion (of bracing and waiting silently). As Baby Suggs says, "Not a house in the county ain't packed to the rafters with some dead Negro's grief."[21] What is provocative is how vivid and complete this construction is, as the affective code creates the illusion of wholeness. Our sense of the house seems precise—or at least its *meaning* is, as we recognize the quiet sense of apprehension. I *have* imagined this house. And in this same way I know the characters, as emotional beings who exist in my mind as emotional constructs. Morrison cites "the unmistakable love call that shimmered around children until they learned better."

Of course an emotion named or evoked in the text does not always require the affective code. The point bears repeating. One can think the idea of an emotion, and no doubt some image-oriented people find ways to visualize the emotion as well. Still, in the heat of reading one cannot intellectualize the scene at the same time that one identifies with the protagonist or narrator. One must feel it. Nor do we have the time to translate emotions into images, even if we could find visual equivalents to all those subtle feelings.

But to return to my point: to Morrison the whole material world is an emotional construct. She equates sensation and emotion, as I say ("The scent of their disapproval lay heavy in the air") and describes even the physical world as the emotion that expresses its meaning: "The weather was warm; the day beautiful. It was April and everything alive was tentative." Dismiss this, if you will, as the pathetic fallacy; in the imagining mind the feeling attributed to the physical world makes it blossom.

Does an examination of the affective code yield insight into this novel? It seems to offer less illumination than a focus on Morrison's tone or the reader's reaction, though it does lead us to Morrison's unique definition of matter. This notion is alien and yet of great interest. Sethe has no Greek gods looking down on her, but she does have a vibrant, spiritualized physical world that charges everything with significance and makes us feel that her unique struggle is somehow metaphysically recognized. *This* is what counts, I think, far more than the ghosts alone, since it shapes every word of Morrison's prose and provides the context within which we interpret the story.

It is significant that this spirituality takes the form of emotion, floating free as a substance in its own right. One could argue that the supernatural aura about *Beloved* refers not to the girl's identity as a ghost but to the palpable, continuing presence of emotion in the world, lingering in the air long after originally felt. Emotion embodies the presence of all who have passed before, remaining in the air. (Sethe calls such feelings "rememories.") In such a world death is not what it seems, but then neither is matter. Because Morrison's universe contains emotion—the emotions left by previous occupants—it *lives*. And that gives the affective code a new and perhaps needed base. If the verbal code has its words on the page, and the visual code has its images in the world, we can now say, of Toni Morrison's novel at any rate, that the affective code has its external correspondent in the emotions that inhabit (and give meaning to) matter.

My original concept had been to write two novellas, to be bound into one volume, which would contrast two approaches to the game of life: one would be the rabbit approach, a kind of dodgy approach—spontaneous, unreflective, frightened, hence my character's name, Angstrom—and the second was to be the horse method of coping with life, to get into harness and pull your load until you drop. And this was eventually "The Centaur."

—John Updike, "Why Rabbit Had to Go"

I can't help suspecting that the odd artsy mythological chapters in the book, which is elsewhere so packed with visual delights, are there . . . to introduce what he called "novelistic space," that feeling, as I understand the term, of having two or more processes going on concurrently among which the reader is shuttled, so that he forgets a little of each process in his exposure to the others, and feels the delight of reacquaintance, and doesn't grow rebellious as quickly.

—Nicholson Baker, *U and I*

16
Imagining *The Centaur:* Fusion and Meaning

JOHN UPDIKE'S *THE CENTAUR,* A MASTERFUL FICTION PUBLISHED IN the early sixties, offers a critical problem suitable to affective criticism. The source of that problem is Updike's portrayal of a double world of classical myth and American culture. The novel offers a protagonist with two distinct identities and takes place simultaneously both on Mt. Olympus and in Alton, Pennsylvania. The protagonist is both the centaur, Chiron, who gives up his immortality to Prometheus, and the high-school teacher, George Caldwell, who devotes his life to supporting his wife and his son. During the three days that car trouble and a snow storm keep George in town, away from his farm home, the novel recounts first the poisoning and then the (largely symbolic) suicide of Chiron and Caldwell.[1]

The simultaneity of these two worlds has made Updike's mythic material a source of controversy. At least a dozen reviewers and critics complain that the mythology is superfluous or confusing. Several believe it makes *The Centaur* a bad book. Still other writers defend the novel's mythology, arguing that it is important to its theme and quality. In *Fighters and Lovers* Joyce Markle claims that the novel "exploits to a greater degree myth's potential for lending significance to reality."[2] In *Rainstorms and Fire: Ritual in John Updike,* Edward P. Vargo argues that the myth involves a ritual search for meaning on the part of the narrator, Peter Caldwell, and that it offers a statement of the unity of heaven and earth, or a world in which the mundane is infused with the divine.

Although I agree with Markle and Vargo, I think that the *idea* of Updike's interpenetrating worlds is less important than the reader's *experience* of it. It is true that the myth makes a thematic point, dramatizing the hidden depths of these many characters, but it operates on the reader's imagination in a specific way, creating the concrete experience that is the special province of the affective code. Can a study of the many emotions in this novel lead to an understanding of Updike's point? Looking variously at subject, tone, reaction, and representation, I will show that affect is necessary to our understanding of this narrative. Like most novels, *The Centaur* finds its meaning in the emotions of the characters, only here those feelings are more complex than usual, since the plot lies in a shift in the emotions of the son, Peter, as well as of George Caldwell himself.

That said, I want also—in this last substantive chapter—to demonstrate how completely *The Centaur* illustrates the need for the affective code. Updike's use of myth provides one more opportunity to glimpse the process by which we construct and display a narrative to ourselves. For in truth *The Centaur* proffers a revealing test of each reader's imagination. Those who find the novel incomprehensible show signs of having imagined it on the visual or intellectual track alone, where it is inevitably disjointed. It is no wonder that they find the novel confusing. Those who praise the novel as Updike's best, on the other hand, seem to have constructed the novel emotionally, which enables them to imagine a coherent whole.[3] In any case, it is clear that the double world of *The Centaur* requires an act of imaginative fusion that is beyond the capability of the visual or ideational codes and so demonstrates the necessity of the affective code. In the following sections I will look first at the characterization of the central character, next at Updike's rather painterly visual images, and then at the plot with its double story, showing that all three levels require the affective code.

I

How are we to judge the protagonist of *The Centaur*, George Caldwell? Because his strength and comic awkwardness are equal to that of Henry Fielding's Parson Adams, George may someday be known as one of the memorable characters in American fiction. Yet George does elicit negative reactions. Early in the novel he carelessly lets a hitchhiker steal the expensive gloves that his son, Peter, had given him for Christmas. Like Peter, the reader is appalled by such carelessness, which Updike assures us is typical of the man. George actually embarrasses his son, who attends the high school where he teaches:

> He had on his overcoat, a tattered checkered castoff with mismatching buttons, which he had rescued from a church sale, though it was too small and barely reached his knees. On his head he wore a hideous blue knitted cap that he had plucked out of a trash barrel at school.[4]

George talks too much, dissipating his authority. He fawns over people, proclaiming his own unworthiness. To Peter and his wife, Cassie, he is a private joke, and to his students he is a public one. Peter is especially embarrassed by George's habit of engaging strangers in personal conversation—George needs approval too desperately to be an attractive character.

Just when we give up on George, however, Updike imbues him with stature. Peter loves George and so does Cassie. Others love him too, including his students and most significantly, his friends, Al and Vera Hummel. Though George "claimed never to learn or remember anything," Peter tells us, he "could read at a terrific speed." George is full of energy, alert to the world and fascinated by it. More than that, he is funny: when a student tells him " 'I like you. All the kids like you,' " George replies, " 'That's my trouble, Deifendorf. . . . I don't *want* you to like me. . . . I want you to be stiff with fear.' " Years later Peter in his New York loft tells his mistress, "I miss only . . . the sudden white laughter that [was] like heat lightning bursts in an atmosphere where souls are trying to serve the impossible. My father for all his mourning moved in the atmosphere of such laughter."

Such contradictions make George Caldwell a good illustration of the skill it takes to read realistic fiction. Like many realists, Updike qualifies his point so strenuously that he obscures it. All of his novels, Updike confesses, say "Yes, but. . . . Yes, in *The Centaur*, to self-sacrifice and duty, but—what of a man's private agony and dwindling?"[5] Having set up George as a bumbler, Updike provides a foundation for respect, creating the shift in reader reaction that forms the real story. George talks too much because he fears he is about to die of cancer. His father died close to the age George is now. George has also seen his horizons shrink. He is alienated from the people of Olinger, to whom he will always be an outsider, and he cannot quit the teaching that makes him sick because he has a mortgage and Peter's impending college education to pay off.

Facts like these make *The Centaur* a study of a person trapped within the role assigned by society to his gender. It is a portrait of the old-fashioned family provider.[6] In a three-day span George endures a toothache, a disabled car, a conflict with his boss (whom he has caught committing theft and adultery), and a paralyzing snowstorm—all on top of the pain he fears is fatal. Yet he does not succumb to depression or bad temper. George suffers all right (he is no fool), but he is courageous and intelligent. He does not snap at his son or blame his wife, who had insisted on the farm, or express bitterness about the high school and its tyrannical principal. Out of love for his family George is willing, as Updike put it in an interview, "to get into harness and pull your load until you drop."[7]

I should add that George is also a superb teacher who speaks to his class with humor and narrative drive. He can make science live because he understands his students, though his insight makes their inattention to his words painful. A master of classroom presentation (even though he has trouble keeping order), George is also compassionate in individual conferences, aware of the difficult lives awaiting these young people.

As one might expect, we know George by the tone of his voice. "He worried about the kid, when he had the time." If George is anxious, embodying the fear of the late Truman era (as Updike has said), he is also breezy—his "when he had the time" reveals all. He has something self-dramatizing about him, as though he were burlesquing his role, which means that his speech takes back what it gives, working off his frustration and anger. George is conflicted, confiding in people even as he pushes them away, a private man who negotiates his health in public. He is both a fool—"that silly sad man," Peter calls him—and a hero.

How can we as readers imagine such a character? Updike describes George as all elbows and angles, which means that we could visualize him as a kind of Icabod Crane. Or we might represent him by the sound of his voice, which indicates the complexity of the man without constructing it in detail. As we have seen several times, we cannot really visualize or verbalize such complexity. We must instead feel the presence of the character. We can visualize or intellectualize parts of George, but the personality that is the whole person requires feeling.

Thus we imagine a complex character by feeling his identity. But note how much more difficult the construction becomes if the character is not only an American high-school teacher but a centaur—a famous centaur, in fact, or Chiron, the teacher of the gods. Although the linear nature of prose requires Updike to offer first George and then Chiron, Updike finds a way to make us imagine George and Chiron at the same instant, within the same being. We witness this point in the opening scene of the novel, when "Caldwell turned and as he turned his ankle received an arrow." The tone is realistic, but the event is fantastic, since high-school teachers do not usually get shot with arrows. We do not know it yet, but the Caldwell who turns is also Chiron, who (as the myth goes) has received a poisoned arrow at a wedding feast.

In pain, George flees from the classroom into a hallway. But something is odd. George thinks of a fellow teacher as "Pholos." He tries "to keep that leg from touching the floor"—not the act of a two-legged creature. And then, Updike writes, "the jagged clatter of the three remaining hooves sounded so loud he was afraid one of the doors would snap open." George is suddenly part horse, depositing a horse apple "on the glimmering varnished boards" of the hallway.

Such sudden shifts teach us how to read this prose, forcing us to compress the two identities into a single being. When George/Chiron seeks medical aid from his friend Al Hummel, the blacksmith/auto mechanic works on the hoof of a horse ("Ronnie, could you get me a soaking wet rag?") and the foot of a person ("carefully holding Caldwell's pants leg up from the wound"). Are we capable of imagining such an act? We *can* visualize a creature half-horse and half-man, since that is the nature of the centaur. But how visualize a centaur who is also a full human being? Literally speaking, I suppose, such a creature would be three-quarters man and one quarter horse. Yet that is absurd. Updike forces us to imagine the two identities as one, but it is not a task we can perform visually. Nor do we have a single idea that unites a high-school teacher and a centaur, let alone a small town and a sacred mountain.

We *can* evade such difficulty. Call the centaur "George/Chiron" and you have labeled him, using a word or idea to gloss over the specifics. Updike really does leave the matter open. Or put George's head on the centaur's trunk, making him only a centaur, and you have solved the problem well enough to get on with your reading. It might be that our feeling of the creature is vague enough to represent him without constructing him in detail, which would be good enough, since the personality is what counts. For some readers, of course, the shift from man to centaur breaks their emotional engage-

ment with the text and so defamiliarizes the character, making him
an object of thought. Some readers feel one of the two identities as
dominant, including the other as an auxiliary feeling tone. They
imagine a high-school teacher who is "horsy," say, or a centaur with
the manner of an American high-school teacher. I find that I can
visualize the horse but not the personality.

But while such evasion permits one to read, it damages the quality
of the imagined novel. Ultimately one must employ the affective
code, which is available to all readers and permits a fusion of the two
identities. Feel George as one emotion and Chiron as another and
you can fuse the two feelings within a single, comprehensive emotion: the feeling of George as Chiron. Feel the *relationship* of man and
centaur, moreover, and you can represent the character by the feeling of that relationship, especially since a horselike awkwardness is
part of George's problem. In either case, the affective code permits
an efficient and concrete representation of the complex being.[8] Of
course, George would have the same voice and so the same set of
emotions and desires whatever his appearance. To represent him
emotionally is to represent him from the inside, where he is the same
person no matter how many legs he may have. We have only to feel
the personality. The person George steps high like the stallion, providing an image, while the centaur Chiron chatters like the person,
providing an emotion.

II

One could argue, then, that Updike requires the reader to use the
affective code. This point is significant because Updike seems to
emphasize the visual. Peter Caldwell, who in later life becomes a
painter—what he calls a "second rate expressionist"—always notes
the look of things, using the visual as his metaphor for thought.
When he had driven as a boy with his father about the countryside,
he says, "my hand twitched, as if a brush were in it." Starting an
engine, he and his father had "listened so intently that a common
picture seemed crystallized between our heads." And now, he says, as
he remembers the three days that comprise the novel, "I can still see
everything."

This emphasis on the visual gives *The Centaur* a painterly quality.
Here is Peter describing his father marching off to school at the end
of the book:

> I turned my face away and looked through the window. In time my father
> appeared in this window, an erect figure dark against the snow. His pos-

ture made no concession to the pull underfoot; upright he waded out through our yard and past the mailbox and up the hill until he was lost to my sight behind the trees of our orchard. The trees took white on their sun side. Two telephone wires diagonally cut the blank blue of the sky. The stone bare wall was a scumble of umber; my father's footsteps thumbs of white in white. (217–18)

Peter catches the play of light and color and line and form—he sees the wires and the stone wall less as meaning than as shape, lines across blue and a "scumble" (a thin overlay) of opaque color. Like Vermeer, whom he admires, Peter describes a scene in which the deep quiet makes time appear to stand still. Again like Vermeer, Peter paints with planes of color: the figure is dark and the snow is white; the trees consist of two planes, one white in the sun, the other dark in the shade. The sky is a blank blue cut by the black wires. In effect Updike offers a scene barren and powerful in its contrasts, and then a hint of delicate color—the "thumbs of white in white," and the "scumble of umber," or the brownish-colored rock washed lightly across the scene.

Thus Updike, who studied painting at the Ruskin School in Oxford, offers his novel to the visual track (or code) of the reader. His bias reminds us of Ernest Hemingway's study of Cezanne and Henry James's equation of paint and print, not to mention the many readers who swear they visualize the text. In their eyes, Updike in this text skillfully embodies the techniques of the painter.[9]

When we look at the matter more closely, however, we discover that even here, on the visual level, emotion dominates our construction of the text. Updike supplements the image, for example, with meaning expressed as emotion, in this case evoked by the contrast of this final walk with the opening one. In George's first walk Updike uses terms that are lush, busy, and complex. The wounded George suffers a pain with "wet wings" and is "heavily sunk in a swamp."[10] But in the concluding walk of the novel, the first part of which I just cited, George rises from the swamp into "a starry firmament." The final walk is a triumphant march, as George becomes Chiron on his way to becoming Sagittarius, freed of his pain and his responsibility and the awful ambiguities of his position. Having suffered as a half-beast, George now enters a plane of pure form that we feel by virtue of the silence and light and absence of color.

What is visual thus takes its meaning from the emotion that it evokes. But Updike goes further to actually represent the scene by emotion, as we can see in another set of parallel scenes. Early in the novel, Peter awakens in his bed to *feel* his parents talking about a momentous subject. "I could not make out its form," he says, "only feel within myself . . . its restless weight of dread." Peter feels "an invisible membranous tension spread through the house," perhaps because Pop Kramer is "throwing an atmosphere." In contrast, Peter later awakes in the Hummel guest room, wondering "what event had spread through the house this aftermath of peaceful, reconciled radiance."

In such parallel passages Updike gives the scene by naming emotions, encouraging us to construct it as the meaning expressed by the emotion. Thus Updike requires the reader to employ the affective code. And he does even more, returning us to the radical hypothesis I proffered in chapter 8. *The Centaur* suggests that the mind employs emotion to represent even the image itself. In Peter's description I *feel* the black line cutting the sky. I *feel* the black figure crossing the white field. When Updike writes that "his posture made no concession to the pull underfoot," I can see a straight back, with the feet lifting high in the snow, but even more, I feel the squared shoulders and the pull of the snow. A few minutes after reading the passage, moreover, I represent the scene as not an image, which has faded, but the emotion, or the feeling of this man trudging through a barren landscape. Or more accurately, I feel the son behind a window watching his father trudge through the snow.[11]

III

The plot of *The Centaur* is not perfect. Updike is inconsistent in his use of myth, turning to it only when it suits him. We don't know how much Peter knows about his father's identity or whether—since Peter sometimes seems to know that he is Prometheus—George Caldwell knows that he is Chiron. And such uncertainties seem to spill over into the plot of *The Centaur* as a whole. During the three days that George is trapped in town, he teaches his class, coaches the swimming team, visits the doctor, and collects tickets at a high-school basketball game. Peter, who is usually (but not always) the narrator, goes to a movie, has lunch in a local teenage dive, and accepts the ministrations of his father. What point ties these several events together? Not a few reviewers and critics complain of confusion. How do these events relate to the mythic material?

The answer lies in the precise fit Updike crafts between the mythic and the "real" levels of the story—a fit revealed by a focus on emotion. For the two worlds use their different idioms to tell essentially the same tale, which is George/Chiron's achievement of peace. Updike establishes the parallel between the two main characters first of all in Peter's personal experience. As Peter slides through these three days in town, he has a recurring feeling that his father and the other Alton adults have a second existence or identity. The world seems exotic and grand to him, as though it were ancient Greece. "I was haunted at that age by the suspicion that a wholly different world, gaudy and momentous, was enacting its myths just around the corners of my eyes." As Updike himself later put it, Peter feels that "the people we meet are *guises,* do conceal something mythic, perhaps prototypes or longings in our mind."[12] Peter finds that his father has a second identity.

Peter regards such feelings as we all do: they are "just feelings," not to be taken seriously. But as Updike makes clear, Peter's feeling of his father's duality is true. Because George really is Chiron, Peter is not deluded—the feeling represents what the novel proclaims to be fact.[13] Peter has yet to learn that his feelings can carry information in the form of an affective code.

Updike reinforces this duality of character by structuring the novel as a series of parallels. George opens and closes the novel with a walk, as we have just seen, and Peter begins and ends his appearance in the book by awakening in bed, feeling the emotional climate of the house. Updike's epigraph of a Karl Barth quote, contrasting heaven and earth, finds substance in symmetrical dualities like Minor's malt shop and its twin, the post office.[14]

And even the actions have a dual existence. In the classroom, Zimmerman's molestation of the student Iris Osgood belongs to both myth, where the sex actually happens, and "reality," where it remains only desire. By offering two parallel versions of the same event, Updike can have fun with the contrast between decorum and desire, or what we present to the world and what we actually feel. Ironically, perhaps, the imaginary world of myth presents our uninhibited or "real" selves, while the ordinary world presents our controlled and so "falsified" selves. As Updike puts it, the novel is "a kind of a gag," permitting him to play with not only language but the uncertainties of identity and perception.[15]

The best example of this duality of plot, and of Updike's skill in presenting it, is the parallel between George's relationships with the goddess Venus and the gym teacher Vera Hummel, who are the same character. In their different idioms, Venus in the locker room (in part one) and Vera in the kitchen (in part eight) enact the same story. In the high-school locker room, where George comes upon Venus emerging from the shower, the goddess stands naked before Chiron and proposes sex. George is a stallion. In Vera's kitchen, in a scene that is, as Peter says, "the strangest of all the strange things I have told," the housewife reveals her attraction to George. She has eyes only for him, laughing at whatever he says. When George kisses Vera goodbye on the cheek, Peter is shocked to see Vera's feet rise "up on their toes as she willingly received the kiss."

The goddess in the locker room asks to be mounted; the housewife in the kitchen rises on her toes. What is broad and violent in the goddess is quiet and suggestive in the PE instructor, and quite a bit more moving.[16] We could argue that the two encounters involve two different emotions—lust and tenderness, say—or that Updike is dramatizing the ultimate mix of all feelings. And yet within the tone and circumstance of their given style, Venus and Vera, who are the same character, dramatize the same basic point. Both find George attractive, a fact that has a significant effect on Peter's attitude toward his dad. In the kitchen Peter learns that Vera, the most glamorous woman in the high school (a virtual goddess), *likes* his father. George effortlessly succeeds in the realm where the boy (as Peter confesses) has to struggle.

IV

Just as the two characters fuse to provide a single protagonist, then, so their actions fuse to form a single plot. For this reason, the true story of *The Centaur* lies within Updike's dual reference: the literal and the mythical levels in this novel are not only complements or contrasts, as various critics have claimed, but *duplicates,* covering the same psychological ground. The character Chiron/George rises in the esteem of both Peter and the gods. It is true, of course, that the two realms, Olympus, Greece, and Alton, Pennsylvania, have little in common. The mythic passages are lyrical, allusive, and extreme, incorporating (like the gods themselves) both the majestic and the vulgar. The realistic passages are quiet, understated, and topical, finding poetic force not in the use of language for its own sake (as in Updike's prose poems about ancient Greece) but in the breathtakingly fresh detail. On the mythic level, Updike revels in sound and shock; on the realistic level, Updike lovingly records the specific facts and emotions of an era.

How can one imagine these two plots simultaneously? Their difference raises the same question we saw in regard to George's character and Updike's physical description, with one exception: a plot encompasses the whole novel, and so is more complex than a single description or character, presenting the reader with an even more difficult problem in mental construction. And the solution lies once again in the affective code: readers use emotion to construct not only characters and places but actions, fusing the double events within a single, complex feeling. We *feel* George walking. We *feel* Chiron choosing death. We imagine the events of this novel in the same medium as we do the characters, forming a consistent whole. This is especially true because of the dependence of a plot on the relationship of its parts: one imagines a plot by means of the feeling of how one part—one event or character—relates to another.

The best example of this point is the concluding passage of *The Centaur*, which I mentioned earlier. George's final walk through the snow is the climax of the novel, as George and Chiron reach their heart's desire, though it has also been the source of some confusion. I just said that Chiron at the end walks to his death and immortality, propelled by Zeus into the heavens as the constellation Sagittarius. In these same sentences George Caldwell walks to his stranded car, in order to return to his duties at school, and in doing so "dies" himself, in the sense that he now gives up any hope for a life of his own. (He most decidedly does *not* have a heart attack, as one critic suggests.)[17] On this final morning, as he returns to the job he dislikes, he accepts the loss of himself, and in doing so, as Updike puts it, "discovered that in giving his life to others he entered a total freedom."

George gains freedom because he need no longer worry about his private dreams, or struggle to assert his *self*—one source of his anxiety. Like Chiron, George can in this way "die" and yet live, freed from ego. He loses his private pain (as Peter later understands) and so triumphs.[18] And he serves others. Clearly he is freed from resentment and regret, receiving like Chiron the reward of personal peace. Once again Updike offers a purely human version of the mythical event, providing a second account of triumphant self-sacrifice.

What makes this fusion possible is the psychology (and so the emotion) shared by the two characters. While Chiron yearns for the death that will end his pain, George, too, feels a desire for death, trapped as he is in a job that makes his stomach ache. While Chiron sacrifices himself for Prometheus, giving the demigod his immortality so that he himself may die, George sacrifices himself for Peter, propelling himself forward biologically. While Chiron finds immortality as a cluster of stars, George will be "immortalized" in Peter's words (which are the novel) and perhaps in a future painting—and certainly in his new-found freedom from the demands of self.

Thus the mythic and the real events find unity in the emotions the two characters feel. Track the feelings and you will identify the parallel, as both characters progress from pain to peace. You will understand that the two characters are the same individual. And you will

perceive the change in Peter's emotions, for he moves from an embarrassed love for his nerdish father to an admiration of the man's
substance: Vera's revelation of her affection for George makes Peter
see him with new eyes.

By the end, moreover, George has risen in the esteem of the gods
themselves—not unlike the novel itself, I would add, which has risen
in the estimation of the reader. For whatever we may think of George
and his double identity, we must recognize the purely aesthetic
power of that duality—to those who imagine the novel successfully.[19]
We have many terms to describe the kind of doubleness Updike
offers: ambiguity, tension, twinning, dialectic, chiaroscuro, binary. To
Samuel Coleridge the fusion of disparate elements defines the basic
function of the imagination. To the structuralists, the binary is the
basic structure of thought. But in all of these theories, the point is the
quality of the reader's experience, and most specifically the vitality or
intensity that such duality creates in the reader's mental construction
of the text.[20] George the man is memorable, but George as Chiron
the centaur is even more so, since his double identity gives him the
power and scope of a great fictional character. Because they are so
similar, Chiron adds immediacy to the portrait of George, giving the
modest high-school teacher the weight of ancient myth, while
George gives Chiron roots in the quotidian. The result is a world that
is not only enriched, enjoying the illusions created by its Riffaterrian
internal reference, but vitally dimensional, with all kinds of depths
and shadows.

V

In such ways a focus on emotion illuminates the relation of the two
story tracks, revealing the point of the story by examining our mental
representation of it. But a focus on the other functions of emotion
within the text also sheds light on the novel—and so illustrates an
affective criticism. Updike portrays several emotions, for example,
that make interesting subjects: the sense of a dual existence and a
teenager's yearning for intimacy; a wife's sweet-sour love for her
husband and a worker's fear of his boss; a woman's fondness for a
man and the American's often typical overfamiliarity with strangers.
And then the novel finds a subject in the emotional strategies of the
characters, as in George's remarkable emotional openness. It gets
him in trouble, since he is "uncool," but it keeps him alive as well,
permitting him to work through his frustrations.[21]

When we focus on Updike's tone, we find that it defines his meaning, since it expresses his view of reality as mixed. Updike celebrates George's strength, but he leaves him in his knit hat and absurdly short coat. As Updike says in his *Paris Review* interview, "Yes," he appreciates George's virtue, "but" what about the devastating personal loss it entails? Like Toni Morrison, Updike makes tone palpable, as in Peter's sense of the emotion that fills the house. And then one could argue that Updike's ultimate purpose in this novel is to capture the feeling or tone of an era. Calling *The Centaur* his "Truman book," Updike explains that "the atmosphere of fright permeating *The Centaur* is to an indicated extent early cold-war nerves."[22]

If Updike gets his subject and tone right, of course, readers will react pretty much as he desires. And in this regard Updike accomplishes one of the most difficult feats in narrative: he makes a genuinely good character interesting. It is the comparison of one's own reaction with that expected by the author, moreover, that is the foundation of literary criticism.[23] Monitor Peter's mixed attitude toward his dad, trying to sort out his contradictory feelings, and you will place yourself at the center of Updike's tale. Compare that with your own reaction to George, and you will have an evaluation of Updike's success in characterizing him.

And finally, a focus on emotion can also serve other critical approaches. The feelings of George and Peter, for example, are precisely what their society has taught them: examine those feelings and you examine social construction. Such emotions are of particular interest to gender studies, as I have suggested, since they illustrate socially shaped gender roles. The portrait of George is a classic study of the traditional family provider. It is significant that George recognizes the strength and frustration of Cassie, acknowledging the career she gave up for him.[24] It is also significant that Cassie seems stronger than George, as though the two characters would give the lie to their stereotypes. One can imagine Cassie in a career and the nurturing George happy as a homemaker.

As for the deconstructionists, out of fashion as they have become, we should note that the emotions expressed in this book qualify its overt statement. While the novel celebrates George and his sense of responsibility, it evokes emotions that undermine that celebration. It is a wonderful thing for George to be freed of ego in his final walk, but he is returning, after all, to the job that is killing him. To be "frozen" *is* a form of death, as Updike makes clear, and so we feel the death of George's self.

A foolish German had said that man thought in words. It was totally false; a pernicious doctrine; the thought flashed into being in a hundred simultaneous forms, with a thousand associations, and the speaking mind selected one, forming it grossly into the inadequate symbols of words. . . .

—Patrick O'Brian, *Post Captain*

17
Conclusion

WHAT IS *The Centaur* to us after we have read it? How do we represent the novel as a whole? Because reading consists of constructing ever larger totalities, one's construction of the completed experience is the reader's ultimate imaginative act. It offers an opportunity to examine the way the three codes combine.

We can expect different people to represent *The Centaur* in different ways. Some will verbalize the experience, as we have seen, labeling all that they imagine and feel as "*The Centaur*." Others will represent the novel by another kind of idea, such as "John Updike's most lighthearted book," which they may or may not put into words. The visualizers among us will undoubtedly employ synecdoche, letting an image of some part of the novel (or the novel's cover) represent the whole. I sometimes think of *The Centaur* as the image of Chiron's hooves on the polished floor of the high-school hallway—an initial, striking image that has stayed with me.[1]

And still other readers, as I have now shown, will represent their reading experience by means of a feeling. Such comprehensive feelings are often fused, incorporating within them the emotions that correspond to several specific elements, including meaning and texture—and idea and image. My own feeling of *The Centaur* includes a sense of not only characters like Peter or George but of experiences like George's final, liberating walk through the snow, in which I feel the largely visual event.[2]

What dictates the code the reader uses at any particular point? In chapter 8 I identified five factors: the disposition of the reader, the code required by the previous paragraph, the nature of the content, the stage of the reading process, and the purpose of the construction. These last two, which overlap, may be the most important, since a passing reference to a book differs greatly from a reconstruction of it. In a literary history, after all, one can represent a novel by its title. But during the extended act of reading, one uses all three codes, constructing abstract ideas, physical objects and (affective) meaning. One must represent not only the various objects in the text (ranging from people to the weather) but the relationships among them and the experience that such relationships provide. One needs as much fluidity—and as broad a range—as possible, requiring not only the unique capabilities of all three codes but the different combinations among them.

How do I *now* construct my memory of the novels we have studied? What is striking is how flexible and opportunistic my imagination is, as it employs whatever code or combination of codes fits the circumstance. I think of *Pride and Prejudice* as a feeling of order and clarity, for example, since that is the special quality of the novel, and so employ the affective code alone, as I have said I do in the case of *The Centaur.* But when I turn to *Beloved,* my basically affective representation is accompanied by a shadowy *image* of the title character. Though I can't make it out, I know that I am visualizing—and that the image is necessary to the feeling. The flickering likeness generates a feeling of indeterminacy, which supports Morrison's point about the character: what I feel defines the meaning of the image, and so works in tandem with it. The image and the emotion in this case are not only complementary to one another but equal.

Image and affect also intermingle in my summarizing construction of *The Portrait of a Lady:* for all of my discussion of representational feeling in that novel, I think of the *Portrait* as a shadowy image of its protagonist. True, Isabel is a feeling of her presence, but she is also a vague, willowy figure in a dark dress surrounded by space. Both the feeling and the image are integral to the other. The image that I imagine is unsubstantial, consisting of light and shadow, and intermingles with the feeling, which is substantial indeed.

The experiential nature of image and feeling makes me form my *idea* of the novel after I have already experienced the other two. But even the original image and feeling are permeated by ideas. I visualize Isabel, for example, as a victim. The idea informs the image, just as the idea of slavery (or of the supernatural) informs my construction of Beloved. In the case of *Adventures of Huckleberry Finn,* I become Huck emotionally, as he sits on the sandy river bottom, and I visualize what he sees. But both the feeling and the imagery include the idea that Huck has just escaped the feud. This idea might take the form of a feeling, of course, and for some of us usually does.[3]

Yet it is also true that some levels of representation require a single code after all. For with the passage of time, the pressures of economy require us to summarize even our most complex mental constructions with a single stroke, which means a single code. And in theory, as we have seen, that code can be any one of the three. Because almost any idea can find expression as an image or a feeling, and almost any feeling can be represented by an image or a set of words, the three codes are roughly interchangeable. Both Paivio and Kosslyn agree on that.

Nevertheless, the capacity of the affective code to distill large amounts of meaning within a single emotion makes it especially efficient in representing the whole. When the thought of *Beloved* flickers through my mind, dominated as it might be by the image of the title character, I am likely to represent the novel as not the image, which takes time to construct, but the feeling of the image, which is instantaneous. That feeling can include all of the other emotions that make up the experience and that have fused to express its meaning. Thus I feel the significance of the book—to me and to others— and that provides a highly effective representation.

For this reason the affective code plays a dominant role in mental construction. Its capacity to distill the whole in a flash of consciousness makes it an almost ideal form of representation, as does its capability to be meaningful, comprehensive, and concrete. And that returns me to an issue I mentioned earlier. Is it possible that my description of the affective code is too modest? Could the affective code be not just one code among three, but the basic code underlying the other two—the "mentalese" that is the cognitive scientist's holy grail?

As the philosopher Michael Tye defines the word, first used by the psychologist Zenon Pylyshyn, "mentalese" is

> an inner language within which mental representation, whatever its stripe, is confined. This inner language is largely unconscious and is not itself a natural public language, although it is translated into such a language when we talk.[4]

Affect fits this description. It is indeed an inner, largely unconscious representation that translates from a private into a public language. And it conforms to Pylyshyn's model in two other ways.[5] It supplies a context for images and ideas, first of all, providing them with a base: I imagine the ideas and images of Updike's novel *within* Peter's feeling of a mysterious duality, employing emotion as the medium within which the other two codes float. And then, from another perspective, I feel my images and my ideas much as I feel my feelings—not a few thinkers claim that thought begins with inner feelings. Emotion really could be the elemental medium, or the basic stuff of all thought.[6]

I know that what I privately call an image is often a feeling. My images are dim and illusory at best, as I have said, and so subordinate to the meaning embodied in the feeling. In truth, only emotion is flexible enough to serve as the common denominator of all three codes, binding the disparate elements of our experience (real or vicarious) into a single whole. Only emotion is comprehensive enough to embody a complete, concrete whole—in a single flash of feeling that expresses the essence of the subject.[7] How often do we grope for the words that express the feeling? I have no doubt that we mentally construct some of the narrative text in the form of emotion and that such affect carries factual data within it. At some point, $e = mc^2$ might well have been a feeling.

Could emotion provide the mind with its basic code or language, then? Such a phenomenon would reconcile the theories of Stephen Kosslyn and Allan Paivio, defining a single, basic mode that employs image or idea as its surface appearance. Paivio would be correct in keeping the codes separate, and Kosslyn would be correct in describing their permanent availability.[8] The notion is highly attractive.

But even now, after examining these several novels, I find that three more or less parallel codes (however they may fuse) makes the most sense. I have, after all, treated the three codes as separate because I experience them that way. It is hard to think of them as different facets of a single mode. Each code represents a particular kind of meaning and so has a separate—and necessary—identity.

That is to say that the affective code, like the other two, is specialized. It may represent the presence of the object and its meaning; it may represent the whole better than any other code; but it does not offer a literal, public duplication of the object in the same way that image or language can do. Word by word and phrase by phrase, emotion represents what we already know as word or image or living experience. I can feel Huck's river because Twain describes it in the text (or names it, calling upon my knowledge of the actual river). My feeling provides a shorthand for the previously represented fact.

Although the affective code achieves a kind of precision, then, it is one quite different from that of mathematics or drawing. Never mind that all three codes are referential by definition, since they construct what is already on the page or in the memory. The leap from the private, felt precision of the affective code to the public representation of a body of individual facts is too great. The mathematician may feel the numerical value, as some have told me, but he writes down the number. Emotion excels, in fact, in the representation of the indeterminate, offering, as in Johnson-Laird's example, a feeling of not each one of the two hundred people, but the general crowd. Emotion gives a sense of the immense or complicated subject without bogging down in specifics. More importantly, it expresses meaning, conveying the significance that controls and shapes the description of the event. And, though I have not proved it, emotion probably serves as the primary "marker" of our memories, making access to them possible—a role of immense significance. Clearly emotion is too important, too necessary in itself, to function as "mentalese."

For such reasons, then, let us claim only that the affective code is an equal partner to the codes of image and idea. To recognize that fact is alone a momentous step, requiring a revision in our model of the mind and so a change in almost all areas of thought—a shift that amounts to nothing less than a new definition of ourselves.

And yet, if I may offer one last qualification, the affective code is not just one of three codes but the first among equals. We often feel emotion without ideas or images, but we seldom have ideas or images without emotion. And the content expressed by the affective code may be more significant than any other—I would argue that the mental states and complex relationships that we know as feelings lie at the center of human experience. In many cases the significance of the object is more important than the object itself.

Once I have mentally constructed the text, moreover, and have reacted to it, I react to my reaction. That means that I complete the act of representing with a feeling of some kind—the emotions that I feel in reaction are pleasant or ugly, attractive or unattractive, boring or stimulating. Such subsequent emotions serve as a judgment of the original experience and so a convenient representation of its significance, which may in turn yield yet another emotional reaction. In this way I come away from my construction of each of these five novels with an emotion that supplies a convenient representation. The affective code trumps the other two codes, resonating in the mind long after the mental idea or image has faded.

Notes

CHAPTER 1. IMAGINING THE TEXT

1. Malcolm Cowley, "Nightmare and Ritual in Hemingway," in *Hemingway: A Collection of Critical Essays*, ed. Robert P. Weeks (Englewood Cliffs, N.J.: Prentice-Hall, 1962), 41.

The passage from Ernest Hemingway is *In Our Time* (New York: Charles Scribner's Sons, 1925), 140. Hemingway's language is vivid because it motivates the reader to both expend energy and imagine in a particular way, in this case sensuously. Readers have to *complete* Hemingway's meaning, and then have to do something even more difficult than that.

2. Hundreds of writers have pondered the imagination. One of the most complete treatments of reading fiction is Richard J. Gerrig's *Experiencing Narrative Worlds*, in which Gerrig calls the act of imaginative construction "performance." I investigate the dominant theories of mental representation in chapters 3 and 4.

3. Hemingway studied Chekhov's use of detail. For analysis of Hemingway's style, see such critics as Earl Rovit, Arthur Waldhorn, Harry Levin, Joseph Flora, Emily Watts, Robert Scholes (in *Semiotics*), Raymond Nelson, and Philip Young.

4. We feel the full weight of each of the objects and actions Hemingway names. In case the reader should miss these sensations, Hemingway repeats his key words, in this single passage using "apricot" five times and "remember" three.

5. Jane Austen, *Pride and Prejudice* (London: Penguin, 1972), 116.

6. Although Nick Adams appears in other stories in this volume, Hemingway describes him only once, in "Cross-Country Snow," where he has a "big back and blonde head." See *In Our Time*, 108.

7. Immanuel Kant, among others, held this view. I find these points discussed in Antonio Damasio, *Descartes' Error* (New York: Putnam, 1994); Victor Nell, *Lost in a Book: The Psychology of Reading for Pleasure* (New Haven: Yale University Press, 1988); and Josef Perner, *Understanding the Representational Mind* (Cambridge: MIT Press, 1991). Even dreaming of a subject lights up the same area of the brain as the waking experience of it.

In *Bright Air, Brilliant Fire* (New York: Basic Books, 1992), Gerald Edelman explains the mental construction of memory as the firing of neurons grouped within patterns: to remember is to fire patterns of synapses similar (though not identical) to those of the original experience.

8. Anton Chekhov, in *Chekhov: The Major Plays*, trans. Ann Dunnigan (New York: Signet Classics, 1964), 164. Mary Warnock elaborates upon this point in *Imagination*, showing that the imagination plays an active role in daily perception. In regard to each detail, readers imagine not separate sensations like light and shadow but the whole object. In regard to the total scene, readers imagine not separate details but the whole spectacle.

For further discussion of Chekhov's comment, see Michael Irwin's *Picturing* (London: George Allen, 1979).

9. Ned Block, *Imagery* (Cambridge: MIT Press, 1981), 4. The psychologist Allan Paivio would probably agree, since he had to survey thousands of psychological experiments in order to form his comprehensive theory of thinking. See his *Mental Representations* (New York: Oxford University Press, 1986). Nor can we know anything on this subject with certainty. As Eva Brann says, "It is that one cannot in principle know one's mind, because it is a covert operation, ultimately a brain function, of which subjective experience is a kind of insubstantial effluvium or vaporous facade to be penetrated by the observer on the way to the scientific object" (*The World of the Imagination* [Lanham, Md.: Rowman and Littlefield, 1991], 233).

10. The mental construction of meaning lies close to what is still the mystery of consciousness. How *do* thoughts arise in the mind? If David Hume was correct in saying that all mental experience is based on the re-presentation of original experience, then the imaginative reconstruction of a text could provide the key to all thought.

11. See David Bleich's *Subjective Criticism* (Baltimore: Johns Hopkins University Press, 1978), 65, and Wolfgang Iser's *The Act of Reading* (Baltimore: Johns Hopkins University Press, 1978), 120. Reader-response critics like Hans Robert Jauss, Michael Riffaterre, Jonathan Culler, and Stanley Fish identify and analyze a blizzard of variables influencing the reader's mental representation of the text.

12. Robert Scholes, *Semiotics and Interpretation* (New Haven: Yale University Press, 1982), 113, 112. Scholes also speaks of "the process by which a perceiver actively constructs a story from the fictional data provided by any narrative medium" (*Semiotics,* 60). In book 9 of *The Republic* Plato says that diegesis, in which the author speaks as himself, is superior to mimesis, which entails taking on the identity of another person (392c–395). Plato worries about the emotion involved in mimesis and the "dishonesty" of imaginatively becoming someone else. As Scholes puts it, to act in a play is mimetic, since one becomes the character; to read a play is diegetic, since one remains as oneself.

CHAPTER 2. THE MENTAL DISPLAY OF MEANING

1. Brann, *World of the Imagination,* 643.

2. In *The Language of Thought* (New York: Thomas Y. Crowell, 1975), philosopher Jerry Fodor argues that representation requires a basic mental language. He wants to show that the human mind is computational.

3. John Searle, "The Mystery of Mind," *New York Review of Books,* 42 (November 16, 1995), 58.

4. As Jane Tompkins puts it, paraphrasing Norman Holland, "People deal with literary texts the same way they deal with life experience" (*Reader-Response Criticism* [Baltimore: Johns Hopkins University Press, 1980], xix). To imagine a tree is to use much the same process as to see a tree. Reading is a new application of an old human capacity—to construct mental models.

5. Stephen M. Kosslyn, *Ghosts in the Mind's Machine* (New York: Norton, 1983), 71. Brann, *World of the Imagination,* 236.

6. I should emphasize that I'm talking about a formal, often conscious, display of meaning. This is different from the unconscious mental models posited by thinkers like Josef Perner or Gerald Edelman, who understand that the mind perceives in the context of defining models. In view of my argument in chapter 13, it is significant that Edelman defines consciousness as the relationship between patterns of the

brain, the comparison taking place so deeply that we are never conscious of it (*Bright Air*, 119).

7. The philosopher Michael Tye would agree. When he feels that he is visualizing, he says, at the same time that his friend is verbalizing, both men know the kind of experience they are having. "I am introspectively aware that I am undergoing a *visual experience* with a certain content, whereas Albert is introspectively aware that he is undergoing *thoughts* with that content" (*The Imagery Debate* [Cambridge: MIT Press, 1992], 124).

8. The philosopher R. G. Collingwood, among others, equates the power to imagine with the power to construct memory. See *Principles of Art* (London: Oxford University Press, 1938), 150. Susanne Langer says the defining mode of fiction is memory (*Feeling and Form* [New York: Scribner's, 1953], 264).

9. If primary representation reflects what is actual, or "caused" by the senses, Perner says, then secondary representation reveals what an object "could be." It is a re-*re*-presentation, having been translated by the mind at least twice, and so includes interpretation, elaboration, speculation, analysis, and revision (*Understanding*, 6–7).

10. Of course, the diegetic display is complicated. The display I experience as I read may be different than the more formal and willed construction of my later memory of it. See chapter 8.

11. Among the early discussions of empathy are those of Wilhelm Dilthey and Theodor Lipps, who coined the German term *Einfuhlung*, or empathy. Lipps believed we identify with objects as well as people. Note that identification does not guarantee sympathy: as Noël Carroll points out, the reader's concerns may differ from those of the protagonist (Hjort and Laver, eds., *Emotion and the Arts* [Oxford: Oxford University Press, 1997], 206).

12. Georges Poulet, "Criticism and the Experience of Interiority," in *The Structuralist Controversy: The Languages of Criticism and the Sciences of Man,* ed. Richard A. Macksey and Eugenio Donato (Baltimore: Johns Hopkins University Press, 1972), 56–72.

13. Feagin cites as her source for simulation theory the philosophers Moran, Gordon, Goldman, and Ripstein. I should add that the philosopher David Novitz makes a similar point in *Knowledge, Fiction, and Imagination* (Philadelphia: Temple University Press, 1987). In an earlier essay, "Imagining Emotions and Appreciating Fiction," Feagin argues that the empathetic reader imagines feeling emotions, recognizing the mental patterns associated with real feeling (in *Canadian Journal of Philosophy* 18 no. 3 [September 1988]: 485–500).

14. In this way, readers vicariously experience events they only simulate, feeling real emotions within situational models. They simulate the state of mind of a character without adopting the beliefs of that character, even temporarily.

Feagin also believes that empathy provides knowledge by placing the knower *inside* of that which is to be known. Robert Yanal offers a thorough examination of this problem in his recently published *Paradoxes of Emotion and Fiction* (University Park: Pennsylvania State University Press, 1999).

15. While writers like Hélène Cixous make empathy a defining feminine trait, I would like to repossess it for men. I am sure Cixous's views are true—empathy not only is a defense of the powerless, who are disproportionately female, but is delegated to women by our society. Yet males also identify with other people in the course of their day, even if they are not open about it. As Darwin well knew, the capacity for empathy belongs to all.

16. "It has often struck me as a curious fact that so many shades of expression are instantly recognized without any conscious process of analysis on our part" (Darwin,

The Expression of the Emotions in Man and Animals [New York: Appleton, 1899], 359). Darwin believed these expressions to be innate and the process of recognition to be unconscious, laying a foundation for an empathetic understanding. Of course, one can "read" the expression of another without sharing it.

17. Nell, *Lost in a Book*, 211. Nell cites J. R. Hilgard, *Personality and Hypnosis* (Chicago: University of Chicago Press), 23. In his book Nell offers a valuable overview of what he calls "reading for pleasure," summarizing the psychological research that exists on such topics as daydreaming and the power of the story. He notes, for example, "the strange duality of the entranced reader's experience, which grants imperative internal reality to the imaginary world while at the same time—even at the height of the reader's involvement—never lays claim to an external reality (as dreams so often do)" (*Lost in a Book*, 212).

18. Wolfgang Iser paraphrases a useful distinction made by Paul Ricoeur between "two separate stages of comprehension. Meaning is the referential totality which is implied by the aspects contained in the text and which must be assembled in the course of reading. Significance is the reader's absorption of the meaning into his own existence" (*Act of Reading*, 151). For a summary of the many meanings of "meaning," see A. C. Grayling, *An Introduction to Philosophical Logic* (Oxford: Blackwell, 1997).

19. Kneepkens and Zwaan explore this point in their article, "Emotions and Literary Text Comprehension," *Poetics* 23 (1994): 26.

20. Iser, *Act of Reading*, 168. Many thinkers suggest this point, including Jerome Bruner in *Acts of Meaning*, who argues that people make meaning by telling narratives, and Allan Paivio, who points out that we perceive in terms of meaning. Wolfgang Iser claims that "apprehension of the text is dependent on gestalt groupings" (*Act of Reading*, 120). Iser locates meaning at the intersection of what the reader already knows and what she recognizes in the text.

21. Meaning serves as a shorthand representation in both imagination and memory. When people talk about books, they cannot remember the whole text so much as the impression that expresses its meaning.

22. I take the meaning from the passage as Chekhov wrote it (assuming that he meant us to construct a scene he offers as an example). Chekhov's brief description is romantic and even overly dramatic, which Chekhov may have meant to reveal an insight into the character who speaks.

Would I employ an American mill as a substitute for the Russian? People often claim to do just that, but I find myself deducing what meaning I can from the text at hand.

CHAPTER 3. THE DEBATE

Parts of this chapter first appeared in Keith Opdahl, "Imagination and Emotion: Toward a Theory of Representation," in *Reader* no. 19 (Spring 1988): 1–20.

1. Although the word "imagination" was used in the Renaissance to refer to a poetical capability and in the eighteenth century to denote the creation of images, especially in the imitation of nature, it was the English romantic poets who defined the word as the unifying capability of the mind. Besides those books explicating Coleridge's theory—notable among which are I. A. Richards's *Coleridge on Imagination* (Bloomington: Indiana University Press, 1960) and John Spencer Hill's *Imagination in Coleridge* (Totowa, N.J.: Rowman and Littlefield, 1978), which offers a compilation of all of Coleridge's remarks on imagination—I would recommend James Engell, *The Creative Imagination* (Cambridge: Harvard University Press, 1981), which explores the theory of the imagination in the eighteenth century; Mary Warnock, *Imagination* (Berkeley and Los Angeles: University of California Press, 1976), which

surveys philosophical thought on the subject, and documents the importance of imagination in daily, practical life; and E. Casey, *Imagining: A Phenomenological Study* (Bloomington: Indiana University Press, 1976), which also investigates the philosopher's treatment of imagination. In *The World of the Imagination*, Eva Brann offers a comprehensive look at the present thought on the subject.

2. See Eva Brann: "Some of the imagery-researchers, like Shepard, were themselves vivid imagers" (*World of the Imagination*, 251).

3. The reader-response critics also assume ideation or visualization: Michael Riffaterre (like David Bleich) believes that the reading process is dominated by language, while I. A. Richards believes that the statement of the text is ideational. Stanley Fish stresses experience, but it is largely an intellectual one. Norman Holland believes that readers examine the text as an expression of their personal style, which means, since style is something felt, that they may represent the text emotionally.

4. Kosslyn, *Ghosts*, 58. As Mark Rollins defines proposition, "all cognition requires a linguistic format; all thought is essentially propositional" (*Mental Imagery* [New Haven: Yale University Press, 1989], xiv). Among the many discussions of this debate I have used Eva Brann's *The World of the Imagination* and Michael Tye's *The Imagery Debate*.

5. I. A. Richards summarizes the great value of the word when he says that "an image (in so far as it represents by being a copy) can only represent things that are like one another. A word on the other hand can equally and simultaneously represent vastly different things" (*Practical Criticism* [New York: Harcourt, Brace, 1929], 364).

6. Richard Rorty also embraces the image, claiming in his first book that "it is pictures rather than propositions, metaphors rather than statements, which determine most of our philosophical convictions" (*Philosophy and the Mirror of Nature* [Princeton: Princeton University Press, 1994], 12). See also David L. Hall, *Richard Rorty* (Albany: State University of New York Press, 1994).

7. Edelman, *Bright Air*, 136.

8. Rudolf Arnheim, *Visual Thinking* (Berkeley and Los Angeles: University of California Press, 1969), 231. One can find innumerable objections to verbalization. The psychologist Jerome Bruner believes that "certain communicative functions or intentions are well in place before the child has mastered the formal language for expressing them linguistically" (*Acts of Meaning* [Cambridge: Harvard University Press, 1990], 71). Daniel Goleman believes babies develop "rough, wordless blueprints" of the world, or memories and patterns that precede thought (*Emotional Intelligence* [New York: Bantam, 1995], 22). David Novitz gives a good summary of such objections in *Knowledge, Fiction and Imagination*.

9. Marvin Minsky, *The Society of Mind* (New York: Simon and Schuster, 1985), 28. See also Dreyfus, *What Computers Still Can't Do* (Cambridge: MIT Press, 1992).

10. In *Bright Air, Brilliant Fire*, Gerald Edelman offers an especially interesting critique of the computational view of the mind. Edelman argues that neurons in the brain form groups (or maps) loosely linked to one another. Far from residing in a single, mechanistic, pigeonhole, a perception stimulates a complex interaction among many groups, firing millions of connections that permit complexity, flexibility, and subtlety.

11. After saying this in *The Pursuit of Signs* (Ithaca: Cornell University Press, 1981), Culler proceeds to interpret the work, saying that literature takes the semiotic codes as its subject. Thus one interprets the work in order to understand that interpretation is passé.

12. Scholes, *Semiotics and Interpretation* (New Haven: Yale University Press, 1982), 25. Future page citations to this volume appear in the text.

13. The act of reader identification is no doubt learned, at least in part, and so is a form of social conditioning. Kinds and degrees of empathy vary from culture to culture. Yet it is not true that we learn everything from our society. Today we find a striking gulf between the humanities, which believes that all is culture, and science, which demonstrates the importance of genetics.

14. The problem is how meaning can be mechanical. To construct meaning involves such complexity, change, and movement, such conflicting values and interpretations, that it is hard to see how a purely mechanical process could cope. We know that the mind must eventually reside in mechanics, but our experience of a living, fluid actuality is also real.

15. Cited in Damasio, *Descartes' Error,* 103.

16. Iser, *The Act of Reading* (Baltimore: Johns Hopkins University Press, 1980), 177. Future page citations to this volume appear in the text.

17. Nell, *Lost in a Book,* 217.

18. What kind of physical experience provides the form of the mental construction? I. A. Richards paraphrases Bertrand Russell, noting that the word "cow" need not call up the image: "It is enough if it excite any considerable set of those feelings, notions, attitudes, tendencies to action and so forth that the actual perception of a cow may excite" (*Practical Criticism,* 363).

19. Alan Richardson, *Mental Imagery* (New York: Springer, 1969), 27. Arnheim, *Art and Visual Perception,* 105. The testimony is overwhelming. Even Michael Irwin says that no one sees a photographic image (*Picturing,* 18). See also Andrew Ushenko, *Dynamics of Art* (Humanities series no. 28 (Bloomington: Indiana University Publications, 1953), 163; Allan Paivio, *Imagery and Verbal Processes* (New York: Holt, Rinehart, 1971), 3; I. A. Richards, *Practical Criticism,* 362; Michael Tye, *Imagery Debate,* 70. Among the research psychologists, Paivio and Gordon Bower believe we have image-codes in our head, giving the semblance of the visual, while Kosslyn and Steven Pinker believe that the mind has, as Anees Sheikh says in *Imagery,* an array-like mechanism that mimics coordinate space.

20. Although this is common wisdom, the philosopher Gilbert Ryle made a persuasive point when he observed that we do not have mental copies of senses like smell or touch (Tye, *Imagery Debate,* 22).

Chapter 4. Double Your Pleasure

1. Although memory is real and fiction is not, their mental construction is similar: the mind represents an absent object by constructing a model of it. When reading, one depends upon a combination of Hemingway's language and one's own memory.

2. Paivio, *Imagery and Verbal Processes,* 8. Future page citations to this volume appear in the text.

3. Paivio, *Mental Representations,* 201.

4. "Language and the verbal system . . . provide precise means (conceptual pegs) for retrieving imaginal memories and guiding the processing of the retrieved information" (Paivio, *Representations,* 201).

5. Kosslyn, *Ghosts,* 59.

6. Ibid., 169. The complexity of Kosslyn's concept permits him to have it both ways. It permits him to talk as though people either visualized or ideated, even though he believes they do both. The mind displays the idea or image to itself, but on the deeper level, the image depends upon the propositional cell. It is a matter of which level we consider. Thus Kosslyn observes that children as they develop move from image to word, presumably as a matter of choice, when the image "is much

practiced and so no longer necessary" (*Ghosts*, 203). Kosslyn does recognize the role of culture in such choices. Interestingly, Johnson-Laird argues that the proposition depends upon the image.

7. Nell, *Lost in a Book*, 217.

8. I mean this in both of the ways that idea and image coexist in Kosslyn's model. The mind constructs meaning in both modes; and the mind bases the image on the underground code of propositions. When Kosslyn considers three alternatives to the construction of meaning, he leaves out the choice Paivio has made: the construction of *either* idea or image.

9. Hemingway, *In Our Time*, 140–41.

10. The word determines the medium. I find that I imagine my "house" as a structure and my "home" as a felt meaning. When first reading a novel, I usually construct the words of the text literally, whether image or idea. When I pick up Kingsley Amis's *Lucky Jim*, for example, I visualize red brick buildings. But once I identify with Jim, I imagine his world less as image than significance or meaning.

11. This notion raises the problem of the reader missing Hemingway's meaning and embracing his own, mistaken one. Not a few critics would read this paragraph as evidence of anxiety. No doubt each of us has his own Hemingway. Then too, some readers are more skillful than others, and some readers are just plain wrong. My concern is how we construct and display content once we have determined what it is. The process would probably be the same whether one misreads or not.

12. Let me repeat that under certain conditions any of these sentences could be rendered as an idea. "They were better than fresh apricots." Say this sentence aloud, and you state an idea. Let *Nick* think it and it is an idea. But let Nick taste the apricots, in the imaginative sense, and it is an experience. In any case, we have by this point entered an identifying mode and taste Nick's apricots along with him.

13. Psychologists tell us that perception involves an initial impression of the whole, which provides the context for the specifics. We interpret any given sentence, of course, according to its context.

Chapter 5. Feeling Our Way

1. Historically, thought about emotion tends to consist of lists of specific emotions, as thinkers attempt to pin them down. The latest (and quite persuasive) list belongs to the Darwinian scholar, Paul Ekman, in *The Face of Man* (New York: Garland, 1980).

2. James Hillman recognizes such difficulties when he writes: "The whole fault [of emotion]—and it runs to bedrock—is the *persistent identification of emotion with subjectivity* and the corollary assumption that the intellect, as the only place of reason, is *not* personal, subjective or an expression of the individual in whom it performs" (*Emotion* [Evanston, Ill.: Northwestern University Press, 1960], 190).

I might add that the affective code offers its own hermeneutic circle. Readers cannot react emotionally to the fictional subject until they construct it, but they cannot construct the subject in the emotional mode until they have felt their reactions.

3. Although the philosopher John MacMurray saw the affective code clearly, almost no one recognizes it today. Certainly not the cognitive scientists, for all their interest in mental representation. Certainly not the philosophers, in spite of such excellent books as Susan Feagin's *Reading with Feeling* (Ithaca: Cornell University Press, 1996). And certainly not the literary critics, who if they think of emotion at all construe it as reaction.

4. Paivio uses the term "code" because the meaning on the page translates into a particular mental language or mode. He uses the term "track" because the reader moves forward, through the passage, switching from one mode to another as the language demands. That is, all people employ both codes, though individuals often favor one mode over the other.

5. Our capacity to feel *of* something is widely recognized. The philosopher José Ortega y Gasset speaks of "cypress-feeling and flame-feeling" (Brann, *World of Imagination*, 531). The critic Victor Shklovsky says that "the aim of art is to convey a feeling of the object, as seeing and not as recognizing" (Iser, *Act of Reading*, 187). In *Emotion Concepts* the psychologist Zoltán Kövecses says that "at the present time we know very little about the relationship between (emotional) expression (in the sense of signals) and (emotional) conceptualization, (if there is anything to be known at all)" (Kövecses, *Emotion Concepts* [New York: Springer-Verlag, 1990], 31).

6. Robert Ornstein observes that "children understand and produce the emotional intonations of language, conveyed by tones, before they understand the content of the speech" (*The Right Mind* [New York: Harcourt Brace Jovanovich, 1997], 154).

7. In actual life, emotion often shifts from an instrumental mode, designed to stimulate action, to a representational mode, in which the instrument comes to "stand for" the source of the emotion. As Matt Cartmill suggests in "The Gift of Gab," our original howl of pain may have come over time to include an identification of its source. In any case, to read or imagine is to adapt emotion to the purpose of mental construction and display. The psychologist Steven Pinker points out in *How the Mind Works* (New York: Norton, 1997) that the display of what we feel is itself adaptive, since signaled feeling can forestall misunderstanding and prevent useless argument.

8. J. Allan Hobson, *The Chemistry of Conscious States* (Boston: Little, Brown, 1994), 153, 157.

9. See Paul Ricoeur, "The Metaphorical Process as Cognition, Imagination, and Feeling," *Critical Inquiry* 5, no. 1 (1978): 156, and *Freedom and Nature* (Evanston, Ill.: Northwestern University Press, 1966), 258. In "The Metaphorical Process" the author equates feeling with mood, schemata, and "split structure," or simultaneous identification and distance from the text. In doing so he does justice to the odd way in which we both feel and do not feel the emotions of the fictional characters.

10. It is no accident that we use the same word, "feel," for sensation as well as emotion: like sensation, emotion is an experience we undergo. The philosopher R. G. Collingwood defines feeling as the larger category within which both sensation and emotion belong. Among several different kinds of feeling, the contemporary neurologist Antonio Damasio recognizes a "background feeling," which he defines as our sense of being itself. It is what we feel "*between* emotions," or the relatively neutral feelings that determine much of our mood (Damasio, *The Feeling of What Happens* [New York: Harcourt Brace, 1999], 149).

Significantly, the roots of "emotion" and "feeling" are parallel. The Latin root of emotion is "movere," to move, and the Indo-European root of "feeling" (the word "pil-pol") is to set in motion with a push. See *The Barnhart Dictionary of Etymology*.

11. As a term, "feeling" is thus a catch-all, referring to all kinds of inner experience. And it has to be, really, since the mind experiences and displays all kinds of things—personal mood and the emotional atmosphere of a room, the act of focusing and the sensation of pleasure. Tie "feeling" to sensation alone and we have no name for a large amount of human experience.

12. What is complicated is the fact that having constructed the author's meaning in the affective code, we then react emotionally to what we have constructed. See chapter 11, where I discuss our feelings about the object we have just felt diegetically.

Wimsatt and Beardsley provide a useful gloss to Robert Solomon's point.

> The emotions correlative to the objects of poetry become a part of the matter dealt with— not communicated to the reader like an infection or disease, not inflicted mechanically like a bullet or knife wound, not administered like a poison, not simply expressed as by expletives or grimaces or rhythms, but presented in their objects and contemplated as a pattern of knowledge. (Wimsatt, W. K. and M. C. Beardsley, *The Verbal Icon* [Lexington: University of Kentucky Press, 1954], 38)

13. Note that if the emotion is attached to its object, it may be equated to it and so represent it.

14. Hemingway, *In Our Time*, 140–41.

15. I don't want to oversimplify. Writers have a wide latitude between identification and distance, even in a passage such as this. Shift the tone just a little, and we will laugh at Nick, pulling back to perceive him from a distance. And of course, readers differ. I have no doubt that some readers would not identify with Nick whatever the language requires, while other readers might identify too closely, losing the capacity for criticism—though Hemingway is just about as accepting of Nick as one could be.

16. In this paragraph alone Hemingway moves from fact to feeling several times, using the feeling to cap (and thus to summarize) the action. Three times he offers a series of verbs and nouns that he completes with a short statement about Nick's inner consciousness or feeling. Nick "drove," "hung," "dipped," "put"—and "tried to remember." He "waited," "opened"—and then "liked." He "emptied," "watched," "drank," and then Hemingway concludes—in the only sentence in which Nick is not the subject—"they were better than fresh apricots." This concluding judgment bites off the paragraph by citing the emotion that summarizes its meaning of pleasure and contentment.

17. If we take the time to remember, pausing at this moment in the narrative to unpack Hemingway's meaning (or our construction of his meaning), we can probably specify all of these small actions. Such feelings of pleasure, after all, are striking and familiar and public. How often have I felt pleasure as the can opener cut crisply through metal?

18. In my view the memory of Hopkins is another obstacle Nick surmounts. Their arguing was unpleasant, and Nick's ability to give the point to Hopkins ("He remembered that was Hopkins's way") reveals his gathering strength. See my interpretation of the story in chapter 9.

I might add that we have to feel this relationship because our attention is focused elsewhere. Nick is thinking about how to make coffee, which makes his awareness of Hopkins a kind of afterthought.

19. Many of those who read fiction probably favor the affective code anyway, as a principle of their daily experience. Other readers adopt the affective code as a base mode only when reading fiction or watching a movie, or when the author's language leaves no other choice. On at least one level, the three modes are interchangeable. I can have an idea of an emotion; a feeling of an idea; an idea of a painting. Yet idea stands alone in its abstraction and capacity for self-awareness while the image is powerful because it corresponds to its subject physically. And the emotion is powerful because it corresponds to the felt meaning of its subject.

20. One could even argue that the mental image is unstable, as it flickers in a kind of twilight zone, while a given emotion is strikingly constant and can be revisited over and over. We often feel the same mood all day.

21. Jane Austen, *Mansfield Park: A Novel, The Novels of Jane Austen*, vol. 3, ed. R. W. Chapman (Oxford: Oxford University Press, 1932), 44.

22. See Ed S. Tan, "Story Processing as an Emotion Episode," in *Naturalistic Text Comprehension*, ed. Herre Van Oostendorp and Rolf A Zwaan (Norwood, N.J.: Ablex, 1994), 184.

23. Damasio, *Feeling of What Happens*, 192.

CHAPTER 6. THE INTELLECTUAL LANDSCAPE I

1. Warnock, *Imagination*, 170; Jean-Paul Sartre, *The Psychology of Imagination* (London: Rider, 1950), 83; William James, *The Principles of Psychology* (Cambridge: Harvard University Press, 1981), vol. 1, 246.

As Allan Paivio puts it, some researchers believe that "words could acquire generalized affect-arousing qualities analogous to referential meaning" (Paivio, *Representations*, 271). The philosopher John MacMurray, quoted in the epigraph to chapter 5, sees the affective code clearly in *Reason and Emotion*, but turns from it to explore emotional reaction and education.

2. Henry James, *The Painter's Eye* (London: Rupert Hurt-Davis, 1956), vol. 2, 185. Warnock, *Imagination*, 116.

3. Samuel Coleridge, *Biographia Literaria*, ed. John Shawcross (London: Oxford University Press, 1954), vol. 2, 3. Although Coleridge discusses the imagination in *Biographia Literaria* without mentioning emotion, and did not incorporate emotion into his systematic thought, it was never far from his mind. He mentions "feelings of being" and describes Wordsworth as "the only man who has effected a compleat and constant synthesis of thought and feeling" (Hill, *Imagination in Coleridge*, 44). Coleridge also said of Wordsworth: "In the consideration of the *particular*, the general significance can be found and contemplated, and that in such contemplation a *feeling* for the thing presented is an essential part" (Warnock, *Imagination*, 81). It is but a short step from this recognition of our feeling of things to an understanding of emotional representation.

4. William Wordsworth, preface, 2d ed., *Lyrical Ballads* in *The Poetical Works of Wordsworth*, ed. Ernest De Selincourt (London: Oxford University Press, 1953), 735. Subsequent citations to this edition are in the text. Wordsworth believed that passion fuses ideas together, providing the mechanism of associationism. He got this notion from David Hartley, who felt the association of ideas by means of emotion provided an elevating path. In Hartley's words, "We shall necessarily be led higher and higher by the association of pleasure with sense impressions of a particular kind" (Warnock, *Imagination*, 120).

5. Most of us would say that we contemplate our memory of the scene until it blossoms in our imagination and we are ready to commit it to paper. We would view the reaction as secondary. To Wordsworth, in contrast, the memory and the reaction are one: the poet ponders not his memory but his original emotional reaction, rekindling *it* as his representation of the experience.

6. Wordsworth, "Lines Composed above Tintern Abbey," in *The Poetical Works of Wordsworth*, 163.

7. As Mary Warnock paraphrases Wordsworth's view, "It is the original function of the imagination to reproduce things, to enable us to think them, and above all to feel them, when they are not actually before our eyes" (*Imagination*, 112). Wordsworth saw "feeling" as one of the ways in which the imagination can "reproduce things."

8. Rudolf Arnheim, "Emotion and Feeling in Psychology and Art," in *Toward a Psychology of Art* (Berkeley and Los Angeles: University of California Press, 1966), 315. Arnheim quotes with approval William James's claim that "a good third of our

psychic life consists in these rapid premonitory perspective views of schemes of thought not yet articulate" (James, *Psychology*, vol. 1, 245).

9. William Hazlitt, "On Genius and Common Sense," from *Tabletalk*, vol. 8, in *The Complete Works of William Hazlitt*, ed. P. P. Howe (London: J. M. Dent and Sons, 1931), 31. Like Wordsworth, Hazlitt gets the word "impression" from Locke and the associationists, who focused on the "impress" of sensation on the mind. Hazlitt too believed that passion modifies sense data, fusing with the perception. Note that he views emotion as a continuum from feeling through passion.

10. Eliot, *The Sacred Wood* (London: Methuen, 1920), 100.

11. Adam Gopnik, "The Power Critic," *The New Yorker*, 74 (March 16, 1998): 75.

In "The Objective Correlative of T. S. Eliot," Eliseo Vivas charges that Eliot confuses the expression of emotion, which belongs to the author, with the arousal of emotion within the reader (in *Creation and Discovery* [New York: Noonday, 1955]). In this he misunderstands Eliot's focus on the reader—the point of the objective correlative—and the distinction between emotion, which is what the author might express in a work, and feeling, which is dispassionately embodied in the work and aroused in the reader. Like Vivas, Eliot has a horror of personal expression.

12. Eliot, *Sacred Wood*, 53.

13. Ibid., 55.

14. Eliot does not *say* that emotion represents. The emotion evoked in the reader could simply be reaction, as Eliot strives to evoke emotions for their own sake. It is the equivalence of language and emotion that makes the code possible, though Eliot does speak as though the emotion felt by the reader *is* the poem, which is to say, the content of the poem as available to the mind.

I might add that the function of emotion in diegesis is obscured in Eliot's writings by the other functions that interest the poet. As critics like C. K. Stead point out, Eliot takes states of feeling as his subject and often evokes feeling for its own sake.

15. Eliot makes it clear that the feelings are discovered in the act of writing. The philosopher Bernard Bosanquet makes a key point in this regard when he says

> We must not suppose that we first have a disembodied feeling, and set out to find an embodiment adequate to it. In a word, imaginative expression creates the feeling in creating its embodiment, and the feeling so created not merely cannot be otherwise expressed, but cannot otherwise exist, than in and through the embodiment which imagination has found for it. (Bernard Bosanquet, *Three Lectures on Aesthetic* [Indianapolis, Ind.: Bobbs-Merrill, 1963], 33–34)

16. Eliot understood the unconscious sources of art quite well. Perhaps because they, as philosophers, specialize in conscious analysis, Collingwood and Langer overestimate the consciousness of creative writing.

17. Collingwood, *Principles of Art*, 162–63.

18. Nöel Carroll puts it this way: Collingwood saw much of art as "an occasion for the artist to work through or clarify some initially vague feeling. This process of clarification is supposed to stand in contrast to the arousal of emotion" (Hjort and Laver, *Emotion and the Arts*, 193).

19. Collingwood talks about the emotional meaning of bodily states and the phenomenon of contagion, arguing that even scientific language is emotional. With the rise of science, he says, "we are not getting away from an emotional atmosphere into a dry, rational atmosphere; we are acquiring new emotions and new means of expressing them" (*Principles of Art*, 269).

20. Ibid., 225.

21. Susanne K. Langer, *Problems of Art* (New York: Charles Scribner's Sons, 1957), 80.

22. Ibid., 91.

23. Ibid., 22.

24. Susanne K. Langer, *Feeling and Form,* 59, 176. Langer leaves no doubt as to her meaning on this point. "Art is the articulation, not the stimulator or catharsis, of feeling; and the height of technique is simply the highest power of this sensuous revelation and wordless abstraction." The work "presents the semblance of feeling so directly to logical intuition that we seem to perceive feeling itself in the work; but of course the work does not contain feeling, any more than a proposition about the mortality of Socrates contains a philosopher" (Langer, *Problems of Art,* 107; *Mind* [Baltimore: Johns Hopkins University Press, 1967], vol. 1, 67).

25. "But a true work of art—certainly any great work—is often above sympathy, and the role of empathy in our understanding of it is trivial" (Langer, *Mind,* vol. 1, 164).

CHAPTER 7. THE INTELLECTUAL LANDSCAPE II

1. See W. K. Wimsatt and Monroe Beardsley, "The Affective Fallacy," in Wimsatt, *The Verbal Icon,* 38. "The more specific the account of the emotion induced by a poem, the more nearly it will be an account of the reasons for emotion, the poem itself, and the more reliable it will be as an account of what the poem is likely to induce in other—sufficiently informed—readers" (34).

2. Because we believe that real experience is sensually more vivid than imagined experience, this is an important point. Pepper means that the moment in the story is exceptionally intense because the text is highly focused. He refers to the dulling of experience by habit, and so means that art makes us pay attention.

3. Stephen Pepper, "Emotion," in *Aesthetic Quality* (New York: Charles Scribner's Sons, 1938), 89.

4. Stephen Pepper, *Principles of Art Appreciation* (New York: Harcourt, Brace, 1949), 119.

5. In Scheler's account, empathy is not a matter of reading cues, as Charles Darwin thought, but an immediate emotional understanding of the other person. We blend completely with that individual. If we have difficulty accepting this point today, Scheler says, it is because civilized people have lost the capacity to empathize.

6. To know an event or object as a felt value is already to represent it by means of that value, which expresses its essence. As Scheler says,

> during the process of intentional feeling, the world of objects "comes to the fore" by itself, but only in terms of its *value*-aspect. The frequent lack of pictorial objects in intentional feeling shows that feeling is originally an "objectifying act" that does not require the mediation of [visual] representation. (In *What is an Emotion?,* ed. Cheshire Calhoun and Robert C. Solomon [Oxford: Oxford University Press, 1984] 225)

We do not "require the mediation of representation" because the emotion itself represents the presence of the object. We feel the presence of the object in the values we express within the emotion.

7. R. B. Zajonc, "Feeling and Thinking," *American Psychology* 35 (1980): 154.

Scheffler does not mean to reject reason, he says, but rather to argue a close and positive association between emotion and knowing. Claiming that the emotions play an important role in creative thinking, stimulating images of all kinds, Scheffler continues: "The emotions serve not merely as a *source* of imaginative patterns; they fulfill also a *selective* function, facilitating choice among these patterns, defining their salient features, focusing attention accordingly" ("Cognitive Emotions," 19). It is this general train of thought that influenced Scheler and that leads Robert Solomon to conclude that emotions are constitutive of our experience.

8. Robert Leeper, *Toward Understanding Human Personalities* (New York: Appleton-Century-Crofts, 1959), 214–15.

9. Leeper, *Toward Understanding*, 222.

10. David Bleich also argues in *Subjective Criticism* that any statement involves motive and is thus subjective and so unverifiable. Language embodies this subjectivity since every word is a motivated act.

11. If perception is inevitably flawed, then how does one understand the values of the society accurately? It is not enough to say that one is conditioned, since that simply defers the problem. To learn one must perceive accurately, and it is not at all clear why the illusions of a society can be shared but not a knowledge of the physical world. Poststructural thought is fascinating but often illogical.

12. How could the mind combine two separate images? It could place one within another, of course, or work out some kind of synthesis, dropping parts of each. On the other hand, if one represents each image as an emotion, one can fuse the two with ease. I make use of this fact in Chapters 11 and 16.

13. Paul Ricoeur, "The Metaphorical Process as Cognition, Imagination, and Feeling," *Critical Inquiry* 5, no. 1 (1978): 143. Future citations to this essay are in the text.

14. Ricoeur also contends that "feelings . . . accompany and complete imagination as *picturing* relationships" ("Metaphorical Process," 156). Ricoeur builds upon William James's very important idea that we feel relationships: in the metaphor we not only *see* the congruence between elements but *feel* it, and this feeling provides a special kind of knowledge, making it part of our experience. Thus the reader of a metaphor knows the metaphoric relation as a feeling. Ricoeur subscribes to the view expressed by Northrop Frye that the whole point of an image lies in the articulation of a mood or feeling.

CHAPTER 8. THE AFFECTIVE CODE

1. In the case of the affective code, T. S. Eliot and Ernest Hemingway would deny this immediacy, positing an intermediate step in which readers translate the words into an image or idea, which in turn evokes an emotion within the reader. Eliot speaks of "a set of objects, a situation, a chain of events which shall be the formula of that *particular* emotion" (*Sacred Wood*, 100). But the process is actually less complicated than that, since we feel the identity of the objects as we read the work. Rather than visualize the "set of objects" named by the author and then react to it, we construct and display in the affective code right away.

2. As Antonio Damasio puts it, "I do not see emotions and feelings as the intangible and vaporous qualities that many presume them to be. Their subject matter is concrete, and they can be related to specific systems in body and brain, no less so than vision or speech" (*Descartes' Error*, 164).

3. Chicago might mean excitement to us, for example, making us react with an anticipation we find pleasurable. In such ways our comprehensive feeling of Chicago carries within it several layers of feeling.

4. See Gunnar Hansson, "Emotions in Poetry: Where are they and How do we find them?" in *Empirical Approaches to Literature and Aesthetics*, ed. R. J. Kreuz and M. S. MacNealy (Norwood, N.J.: Ablex, 1986), 279. "Readers of poetry, even if they are not very experienced readers, do see the difference between what has been called 'ap-

praisal of the object,' that is, the meaning they have given to the text, and the feelings that they report to have been evoked in the reading of the text."

5. Brann, *World of the Imagination,* 769.

6. Emotion lies on the border between consciousness and awareness. While consciousness occupies the foreground of my attention, awareness lies at the periphery, available to me only if I choose to focus on it. Thus awareness can furnish meaning to the perception subtly or unobserved, as a feeling of context. I am *conscious* of the walnut tree out my window but only *aware* of the surrounding neighborhood. Because I can be aware of the neighborhood without being conscious of it, moreover, I automatically absorb its meaning as part of my perception of the tree. My feeling of the buildings' presence supplements my conscious perception.

7. Robert Solomon, *The Passions* (South Bend, Ind.: University of Notre Dame Press, 1983), 194. Max Scheler (like William James) believed that this kind of meaning exists in the objects themselves. Such feelings are not projections but discoveries. In *Emotion* James Hillman quotes J. Drever, who says that "this [affective] element is the primary and original factor without which Meaning, as such, could never arise and which actually . . . converts bare sensation into experience" (*Emotion,* 193).

8. Damasio, *Descartes' Error,* xii.

9. This point is worth stressing. It is possible, for example, not to see but to feel Nick feeding the fire, since as any dancer knows, human gesture translates into emotion. Nick "put some more chips under the grill onto the fire." One can feel Nick bend forward, rotating his wrist to slide the chip beneath the grill. It is also possible to translate Hemingway's words as their intellectual meaning, especially if one has not identified with Nick. Taken by itself, Hemingway's sentence states an idea, which can work as such within the fabric of the imagined (and so concrete) construction.

10. One could define all the contents of a mind as idea, in which case even a feeling would be an idea. I define the "idea" as an intellectual abstraction. Although the codes intermingle, the presence of one of these codes sometimes drives out the others: when I look *at* something, the emotional distance tends to diminish my feeling of its presence (though it would not preclude my private reaction to it). When I think an idea, the same process occurs: the intellectual mode makes me feel the presence of the object only slightly (though I can, of course, choose to feel rather than ideate). And when I have a feeling of the ball, the immediate experience, having caught me up, diminishes any tendency to look at or think about—though again, I can switch tracks at any time. Mary Warnock makes a similar point, observing that we focus on the image whenever it is present, feeling emotion most strongly when the image is gone (*Imagination,* 116).

11. To the extent that this amorphous body represents the background, it need be only a general presence. But it also forms the foreground and so must include sharply defined particulars.

12. This memory carries a great deal of information and yet is brief, offering a flash of meaning that can stand alone. Thus it requires qualities very different from the construction of particulars, or even a working sense of the whole.

13. In their different ways, R. G. Collingwood, Robert Solomon, and Eva Brann associate sensation and feeling.

14. I do think that one of the codes can be dominant in a passage, making the key to the interaction of the three codes the variation in their strength. At different times, ideas, images, and feelings can be strong or dim, and so fill dominant or subordinate roles.

15. The use of literature as evidence about real life is not uncommon. One thinks of historians like Peter Stearns and sociologists like Norman Denzin, who use novels

as social documents, and of literary critics like I. A. Richards and David Bleich, who polled their students to develop insights into reading. The advantages of studying a fictional text are considerable. It provides what William James says is the only way to examine a cognitive emotion, by reconstructing the experience, bit by bit (in James F. Brown, *Affectivity, Its Language and Meaning* [Washington, D.C.: University Press of America, 1982], 137). It is an empirical method not unlike that in experimental psychology, where the researcher relies on the subject's report of her experience. Gerald Edelman argues that reports of the subjective can be correlated and so substantiated by many sources. Such correlation means that "we can then take human beings to be the best canonical referent for the study of consciousness" (*Bright Air*, 114).

16. We speak of a skillful use of language or theme or image. Why not of emotion? Writers use language to evoke emotions, which may or may not fulfill their functions within the text.

17. These novels (like perhaps all novels) also take emotion as their subject. They present characters who are first harmed and then helped by their emotional nature. Some of these authors, like Ernest Hemingway and Henry James, would probably accept the premise of this book, while others, like Jane Austen and Mark Twain, would not.

Does the preferred code of an author tell us something about her novel and our mental display of it? In the next few chapters I will ask whether an examination of the code implied by the author's language can be illuminating. Some novelists lean heavily on the visual, as Michael Irwin tells us in *Picturing*, and others emphasize the verbal. Still others emphasize the affective code. Does examining such predilections offer any special insight?

CHAPTER 9. LANGUAGE AS EMOTION

1. Ernest Hemingway, *Death in the Afternoon* (New York: Charles Scribner's Sons, 1932), 192, 2. Jackson Benson notes Hemingway's concern with emotion, arguing that "any discussion of the development of Hemingway's fiction must concern itself with the ways in which Hemingway attempted to express and control the emotions that gnawed at him and threatened to devour both him and his art" (*Ernest Hemingway: New Critical Approaches* [Durham, N.C.: Duke University Press, 1990], 22).

2. The omnipresence of this emotion raises a difficult issue. What is the connection between a writer's skill and the affective code? If readers construct meaning out of emotion anyway, what difference does the quality of the writer's language make? Or does affective construction offer advantages that go to the power of the imagined text? I would like to believe that the writer's skill in employing the affective code helps determine the quality of the text.

3. Max Scheler, *The Nature of Sympathy*, trans. Peter Heath (New Haven: Yale University Press, 1954), 12–15. Pepper, *Principles of Art Appreciation*, 128–34.

4. It is worth noting that some emotions are governed by physical laws, such as our emotional response to particular colors.

5. Significantly, the person feeling the original emotion does not have to *do* anything to convey the emotion: his companion feels it automatically. One can control this tendency, of course, though the behavior of groups, which live by the rule of contagion, suggests that it takes effort. In the case of fiction, the long narrative permits the feelings to gain definition and strength. And then in real life we build up a repertoire of familiar feelings. I enjoy the same feeling of quiet and anticipation each morning as I drink my coffee. I feel the same antipathy toward the

editorial opinions of my local newspaper. My daily routine brings me hundreds of well-worn emotions like these, familiar and mild and ready to be used by the imagination.

6. The quotes in this section are from, in order, Hemingway, *In Our Time,* 149, 134 and F. Scott Fitzgerald, *The Great Gatsby* (New York: Charles Scribner's Sons, 1925), 64.

7. Sometimes the overtly stated idea and the dramatized meaning conflict. To think the idea of an apple is vastly different from imagining oneself biting into its brittle flesh. And yet in fiction the two modes often complement each other, defining one of the great advantages of literature over philosophy. Nor are the two modes ever pure in actual experience: to imagine is to think certain ideas; to think or ideate is to feel certain feelings.

8. I might add that it is contagion that unites the named and the shown emotion. That is, we feel the named emotion, as I have said, and especially when we identify with the text. And we feel the shown or dramatized emotion as a matter of course.

9. Ernest Hemingway, *In Our Time,* 134.

10. We may assume that Nick was wounded in the war, since the other stories lay that background.

11. We also know Nick's feelings by the emotion embodied in the form or style. As Earl Rovit puts it: "That Hemingway is able to insinuate this desperate restraint by making his prose the stylistic equivalent of that restraint is the triumph of the story" (*Ernest Hemingway* [New York: Twanyne, 1963], 81). We are familiar with the lyric poet who describes himself by describing a vista. The poet's mood determines what he sees; the scene before him in turn affects his mood—permitting the writer (whether of poetry or prose) to give the setting and the mind of the narrator in a single description. I might add that Alfred Kazin, too, stresses Nick's "drive to make order" ("Young Man, Old Man," *Reporter* 29 [December 19, 1963], 35).

12. Nick believes that such self-discipline is healing, and the fact is that Hemingway's description of nature is a fantasy. The pine groves rise like small cathedrals, providing shelter, and the river water is pure to drink. When Nick cleans his fish, in a passage that is almost an emotional climax to the story, coming but one paragraph from the end, he discovers order as well as purity: the insides of the fish come out in a single piece, with "gray-white strips of milt, smooth and clean."

13. Raymond S. Nelson, *Hemingway: Expressionist Artist* (Ames: Iowa State University Press, 1979), 58. Keith Carabine, "Big Two-Hearted River: A Re-interpretation," Hemingway *Review* 1, no. 2 (Spring 1982): 43. Chamal Nahal, *The Narrative Pattern in Ernest Hemingway's Fiction* (Rutherford, N.J.: Fairleigh Dickinson University Press, 1971).

14. Saul Bellow, "Hemingway and the Image of Man," *Partisan Review* 20 (May–June 1953): 340.

15. Among the critics who discuss the emotion in this text are Earl Rovit, Raymond Nelson, Arthur Waldhorn, and Richard Hovey. Robert Paul Lamb confirms my point when he writes that "Hemingway searches for the critical detail that will convey a scene's emotional essence" ("Fishing for Stories: What 'Big Two-Hearted River' is Really About," *Modern Fiction Studies* 37, no. 2 [Summer 1991]: 174).

16. I find it corny when the critic discovers the writer's subject to be the process of writing itself. The world contains much more than the creation of fiction. Yet "Big Two-Hearted River" is a tour-de-force, containing but one character, no dialogue, and no explanation. Thus Nick's solitary quest for healing provides a rare glimpse of the equivalence of language and feeling. Denied any other expression of his emotions, it would seem, Nick falls back upon the affective code, working out his feelings by employing the external world as proxy.

17. William James, "The Place of Affectional Facts," in *Writings 1902–10* (New York: Library of America, 1987), 1209.

18. William James, *Principles of Psychology*, vol. 1, 245–46.

19. We could speculate about a larger application of this principle. If Ferdinand de Saussure is correct in saying that all language finds its meaning in the relationship among words, then every word finds its meaning in terms of a relationship we know as an emotion. We can know "up" and "down" both visually and ideationally, of course. But it makes sense to understand that we also know "up" in terms of our feeling of its relationship to "down."

In any case, a great deal of any text consists of relationship, which means (if James is right) that a great deal of a text must be emotion. I develop this idea in chapter 13.

20. I'm indebted in this discussion to Charles Guignon's essay on Heidegger, "Moods in Heidegger's *Being and Time*," in *What is an Emotion?*, ed. Cheshire Calhoun and Robert C. Solomon (New York: Oxford University Press, 1984).

21. This sentence offers a simple statement of fact, asking for no emotional reaction. Nick does this thing and that. Yet even this absence of emotion generates a tone of its own, requiring construction. We know Nick's reliance on barren specifics as a strong feeling of the matter-of-fact. It is as though the nail and the dipped pot were only a means to express the feeling of poetic flatness that is Hemingway's meaning.

22. Solomon, *The Passions*, 159.

CHAPTER 10. SHARED EMOTION

1. One could say that emotion provides the mind with a second language that competes with the verbal. Interestingly enough, while our health does not require us to see or think, it does require us to feel, and so to express emotions that reveal a great deal.

2. Stephen Pepper says that to create agreement we "see to it that identical stimuli such as printed words produce similar responses in different minds" (*Principles of Art*, 126–27). This is the same for emotion as for ideas and obviously involves the writer's skill and clarity as well as the commonality of readers.

3. A few Austen critics have shown an interest in the reader's mental construction of the text. See Kenneth L. Moler, who examines the constructional capacities of image and sound, and Toby Tanner.

Let me qualify my premise at this point. We each feel certain emotions uniquely, but we also feel many emotions in common. Within a narrow range we may all feel a family of similar emotions—my point is simply that such emotions, unique though they may be, are enough alike to provide a shared understanding of the characters and text. Of course, the more homogeneous the body of readers, the larger the degree of sharing.

4. Charlotte Brontë, "Letter to W. S. Williams," April 1850, in *Jane Austen, The Critical Heritage*, ed. B. C. Southam (London: Routledge and Kegan Paul, 1968), 128.

5. Tudja Crowder, for example, says that the formal structure of the novel implies that the emotions are logical.

6. Jane Austen, *Pride and Prejudice* (London: Penguin, 1972), 277. Subsequent citations to this volume appear in the text.

7. James Thompson, as just one example, says that "the subject of Jane Austen's fiction to a large degree is feelings" (*Between Self and World* [University Park: Pennsylvania State University Press, 1989], 2).

8. Marilyn Butler, *Jane Austen and the War of Ideas* (Oxford: Clarendon, 1987), 216, 217.

9. Alison Sulloway, *Jane Austen and the Province of Womanhood* (Philadelphia: University of Pennsylvania Press, 1989), 129.

10. Elizabeth also feels, when Darcy and his sister come to visit her at the Inn near Pemberley, that she has "much to do. She wanted to ascertain the feelings of each of her visitors, she wanted to compose her own, and to make herself agreeable to all."

11. Elizabeth is emotionally sophisticated. When Georgianna and Darcy come to visit, Elizabeth understands that "where she feared most to fail, she was most sure of success, for those to whom she endeavored to give pleasure were prepossessed in her favor." For a nervous young woman at such a time this is a remarkable insight. Of course, Elizabeth has more difficulty reading her own emotions. Referring to Elizabeth's feelings about Darcy, Austen writes, the evening "was not long enough to determine her feelings towards *one* in that mansion; and she lay awake two whole hours, endeavoring to make them out." As Austen traces Elizabeth's journey from embarrassment to resentment to gratitude to love, she portrays an awakening that is nondramatic but psychologically sound. Darcy's love is contagious: once she recognizes them, his feelings toward Elizabeth awaken similar feelings toward him in her.

12. Mary Poovey objects to the narrative celebration of marriage and a bourgeois life, while Marilyn Butler argues that Elizabeth never understands that her judgments are based on faulty emotions. Butler believes *Pride and Prejudice* to be the least conservative of Austen's novels. Claudia Johnson argues that the political issues become gender issues, so that the private lives of the characters are really illustrations of public questions. She feels that Austen "consents to conservative myths, but only in order to possess them and to ameliorate them from within" (*Jane Austen* [Chicago: University of Chicago Press, 1988], 83).

13. Nancy Armstrong documents the growing acceptance of emotion in male protagonists. "It was at first only women who were defined in terms of their emotional natures," she says, but then characters such as Heathcliff and Rochester accepted emotional relationships (*Desire and Domestic Fiction: A Political History of the Novel* [New York: Oxford University Press, 1987], 4). Significantly, they are as obsessively emotional as Darcy.

14. Deny the expression of emotion, on the other hand, and you may repress the feeling of it. As Saul Bellow's Augie March remarks, there is no "fineness of suppression." Yet men do hide what they feel and so appear less emotional than they are. Because the repressed always finds an outlet, moreover, repression may well make men more rather than less emotional.

15. Elizabeth at Pemberley discovers not only Darcy's good taste but the internal economy of his emotions. The housekeeper makes it clear that Darcy—the scowling, tongue-tied Darcy—is really generous and good-tempered. The housekeeper all but brags that he has a sunny disposition.

16. I should add that understanding expression and gesture varies according to the occasion. Some expressions of emotion are clear, as in a hand raised in anger, while others are unfathomable. Thus the same person can understand one expression and not another.

17. R. Harré, *The Social Construction of Emotion* (Oxford: Basil Blackwell, 1986), 290. Michael Steig in *Stories of Readings* (Baltimore: Johns Hopkins University Press, 1989) shows that groups of American students share an understanding of the affective dimension of a text.

18. People who cannot read the emotions registered on faces get into trouble with their companions. Mistake fear for anger, as do some victims of Huntington's disease, for example, and the result is chaos. Many would agree that emotion is an

elementary appraisal of our experience; lose it and you lose a valuable guide to behavior.

19. James Thompson analyzes the historically determined emotions surrounding everything from clothes to marriage to breakfast. He seeks, he says,

> to historicize Austen's language, as well as the feeling expressed in it, by examining emotion in Austen's fiction in the light of a wide range of historical circumstances, social and economic as well as literary (Thompson, *Between Self and World* [University Park: Pennsylvania State University Press, 1989], 5).

Thompson shows how feelings such as pride followed by humiliation find definition in religious and social lessons of the period.

20. Among others, Samuel Kliger discusses the relationship between art and nature. The point is to create the illusion of an orderly or perfect world that occurs naturally, without either domination or subordination. The sharing of an emotion like this is difficult, of course, because people differ. As I now write, I have intellectualized the scene to the point of not feeling anything. But the reader identifying with Elizabeth reacts to this scene with her, feeling what she does. What is this feeling? It is a sense of a lovely natural scene improved by an unobtrusive hand, including feelings of harmony and ease.

21. As Melvin Mudrick argues, the story portrays Elizabeth learning to master her subversive or antisocial emotions ("Irony as Discrimination: *Pride and Prejudice*," in *Jane Austen,* ed. Ian Watt [Englewood Cliffs, N.J.: Prentice-Hall, 1963], 84). This view parallels the argument that Elizabeth learns to be objective or rational (and tends to support the notion that Austen is a cultural conservative).

22. Many emotions are too closely tied to our need for survival not to have biological roots. As Barbara Ehrenreich and Janet McIntosh have reported, members of the physical sciences claim that the debate between nurture or nature is finished: it is neither one alone but both, interacting in complex ways. Thinkers in the humanities, on the other hand, deny the role of the physiological, even as geneticists and neurologists make momentous discoveries. But as Ehrenreich and McIntosh suggest, if human beings do not share an essential nature, the claim that we are all alike falls.

23. Paul Ekman, *The Face of Man,* 137.

24. Not a few cognitive scientists believe with Roger Schank that the mind uses scripts, or patterns of behavior that form a mental unit. Members of a culture would tend to share these schemata, which, as Keith Oatley suggests, might include as scripts specific emotions. (See Oatley, "Emotion," in *The Blackwell Dictionary,* ed. Michael Eysenck [Oxford: Blackwell, 1990], 133).

25. In Nussbaum's words, "narratives contain emotions in their very structure." "Their very forms are themselves the sources of emotional structure, the paradigms of what, for us, emotion *is*" ("Narrative Emotions: Beckett's Genealogy of Love," *Ethics* 98, no. 2 [January 1988]: 252, 236).

26. Virginia Woolf, *The Common Reader* (New York: Harcourt, Brace, 1925), 174.

27. D. W. Harding also calls Elizabeth a Cinderella. Another critic who sees a great deal of implied emotion in the novel is Dennis W. Allen.

28. Pepper, "Emotion," 97.

Chapter 11. Precise Emotion

1. Few would disagree with this. Tony Tanner observes that "if Huck reflected, moralized, and sermonized we would weary of him very soon: but this of course, as

Tom Sawyer points out, is the one thing Huck cannot do" (*The Reign of Wonder* [Cambridge: Cambridge University Press, 1965], 169). Richard Bridgman observes that Huck "is notably not a thinker. His powers of generalization are almost nil." Bridgman also observes that "whereas the Jamesian characters discuss states of being . . . Huck and the other characters in his book talk about things" (*Colloquial Style in America* [New York: Oxford University Press, 1966]). Harold Beaver says that Huck's "response is *all* feeling. It is solely by feeling. It is nothing but feeling" (*Huckleberry Finn* [London: Unwin Critical Library, 1987], 96).

It is worth noting that Huck uses "think" in the sense of "conjuring" or "constructing."

2. Mark Twain, *Adventures of Huckleberry Finn* (New York: Penguin, 1981), 3. Subsequent citations to this volume appear in the text.

Like Jane Austen in *Pride and Prejudice*, Mark Twain finds humor in feigned or spurious emotion, illustrating again the readers' shared understanding of human feeling. Coincidentally, both of their protagonists are young people who are wronged by their elders and who provide the moral norm of their novels. Although Austen offers dialogue and states of mind while Twain offers the physical world, both employ the affective code. To me, the reality of *Pride and Prejudice* lies behind the words, making the reader travel through the language to the scene, while the actuality of *Huck Finn* is so immediate (in this first-person narration) that it lies on the surface of the words.

3. Huck will later choose to protect Jim as a result of weighing two different emotions, which means that he makes decisions on the basis of emotion, too. It is significant that millions of readers have felt that this portrayal of the mind is convincing.

4. Hemingway, *The Green Hills of Africa* (New York: Charles Scribner's Sons, 1935), 22. There is a sense in which Huck, like Nick Adams, needs to control his feelings by controlling the content of his thought and sensation. Thus he tries "to think of something cheerful."

5. How do I construct this scene by the window? Let me review my experience. Because Huck tells what he hears, I do not visualize it, in spite of the helpfully imagistic, "I set down in a chair by the window." But I do not *hear* these sounds, either. I do not reproduce leaves rustling, whether mournful or not, or an owl "who-whooing" (though Twain gives me the literal sound). I feel these sounds as emotions in which meaning dominates.

Once I have read this passage, I represent it in my memory as a sense of the whole: call it the feeling of Huck-feeling-lonesome-and-scared-by-the-window. My feeling includes not only what Huck feels, which I know because of my identification with him, but what I feel about the passage.

Can I think this passage? Huck concentrates on his emotions so strongly, I should think it almost impossible. Do I *see* the spider shrivel in the flame? I can, with effort, but even in this graphic instance, I feel the shriveling more than I see it.

6. Another way of saying this is to note the different kinds of emotional source: we feel Twain's content—the objects, actions, characters that Huck names—and we feel the form in which he puts them; we also feel the relationship among them, a point I develop in chapter 13.

7. Samuel Clemens, *The Love Letters of Mark Twain*, ed. Dixon Wecter (New York: Harper and Brothers, 1949), 165. The pulsation provides the text with a variety and liveliness that we feel. It also provides a certain realism to the dialogue, since speakers often repeat themselves, rhythmically returning to a key (but inconsequential) word. "But that ain't no matter," Huck says, using "that" in the opening para-

graph of the novel in three different ways. "That book was made by Mr. Mark Twain," who stretched the truth, but "that is nothing." Huck's rhythms give us a sense of who he is.

8. I think I can name these as emotions. Perhaps I should say feelings *of* order, ease, fluidity, and recognition—I register these qualities in the affective code, which does not make them emotions in themselves. My feeling of order is quite clear to me, however, and stands as an emotion in its own right, as do my feelings of fluidity and ease and recognition. The fact that these feelings of a quality appear to be emotions in their own right offers a kind of evidence for the emotional code.

9. Norman K. Denzin, *On Understanding Emotion* (San Francisco: Jossey-Bass, 1984), 56. Although this is not one of our stock ideas, it is not really new. It is embraced by, among others, John Dewey and R. G. Collingwood. Roland Barthes claims at one point that a detail exists in the text not so much for itself "but to signal 'trueness' or 'realness'" (in A. D. Nuttall, *A New Mimesis* [London: Methuen, 1983], 56). Norman Denzin formulates the point by distinguishing between "core" and "circling" emotions (*On Understanding Emotion*, 99).

10. Again let us remember that Huck's riverbank is a place we imaginatively *enter,* which means we must construct it in such a way that it is "there," a place within our imagination that we can visit and revisit.

11. Huck feels a growing pleasure at his ability to recognize things. He suspects that something is so and so, and then, as the light grows, discovers that it is indeed. Such confirmation strikes a deep chord: we take a profound pleasure in confirmation. The dark and the mist are confusing and the achievement of clarity hits a nerve even deeper than, say, the delightful birdsong, involving as it does the consciousness that enables our species to survive.

12. Langer, *Feeling and Form*, 52.

13. Pepper, *Principles*, 135–38. It is interesting that contrast plays a central role in all meaning, since we always understand a term in contrast to what it is not. Note that each of these organizations evokes an emotion on its own. The reader has a feeling of a single theme, of contrast, of gradation, of natural sequence—one has a feeling of the form. In the course of reading, such feelings enter the mix so unobtrusively we are not aware of them.

14. As my use of Pepper's other term, "fusion," suggests, things are not really this simple. The dominant emotion may well absorb (or "fuse") all of the secondary emotions within it. While natural sequence and gradation are sequential, contrasting emotions often combine to form an aggregate.

15. Stephan Strasser, *Phenomenology of Feeling*, trans. Robert E. Wood (Pittsburgh: Duquesne University Press, 1977), 98. Because these strata do not exist in space, Strasser says, they can coexist. They are developmental, the higher encompassing the lower. He considers the possibility that they can unite on the horizontal plane (resorting to a spacial metaphor) or exist in a subordinate-dominant mode. See his discussion in chapter 6 of *Phenomenology of Feeling*.

Huck in the river dawn passage follows something like these strata, as he moves from his personal needs to the first light to a loss of self within the scene. Yet Strasser's point is that readers feel these three levels of emotion simultaneously, the higher levels containing the lower. Because of such "vertical binding," Strasser believes that emotion "mediates" between our unconscious and our conscious (or self-conscious) experience (*Phenomenology*, 98).

16. Langer, *Problems of Art*, 22.

17. Although Pepper stresses sequence in *Principles of Art Appreciation*, he does speak of fusion:

But the distinctive over-all character of each picture remains as something different from the characters of the elements. This intuitively grasped character of the total picture is its fused quality. And to grasp that character is to react emotionally to the picture rather than analytically. (Pepper, *Principles*, 119)

Other thinkers talk about combining emotion into new wholes. See Iser (*The Act of Reading*, chapter 5); Nussbaum ("Narrative Emotions," 236); Harré (*Social Construction*, 3); Dunlop (*The Education of Feeling and Emotion*, 104); Denzin (*Understanding Emotion*, 56); Eliot ("Tradition," 53–54); and Ricoeur ("Metaphor," 155–59). The James-Lange theory of emotion defines a fusion of sensation. And of course T. S. Eliot talks of fusion. One is reminded that Locke and Hartley saw the combination of simple ideas into complex ones to be a key principle.

18. This feeling of awe is a general reaction, but it is not sloppy. In the passage it is bound tightly to the forms emerging from the darkness. It is tied to Huck and to this river at this time. In a sense this emotion of awe organizes or synthesizes all of the other emotions at this point, representing them on the instant. What is the river dawn in my mind? It is a feeling of forms emerging from darkness, which I know as a feeling of awe based on my fused sense of a vast time and a peculiar intimacy. It is a flash of feeling that opens up into a large and complex world, represented by all of the other emotions involved.

19. Note that the mental construction is not static, as Huck adds to it, bit by bit. He first gives us a sense of the whole, or what I have so far called an "impression," telling us that the "days swum by," and then fills in that general idea with particulars.

Janet McKay reminds us that Huck's use of conjunctions between the clauses provides a smooth and even rhythm (*Narrative and Discourse in American Realistic Fiction*, [Philadelphia: University of Pennsylvania Press, 1982], 155). Huck also stresses words like "see," which he repeats over and over, and "away," as he looks "away over the water" and the river softens "away off," the dark spots appearing "ever so far away." Besides capturing the fumbling sincerity of a young boy, such repetition reinforces our sense of ease and comfort.

20. The elements of the river dawn come so thick and fast that only the affective code can cope with them. For all of Huck's emphasis on sight, we do not have the time to construct a detailed image, and as I have said, the concrete nature of the imagination rules out abstract idea. Nor do we have the time to construct the rush of sensations, taste, smell, sight, feel, and sound, settling instead for their emotional equivalent, the feeling of having those feelings. And then, as I have just said, Twain's thesis is nothing less than an emotion: one might be able to visualize days that "slid along so quiet and smooth and lovely," and we know rationalistic readers who will insist on thinking the idea. But it is a feeling—that highly precise feeling—that many readers will feel as they proceed through the passage.

CHAPTER 12. OBJECTIVE EMOTION

Parts of this chapter were published in my article, "'The Rest is Just Cheating': When Feelings Go Bad in *Adventures of Huckleberry Finn*," *Texas Studies in Language and Literature* 32, no. 2 (Summer 1990): 277–96. Copyright 1990 by University of Texas Press. All rights reserved.

1. William James, *The Varieties of Religious Experience*, in *Writings 1902–10* (New York: Library of America, 1987), 446.

2. Leo Marx, "Mr. Eliot, Mr. Trilling, and *Huckleberry Finn*," in *The Adventures of Huckleberry Finn*, eds. Sculley Bradley, Richmond Beatty, E. Hudson Long, and

Thomas Cooley (New York: Norton, 1977) 343. An almost independent canon of criticism has grown up around the ending. T. S. Eliot and Lionel Trilling are among the most famous defenders of it, while Leo Marx makes the basic case against it. John Seelye claims Twain played a practical joke on the reader. Harold Kolb says that "Jim's debasement and Huck's suppression" are Twain's subject. ("Mark Twain, Huck Finn, and Jacob Blivens: Gilt-Edged, Tree-Calf Morality in *The Adventures of Huckleberry Finn*," *Virginia Quarterly Review* 55 [1979]: 653–69). George C. Carrington argues that the ending exemplifies people constructing their own meaning, while Richard Bridgman observes that the ending "fails to generate power" (*The Dramatic Unity of Huckleberry Finn* [Columbus: Ohio State University Press, 1976]; Bridgman, *Colloquial Style,* 104). Edward J. Piacentino explains that Twain returned the ending to the comic mode ("The Ubiquitous Tom Sawyer: Another View of the Conclusion of *Huckleberry Finn*," *Cimarron Review* 37 (October 1979), while James M. Cox argues ingeniously that Huck can receive no reward for his moral behavior (*Mark Twain: The Fate of Humor* [Princeton: Princeton University Press, 1966]).

3. Richard Hill, "Overreaching: Critical Agenda and the Ending of *Huckleberry Finn*," *Texas Studies in Language and Literature* 33, no. 4 (Winter 1991): 508.

4. My quotations are from the Penquin Classic Edition: *The Adventures of Huckleberry Finn* (New York: Penguin, 1985). Subsequent citations from this volume appear in the text.

5. It is actually the last fifth of the novel that is racist. Jim becomes a stereotype and a plaything for the white boys.

6. James Lloyd tells us that people cry in the novel seventy-one times, and the reason, I would suggest, is that the novel portrays contrasting emotions (Lloyd, "The Nature of Twain's Attack on Sentimentality in *The Adventures of Huckleberry Finn,*" *Mississippi Studies in English* 13 [1972]: 60). Twain shows emotion out of control in the Grangerford-Shepherdson feud and the Sherburn-Boggs shooting. He has a keen eye for pretentious or sentimental feeling, as in his portrayals of Emmeline Grangerford, pap Finn, the duke and king (who both prey on others by exploiting their emotions), and Tom Sawyer.

7. Albert von Frank says that Huck is like an adult in a child's body and becomes childlike when he is on the raft with Jim.

8. The loss of Huck creates all sorts of changes, not the least of which is the loss of Huck's world, which means a loss of context, which in turn affects our view of the subject and alters the illusion we obtain. Just as a specific color appears to be different against differently colored backgrounds, so a single event appears differently within different surroundings. In the last third of the novel, Twain drops any detailed description of the Mississippi River, placing Huck in the benign environment of the Phelps farm, and loses his stunning villains, replacing them with the kindly Phelps. At such a place and among such people, Huck's anger now seems unjustified.

9. Richard Poirier observes that "the novel is remarkable for the degree to which the hero's voice—from which his point of view is deduced—becomes increasingly inaudible" (*A World Elsewhere* [New York: Oxford University Press, 1966], 179).

10. The feelings surrounding the thesis "And they all look alike" are dismissive, revealing Twain's own boredom. He clearly regards the farm with distaste.

11. Hemingway, *Green Hills*, 22.

12. Samuel Clemens, 1895 Notebook. Notebook 35, Typescript p. 35. Mark Twain Papers, University of California Library at Berkeley, 35. Also, T. S. Eliot, "Mark Twain's Masterpiece," in *Huck Finn Among Critics,* ed. Thomas Inge (Frederick, Md.: University Publications of America, 1985) 105.

Leo Marx hints at a shift in tone and style. "The major characters themselves are forced to play low comedy roles." Marx also recognizes a shift in emotion, commenting that "during the final extravaganza we are forced to put aside many of the mature emotions evoked earlier" (Marx, "Mr. Eliot, Mr. Trilling, and *Huckleberry Finn,*" Bradley, Beatty, Long, and Cooley, 340).

13. Huck reacts to the abuse that he receives by turning his emotions back upon himself. Rather than lash out at others, he turns his anger and resentment against himself, where they generate his melancholy.

Nor do these feelings distort or invalidate his perception, as one would expect, since they imbue it with integrity. Huck's sadness keeps him from appearing simple-minded and enriches his prose, creating those shadows and highlights that create the effect of dimension. It provides a hint of despair, trembling just beneath the surface of Huck's style, to create a complexity and energy that heighten Huck's joy and add a thoughtful cast to his comments. In the form of repressed anger, moreover, which is also there, Huck's emotion supplies energy, driving the text forward.

14. This is Robert Solomon's argument, as I have said, and some of his other ideas are applicable to this chapter. Although we like to think of emotion as involuntary, we can control it: even feigning an emotion can produce the real thing. And then what we feel reflects (perhaps even creates) who we are, so that our emotions become a basis for judgment of us. The larger point, in terms of objectivity, is the dependence of perception upon our disposition or mood: Huck *feels* fair-minded. He *feels* dispassionate. If rationality is the feeling of being rational, as William James says, then objectivity would be a feeling of fidelity to the object as itself.

15. To show that the Grangerford house "was so nice and had so much style," for example, Huck explains that it "didn't have an iron latch on the front door, nor a wooden one with a buckskin string, but a brass knob to turn, the same as houses in town. There warn't no bed in the parlor." Such details work impressionistically to evoke the scene all by themselves, especially since they are exactly what Huck would have noticed in the confusion of his nighttime arrival. And yet their true value lies in their interaction with the emotion that Huck names, as they give it a physical cause and so credence.

16. Hillman, *Emotion,* 191; Langer, *Feeling and Form.* So do James Hillman, Max Scheler, and Jean-Paul Sartre, among others. In *What is Literature?* Sartre writes,

> If the poet injects his feelings into his poem, he ceases to recognize them; the words take hold of them, penetrate them, and metamorphose them; they do not signify them, even in his eyes. Emotion has become thing; it now has the opacity of things. (*What is Literature?*, trans. Bernard Frechtman [New York: Philosophical Library, 1949], 19)

CHAPTER 13. RELATION IN *THE PORTRAIT OF A LADY*

1. Bridgman, *Colloquial Style in America,* 106.

2. Henry James, "The Art of Fiction," in *Theory of Fiction: Henry James,* ed. James E. Miller, Jr. (Lincoln: University of Nebraska Press, 1962) 41.

3. While some critics do not like Isabel Archer, others complain that her portrayal is inadequate. Millicent Bell, for example, claims that "what we lack is, precisely, a 'portrait,' a spacial arrangement of our impressions, something arrived at by a hundred strokes of the brush, but finally stable" (*Meaning in Henry James* [Cambridge: Harvard University Press, 1991], 93).

We should not be surprised that contemporary critics look askance at Isabel, who rejects the social construction they hold dear. In her famous exchange with Madame Merle, which I quote in section III, Isabel insists that her identity is separate from her appearance in the world. If ever a young lady felt the lash of contingency, however, it is Isabel, who is manipulated by Mrs. Touchett, Ralph, Merle, and Osmond. The critics Virginia Smith and Donald Mull argue that the theme of *Portrait* is the nature of the self. (I might add that the quality of James criticism is exceptionally high.)

4. As Todorov points out, fictional characters use their imaginations, offering in their fictional experience a model of the author's activity. Nicola Bradbury in *Henry James: The Later Novels* (Oxford: Clarendon, 1979) points to an analogy between the processes of "seeing" (by the characters) and of "representation" (by the writer).

5. Nina Baym, "Revision and Thematic Change in *The Portrait of a Lady*," *Modern Fiction Studies* 22, no. 2 (Summer 1976): 187. Joel Porte, "Introduction," *New Essays on the* Portrait of a Lady (Cambridge: Cambridge University Press, 1990), 9.

Unless otherwise noted, citations to *The Portrait of a Lady* are to the Signet Classic edition (New York: New American Library, 1963). This is the text of the 1881 edition. For the preface and the 1908 edition I use the Modern Library edition (New York: Random House, 1966). When I quote from the 1908 edition, I add the initials "ML." Subsequent quotations from these works appear in the text.

6. When Isabel first sees Mrs. Touchett, for example, her mentor has "a face with a good deal of rather violent point" (ML, 24). This phrase describes not only the woman's features, with their thin nose and narrowing chin, but Isabel's emotional construction of her. To Isabel the feeling of "violent point" captures the rigidity and abruptness of Mrs. Touchett's manner.

7. It is Osmond's personal style that makes Isabel choose him ("his 'style' was what the girl had discovered"), and it is Isabel's contribution to his style that persuades Osmond to marry her ("she would publish it to the world without his having any of the trouble") (ML, 305).

Dorothea Krook makes the crucial point that Osmond really *likes* Isabel, offering the most sympathetic view of him I know (*The Ordeal of Consciousness in Henry James* [Cambridge: Cambridge University Press, 1962], 54). Nina Baym points out that Osmond in the 1881 version is really in love, making him a more ambiguous figure than he is in 1908. William T. Stafford argues that Osmond is witty and eloquent ("*The Portrait of a Lady:* The Second Hundred Years," *The Henry James Review* 2 [Winter 1981]: 98).

8. Henry James, "The Real Thing," in *The Complete Tales of Henry James*, ed. Leon Edel, vol. 8 (Philadelphia: J. B. Lippincott, 1963), 245.

9. Osmond makes sure that the Isabel who feels oppressed by Warburton and Caspar may enjoy his love without suffering a lover's demands. When she leaves him for the several months that might mean forever, he remains generous (if plaintive). "'Go everywhere,' he said at last, in a low, kind voice: 'do everything; get everything out of life. Be happy—be triumphant.'"

Osmond has learned to imply rather than state, knowing that people automatically infer the whole from the part. He knows that the enveloping emotion or tone determines meaning, and that we really do let a single emotion represent the total person. Osmond is thus the master of the impression, providing the hint that his audience will complete. His intelligence finds expression not in ideas but emotion, which is the realm in which Osmond seeks power. "Success, for Gilbert Osmond, would be to make himself felt."

10. In this image, Osmond understands Isabel's love of freedom (though he misjudges it) and her need to serve, which explains his use of Pansy in the courtship. He also understands the emotion that is the key to Isabel's character: her love of a cozy and peaceful privacy. It is precisely such an attractive but circumscribed life, not unlike those hours she spent in the alcove of her parent's house in Albany, that Osmond offers her.

11. Osmond's sudden and extreme behavior defamiliarizes his act, but once it is done, he is so confident of being understood that he can deny his meaning. While a lesser stylist might openly state his point, telling Isabel how easy it is to separate her from Pansy, Osmond insists that Isabel must visit Pansy, though "not too often." This quiet denial of the obvious meaning of Osmond's action skillfully enhances its power: Osmond's mild (and self-satisfied) tone heightens Isabel's sense of his malice. By creating a gap, Osmond also pulls his audience into the Iserian "text."

12. Henry James, preface, *Portrait of a Lady*, (ML, xli).

13. Osmond leaps to his feet, and Madame Merle takes Isabel aside to urge that she persuade Warburton to marry Pansy. Later Osmond does so too, using much the same language as Merle: "You have great influence with him."

14. Charles Anderson, *Person, Place, and Thing in Henry James' Novels*, (Durham, N.C.: Duke University Press, 1977) 122. Stowell, *Literary Impressionism, James and Chekhov* (Athens: University of Georgia Press, 1980), 181. Paul B. Armstrong, *The Phenomenology of Henry James* (Chapel Hill: University of North Carolina Press, 1983), 122–28.

15. Armstrong, *Phenomenology of Henry James*, 39. Like the critics Kirschke and Stowell, Paul Armstrong stresses the way in which Isabel infers the truth from her "impression horizons," filling in the whole from the part according to the principles of agreement and harmony. Armstrong uses Husserl to explicate the mind's propensity to complete its partial knowledge, constructing the hidden sides of the cube. To this I would add that, as I have said, the impression is often an emotion that represents the whole. No less an authority than the philosopher David Hume would agree. The emotional "impression" that might seem frivolous (it's only an impression) or sloppy (don't be so impressionistic) or unstable (he's so impressionable) is in truth a process of imagination and memory that provides insight.

In this remarkable feat of representation, I might add, Isabel does nothing less than review and represent several years of a complex relationship, an act illustrating the specific advantages of emotion as a form of consciousness (and so mental construction). James makes us believe that we have witnessed the marriage, even though he gives but a few pages of summary. He describes not action, or the spouses together, but the emotion that represents the union, or how it feels to be married to Osmond. While such a feeling is not as complete as several chapters showing the marriage, it conveys a great deal. Note that Isabel here is herself a novelist (or narrator), representing a body of experience.

16. It is possible that Isabel returns to Osmond at the end like a battered wife, clinging to the man who has abused her. But she has done battle with him over Pansy and shows every sign of doing so in the future. And she now knows that he cheated her, which gives her a moral advantage.

17. Leon Edel, *Henry James* (Philadelphia: J. B. Lippincott, 1953–72), vol. 2, 433; F. W. Dupee, *Henry James* (New York: Sloane, 1956), 122; Virginia Llewellyn Smith, *Henry James and the Real Thing* (New York: St. Martin's, 1996), 33; James, preface, xxxiv, xxxiii. Henry James had a clear sense of Isabel developing in the course of the novel, a "seed" that he wanted "to grow as tall as possible, to push into the light and air and thickly flower there" (preface, xxix).

Part of the problem lies in the fact that Isabel's parents are dead. To have seen her mother or her father, who was a dilettante like Osmond, would have told us a great deal. In a way, Isabel is an orphan who must create herself, and Ralph's largess permits her to do so—which is why the disappointment is so great.

18. Henry James, preface, xxxiii. Isabel commits herself; she acts; she tastes disappointment—in a real sense, James's portrait is a masterpiece in its fidelity to the way felt experience in real life deepens character. Isabel's confession of her real

feelings to the dying Ralph dramatizes this theme admirably: by the end of the novel, Isabel is emotionally open to the "tangle" she once shut out. She is real because she has felt deeply.

19. Donald Mull observes that Osmond seems autonomous, or free of contingency, which would make him that much more attractive to Isabel. She believes Osmond would be simply himself.

20. Like a good painter, James gives a carefully defined foreground, middle distance, and vista. And just as a three-dimensional scene seems more real than a flat one—more vivid or fresh, as it leaps from the canvas—so James's chiaroscuristic scene springs to life. "Real dusk would not arrive for many hours; but the flood of summer light had begun to ebb, the air had grown mellow, the shadows were long upon the smooth, dense, turf."

Several critics talk about space in literature. Joseph Frank is interested in the formal space within the novel, while Joseph Kestner argues that *The Portrait of a Lady* is about "pictorial illusion" (*The Spaciality of the Novel* [Detroit: Wayne State University Press, 1978], 77).

21. Henry James, preface, xxxvi.

22. Edelman, *Bright Air*, 119. What does James mean by "relation"? The context of his remark points to several meanings. The secondary characters think *about* Isabel, pondering her relation to them. They also think about themselves, pondering their relation to her—or that to which she assigns them. Each ponders what she seems to think about him, as well as her effect upon him. Critics have often misunderstood James's comment, "'Place the centre of the subject in the young woman's own consciousness,' I said to myself, 'and you get as interesting and as beautiful a difficulty as you could wish'" (preface, xxxvi). *Portrait* spends little time in Isabel's own consciousness: it is the other characters who (with great difficulty) examine this "subject," which is Isabel's feelings.

A specific relation is a world unto itself, belonging to neither of the two related elements. It is at once abstract, existing as an idea, and concrete, representing what is physically real. Perhaps the key to relation is its complexity: set an apple next to a pear and they "relate" in dozens of ways. The relation might be a comparison of (or an interaction between) the two colors or shapes or tastes, but it is in any case multidimensional. What counts is the context, or what one intends. The relation is so subtle that we have no language for it. Dictionaries define this meaning of relation as "connection."

23. In the case of reading, it is not enough to imagine two objects. One must mentally construct the relationship between them. The relation might be implied by imagining only the objects, of course, but we know their meaning as the feeling of their relationship. I don't mean that substance does not count. It matters greatly whether the animal outside my tent is a dog or a grizzly. But so does its precise relationship to me.

24. Images or ideas cannot do justice to even the simple relationship I have with a neighborhood dog. I can picture the dog leaping up on the fence to be petted, and I can conceptualize its friendliness, putting it into words. Yet even this uncluttered relationship is more complicated than space or idea can portray quickly. It involves the neighborhood in which we meet, my state of mind, the dog's temperament, and my daily routine. It involves the dog's relation to its owners and my attitude toward animals.

25. William James, *Principles of Psychology*, vol. 1, 245–46. In his use of the word "feeling," William James conflates sensation and emotion, but then he believed emotion to be just another name for sensation. Clearly he saw that the mind experiences the meaning of relation as a precise and subtle feeling.

26. A large number of thinkers focus on relationships, some even arguing that the relation among objects is more important than the objects themselves. See Susanne Langer, Northrop Frye, and Paul Ricoeur. I've already mentioned psychologists and cognitive theoreticians like Josef Perner, who define perception as the comparison of the present sensation to our mental model of the subject (see chapter 2). Stephen E. Palmer makes it clear that mental representation is representation of *relations*. Susanne Langer goes even further in the first volume of *Mind:* "Even a non-representational picture is an image—not of physical objects, but of those inward tensions that compose our life of feeling" (*Mind,* 145).

27. Iser, *Act of Reading,* 182.

28. The sadness felt by the characters at the beginning of the novel, and the fact that Touchett's house is made more beautiful by its scars, suggests that James's theme is the beauty that flows from absence or pain. Beauty lies in the waning light. It is significant that the ladies who might serve as mentors to Isabel—Mrs. Touchett, Madame Merle, and (improbably) Countess Gemini—are all unhappy. The woman who does achieve happiness, the humorous Henrietta, is not a lady.

29. Michael Riffaterre, *Fictional Truth* (Baltimore: Johns Hopkins University Press, 1990), 10.

30. James, preface, xxxvi.

31. James's title, after all, is not "The Portrait of Isabel." Note how little James tells us of Isabel's looks and how thoroughly he dramatizes her measured, civilized behavior. Of course, when Isabel defines herself as the division between inner and outer, she defines herself as a relationship: James really does create her in terms of her relationship to herself and others.

Chapter 14. An Affective Criticism

1. One could view Wayne Booth's *Rhetoric of Fiction* as a precursor of affective criticism, in that he dispels the illusion of an objective novel, discussing the necessity of revealed emotion to reader understanding.

2. Literary studies have no extended contemporary analysis of emotion within literature. Neal Oxenhandler provides an excellent starting point in his essay "The Changing Concept of Literary Emotion," but it is still to philosophers that one must look for guidance.

3. Graff, "Disliking Books at an Early Age," 46.

4. Rather than serve as illustration, literature is a way of discovering truth. It is a process of problem-solving based on the examination of alternative solutions constructed in concrete form—precisely the trial-and-error psychologists perceive at the root of human creativity. While other disciplines achieve their insight by narrowing their focus, literature broadens it, offering a model of the world that includes as many dimensions of the subject as possible. Its great strength lies in its concreteness, which (though embodied in language) captures the truths available to the concrete alone, and in the creativity of the imagination, as it discovers new possibilities in its reconstruction of the real.

5. I've already discussed Hemingway's use of the feeling of convalescence as a subject, and have examined Jane Austen's study of emotion in general. Emotions can be not only interesting, as when Madeline sinks to the floor in church in Saul Bellow's *Herzog,* but the very point of the work, as in the protagonist's discovery of an emotional pattern within himself (as in *Herzog* again), or in the portrayal of a telling attitude toward emotion, as in Samuel Beckett's work.

6. For this reason if none other, the tone of what is said can be more important than the content. This is true of human conversation and it is certainly true of the novel, in which facts can serve merely as the expression of an emotion—a means by which to convey approval or anger or desire. Imagine an event in which the characters feel nothing: except for the strangeness of such an event (which would convey a meaningful emotion of its own), the scene would appear peculiarly barren.

7. How do tone and subject interact? The choice of the subject alone can set tone, whether it be a slum in Calcutta or the Upper East Side of New York City. Conversely, tone is the text's evaluation of the subject: take the subject straight and you say one thing; take it ironically and you take it another way. Because tone evaluates the subject, it helps define it. And in any case, tone is the means by which the author positions the reader vis-à-vis the text, insuring that he or she has the experience the writer desires.

8. How does reaction interact with subject and tone? The author would use subject and tone to elicit the desired response in the reader, of course, and the reader judges the author's choice of subject and tone by virtue of the reaction the reader feels. What is noteworthy is the effect on reaction by the mere choice of subject—not a few writers have gained audiences by writing about the right thing. An otherwise disjointed subject and tone, moreover, can be united in the reader's reaction. We desire to feel, and so seek out occasions to react emotionally, whether it be in a football stadium or a horror movie.

9. Richards believed that science offers a statement of fact while the poem offers a "pseudostatement," which finds its point not in what it says but how it affects the reader.

10. Selden, *A Reader's Guide to Contemporary Theory,* 107.

11. Jane Tompkins explores this idea in her essay "The Reader in History" (*Reader-Response Criticism,* 201–26). She shows that criticism has historically examined the connection between aesthetics and power. The novelist persuades the reader to construct the text in a certain way, and this is a form of power obtained by means of language. For an applied affective criticism, one might look at Tompkins's "Me and My Shadow."

12. A focus on emotion permits one to judge the work on the terms set by the novel itself. Does the narrative justify sympathy for this character or group? Does the narrative portray a Mrs. Bennet who deserves the contempt Austen appears to request? If one looks at emotion as the writer's judgment, then the emotion created in the reader by the text is the measure of the author's success in the text. At the same time, writers include in the work what they do not consciously intend, which means that the emotion felt by the reader may reveal the unconscious or hidden meaning of the text. If this response conflicts with the judgment signalled by the author, even though the text actually justifies it, the reader becomes confused and irritated.

13. R. W. Hepburn, "The Arts and the Education of Feeling and Emotions," 485. Margaret Phillips, *The Education of the Emotions through Sentiment Development* (London: Allen and Unwin, 1937). Quoted in Dunlop, *The Education of Feeling and Emotion,* 106–7. Langer, *Mind,* vol. 1, 147.

14. In his book *Emotion,* the philosopher William Lyons distinguishes between evaluation, which is rational, and appraisal, which is emotional. In many cases reason and emotion are complementary, both leading to the same judgment.

15. Twain, *Huck Finn,* 29.

16. Some thinkers claim that we have evolved to perceive dishonesty in others, since that has an impact on our survival. Certainly we have considerable agreement on what emotions are appropriate. As Noël Carroll puts it, "within the boundaries of certain cultures, there are certain criteria concerning which emotional responses

are normatively correct—that is, which emotions certain situations are supposed to elicit" (Hjort and Laver, *Emotion and the Arts,* 206).

17. Mitchell, "Nobody but our Gang warn't Around," 88, 92–93.

18. Many philosophers define moods as emotions without objects. Thus we have a disposition toward feeling a certain way, whether it be "blue" or "excited." Yet I think Heidegger is correct in tying a mood to a specific source. In a way a mood takes as its object one's desire or need. In this sense, a mood is about one's inner state, to which Heidegger adds the notion of one's situation in the world.

What about those people who *want* to feel and so pump up their emotions? We do have the ability to conjure up a feeling for its own sake—when we *try* to feel an emotion, we often discover that it materializes—though actors do speak of visualizing the object or circumstance that provides the emotion.

19. As Jane Tompkins puts it in *Sensational Designs,* much of what we today consider unjustified emotion in the "sentimental novel" was justified at the time by the then current values and controlling myths. Tompkins insists rightly that emotion in itself is not "bad," and that we are too quick to dismiss feelings we do not immediately understand. The word "sentimental" may refer either to the presence of emotion, as in a given tradition, or to the excessive or unjustified use of emotion, and it is in the second sense that I use the word. In his essay in Hjort and Laver, Robert Solomon defends even "unjustified" emotions, since, among other things, they give pleasure.

Chapter 15. A Critic's Notebook

1. At one time, Morrison has said, *Jazz* and *Beloved* were parts of one novel. She found *Beloved* to be so confusing that she could not finish it. When she turned 275 pages in to her editor, seeking help, he saw that the manuscript already formed a finished tale—the novel that we know (in *Conversations* with Toni Morrison, ed. Danielle K. Taylor-Guthrie [Jackson: University Press of Mississippi, 1994], 240).

2. "A Gravestone of Memories," *Newsweek* 110 (September 28, 1987), 74.

3. Mervyn Rothstein, "Toni Morrison, in Her New Novel, Defends Women," *New York Times* (August 26, 1987), sec. C, p. 17. (Henceforth I will abbreviate the *Times* as *NYT.*)

4. Toni Morrison, *Beloved* (New York: New American Library, 1987), 7. Subsequent citations to this volume appear in the text.

5. Deborah Ayer makes this point.

6. "One of the nicest things women do is nurture other people, but it can be done in such a way that we surrender anything like a self. You can surrender yourself to a man and think that you cannot live or be without that man; you have no existence. And you can do the same thing with children. . . . It seemed that slavery presented an ideal situation to discuss the problem" (*Conversations,* 254). Sethe feels that she owns her children; at other times she sees them as literally part of herself.

7. Karen Carmean puts it this way: "Morrison meant for Beloved to be a kind of 'mirror' character who would reflect the inner lives of the characters with whom she made contact" (*Toni Morrison's World of Fiction* [Troy, N.Y.: Whitston, 1993] 85).

This theme does not mean that Morrison views emotion as a negative force. Morrison makes this clear in the character of Ella, who is described as an enemy of emotion. "Nobody loved her and she wouldn't have liked it if they had, for she considered love a serious disability." Ella is hard-headed and practical—and chronically wrong. Although she is responsible for saving Sethe, since she leads the women in the exorcism, she originally suspected Sethe of all sorts of transgressions.

"'Well, who can tell what all went on in there? Look here, I don't know who Sethe is or none of her people'" (187).

8. Like Elizabeth Bowen, who announced the "Death of the Heart," T. S. Eliot also believed that modern people have lost the capacity to feel, which is why they live in a wasteland. In an account that may be the most convincing treatment of the theme, Toni Morrison shows that people shut off feelings that are too painful. It is worth noting that Morrison has a special pride in her own emotion:

> I really think the range of emotions and perceptions I have had access to as a black person and as a female person are greater than those of people who are neither. I really do. So it seems to me that my world did not shrink because I was a black female writer. It just got bigger. (Rothstein, *NYT*, sec. C, 17)

9. I don't mean that one accepts the tone of a work blindly. As I have said, one adopts the tone provisionally, reserving judgment, and that judgment is severe: if the author is too far off base in her evaluation of the material, we will quit reading.

10. Stanley Crouch, "Aunt Medea," *New Republic* 197 (October 19, 1987): 41, 42.

11. Bernard Bell identifies "five different but related linguistic codes. . . . Standard American English; rural black vernacular English; black feminist discourse; black patriarchal discourse; white male hegemonic discourse" (in Barbara Solomon, ed., *Critical Essays on Toni Morrison's* "Beloved" [New York: G. K. Hall, 1998], 14).

12. Morrison says she *wanted* a calm narrative voice. See Carol Kolmerten, Stephen Ross, and Judith Wittenberg, eds., *Unflinching Gaze: Morrison and Faulkner Reenvisioned* (Jackson: University Press of Mississippi, 1997), 93.

13. For an extended discussion of this point, including the stream motif, see Elizabeth House's essay, "Toni Morrison's Ghost: The Beloved Who is Not Beloved," *Studies in American Fiction* 18, no. i (Spring 1980). Interestingly, Robert L. Broad says in another connection that Beloved's comments "are far easier to comprehend if Beloved's anger stems from a trauma completely different in time, place, and nature from the expected one" ("Giving Blood to the Scraps," *African American Review* 28, no. 2 [Summer 1994]: 191).

Morrison herself includes both views of Beloved. "Literally she is what Sethe thinks she is, her child returned to her from the dead. . . . She is also another kind of dead which is not spiritual but flesh, which is, a survivor from the true, factual slave ship" (*Conversations,* 247).

14. "I just imagined the life of a dead girl which was the girl that Margaret Garner killed. . . . I just imagined her remembering what happened to her, being some place else and returning, knowing what happened to her. And I call her Beloved" (Kolmerten et al., *Unflinching Gaze,* 182).

15. Since I wrote these comments, Barbara Solomon has published Terry Otten's excellent essay "Transfiguring the Narrative: *Beloved*—from Melodrama to Tragedy," in *Critical Essays on Toni Morrison's* "Beloved" (New York: G. K. Hall, 1998). Otten argues that Morrison moves from the slave narrative of Sethe's escape to a tragic story. As a tragic figure, Sethe experiences conflict within herself, obsession with the presence of the past, a movement toward reenactment, ritual, and the ambiguity of victory and defeat. She also suffers from hubris, while the community acts as a Greek chorus. I would add that the extreme (and absolute) nature of Sethe's decision—whether to permit her children to return to slavery or death—also sets a tragic tone. Otten shows that Morrison was quite conscious of the Greek tradition.

16. One could say that Morrison turns the screw another turn, using not the children James employed but a baby. In both fictions the supernatural and the sexual offer competing interpretations, and it is difficult to prove one to the exclusion of the other. Although both authors use childhood sexuality and sexual repres-

sion, Morrison does not employ a narrator or a single point of view, let alone the device of an old manuscript. Unlike James, Morrison embraces the supernatural openly, connecting it to the natural by means of emotion.

It is relevant that, as Deborah Guth reminds us, "Dearly Beloved" is the opening of the marriage service. See Guth, *Journal of Narrative Technique* 24, no. 2 (Spring 1994): 83.

17. Beloved is perversely impersonal in sex because she has been damaged. When she asks for sex from Paul D, she uses the same phrase she used to describe the sexual abuse of the white men. Paul D's susceptibility to her, on the other hand, reveals *his* damage, just as Sethe's vulnerability reveals hers. Throughout the novel, whether it be Denver's marriage or the fellatio forced each morning upon the chain gang, Morrison uses sex as the barometer of invasion and humiliation.

18. Some will say that the experience of a black female slave is too great a stretch for a white male. Yet the glory of fiction is its ability to transfer the reader vicariously into unknown situations. I feel confident that Morrison's skill leads me to a reasonably accurate understanding of Sethe's life. I miss a great deal, obviously, and as a male might be less skillful empathetically than a woman who has had to identify all her life with predominantly male protagonists. On the other hand, individuals probably differ more among themselves than within their genders. And I do think that reader identification can take one a long way.

19. One could also view Beloved as the essence of femininity driven to excess or madness. Morrison does not push this theme, but the three women in the cabin form a purely female society that enjoys the absence of the men who have abused them. The episode begins as an idyll. Is it possible that the bulging Beloved is pregnant? It seems to be so.

20. Rothstein, *NYT*, sec. C, p. 17. Morrison observes, "there are certain emotions that are useful for the construction of a text, and some are too small. Anger is too tiny an emotion to use when you're writing, and compassion is too sloppy. Almost everything that makes you want to write, or feel like writing, is not useful in the act of writing. So it's the mediation between those two states, the compulsion and all those feelings, that make you compelled."

Barbara Solomon observes that many critics study the images of this novel, finding in them structure and interpretation.

21. Morrison is quite aware of this spirituality. In addition to the African American's practical knowledge, she says, "there was this other knowledge or perception, always discredited but nevertheless there, which informed their sensibilities and clarified their activities" (*Conversations*, 226).

CHAPTER 16. IMAGINING *THE CENTAUR*

Parts of this chapter first appeared in Keith Opdahl, "John Updike and the Realistic Tradition," *Contemporary American Fiction*, eds. Malcolm Bradbury and Sigmund Ro (London: Edward Arnold, 1987), 1–15.

1. I like to think of John Updike as the heir to Saul Bellow. Updike really does write as though (as Bellow put it) "the development of realism in the nineteenth century is still the major event of modern literature" (*Writers at Work*, 3rd series, ed. George Plimpton [New York: Viking, 1968], 180). I say this even though Updike has criticized Bellow's didacticism and Bellow didn't much like *The Centaur* when he reviewed it in *The Great Ideas Today*. Yet Updike's fiction accomplishes the feat he attributes to Bellow: to take "mimesis to a layer or two deeper than it has gone

before" (*Hugging the Shore,* [New York: Knopf, 1983], 263). Like Bellow, Updike describes not only the surface detail of American life but a second, transcendent world that shines through it. While Bellow glimpses a hidden force in the subterranean tremor of a passing subway, Updike describes the snowflakes falling beneath parking lot lights, forming millions of rushing, "ghostly" shadows on the ground.

2. Joyce Markle, *Fighters and Lovers* (New York: New York University Press, 1973), 63. Among those who complain of the mythology, we find George Steiner, Richard Gilman, Granville Hicks, and Norman Podhoretz. John Aldridge complains that Updike assumed that "all one needed to do was bring together some mythological figures and some contemporary characters, and say that they were parallels, without troubling to create a dramatic situation in which they actually *became* parallels and therefore meaningful" ("The Private Vice of John Updike," in *Time to Murder and Create: The Contemporary Novel in Crisis* [New York: David McKay, 1966], 168). I will show that this statement is exactly wrong.

Those critics who accept the mythic tend to come later, notable among whom is Robert Detweiler, who takes a middle position, claiming the mythic is a matter of gestalt: "One sacrifices a coherent story line for the impact of a total imaginative-emotional approach, but it is a worthwhile trade" (*John Updike* [New York: Twayne, 1972], 84).

3. Quite a few critics understand that emotion plays an important role in the imagining of this novel. See Detweiler, Mellard, and Markle.

4. John Updike, *The Centaur* (New York: Fawcett Crest, 1963), 53. Subsequent citations to this volume appear in the text.

5. John Updike, *Writers at Work,* 4th series, ed. George Plimpton (New York: Penguin, 1976), 440.

6. Caldwell is based upon Updike's own father, interestingly enough, who reacted to that fact characteristically. When someone objected to the portrait in *The Centaur,* Updike reports, Wesley Updike responded, "No, it's the truth. The kid got me right" (Updike, *Writers at Work,* 432).

7. John Updike, "Why Rabbit Had to Go," *New York Times Book Review* (August 5, 1990), 1.

8. We represent George the man as an emotion, feeling the potentiality of the centaur even as we do so. And we construct Chiron as an emotion, too—the Olympian teacher whose poisoning puts him into constant pain—but within an emotional nimbus embodying the identity of George. I suppose that one could also visualize George while feeling the presence of Chiron. Or visualize Chiron while feeling the identity of George. To construct both characters in the affective code seems advantageous, however, since feelings blend together so easily.

9. Perhaps the best example of this skill is Updike's creation of the effect of three dimensions—a technique we have already witnessed in *Portrait.* Like a good painter, Updike dramatizes the existence of two or more planes of space. The scene is framed in the window—a device that in itself dramatizes distance—and describes a figure passing through space until he travels out of sight. Updike describes George's movements as a diagonal, moving *into* the canvas ("out through our yard and past the mailbox and up the hill"), and then again dramatizes space by means of blocking: George comes into our vision from outside the window frame and disappears behind trees. Updike employs contrast ("figure dark against the snow") and even chiaroscuro, denoting the way the "trees took white on their sun side" to draw the play of light on spacial forms.

10. George feels the arrow as "a metallic scratch and a stiff rustle," as "the feathers brushed the floor." "How strange he had grown," Updike writes, giving a key pattern in the novel. "His top half felt all afloat in a starry firmament of ideals and young

voices singing; the rest of his self was heavily sunk in a swamp where it must, eventually, drown."

11. Could what seems visual in the mind's eye be represented by emotion, so that we actually *feel* what we think we "see"? In a manner reminiscent of Henry James and Toni Morrison, Updike uses images to create emotions in the reader, speaking of "brown air" or a "white voice." He also depends upon emotion to embody certain important technical effects, such as the illusion of three dimensions. If the eye views a canvas as flat unless cued by the mind to view it dimensionally, as psychologists claim, then that cue could well be the feeling of dimensional space.

12. Updike, *Writers at Work*, 442.

13. Walking behind George in the snow, Peter imagines that "his was the shape of the neck and head of a horse I was riding." Elsewhere George walks quickly and restlessly, like a stallion in a corral, giving Peter the sense that his father is horselike. In the office of Doc Appleton, who is actually Apollo, Peter overhears the phrase "hydra-venom."

Significantly, Peter's feelings give us as readers an emotional construction of this special world. *We* feel the presence of ancient Greece. *We* feel the sense of George in guise. What is the theme of *The Centaur*? It is precisely this feeling of a hidden world, which permeates our sense of Peter's Alton, Pennsylvania. In Peter, Updike offers a character who resists the affective code and in doing so lives in a limited or narrow world. Peter naturally embraces the visual or rational as the "real" world, dismissing the emotional (however much it may haunt him), while the reader imagines both the visual and the emotional levels, taking his or her cue from the feeling of the double level, feeling both the high school hangout, say, and the shadowy movements of the Minotaur.

14. Updike also alternates points of view, shifting between Greece and Pennsylvania, in a way that makes them easy equivalents. In chapter 6, for example, Peter is Prometheus, entertaining a group of visitors "as I lay on my rock," until suddenly "the bell rang" and "I sat opposite Johnny Dedman," who is showing pornographic playing cards in the high-school cafeteria. We realize that Prometheus has been Peter Caldwell all along.

15. This fact contradicts the view of critics such as James E. Mellard, who claims the whole novel to be Peter's reminiscence (and that the mythic is thus a metaphor in Peter's mind). In contrast to Mellard, I see good reason to take Updike's point of view literally. Updike alternates an omniscient point of view (often limited to George's third person) with the first-person point of view of Peter himself. While part of the novel is Peter's later reminiscence, part of it exists independently, containing information Peter could not know.

16. Is it possible that George and Vera have had sexual relations? The two were earlier alone in the kitchen, and Peter awakes to a house humming with an unusual (and suggestive) radiance. The point is unlikely, though it underlines the similarity of the two Venus stories.

17. "By the way, I must repeat that I didn't mean Caldwell to die in *The Centaur;* he dies in the sense of living, of going back to work, of being a shelter for his son" (*Writers at Work*, 433).

18. Peter at the end of the novel confesses to a submission that plays a key role in his art and that he may have learned from his father. "It came upon me that I must go to Nature disarmed of perspective and stretch myself like a large transparent canvas upon her in the hope that, my submission being perfect, the imprint of a beautiful and useful truth would be taken."

19. Several of the later critics recognize this connection between duality and intensity. Thus George W. Hunt observes that "this paralleling of realism with myth at

times takes on a double focus, a simultaneity of the two perspectives that is itself a fine stylistic achievement" (*John Updike and the Three Secret Things: Sex, Religion and Art* [Grand Rapids, Mich.: W. B. Eerdmans, 1980], 50). Other critics like Detweiler and Mellard understand that the novel must be imagined emotionally.

20. One can speculate on just which of these dualities creates vitality. Some believe the mind simply works that way. We see in "pairs." Others argue that duality belongs to what we could call the arithmetic of language: we know "up" in terms of a Sausserian "down," and so always understand in pairs. Physiologically, perception offers sensation in a binocular fashion, enabling us to triangulate the source of the sound, or sight, or smell. Such closely related duality might make such constructions more vital.

21. Elizabeth Bennet misunderstands her feelings about Darcy; Huck Finn ignores his own anger and fear; Isabel Archer does not understand her own sexuality; and even Sethe represses an immense and multifaceted pain. Against this background, George's openness is refreshing. He deals with his feelings by expressing them. And he understands them. Updike, too, is "open" in his descriptions of the emotional climate, as he treats the "atmosphere"—which defines the meaning of the moment—in a palpable way.

22. Updike, *Writers at Work*, 444.

23. I do not mean to claim that readers construct this novel in the affective code exclusively. The nature of the centaur is largely visual, asking us to form an image. And the dual world, with its running pun, asks for intellectualization.

24. Updike portrays the female trapped in her social role. Cassie gave up the stage for George, who tells Peter she is a real "femme," by which he means a strong and femininely charismatic person. Of course, George is also a type, a plodder, who reaches his goal by persistence; but that means he is loyal to the needs of his family.

CHAPTER 17. CONCLUSION

1. Even so, much of this image is really the feeling of incongruity. The point of the image lies in its significance, which we know as affect.

2. Sometimes feelings work as synecdoche, as the localized emotion represents the larger whole. One might represent the complete novel as Peter's sense of a familiar but hidden world, for example, a feeling that on at least one level gives the novel meaning. To someone else, the representing emotion may involve gender roles, since George is caught up in his role as a provider (and Cassie is isolated in that farmhouse).

3. The three codes relate to one another in different ways. As I vicariously sit within the shadow of the river bank, the willows dark behind me, I look out on the blazing light of the river—a perfect visual correlative to the feeling of safety. The images of light and dark reinforce Twain's original emotional meaning. In other cases, the image and idea qualify or conflict with the feeling, forming what amounts to a kaleidoscope of codes confirming, modifying, or negating one another.

4. Michael Tye, *Imagery Debate*, 64.

5. Others suggest ideas similar to this. "Emotion might be the ground of images, imagination and thought," James Hillman says, and no less an expert than Susanne Langer agrees, noting that in "the image of feeling created by artists in every kind of art . . . serves to hold the reality itself for our labile and volatile memory, as a touchstone to test the scope of our intellectual constructions" (Hillman, *Emotion*, 175; Langer, *Mind*, vol. 1 xix). If such statements are true, then it is no accident that emotion represents the object as a whole. Because we know the context as a feeling or emotion, our emotion literally "serves to hold the reality."

6. Most people would agree that meaning enters the conscious mind from some dim or unconscious region. We feel it before we give it voice. Hence, Harold Osborne observes, "feeling seems as it were to grope ahead of perception and to put out cognitive tentacles in advance of clear apprehension" ("The Quality of Feeling in Art," *British Journal of Aesthetics* vol. 3 no. 1 [1963], 47). Edith Stein says that "knowledge not yet realized is felt as a value. This feeling of value is the source of all cognitive striving. . . . An object proffers itself to me as dark, veiled, and unclear. It stands there as something which demands exposure and clarification" (Edith Stein, *On the Problem of Empathy,* trans. W. Stern [The Hague: Nijhoff, 1970], 97–98).

I might add that the distinction between image and feeling in this netherworld of burgeoning thought is not at all clear. I also "see" a flickering image, as I said earlier: it is just that the emotion expresses the meaning in a more precise and "solid" way than the image.

7. We may now understand that Stanley Fish's description of the sentence applies to not only idea but emotion: as one reads through the sentence, the words trigger first one feeling and then another. But while ideas tend to replace one another with finality, feelings tend to linger, overlapping and even fusing with what follows. The feeling expressed by the first part of the sentence not only modifies its successor but is itself modified.

8. The philosopher Eva Brann sums up the majority view when she suggests that what seems to be a representational emotion is really an image. Are such emotions, she asks, "inherently amorphous, unobjective? Are they perhaps images of a sort, or are they the cause of images, or possibly their effect?" (*World of Imagination,* 761). Nevertheless, Brann leaves the door open, concluding that the matter of affective display is an open question.

Bibliography

(See separate sections for criticism of the novels studied here.)

Altieri, Charles. "Sensibility, Rhetoric and Will: Some Tensions in Contemporary Poetry." *Contemporary Literature* 23 (Fall 1982): 451–79.

Armstrong, Paul B. *The Challenge of Bewilderment*. Ithaca: Cornell University Press, 1987.

Arnheim, Rudolf. *Art and Visual Perception*. Berkeley and Los Angeles: University of California Press, 1954.

———. "Emotion and Feeling in Psychology and Art." *Toward a Psychology of Art*. Berkeley and Los Angeles: University of California Press, 1966.

———. *Visual Thinking*. Berkeley and Los Angeles: University of California Press, 1969.

Arnold, Magda. *Emotion and Personality*. Vol. 1. New York: Columbia University Press, 1960.

———. *Feelings and Emotions: The Loyola Symposium*. New York: Academic Press, 1970.

Austen, Jane. *Mansfield Park: A Novel*. Vol. 3 of *The Novels of Jane Austen*. Edited by R. W. Chapman. Oxford: Oxford University Press, 1923.

———. *Pride and Prejudice*. London: Penguin, 1972.

Barth, John. "The Literature of Exhaustion." *The Atlantic* 220 (August 1967): 29–34.

Bellow, Saul. *Herzog*. New York: Viking, 1964.

———. "Literature." *The Great Ideas Today*, 135, 79. New York: Encyclopedia Britannica, 1963.

———. "Hemingway and the Image of Man." *Partisan Review* 20 (May–June 1953): 338–42.

Bleich, David. *Readings and Feelings*. Urbana: National Council of Teachers of English, 1975.

———. *Subjective Criticism*. Baltimore: Johns Hopkins University Press, 1978.

Block, Ned. *Imagery*. Cambridge: MIT Press, 1981.

Boruah, Bijoy. *Fiction and Emotion*. Oxford: Clarendon, 1988.

Bosanquet, Bernard. *Three Lectures on Aesthetic*. Indianapolis, Ind.: Bobbs-Merrill, 1963.

Bradbury, Malcolm. "Neorealist Fiction." In *Columbia Literary History of the United States*, edited by Emory Elliott. New York: Columbia University Press, 1988.

———. "Preface." In *Contemporary American Fiction*, edited by Malcolm Bradbury and Sigmund Ro. London: Edward Arnold, 1987.

Brann, Eva. *The World of the Imagination*. Lanham, Md.: Rowman and Littlefield, 1991.

271

Broad, C. D. "Emotion and Sentiment." *Journal of Aesthetics and Art Criticism* 13 (1954): 203–4.

Brodsky, Claudia. *The Imposition of Form: Studies in Narrative Representation and Knowledge.* Princeton: Princeton University Press, 1987.

Brown, James F. *Affectivity, Its Language and Meaning.* Washington, D.C.: University Press of America, 1982.

Bruner, Jerome. *Acts of Meaning.* Cambridge: Harvard University Press, 1990.

Buck, Ross. *The Communication of Emotion.* New York: Guilford Press, 1984.

Calhoun, Cheshire, and Robert C. Solomon, eds. *What is an Emotion?* Oxford: Oxford University Press, 1984.

Cartmill, Matt. "The Gift of Gab." *Discover* 19 (November 1998): 56–64.

Casey, Edward. *Imagining: A Phenomenological Study.* Bloomington: Indiana University Press, 1976.

Chalmers, David. *The Conscious Mind.* Oxford: Oxford University Press, 1996.

Chekhov, Anton. *Chekhov: The Major Plays.* Translated by Ann Dunnigan. New York: Signet Classic, 1964.

———. *Letters.* Edited by Abraham Yarmolinsky. New York: Viking, 1973.

Chodorow, Nancy. *The Reproduction of Mothering.* Berkeley and Los Angeles: University of California Press, 1978.

Clemens, Samuel. *The Adventures of Huckleberry Finn.* New York: Penguin, 1985.

———. "Old Times on the Mississippi." In *Great Short Works of Mark Twain,* edited by Justin Kaplan. New York: Harper and Row, 1967.

Coleridge, Samuel. *Biographia Literaria.* Vols. 1 and 2. Edited by John Shawcross. London: Oxford University Press, 1954.

Collingwood, R. G. *The Principles of Art.* London: Oxford University Press, 1938.

Coover, Robert. "Interview." In *Anything Can Happen: Interviews with Contemporary American Novelists,* edited by Tom LeClair and Larry McCaffery. Urbana: University of Illinois Press, 1983.

Culler, Jonathan. *On Deconstruction.* Ithaca, N.Y.: Cornell University Press, 1982.

———. *The Pursuit of Signs.* Ithaca: Cornell University Press, 1981.

Cummins, Robert. *Meaning and Mental Representation.* Cambridge: MIT Press, 1989.

Damasio, Antonio. *Descartes' Error.* New York: Putnam, 1994.

———. *The Feeling of What Happens.* New York: Harcourt Brace, 1999.

Darwin, Charles. *The Expression of the Emotions in Man and Animals.* New York: Appleton, 1899.

DeLillo, Don. *The New Yorker* 73, no. 27 (September 15, 1997): 47.

Denzin, Norman K. *On Understanding Emotion.* San Francisco: Jossey-Bass, 1984.

Diamond, Elin. "Realism and Hysteria: Toward a Feminist Mimesis." *Discourse* 13, no. 1 (Fall–Winter 1990–91): 59–93.

Donovan, Josephine. *Feminist Literary Criticism.* Lexington: University Press of Kentucky, 1975.

Dreyfus, Hubert L. *What Computers Still Can't Do.* Cambridge: MIT Press, 1992.

Dunlop, Francis. *The Education of Feeling and Emotion.* London: George Allen and Unwin, 1984.

Edelman, Gerald M. *Bright Air, Brilliant Fire.* New York: Basic Books, 1992.

Ekman, Paul. *The Face of Man.* New York: Garland, 1980.

————,and Richard J. Davidson, eds. *The Nature of Emotion*. New York: Oxford University Press, 1994.

Eliot, T. S. "Hamlet and His Problems." In *The Sacred Wood*. London: Methuen, 1920.

————. *Selected Essays*. 2d ed. New York: Harcourt, Brace, 1950.

————. "Tradition and the Individual Talent." In *The Sacred Wood*. London: Methuen, 1920.

Emmott, Catherine. *Narrative Comprehension*. Oxford: Clarendon, 1997.

Engell, James. *The Creative Imagination*. Cambridge: Harvard University Press, 1981.

Esrock, Ellen J. *The Reader's Eye*. Baltimore: Johns Hopkins University Press, 1994.

Feagin, Susan. *Reading with Feeling*. Ithaca: Cornell University Press, 1996.

————. "Imagining Emotions and Appreciating Fiction." *Canadian Journal of Philosophy* 18, no. 3 (September 1988): 485–500. [Reprinted in Hjort and Laver, *Emotion and the Arts*, 50–60.]

Fish, Stanley E. "Literature in the Reader: Affective Stylistics." In *Reader Response Criticism*, edited by Jane P. Tompkins. Baltimore: Johns Hopkins University Press, 1980. [Reprinted from *New Literary History* 2, no. 1 (Autumn 1970): 123–62.]

Fitzgerald, F. Scott. *The Great Gatsby*. New York: Charles Scribner's Sons, 1925.

Flaxx, Jane. "The Patriarchal Unconscious." In *Discovering Reality*, edited by Sandra Harding and Merrill B. Hintikka. Dordrecht, Holland: D. Reidel, 1983.

Fodor, Jerry A. *The Language of Thought*. New York: Thomas Y. Crowell, 1975.

Fortenbaugh, W. W. *Aristotle on Emotion*. London: Gerald Duckworth, 1975.

Foucault, Michel. *The History of Sexuality*. Vol. 1. Translated by Robert Hurley. New York: Pantheon, 1978.

Frank, Joseph. "Spatial Form in Modern Literature." *Sewanee Review* 53 (1945): 221–40; 433–56; 643–53. [Reprinted in *The Widening Gyre* (New Brunswick, N.J.: Rutgers University Press, 1963).]

Freedman, Ralph. *The Lyrical Novel*. Princeton: Princeton University Press, 1963.

Frings, Manfred S. *Max Scheler*. Pittsburgh: Duquesne University Press, 1965.

Frye, Northrop. *The Well-Tempered Critic*. Bloomington: Indiana University Press, 1962.

Gablik, Suzi. *Has Modernism Failed?* New York: Thames and Hudson, 1984.

Gardiner, H. M., Ruth Clark Metcalf, and John G. Beebe-Center, eds. *Feeling and Emotion: A History of Theories*. New York: American Book Co., 1937.

Gerrig, Richard J. *Experiencing Narrative Worlds*. New Haven: Yale University Press, 1993.

Goleman, Daniel. *Emotional Intelligence*. New York: Bantam, 1995.

Gombrich, E. H. *Art and Illusion*. Princeton: Princeton University Press, 1972.

Goodman, Nelson. *Languages of Art*. Indianapolis, Ind.: Bobbs-Merrill, 1968.

Gopnik, Adam. "The Power Critic." *The New Yorker* 74 (March 16, 1998): 70–78.

Graff, Gerald. "Disliking Books at an Early Age." *Lingua Franca* 6 (September–October 1992): 46. [Reprinted in *Beyond the Culture Wars* (New York: Norton, 1992).]

Grayling, A. C. *An Introduction to Philosophical Logic*. Oxford: Blackwell, 1997.

Guignon, Charles. "Moods in Heidegger's *Being and Time*." In *What is an Emotion?*, edited by Cheshire Calhoun and Robert C. Solomon. New York: Oxford University Press, 1984.

Hall, David L. *Richard Rorty.* Albany: State University of New York Press, 1994.

Hansson, Gunnar. "Emotions in Poetry: Where Are They and How Do We Find Them?" In *Empirical Approaches to Literature and Aesthetics,* edited by R. J. Kreuz and M. S. MacNealy. Norwood, N.J.: Ablex, 1986.

Harré, R., ed. *The Social Construction of Emotion.* Oxford: Basil Blackwell, 1986.

Hazlitt, William. "On Genius and Common Sense" and "On Genius and Common Sense, The Same Subject Continued." From *Tabletalk,* vol. 8. In *The Complete Works of William Hazlitt,* edited by P. P. Howe. London: J. M. Dent and Sons, 1931.

Heidegger, Martin. *Being and Time.* Translated by John MacQuarrie and Edward Robinson. New York: Harper and Row, 1962.

Hemingway, Ernest. *Death in the Afternoon.* New York: Charles Scribner's Sons, 1932.

———. *In Our Time.* New York: Charles Scribner's Sons, 1925.

———. In *Writers At Work,* edited by George Plimpton, 215–40. 2d series. New York: Viking, 1965.

Hepburn, R. W. "The Arts and the Education of Feeling and Emotions." In *Education and the Development of Reason,* edited by R. F. Dearden, P. H. Hirst and R. S. Peters. London: Routledge and Kegan Paul, 1972.

Hill, John Spencer. *Imagination in Coleridge.* Totowa, N.J.: Rowman and Littlefield, 1978.

Hillman, James. *Emotion.* Evanston, Ill.: Northwestern University Press, 1960.

Hirsch, E. D. *Validity in Interpretation.* New Haven: Yale University Press, 1967.

Hite, Shere. *Woman and Love.* New York: Alfred A. Knopf, 1987.

Hjort, Mette, and Sue Laver, eds. *Emotion and the Arts.* Oxford: Oxford University Press, 1997.

Hobson, J. Allan. *The Chemistry of Conscious States.* Boston: Little, Brown, 1994.

Hochschild, Arlie Russell. *The Managed Heart.* Berkeley and Los Angeles: University of California Press, 1983.

Holland, Norman. "Affect." In *Dynamics of Literary Response.* New York: Oxford University Press, 1968.

———. *Five Readers Reading.* New Haven: Yale University Press, 1975.

Home, Henry Lord Kames. *Elements of Criticism.* Vol. 1. New York: Garland, 1972.

Hume, David. *A Treatise of Human Nature.* Oxford: Clarendon Press, 1958.

Ingarden, Roman. *The Literary Work of Art.* Translated by George G. Grabowicz. Evanston, Ill.: Northwestern University Press, 1973.

Irwin, Michael. *Picturing.* London: George Allen, 1979.

Iser, Wolfgang. *The Act of Reading.* Baltimore: Johns Hopkins University Press, 1978.

———. "Interaction Between Text and Reader." In *The Reader in the Text,* edited by Susan R. Suleiman and Inge Crosman. Princeton: Princeton University Press, 1980.

Izard, Carroll E. *The Psychology of Emotions.* New York: Plenum Press, 1992.

Jakobson, Roman. "On Realism in Art." In *Readings in Russian Poetics: Formalist and Structuralist Views,* edited by Ladislav Matejka and Krystyna Pomorska. Cambridge: MIT Press, 1971.

Jaggar, Alison M. "Love and Knowledge." *Inquiry* 32 (June 1989): 151–76. [Reprinted in *Gender/Body/Knowledge,* edited by Alison M. Jaggar and Susan R. Bordo (New Brunswick, N.J.: Rutgers University Press, 1989).]

James, William. "The Place of Affectional Facts." In *Writings 1902–10*. New York: Library of America, 1987.

———. *The Principles of Psychology*. 3 vols. Cambridge: Harvard University Press, 1981.

———. The *Varieties of Religious Experience*. In *Writings 1902–10*. New York: Library of America, 1987.

———. *The Writings of William James*. Edited by John J. McDermott. New York: Random House, 1967.

Johnson, Mark. *The Body in the Mind*. Chicago: University of Chicago Press, 1987.

Johnson-Laird, P. N. *Mental Models: Towards a Cognitive Science of Language, Inference, and Consciousness*. Cambridge: Harvard University Press, 1983.

Josipovici, Gabriel. *The World and the Book*. Stanford, Calif.: Stanford University Press, 1971.

Katz, Jack. *How Emotions Work*. Chicago: University of Chicago Press, 1999.

Kazin, Alfred. *Bright Book of Life*. Boston: Little, Brown, 1973.

Kenny, Anthony. *Action, Emotion and Will*. London: Routledge and Kegan Paul, 1963.

Kintsch, Walter. "The Role of Knowledge in Discourse Comprehension." *Psychological Review* 95, no. 2 (April 1988): 163–82.

Klinkowitz, Jerome. *Literary Disruptions*. Urbana: University of Illinois Press, 1975.

Kneepkens, E. W. E. M., and Rolf A. Zwaan. "Emotions and Literary Text Comprehension." *Poetics* 23 (1994): 125–38.

Kosslyn, Stephen M. *Ghosts in the Mind's Machine*. New York: Norton, 1983.

———. *Image and Brain: The Resolution of the Imagery Debate*. Cambridge: MIT Press, 1994.

———. "Stalking the Mental Image." *Psychology Today* 19 (May 1985): 24–28.

Kövecses, Zoltán. *Emotion Concepts*. New York: Springer-Verlag, 1990.

Kreuz, R. J., and M. S. MacNealy, eds. *Empirical Approaches to Literature and Aesthetics*. Norwood, N.J.: Ablex, 1996.

Langer, Susanne. *Feeling and Form*. New York: Charles Scribner's Sons, 1953.

———. *Mind*. Baltimore: Johns Hopkins University Press, 1967.

———. "Expressiveness." In *Problems of Art*. New York: Charles Scribner's Sons, 1957.

Lazarus, Richard S. "Thoughts on the Relations between Emotion and Cognition." *American Psychologist* (September 1982): 1019–24.

Lemon, Lee, and Marion J. Reis. *Russian Formalist Criticism: Four Essays*. Lincoln: University of Nebraska Press, 1965.

Leeper, Robert. *Toward Understanding Human Personalities*. New York: Appleton-Century Crofts, 1959.

Lentricchia, Frank. *After the New Criticism*. Chicago: University of Chicago Press, 1980.

———, ed. *Introducing Don DeLillo*. Durham, N.C.: Duke University Press, 1992.

Levine, George. *The Realistic Imagination*. Chicago: University of Chicago Press, 1981.

Lukacs, Georg. *Studies in European Realism*. New York: Grosset and Dunlap, 1964.

Lyons, William. *Emotion*. Cambridge: Cambridge University Press, 1980.

Lyotard, Jean-François. *The Post-Modern Condition*. Translated by Geoff Bennington and Brian Massumi. Minneapolis: University of Minnesota Press, 1984.

MacMurray, John. *Reason and Emotion*. London: Faber, 1935.

Mahoney, John L. *The Logic of Passion: The Literary Criticism of William Hazlitt*. Bronx, N.Y.: Fordham University Press, 1981.

Mailloux, Steven. *Interpretive Conventions*. Ithaca: Cornell University Press, 1992.

Markman, Arthur B. *Knowledge Representation*. Mahwah, N.J.: Lawrence Erlbaum Associates, 1999.

Marquez, Gabriel García. "Fantasy and the Artistic Creation in Latin America and the Carribbean." Translated by Elena Brunet. *Harper's* 270 (January 1985): 15.

Martin, Wallace. *Recent Theories of Narrative*. Ithaca: Cornell University Press, 1986.

McLeod, Susan. *Notes on the Heart*. Carbondale: Southern Illinois University Press, 1997.

Miller, James E., ed. *Theory of Fiction: Henry James*. Lincoln: University of Nebraska Press, 1962.

Miller, Jonathan. "Profile," with Penelope Gilliat. *The New Yorker* 65 (April 17, 1989): 82.

Miller, J. Hillis. "The Geneva School." *Critical Quarterly* (Winter 1966). [Reprinted in *Modern French Criticism,* edited by John K. Simon. Chicago: University of Chicago Press, 1972.]

———. *Fiction and Repetition*. Cambridge: Harvard University Press, 1982.

Minsky, Marvin. *The Society of Mind*. New York: Simon and Schuster, 1985.

Mitchell, Lee Clark. "'Nobody but our Gang warn't Around': The Authority of Language in *Huckleberry Finn*." In *New Essays on Adventures of Huckleberry Finn,* edited by Louis J. Budd. Cambridge: Cambridge University Press, 1985.

Nell, Victor. *Lost in a Book: The Psychology of Reading for Pleasure*. New Haven: Yale University Press, 1988.

Norman, Liane. "Risk and Redundancy." *PMLA* 90, no. 2 (March 1975): 285–91.

Novitz, David. "Fiction, Imagination and Emotion." *Journal of Aesthetics and Art Criticism* 38 (1980): 279–88.

———. *Knowledge, Fiction, and Imagination*. Philadelphia: Temple University Press, 1987.

Nussbaum, Martha. "Narrative Emotions: Beckett's Genealogy of Love." *Ethics* 98, no. 2 (January 1988): 225–54.

Nuttall, A. D. *A New Mimesis*. London: Methuen, 1983.

Oatley, Keith. "Emotion." In *The Blackwell Dictionary of Cognitive Psychology,* edited by Michael W. Eysenck. Oxford: Blackwell, 1990.

——— and Mitra Gholamain. "Emotions and Identification." In *Emotion and the Arts,* edited by Mette Hjort and Sue Laver. Oxford: Oxford University Press, 1997.

Oostendorp, H. Van and Rolf A. Zwaan, eds. *Naturalistic Text Comprehension*. Norwood, N.J.: Ablex, 1994.

Opdahl, Keith M. "Imagination and Emotion: Toward a Theory of Representation." no. 19: Reader (Spring 1988): 1–20.

———. "Saul Bellow and the Function of Representational Feeling." *delta* 19 (October 1984): 29–45.

Ornstein, Robert. *The Right Mind*. New York: Harcourt Brace Jovanovich, 1997.

Ortony, Andrew. "Value and Emotion." In *Memories, Thoughts and Emotions,* edited by Andrew Ortony and others. Hillsdale, N.J.: Lawrence Erlbaum Associates, 1991.

Osborne, Harold. "The Quality of Feeling in Art." *British Journal of Aesthetics* 3, no. 1 (1963): 38–53.

Osgood, Charles E. *Lectures on Language Performance*. New York: Springer-Verlag, 1980.

Oxenhandler, Neal. "The Changing Concept of Literary Emotion." *New Literary History* 20, no. 1 (Autumn 1988): 105–21.

Paivio, Allan. *Imagery and Verbal Processes*. New York: Holt, Rinehart, 1971.

———. *Mental Representations*. New York: Oxford University Press, 1986.

Palmer, Stephen E. "Fundamental Aspects of Cognitive Representation." In *Cognition and Categorization*, edited by Eleanor Rosch and Barbara Lloyd. Hillsdale, N.J.: Lawrence Erlbaum Associates, 1978.

Pepper, Stephen. *Aesthetic Quality*. New York: Charles Scribner's Sons, 1938.

———. *Principles of Art Appreciation*. New York: Harcourt, Brace, 1949.

Perner, Josef. *Understanding the Representational Mind*. Cambridge: MIT Press, 1991.

Pinker, Steven. *How the Mind Works*. New York: Norton, 1997.

Polanyi, Michael. *The Tacit Dimension*. Garden City, N.Y.: Doubleday, 1966.

Poulet, Georges. "Criticism and the Experience of Interiority." In *The Structuralist Controversy: The Languages of Criticism and the Sciences of Man*, edited by Richard A. Macksey and Eugenio Donato. Baltimore: Johns Hopkins University Press, 1972.

Preminger, Alex, and T. V. E. Brogan. *The New Princeton Encyclopedia of Poetry and Poetics*. Princeton: Princeton University Press, 1993.

Prince, Gerald. "Introduction to the Study of the Narratee." In *Reader-Response Criticism*, edited by Jane P. Tompkins. Baltimore: Johns Hopkins University Press, 1980.

Pylyshyn, Zenon. "The Imagery Debate. Analog Media versus Tacit Knowledge." In *Imagery*, edited by Ned Block. Cambridge: MIT Press, 1981.

Richards, I. A. *Coleridge on Imagination*. Bloomington: Indiana University Press, 1960.

———. *Practical Criticism*. New York: Harcourt, Brace, 1929.

———. *Science and Poetry*. New York: Norton, 1926.

Richardson, Alan. *Mental Imagery*. New York: Springer, 1969.

Ricoeur, Paul. *Freedom and Nature*. Evanston, Ill.: Northwestern University Press, 1966.

———. "The Metaphorical Process as Cognition, Imagination, and Feeling." *Critical Inquiry* 5, no. 1 (1978): 143–60.

Riffaterre, Michael. *Fictional Truth*. Baltimore: Johns Hopkins University Press, 1990.

Rollins, Mark. *Mental Imagery: On the Limits of Cognitive Science*. New Haven: Yale University Press, 1989.

Rorty, Amélie, ed. *Explaining Emotions*. Berkeley and Los Angeles: University of California Press, 1980.

Rorty, Richard. *Philosophy and the Mirror of Nature*. Princeton: Princeton University Press, 1994.

Rosaldo, Michelle S. "Towards an Anthropology of Self and Feeling." In *Culture Theory: Essays on Mind, Self, and Emotion*, edited by Richard Shweder and Robert LeVine. Cambridge: Cambridge University Press, 1984.

Rosenblatt, Louise. *Literature as Exploration*. New York: Nobel, 1968.

Ruthrof, Horst. *The Reader's Construction of Narrative*. London: Routledge and Kegan Paul, 1981.

Ryle, Gilbert. *The Concept of Mind*. London: Huchinson's University Library, 1949.

Sartre, Jean-Paul. *The Psychology of Imagination*. London: Rider, 1950.

———. *Sketch for a Theory of the Emotions*. Translated by Phillip Mairet. London: Methuen, 1962.

————. *What is Literature?* Translated by Bernard Frechtman. New York: Philosophical Library, 1949.

Schank, Roger. *The Connoisseur's Guide to the Mind.* New York: Summit Books, 1991.

Scheffler, Israel. "In Praise of the Cognitive Emotions." *Thinking* 3, no. 2 (1981): 16–23.

Scheler, Max. *The Nature of Sympathy.* Translated by Peter Heath. New Haven: Yale University Press, 1954.

Searle, John. "The Mystery of Mind." *New York Review of Books* 42 (November 2, 1995): 60–66 and (November 16, 1995): 54–61.

Scholes, Robert. *Semiotics and Interpretation.* New Haven: Yale University Press, 1982.

Sedgwick, Eve Kosofsky. *Epistemology of the Closet.* Berkeley and Los Angeles: University of California Press, 1990.

Selden, Raman. *A Reader's Guide to Contemporary Theory.* 2d ed. Lexington: University of Kentucky Press, 1989.

Sheikh, Anees, ed. *Imagery—Current Theory, Research, and Application.* New York: Wiley, 1983.

Shepard, Roger N., and Lynn A. Cooper. *Mental Images and Their Transformations.* Cambridge: MIT Press/Bradford Books, 1982.

Shibles, Warren A. *Emotion in Aesthetics.* Dordrecht: Kluwer Academic Publishers, 1995.

Shklovsky, Victor. "Art as Technique." In *Russian Formalist Criticism: Four Essays,* translated by Lee T. Lemon and Marion J. Reis. Lincoln: University of Nebraska Press, 1965.

Smith, F. *Understanding Reading.* 5th ed. Hillsdale, N.J.: Lawrence Erlbaum Associates, 1994.

Solomon, Robert. *The Passions.* South Bend, Ind.: University of Notre Dame Press, 1983.

Sontag, Susan. *Against Interpretation.* New York: Farrar, Straus, 1966.

Spilka, Mark. *Towards a Poetics of Fiction.* Bloomington: Indiana University Press, 1977.

Stead, C. K. *The New Poetic: Yeats to Eliot.* Philadelphia: University of Pennsylvania Press, 1987.

Stearns, Peter N. *American Cool.* New York: New York University Press, 1994.

————. *Jealousy: The Evolution of an Emotion in American History.* New York: New York University Press, 1989.

Steig, Michael. *Stories of Reading.* Baltimore: Johns Hopkins University Press, 1989.

Stein, Edith. *On the Problem of Empathy.* Translated by W. Stern. The Hague: Nijhoff, 1970.

Stern, Joseph Peter. *On Realism.* London: Routledge and Kegan Paul, 1973.

Stotland, Ezra, Kenneth Mathews, Stanley Sherman, Robert Hansson, and Barbara Richardson, eds. *Empathy, Fantasy and Helping.* Beverly Hills, Calif.: Sage, 1978.

Strasser, Stephan. *Phenomenology of Feeling.* Translated by Robert E. Wood. Pittsburgh: Duquesne University Press, 1977.

Tan, Ed S. "Story Processing as an Emotion Episode." In *Naturalistic Text Comprehension,* edited by H. van Oostendorp and Rolf Zwaan. Norwood, N.J.: Ablex, 1994.

Tanner, Tony. *The Reign of Wonder: Naivety and Reality in American Literature.* Cambridge: Cambridge University Press, 1965.

Titchener, Edward B. *Lectures on the Experimental Psychology of the Thought-Processes.* New York: Macmillan, 1926.

Todorov, Tzvetan. *The Poetics of Prose.* Translated by Richard Howard. Ithaca: Cornell University Press, 1977.

Tolstoy, Leo. *What is Art?* Translated by Aylmer Maude. London: Oxford University Press, 1930.

Tompkins, Jane. "Criticism and Feeling." *College English* 39 (October 1977): 169–78.

———. "Me and My Shadow." *New Literary History* 19 (Fall 1987).

———, ed. *Reader-Response Criticism.* Baltimore: Johns Hopkins University Press, 1980.

———. "The Reader in History." In *Reader-Response Criticism,* edited by Jane Tompkins. Baltimore: Johns Hopkins University Press, 1980.

———. *Sensational Designs.* New York: Oxford University Press, 1985.

Tuveson, Ernest Lee. *The Imagination as a Means of Grace.* Berkeley and Los Angeles: University of California Press, 1960.

Twain, Mark. *The Adventures of Huckleberry Finn.* New York: Penguin, 1981.

Tye, Michael. *The Imagery Debate.* Cambridge: MIT Press, 1992.

Ushenko, Andrew Paul. *Dynamics of Art.* Bloomington: Indiana University Publications, Humanities Series, no. 28, 1953.

Vivas, Eliseo. "The Objective Correlative of T. S. Eliot." In *Creation and Discovery.* New York: Noonday, 1955.

von Helmholtz, Hermann. *Handbuch der Physiologischen Optik.* 2d. Edition. Hamburg and Leipzig: Leopold Voss, 1896. [Translated and quoted by E. H. Gombrich in "Standards of Truth: The Arrested Image and the Moving Eye." In *The Language of Images,* edited by W. J. T. Mitchell. Chicago: University of Chicago Press, 1980.]

Warnock, Mary. *Imagination.* Berkeley and Los Angeles: University of California Press, 1976.

Watson, J. B. *Psychology from the Standpoint of a Behaviorist.* Philadelphia: Lippincott, 1919.

Webster's Seventh New Collegiate Dictionary. Springfield, Mass.: G. and C. Merriam, 1987.

Wimsatt, W. K. "The Affective Fallacy." In *The Verbal Icon.* Lexington: University Press of Kentucky, 1954.

Woodward, Kathleen. "Freud and Barthes: Theorizing Mourning, Sustaining Grief." *Discourse* 13, no. 1 (Fall–Winter 1990–91): 93–110.

———, ed. A Special Issue on the Emotions. *Discourse* 13, no. 1 (Fall–Winter 1990–91).

Wordsworth, William. "Preface," *Lyrical Ballads.* In *The Poetical Works of Wordsworth,* edited by Ernest De Selinecourt. 2d ed. London: Oxford University Press, 1953.

Wright, John. "His Fantastic is Credible." *Indianapolis Star* (Sunday, November 3, 1991): F7.

Wright, Walter F. "Tone in Fiction." In *The Theory of the Novel,* edited by John Halperin. New York: Oxford University Press, 1974.

Yanal, Robert J. *Paradoxes of Emotion and Fiction.* University Park: Pennsylvania State University Press, 1999.

Young, Paul. *Motivation and Emotion: A Survey of the Determinants of Human and Animal Activity.* New York: J. Wiley, 1961.

Zajonc, R. B. "Feeling and Thinking." *American Psychology* 35 (1980): 151–79.

Zwaan, R. A. *Aspects of Literary Comprehension.* Amsterdam: John Benjamins, 1993.

CRITICISM OF THE SHORT STORY AND SPECIFIC NOVELS

"Big Two-Hearted River"

Benson, Jackson. *New Critical Approaches to the Short Stories of Ernest Hemingway.* Durham, N.C.: Duke University Press, 1990.

———. *Hemingway.* Minneapolis: University of Minnesota Press, 1989.

Carabine, Keith. "'Big Two-Hearted River': A Re-interpretation." *Hemingway Review* 1, no. 2 (Spring 1982): 39–44.

Cowley, Malcolm. "Nightmare and Ritual in Hemingway." In *Hemingway: A Collection of Critical Essays,* edited by Robert P. Weeks. Englewood Cliffs, N.J.: Prentice-Hall, 1962.

Flora, Joseph. *Ernest Hemingway: A Study of the Short Fiction.* Boston: Twayne, 1989.

Gaggin, John. *Hemingway and Nineteenth-Century Aestheticism.* Ann Arbor, Mich.: UMI Research Press, 1988.

Grebstein, Sheldon. *Hemingway's Craft.* Carbondale: Southern Illinois University Press, 1973.

Kazin, Alfred. "Young Man, Old Man." *Reporter* 29 (December 19, 1963): 35–36.

Lamb, Robert Paul. "Fishing for Stories: What 'Big Two-Hearted River' is Really About." *Modern Fiction Studies* 37, no. 2 (Summer 1991): 161–81.

Levin, Harry. "Observations on the Style of Ernest Hemingway." *Kenyon Review* 13 (1951): 581–609.

Lynn, Kenneth. "Hemingway's Private War." *Commentary* 72, no. 1 (July 1981): 24–33.

Mellow, James R. *Hemingway: A Life without Consequences.* Boston: Houghton Mifflin, 1992.

Nahal, Chamal. *The Narrative Pattern in Ernest Hemingway's Fiction.* Rutherford, N.J.: Fairleigh Dickinson University Press, 1971.

Nelson, Raymond S. *Hemingway: Expressionist Artist.* Ames: Iowa State University Press, 1979.

Rovit, Earl. *Ernest Hemingway.* New York: Twayne, 1963.

Stewart, Jack S. "Christian Allusions in 'Big Two-Hearted River.'" *Studies in Short Fiction* 15 (1978): 194–96.

Waldhorn, Arthur. *A Reader's Guide to Ernest Hemingway.* New York: Farrar, Straus, and Giroux, 1972.

Watts, Emily. *Ernest Hemingway and the Arts.* Urbana: University of Illinois Press, 1971.

Williams, Wirt. *The Tragic Art of Ernest Hemingway.* Baton Rouge: Louisiana State University Press, 1981.

Young, Philip. *Ernest Hemingway: A Reconsideration.* University Park: Pennsylvania State University Press, 1966.

Pride and Prejudice

Allen, Dennis W. "No Love for Lydia: The Fate of Desire in *Pride and Prejudice.*" *Texas Studies in Language and Literature* 27, no. 4 (Winter 1985): 425–43.

Armstrong, Nancy. *Desire and Domestic Fiction: A Political History of the Novel.* New York: Oxford University Press, 1987.

Brontë, Charlotte. "Letter to W. S. Williams." April 1850. In *Jane Austen: The Critical Heritage,* edited by B. C. Southam. London: Routledge and Kegan Paul, 1968.

Butler, Marilyn. *Jane Austen and the War of Ideas.* Oxford: Clarendon, 1987.

Crowder, Tudja. "The Rational Treatment of Emotion: An Essay on Jane Austen's Style." *Spectrum* 5 (1961): 91–96.

Ehrenreich, Barbara, and Janet McIntosh. "The New Creationism." *Nation* 264, no. 22 (1997): 11–16.

Harding, D. W. "Regulated Hatred: An Aspect of the Work of Jane Austen." In *Jane Austen,* edited by Ian Watt. Englewood Cliffs, N.J.: Prentice-Hall, 1963. [Reprinted from *Scrutiny* 7 (1940): 346–62.]

Johnson, Claudia L. *Jane Austen.* Chicago: University of Chicago Press, 1988.

Kliger, Samuel. "Jane Austen's *Pride and Prejudice* in the Eighteenth-Century Mode." In *Twentieth Century Interpretations of "Pride and Prejudice,"* edited by E. Rubinstein. Englewood Cliffs, N.J.: Prentice-Hall, 1969.

Moler, Kenneth L. *Pride and Prejudice: A Study in Artistic Economy.* Boston: Twayne, 1990.

Morgan, Susan. *In the Meantime.* Chicago: University of Chicago Press, 1980.

Mudrick, Melvin. "Irony as Discrimination: *Pride and Prejudice.*" In *Jane Austen,* edited by Ian Watt. Englewood Cliffs, N.J.: Prentice-Hall, 1963.

Poovey, Mary. *The Proper Lady and the Woman Writer.* Chicago: University of Chicago Press, 1984.

Sulloway, Alison. *Jane Austen and the Province of Womanhood.* Philadelphia: University of Pennsylvania Press, 1989.

Tanner, Tony. "Introduction." *Pride and Prejudice.* Baltimore: Penguin Books, 1972.

———. *Jane Austen.* Cambridge: Harvard University Press, 1986.

Thompson, James. *Between Self and World.* University Park: Pennsylvania State University Press, 1989.

Woolf, Virginia. *The Common Reader.* New York: Harcourt Brace, 1925. [Reprinted in *Jane Austen,* edited by Ian Watt. Englewood Cliffs, N.J.: Prentice-Hall, 1963.]

Adventures of Huckleberry Finn

Beaver, Harold. *Huckleberry Finn.* London: Unwin Critical Library, 1987.

Beidler, P. D. "Realistic Style and the Problem of Context in *The Innocents Abroad* and *Roughing It.*" *American Literature* 52 (March 1980): 33–49.

Bellamy, Gladys. *Mark Twain as a Literary Artist.* Norman: University of Oklahoma Press, 1950.

Blair, Walter. *Mark Twain and Huck Finn.* Berkeley and Los Angeles: University of California Press, 1960.

Bloom, Harold. *Mark Twain's "The Adventures of Huckleberry Finn."* New York: Chelsea House, 1986.

Brenner, Gerry. "More than a Reader's Response: A Letter to 'De Ole True Huck.'" In *Adventures of Huckleberry Finn,* edited by Gerald Graff and James Phelan. Boston: Bedford/St. Martin's Press, 1995.

Burns, Graham. "Time and Pastoral: *The Adventures of Huckleberry Finn.*" *Critical Review* 15 (1972): 53–63.

Carrington, George C. *The Dramatic Unity of Huckleberry Finn.* Columbus: Ohio State University Press, 1976.

Clemens, Samuel. *Mark Twain's Letters.* Edited by Albert Bigelow Paine. New York: Harper and Brothers, 1917.

———. *The Love Letters of Mark Twain.* Edited by Dixon Wecter. New York: Harper and Brothers, 1949.

———. *The Mark Twain-Howells Letters, 1872–1910.* Edited by Henry Nash Smith and William M. Gibson. Cambridge: Harvard University Press, 1960.

———. 1895 Notebook. Notebook 35. Typescript p. 35. Mark Twain Papers. University of California Library at Berkeley.

Clerc, Charles. "Sunrise on the River: 'The Whole World' of *Huckleberry Finn*." *Modern Fiction Studies* 14 (Spring 1968): 67–78.

Cox, James M. *Mark Twain: The Fate of Humor.* Princeton: Princeton University Press, 1966.

Eliot, T. S. "Mark Twain's Masterpiece." Introduction to *The Adventures of Huckleberry Finn.* London: Cresset Press, 1950. [Reprinted in *Huck Finn Among the Critics,* edited by Thomas Inge. Frederick, Md.: University Publications of America, 1985.]

Feinstein, G. W. "Mark Twain's Idea of Story and Structure." *American Literature* 18 (1946): 160–63.

Frank, Albert J. von. "Huck Finn and the Flight from Maturity." *Studies in American Fiction* 7 (Spring 1979): 1–15.

Gibson, William. *The Art of Mark Twain.* New York: Oxford University Press, 1976.

Graff, Gerald, and Richard Phelan, eds. *Adventures of Huckleberry Finn.* Boston: Bedford/St. Martin's Press, 1995.

Hemingway, Ernest. *The Green Hills of Africa.* New York: Charles Scribner's Sons, 1935.

Hill, Richard. "Overreaching: Critical Agenda and the Ending of *Adventures of Huckleberry Finn*." *Texas Studies in Language and Literature* 33, no. 4 (Winter 1991), 492–513. [Reprinted in *Huck Finn Among the Critics,* edited by Thomas Inge. Frederick, Md.: University Publications of America, 1985.]

Kolb, Harold H. Jr. "Mark Twain, Huck Finn, and Jacob Blivens: Gilt-Edged, Tree-Calf Morality in *The Adventures of Huckleberry Finn*." *Virginia Quarterly Review* 55 (1979): 653–69.

Krause, S. J. "Twain's Method and Theory of Composition." *Modern Philology* 56 (1959): 167–77.

Krauth, Leland. "Mark Twain: The Victorian of Southwestern Humor." *American Literature* 54, no. 3 (1982): 368–84.

Lloyd, James B. "The Nature of Twain's Attack on Sentimentality in *The Adventures of Huckleberry Finn*." *University of Mississippi Studies in English* 13 (1972): 59–63.

Lucas, F. L. *Style.* New York: Collier, 1962.

Lynn, Kenneth. *Mark Twain and Southwestern Humor.* Boston: Little, Brown, 1959.

Marx, Leo. "Mr. Eliot, Mr. Trilling, and *Huckleberry Finn*." *American Scholar* 22, no. 4 (Autumn 1953). [Reprinted in *The Adventures of Huckleberry Finn,* edited by Sculley Bradley, Richmond Beatty, E. Hudson Long, and Thomas Cooley. New York: Norton, 1977.]

———. "The Pilot and the Passenger: Landscape Conventions and the Style of *Huckleberry Finn*." *American Literature* 28 (1956): 129–46.

McKay, Janet. *Narration and Discourse in American Realistic Fiction.* Philadelphia: University of Pennsylvania Press, 1982.

Opdahl, Keith. "'The Rest is Just Cheating': When Feelings Go Bad in *Adventures of Huckleberry Finn.*" *Texas Studies in Language and Literature* 32, no. 2 (Summer 1990): 277–96.

———. "'You'll Be Sorry When I'm Dead': Child-Adult Relations in *The Adventures of Huckleberry Finn.*" *Modern Fiction Studies* 25 (Winter 1979–80): 613–24.

Piacentino, Edward J. "The Ubiquitous Tom Sawyer: Another View of the Conclusion of *Huckleberry Finn.*" *Cimarron Review* 37 (October 1979): 34–43.

Poirier, Richard. *A World Elsewhere.* New York: Oxford University Press, 1966.

Quirk, Tom. *Coming to Grips with Huckleberry Finn.* Columbia: University of Missouri Press, 1993.

Robinson, F. G. "Silences in *Adventures of Huckleberry Finn.*" *Nineteenth Century Fiction* 37 (June 1982): 50–74.

Rubin, Louis D., Jr. *The Teller in the Tale.* Seattle: University of Washington Press, 1967.

Scafella, Frank. "Models of the Soul: Authorship as Moral Action in Four American Novels." *Journal of the American Academy of Religion* 44 (1976): 459–75.

Seelye, John. Introduction to *Adventures of Huckleberry Finn.* New York: Penguin, 1985.

Smith, Henry Nash. *Mark Twain: The Development of a Writer.* Cambridge: Harvard University Press, 1962.

Trilling, Lionel. "Introduction to *Huckleberry Finn.*" In *The Art of Huckleberry Finn,* edited by Hamlin Hill and Walter Blair. San Francisco: Chandler, 1962. [Reprinted in *The Adventures of Huckleberry Finn,* edited by Sculley Bradley, Richmond Beatty, and E. Hudson Long. New York: Norton, 1961.]

Wagner, Jeanie. "*Huckleberry Finn* and the History Game." *Mark Twain Journal* 20 (Winter 1979–80): 5–10.

The Portrait of a Lady

Anderson, Charles. *Person, Place and Thing in Henry James's Novels.* Durham, N.C.: Duke University Press, 1977.

Armstrong, Paul B. *The Phenomenology of Henry James.* Chapel Hill: University of North Carolina Press, 1983.

Baym, Nina. "Revision and Thematic Change in *The Portrait of a Lady.*" *Modern Fiction Studies* 22, no. 2 (Summer 1976): 183–200.

Bell, Millicent. *Meaning in Henry James.* Cambridge: Harvard University Press, 1991.

Bradbury, Nicola. *Henry James: The Later Novels.* Oxford: Clarendon, 1979.

Bridgman, Richard. *The Colloquial Style in America.* New York: Oxford University Press, 1966.

Buitenhuis, Peter. *The Grasping Imagination: The American Writings of Henry James.* Toronto: University of Toronto Press, 1970.

Cameron, Sharon. *Thinking in Henry James.* Chicago: University of Chicago Press, 1989.

Chatman, Seymour. *The Later Style of Henry James.* Oxford: Basil Blackwell, 1972.

Cox, C. B. *The Free Spirit.* London: Oxford University Press, 1963.

Dupee, F. W. *Henry James.* Rev. ed. New York: Sloane, 1956.

Edel, Leon. *Henry James.* 5 vols. Philadelphia: Lippincott, 1953–1972.

Fogel, Daniel Mark, ed. *A Companion to Henry James Studies.* Westport, Conn.: Greenwood, 1993.

Fowler, Virginia. *Henry James's American Girl.* Madison: University of Wisconsin Press, 1984.

Freedman, Jonathan, ed. *The Cambridge Companion to Henry James.* Cambridge: Cambridge University Press, 1998.

Gargano, James W. "The Middle Years." In *A Companion to Henry James Studies,* edited by Daniel Mark Fogel. Westport, Conn.: Greenwood, 1993.

Goetz, William. *Henry James and the Darkest Abyss of Romance.* Baton Rouge: Louisiana State University Press, 1986.

Grover, Philip. *Henry James and the French Novel.* New York: Barnes and Noble, 1973.

Habegger, Alfred. *Gender, Fantasy and Realism in American Literature.* New York: Columbia University Press, 1982.

———. *Henry James and "The Woman Business."* Cambridge: Cambridge University Press, 1989.

Holland, Laurence. *The Expense of Vision.* Princeton: Princeton University Press, 1964.

Hutchinson, Stuart. *Henry James, an American, as Modernist.* Totowa, N.J.: Barnes and Noble, 1983.

James, Henry. "The Art of Fiction." In *Theory of Fiction: Henry James,* edited by James E. Miller, Jr. Lincoln: University of Nebraska Press, 1962.

———. *The Painter's Eye.* Edited by John Sweeney. London: Rupert Hart-Davis, 1956.

———. "Preface." *The Portrait of a Lady* (1908). New York: Modern Library ed. 1966.

———. *The Portrait of a Lady* (1881). New York: Signet Classic, New American Library, 1963.

———. "The Real Thing." In *The Complete Tales of Henry James,* edited by Leon Edel. Vol. 8. Philadelphia: Lippincott, 1963.

Kappeler, Susanne. *Writing and Reading in Henry James.* New York: Columbia University Press, 1980.

Kaston, Carren. *Imagination and Desire in the Novels of Henry James.* New Brunswick, N.J.: Rutgers University Press, 1984.

Kestner, Joseph. *The Spatiality of the Novel.* Detroit: Wayne State University Press, 1978.

Kirschke, James J. *Henry James and Impressionism.* Troy, N.Y.: Whitson, 1981.

Kronegger, Maria Elisabeth. *Literary Impressionism.* New Haven, Conn.: College and University Press, 1973.

Krook, Dorothea. *The Ordeal of Consciousness in Henry James.* Cambridge: Cambridge University Press, 1962.

Miller, James E., Jr., ed. *Theory of Fiction: Henry James.* Lincoln: University of Nebraska Press, 1962.

Mull, Donald. *Henry James's "Sublime Economy."* Middletown, Conn.: Wesleyan University Press, 1973.

Poole, Adrian. *Henry James.* New York: St. Martin's, 1991.

Poirier, Richard. *The Comic Sense of Henry James.* New York: Oxford University Press, 1960.

Porte, Joel, ed. *New Essays on* The Portrait of a Lady. Cambridge: Cambridge University Press, 1990.

Rowe, John Carlos. *The Theoretical Dimensions of Henry James.* Madison: University of Wisconsin Press, 1984.

Sabiston, Elizabeth. *The Prison of Womanhood.* New York: St. Martin's, 1987.

Schneider, Daniel. *The Crystal Cage*. Lawrence: Regents Press of Kansas, 1978.

Segal, Ora. *The Lucid Reflector*. New Haven: Yale University Press, 1969.

Smith, Virginia Llewellyn. *Henry James and the Real Thing*. New York: St. Martin's, 1996.

Stafford, William T. "*The Portrait of a Lady*: The Second Hundred Years." *The Henry James Review* 2 (Winter 1981): 91–100.

Stowell, H. Peter. *Literary Impressionism, James and Chekhov*. Athens: University of Georgia Press, 1980.

Veeder, William. *Henry James: The Lessons of the Master*. Chicago: University of Chicago Press, 1975.

Wallace, Ronald. *Henry James and the Comic Form*. Ann Arbor: University of Michigan Press, 1975.

Walton, Priscilla. *The Disruption of the Feminine in Henry James*. Toronto: University of Toronto Press, 1992.

Ward, J. A. *The Search for Form: Studies in the Structure of James's Fiction*. Chapel Hill: University of North Carolina Press, 1967.

Weinstein, Philip M. *Henry James and the Requirements of the Imagination*. Cambridge: Harvard University Press, 1971.

Woolf, Judith. *Henry James: The Major Novels*. Cambridge: Cambridge University Press, 1991.

Beloved

"A Gravestone of Memories." *Newsweek* 110 (September 28, 1987): 74–75.

Ayer, Deborah (Sitter). "The Making of a Man: Dialogic Meaning in *Beloved*." *African American Review* 26, no. 1 (1992): 17–29. [Reprinted in *Critical Essays on Toni Morrison's "Beloved,"* edited by Barbara Solomon. New York: G. K. Hall, 1998.]

Bloom, Harold, ed. *Toni Morrison*. New York: Chelsea House, 1990.

Broad, Robert L. "Giving Blood to the Scraps." *African American Review* 28, no. 2 (Summer 1994): 189–96.

Carmean, Karen. *Toni Morrison's World of Fiction*. Troy, N.Y.: Whitston, 1993.

Crouch, Stanley. "Aunt Medea." *The New Republic* 197 (October 19, 1987): 38–43.

Edwards, Thomas R. "Ghost Story." *New York Review of Books* 34 (5 November 1987): 18.

Furman, Jan. "Sethe's Re-memories: The Covert Return of What is Best Forgotten." In *Critical Essays on Toni Morrison's "Beloved,"* edited by Barbara Solomon. New York: G. K. Hall, 1998.

Gates, H. L., Jr., and K. A. Appiah, eds. *Toni Morrison: Critical Perspectives Past and Present*. New York: Penguin, 1993.

Guth, Deborah. *Journal of Narrative Technique* 24, no. 2 (Spring 1994): 83–97. [Reprinted in *Critical Essays on Toni Morrison's "Beloved,"* edited by Barbara Solomon. New York: G. K. Hall, 1998.]

House, Elizabeth B. "Toni Morrison's Ghost: The Beloved Who is Not Beloved." *Studies in American Fiction* 18, no. 1 (Spring 1990): 17–26. [Reprinted in *Critical Essays on Toni Morrison's "Beloved,"* edited by Barbara Solomon. New York: G. K. Hall, 1998.]

Hudson-Weems, Clenora, and Wilfred D. Samuels, eds. *Toni Morrison*. New York: Twayne, 1990.

Kastor, Elizabeth. "Toni Morrison's *Beloved* Country: The Writer and Her Haunting Tale of Slavery." *Washington Post* (5 October 1987): 1, 12.

Kolmerten, Carol, Stephen Ross, and Judith Wittenberg, eds. *Unflinching Gaze: Morrison and Faulkner Re-envisioned.* Jackson: University Press of Mississippi, 1997.

Morrison, Toni. *Beloved.* New York: New American Library, 1987.

Otten, Terry. "Transfiguring the Narrative: *Beloved*—from Melodrama to Tragedy." In *Critical Essays on Toni Morrison's "Beloved,"* edited by Barbara Solomon. New York: G. K. Hall, 1998.

Rigney, Barbara Hill. "'Breaking the Back of Words': Language, Silence, and the Politics of Identity in *Beloved.*" In *The Voices of Toni Morrison.* Columbus: Ohio State University Press, 1991. [Reprinted in *Critical Essays on Toni Morrison's "Beloved,"* edited by Barbara Solomon. New York: G. K. Hall, 1998.]

Rothstein, Mervyn. "Toni Morrison, in Her New Novel, Defends Women." *New York Times* (August 26, 1987): C-17.

Sale, Roger. "Toni Morrison's *Beloved.*" *Massachusetts Review* 29, no. 1 (Spring 1988): 71–86.

Smith, Amanda. *Publisher's Weekly* 21 (August 1987): 51. [Cited in *Toni Morrison,* edited by Harold Bloom. New York: Chelsea House, 1990.]

Snitow, Ann. "Death Duties: Toni Morrison Looks Back in Sorrow." *The Village Voice Literary Supplement* 58 (September 8, 1987): 25–26. [Reprinted in *Critical Essays on Toni Morrison's "Beloved,"* edited by Barbara Solomon. New York: G. K. Hall, 1998.]

Solomon, Barbara, ed. *Critical Essays on Toni Morrison's "Beloved."* New York: G. K. Hall, 1998.

Taylor-Guthrie, Danille K., ed. *Conversations with Toni Morrison.* Jackson: University Press of Mississippi, 1994.

The Centaur

Aldridge, John. "The Private Vice of John Updike." In *Time to Murder and Create: The Contemporary Novel in Crisis.* New York: David McKay, 1966.

Bellow, Saul. In *Writers at Work,* edited by George Plimpton, 175–96. 3d series. New York: Viking, 1968.

Bloom, Harold, ed. *John Updike.* New York: Chelsea House, 1987.

Detweiler, Robert. *John Updike.* New York: Twayne, 1972.

Gilman, Richard. "The Youth of an Author." *The New Republic* 13 (April 1963): 27.

Hicks, Granville. "Pennsylvania Pantheon." *Saturday Review* 46 (February 2, 1963): 27.

Howard, Jane. "Can a Nice Novelist Finish First?" *Life* 61 (November 4, 1966): 74–82.

Hunt, George W. *John Updike and the Three Secret Things: Sex, Religion, and Art.* Grand Rapids, Mich.: William B. Eerdmans, 1980.

Markle, Joyce. *Fighters and Lovers.* New York: New York University Press, 1973.

Mellard, James M. "The Novel as Lyric Elegy: The Mode of Updike's *The Centaur.*" *Texas Studies in Language and Literature* 21 (1979): 112–27. [Reprinted in *John Updike,* edited by Harold Bloom. New York: Chelsea House, 1987.]

Neary, John. *Something and Nothingness.* Carbondale: Southern Illinois University Press, 1992.

Newman, Judie. *John Updike.* New York: St. Martin's, 1988.

Opdahl, Keith. "John Updike and the Realistic Tradition." In *Contemporary American Fiction,* edited by Malcolm Bradbury and Sigmund Ro. London: Edward Arnold, 1986.

Plath, James, ed. *Conversations with John Updike.* Jackson: University Press of Mississippi, 1994.

Podhoretz, Norman. "A Dissent on Updike." *Show* 3 (April 1963): 49–52.

Rhode, Eric. "John Updike Talks about the Shapes and Subjects of His Fiction." *Listener* 81 (June 19, 1969): 862–64. [Reprinted in *Conversations with John Updike,* edited by James Plath. Jackson: University Press of Mississippi, 1994.]

Searles, George J. *The Fiction of Phillip Roth and John Updike.* Carbondale: Southern Illinois University Press, 1985.

Schiff, James A. *John Updike Revisited.* New York: Twayne, 1998.

Steiner, George. "Half Man, Half Beast." *The Reporter* 28 (March 14, 1963): 52.

Updike, John. In *Writers at Work,* edited by George Plimpton, 431–54. 4th series. New York: Penguin, 1976.

———. *The Centaur.* New York: Alfred A. Knopf, 1963.

———. "Toppling Towers Seen by a Whirling Soul." *The New Yorker* (February 22, 1982), 120–28. [Reprinted in *Hugging the Shore* by John Updike. New York: Alfred A. Knopf, 1983.]

———. "Why Rabbit Had to Go." *New York Times Book Review* (August 5, 1990): sec. 7-1, 24–25.

Vargo, Edward P. "The Necessity of Myth in Updike's *The Centaur.*" *PMLA* 85 (1973): 452–60. [Reprinted in *Rainstorms and Fire: Ritual in the Novels of John Updike.* Port Washington, N.Y.: Kennikat Press, 1973.]

Index

Acker, Kathy, 93

Act of Reading, The (Iser), 42

Adams, Nick ("Big Two-Hearted River"), 19, 96, 113, 189; context of, 116, 117; emotional contagion of, 114; emotions of, 117–19; empathy with, 53; identification with, 30, 67; and judgment, 122; mental representation of, 53, 59, 103; mood of, 121; reader's experience of, 52; and socially constructed values, 122; state of mind of, 118; vicarious experience of, 53

Addison, Joseph: on emotional reaction, 79

Adventures of Huckleberry Finn (Twain), 107; contrasts in, 145; emotion in, 148–51, 161, 162, 197; emotional representation in, 142–44, 160, 231; exposition, 156; interpretations of, 154–57, 197–99; language of, 155, 206; mental construction of, 156; objective correlative in, 142; the Phelps episode, 154; quality in, 157; style, 144, 145, 158–60; tone, 160

Aesthetic Quality (Pepper), 88

affect. *See* emotion

After the New Criticism (Lentricchia), 191

American Cool (Stearns), 195

Anderson, Charles: on mental construction, 170; *Person, Place and Thing*, 170

Archer, Isabel (*Portrait of a Lady*): and the affective code, 176, 177–78; characterization of, 166, 171–72, 173–79, 194, 212, 231; dual existence of, 173, 174–75; as emotional, 166; and emotional understanding, 171; interpretations of, 166, 171, 174; and judgment, 167; mental construction of, 166–67, 168, 170; and Osmond, 168, 169, 171; reader identification with, 176; reader's construction of, 166, 172, 173, 176, 177, 179, 231; and relationships, 166, 174, 175, 176

Armstrong, Paul: on mental construction of Isabel Archer, 170; *The Phenomenology of Henry James*, 170

Arnheim, Rudolph, 41; on judgments, 77–78; on mental imagery, 45; on verbal thinking, 36; *Visual Thinking*, 36

Arnold, Magda: on emotion as appraisal, 91

art: as affective communication, 82; as expression of emotion, 82–84, 85; as impersonal, 84; and science, 164; experience in, 88; verisimilitude of, 164

Aspects of Literary Comprehension (Zwaan), 56

Associationists, British 33

Austen, Jane, 107; and the biological, 137; characterization, 203; compared to Henry James, 137; and emotion, 124, 125; and Hemingway, 20; *Mansfield Park*, 69; style of, 20, 125–26; use of the affective code, 69–70; use of emotion in *Pride and Prejudice*, 126, 129–30

Baby Suggs (*Beloved*): emotional damage of, 204, 209; and feeling, 204

Baym, Nina: on Isabel Archer, 166

Beardsley, Monroe, 101; on emotion in literary studies, 86–87; on the objective correlative, 87

288

35, 40; theory of mental construction, 48

Kristeva, Julia: on language and desire, 192

Lacan, Jacques: on language and desire, 192

Langer, Susanne K., 94, 122; on composite emotion, 146, 148; critique of, 84–85; on emotional experience, 83; on emotion in art, 83; on emotion as impersonal, 83; on emotion in judgment, 196; *Form and Feeling*, 83, 84; on memory, 237 (8); on mild emotions, 126; *The Mind*, 83; *Philosophy in a New Key*, 83; *Problems of Art*, 83; on virtual emotion, 84, 163

language: in *Beloved*, 202, 206, 215; and context, 36; credibility of, 155; as directive, 50, 66; and desire, 192; effect on mental codes, 50, 54; and emotion, 79, 81, 84, 106, 112–13, 120; and emotional construction, 166; of Henry James, 166; of Huck Finn, 44–47, 149, 150, 155; and imagination, 35; limitations of, 83; and meaning, 36, 72, 92; mental construction of, 175; as objective representation, 35; and relation, 175

Laver, Sue: *Emotion and the Arts*, 11, 184

Lawrence, D. H.: *Women in Love*, 187

Leeper, Robert: on emotion and experience, 91

Lentricchia, Frank: *After the New Criticism*, 191; on reader-response criticism, 191

Literary Impressionism (Stowall), 170

Literary Work of Art, The (Ingarden), 41

Lyons, William, 9, 62, 92; on emotion as choice, 189

Lyotard, Jean-Francois: *The Post-Modern Condition*, 193

Lyrical Ballads (Wordsworth): "The Preface," 76–78

MacMurray, John, 163

magnetic resonance imaging: and locations of mental function, 20

Mailer, Norman: author's use of emotion, 195; *Tough Guys Don't Dance*, 195

Mailloux, Steven, 41

Mandler, George, 72

Mansfield Park (Austen): affective code in, 69–70

Markle, Joyce: *Fighters and Lovers*, 218; on mythology in *The Centaur*, 218

Markman, Arthur B.: *Knowledge Representation*, 11

Marx, Karl: on emotion, 62

McCormick, Katherine (*Riven Rock*), 11

meaning: and the affective code, 101; construction of, 42, 55–56, 64; creation of, 92; definition of, 31; embodied, 66; and emotion, 59, 124; as experiential, 55; as fluid, 38; and imagination, 31–32, 45, 54; implied, 42; and intuition, 38; and language, 36, 92; the mind's creation of, 92, 255 (13); as representation, 32; as shorthand, 31; as social convention, 40; as subjective, 38; uses of, 32

Meaning and Representation (Cummins), 36

memory: emotion in, 88, 150; Kosslyn's theory of retrieval, 49–50; and mental codes, 103; mental construction of, 49, 231; as motivator, 91; Paivio on, 50; in poetry, 77; representation of, 24, 49, 52, 78, 104; duration, 49; as synthesis, 54

Mental Models (Johnson-Laird), 26, 55

Mental Representations (Paivio), 37, 47

mentalese: definition of, 232

metaphor: and emotion, 95; and emotional representation, 170, 173; as mediator, 95; and objectivity, 95

Miall, David S.: 72, 112, 184

Miller, J. Hillis, 191

Mind, The (Langer), 83, 84, 122

mind: and construction of meaning, 154; definition of, 34. *See also* mental model, mental construction

Minsky, Marvin, 37

Mitchell, Lee Clark: on *Adventures of Huckleberry Finn*, 198; on emotional referents, 198–99

model, mental, 26, 55; and emotions, 29; as representation, 27, and context, 55; and subjectivity, 55; as unconscious, 55. *See also* mental construction

modernism: attitudes toward emotion, 80